THE
TUTOR
BOOK

**Longman Series in
College Composition and Communication**

Advisory Editor: Harvey Wiener
LaGuardia Community College
The City University of New York

THE TUTOR BOOK

Marian Arkin
LaGuardia Community College
The City University of New York

Barbara Shollar
College of New Rochelle

Longman

New York & London

The Tutor Book

Longman Inc., 19 West 44th Street, New York, N.Y. 10036
Associated companies, branches, and representatives throughout the world.

Developmental Editor: Gordon T. R. Anderson
Editorial and Design Supervisor: Joan Matthews
Interior Design: Angela Foote
Production Supervisor: Ferne Y. Kawahara
Manufacturing Supervisor: Marion Hess
Composition: Intergraphic Technology Inc.
Printing and Binding: Interstate Book Manufacturers, Inc.

Library of Congress Cataloging in Publication Data

Arkin, Marian, 1943–
    The tutor book.

    Includes bibliographies and index.
    1. Tutors and tutoring. I. Shollar, Barbara.
II. Title.
LC41.A68   371.3'94   81-13697
ISBN 0-582-28233-0   AACR2

Manufactured in the United States of America
9 8 7 6 5 4 3 2 1

To Betty Arkin Orenstein
and the memory of Will Haber

To the Group: Jim, Jerry, Joanne,
Charles, and Bob
and to the Memory of Ethel Hofrichter

CONTENTS

Acknowledgments   *xi*
Foreword   *xiii*
Preface   *xv*

1. Tutoring and Peer Tutoring: An Introduction   1

Definitions 1
Why Tutor? 4
Collaborative Learning 6
Tutor Preparation 9
The Ethics of Tutoring 16

Readings
1. Charles Dickens, *Hard Times* 19
2. Porter and Wolfe, "Autobiography and the Classroom" 23
3. Thom Hawkins, *Benjamin: Reading and Beyond* 29
4. Philip G. Hansen, "What to Look for in Groups" 36

Bibliography 39

2. Beginning to Tutor   41

Preparing for the Tutoring Session 41
The Initial Interviews 44
The Tutorial Relationship: Roles, Expectations, and
    Models 52
Beginning to Evaluate 53

Readings
5*a*. Antonia Retamar, "Tutoring Maria: A Case Study" 58
5*b*. Renee Bresnick, "Edward" 61

Bibliography 62

3. Tutoring Handicapped Students   64

Deaf Students 65

Visually Handicapped Students 69
Students with Other Physical Impairments 72
Students with Learning Disabilities 72

Readings
6. Howard T. Hofsteater, "An Experiment in Preschool
   Education" 75

Bibliography 83

4. The Tutorial Session   84

The Role of Planning 84
Components of a Good Session 88
Making a Good Session 89
Audiovisual Aids: A Glossary of Hardware 105

Readings
7. Plato, "Meno" 109
8*a*. Pask et al., "Numerical Intuition" 115
8*b*. Arlene Hartman *The Calculator Game Book for Kids of All
    Ages* 117
8*c*. Pask et al., "Reluctance," and "Conjugal
    Reluctance" 120

Bibliography 126

5. Tutoring in Multicultural Settings   127

Cultural Understanding 127
Second-Language Learners 129

Readings
 9. Langston Hughes, "Coffee Break" 134
10. Richard Rodriguez, "Going Home Again: The New
    American Scholarship Boy" 136
11. J. S. Kleinfeld, "Intellectual Strengths in Culturally
    Different Groups: An Eskimo Illustration" 144

Bibliography 153

6. Tutoring-Counseling   154

Dealing with the Whole Student 154
Motivation 154
Counseling Approaches 160
A Word of Caution about Counseling 171
Self-Understanding 171

Readings
12. Carl R. Rogers, "Freedom To Learn" 176
13. "Task-Centered Casework" 185

Bibliography 193

7. Roleplaying Tutoring Problems   194

Roleplaying 194
Potential Problem Areas   202

Readings
14. R.K. Narayan, *My Days: A Memoir*   220
15. Wendy M. Ferguson, Case Study: Patricia Bauer   211
16. Ann Cornelisen, *Women of the Shadows*   225

Bibliography 232

8. Learning   233

A Tutorial Protocol   233
Stimulus-Response Theory   234
Cognitive Theory 239

Readings
17. A. R. Luria, *The Making of Mind*   250
18. Sylvia Scribner and Michael Cole, "Cognitive Consequences of Formal and Informal Education" 254
19. Gaylen Carlson, *Development of Reasoning in Science* 266

Bibliography 269

9. Tutoring Adults   270

Social Aspects: Work, Family, and Education   270
Physiological Factors 272
Adult Intelligence 273

Readings
20. Donald Barthelme, "Me and Miss Mandible"   277

Bibliography 284

10. Evaluation   285

Theoretical Considerations 285
Practical Applications: The End-term Evaluation 286

Readings
21. Kathy Blasius, "Tutor-Counseling Self-Evaluation"   298

Summary 306
Bibliography 306

Index 307

ACKNOWLEDGMENTS

Grateful acknowledgment is made to the following for their permission to reprint:

"About New York—A Diarist and the City, From Apple to Zest" by William E. Farrell, Feb. 25, 1981. © 1981 by The New York Times Company. Reprinted by permission of the New York Times.

"Autobiography and the Classroom" from *The Voice Within: Reading and Writing Autobiography* by Roger Porter and Howard Wolf. Copyright © 1973 by Roger Porter. Reprinted by permission of the authors.

"Benjamin: Reading and Beyond" by Thom Hawkins. Copyright © 1972 by Charles Merrill Co. Copyright © 1980 by Thom Hawkins. Reprinted by permission of the author.

"What to Look for in Groups: An Observation Guide," pp. 21-24. Reprinted from: J.W. Pfeiffer and J.E. Jones (Eds.), *The 1972 Annual Handbook for Group Facilitators*. San Diego, CA: University Associates, 1972. "This structured experience and the accompanying observation guide were contributed by Philip G. Hansen, V.A. Hospital, Houston, Texas." Used with permission.

"Talking Machine Center to Aid Blind Lawyers in Justice Dept.," December 7, 1980. © 1980 by the New York Times Company. Reprinted by permission of The New York Times.

"An Experiment in Preschool Education" by Howard T. Hofsteater. Originally printed in the Gallaudet College Bulletin, No. 1, Vol. 8, February 1959. Reprinted by permission of National Association of the Deaf.

Excerpts from Plato: PROTAGORAS & MENO, trans. W.K.C. Guthrie (Penguin Classics, 1956) pp. 130-138. Copyright © W.K.C. Guthrie. Reprinted by permission of Penguin Books Ltd.

"Numerical Intuition," "Reluctance" and Figure 10, page 156, and "Conjugal Reluctance" from CALCULATOR SATURNALIA, by Gordon Pask, Ranulph Glanville, and Mike Robinson. Copyright © 1980 by Gordon Pask, Ranulph Glanville, Mike Robinson, John Gage, Stephen Gage, and Peter Jackson. Illustrations copyright © 1980 by Gordon Pask. Reprinted by permission of Random House, Inc.

Excerpts from THE CALCULATOR GAME BOOK FOR KIDS OF ALL AGES by Arlene Hartman. Copyright © 1977 by Arlene Hartman. Reprinted by arrangement with the New American Library, New York, New York.

"Coffee Break" from SIMPLE'S UNCLE SAM by Langston Hughes. Copyright © 1965 by Langston Hughes. Reprinted by permission of Hill and Wang, a division of Farrar, Straus and Giroux, Inc.

FOREWORD

Few books are needed in our profession at the present moment as this book is. Few members of our profession are as qualified to write it as Marian Arkin and Barbara Shollar are. Their academic training and their experience as teachers prepare them to write effectively about tutoring because to do so requires both understanding students' needs today and understanding our own needs as professionals committed to scholarship and the growth of knowledge.

Of these requisites for writing a good book on tutoring, though, experience is the more telling. This is because although people have tutored each other since time immemorial, our effort to understand, organize, and institutionalize that process on a large scale in this country is barely a decade old. In this respect every American teacher and educator who teaches and supervises tutors is something of an amateur.

The main reason we are so is that collaborative learning is still uncommon and poorly understood in American education. As this book makes clear, tutoring—especially peer tutoring—is one kind of collaborative learning. In collaborative learning, those who set out to learn invest each other with the authority and responsibility to help each other learn. Most of us do not know much about how to make this happen, because there is a lot we do not yet know about how to organize the exchange of authority and responsibility among peers. We barely know how to do it well ourselves. We know very little of what its educational and cultural implications might be. This book is a solid contribution to our effort to understand and practice collaborative learning in one of its most important and prevalent forms: tutoring.

I know first hand the practical work the book grows out of. I have met and talked with peer tutors the authors have taught. At my invitation, Marian Arkin and several of her tutors explained their work at the FIPSE-funded, 1980-1981 Brooklyn College Summer Institute in Training Peer Tutors. What they brought to the Institute was the intelligence, insight, experience, and sense of caring that is so evident in this book. Teachers attending the Institute from all over the country—colleges and universities Florida to Washington state, Maine to Arizona—received them enthusiastically.

Few readers will find that everything in the book reflects their own experience or expresses their own point of view. No book as ambitious as this one could possibly do so. But I think most readers will find the book useful at every turn. It is thorough and well informed. It puts tutoring—especially peer tutoring—into its appropriate educational context. It is, above all, practical: it tells tutors how to do a good job tutoring, and it provides teachers with an excellent tool to use in teaching tutors. Finally, it has its roots in the concrete experience of its authors and their tutors working and learning collaboratively. A book written in that way should grow in the hands of those who use it. That is what I believe this book will do.

Kenneth A. Bruffee

PREFACE

This book came about as a result of a disagreement. The authors were on a panel in which they presented what seemed to be disparate conceptions of learning centers and tutorial programs. However, as we talked after the conference about our respective peer-tutoring classes and tutorial programs, we discovered quite a few common elements in our approaches. In fact, the premise on which our courses and on which the centers we direct are based turned out to be very similar. And so, our collaboration began: first as a series of discussions, during which we aimed to expand our repertoires of methods; later came the idea of a book which would synthesize our experiences. This book, then, is a compilation of all we knew about tutoring when we started our meetings and all we learned through the process of collaboration.

Indeed, the book is as much about the process of collaboration as it is about tutoring. To be a real learning process, the tutorial must first be a collaboration between tutor and tutee, and then, ideally, in the academic world, between tutor and teacher. Collaboration must also occur during the training of tutors in a lab, or course, or program. Finally, we earnestly hope you will see your use of this book as a collaboration. While we offer you the fruits of our experience we acknowledge that your experiences may lead you in different directions and to different conclusions. As with any process, tutoring thrives on flexibility and openness to change.

Tutoring and peer tutoring are hardly recent educational practices. Traditionally, experts and scholars have passed on their knowledge to apprentices, and students have been helping one another learn for centuries. In some circles, this has recently been defined as part of *andragogy,* the theory and method of adult learning, which assumes that adults can and do take increasing responsibility for their own education. The thousands of peer-tutoring programs and courses which have sprung up in the business world as well as in educational and public settings in the last ten to twenty years attest to this. These assume that tutors are learners who benefit personally and academically by tutoring their fellow students—and that their tutees can learn as much in such a collaborative program as in a traditional teaching situation, and perhaps more.

The book is addressed to tutors and peer tutors in higher education and adult education programs in public and corporate training programs. It may be used as a training text for teachers and group leaders or as a course text for trainees. It is both comprehensive and self-contained, drawing from and integrating the knowl-

xv

edge and insights of many fields and anthologizing readings—both classical and comtemporary—from these disciplines.

Our book is intended to contribute to the development of collaborative learning and to give the tutoring process coherence and substance by systematizing it, grounding it in theory, and combining sound theory with successful practice. We hope it will enable tutors to understand as well as put into practice the theories, techniques and skills they are learning.

Included in each chapter is a *text* covering an aspect of tutoring. Both theoretical and practical material are presented. The text section also includes charts, sample forms, checklists, and evaluations, where appropriate. Many of these can be reproduced for use in the classroom or training program or in the tutorial itself. *Class Projects* provide for skills development and group discussion; *Lab Applications* are designed for immediate use in a learning skills or subject-area center, or in the tutorial. Both of these give the tutor a chance to apply and reinforce theoretical discussion and help guide the tutorial process. All of these projects and applications help develop analytic and reasoning abilities, nurture creativity, and promote active involvement. Some of the projects and applications are long term, to be done over a period of time, up to a term or year; others are short term. We do not assume that all tutors will do all the projects: some may be done by the groups as a whole, others by subgroups, still others by individuals interested in pursuing some specialty. They are intended to be used selectively, according to the interests of the tutors and the focus of the program; they may even stimulate you to develop other projects we have not thought of. In any case, they should enhance tutoring and training, and they can contribute to the materials available in the lab and to the structure and substance of the tutoring program.

To illustrate and supplement the material in each chapter are *readings* from a variety of disciplines: English and American Literature, Sociology and Cultural Anthropology, Education and Social Work, Psychology, Math and Science, and Philosophy. The different genres include: personal and literary essays, autobiographical memoirs, case studies, fiction, research articles, games, and philosophic dialogues. Some selections are student work. Each of these readings is prefaced by questions to guide reading and group discussion. (We have not attempted to make the readings consistent in style, preferring to retain the format of their original publication and discipline.)

The first chapter introduces the tutor to the concept of tutoring by exploring who tutors are and how they relate to other members of an educational enterprise. More specifically, it discusses peer tutors, how they benefit from tutoring, and how they, in turn, can help their tutees. It includes background on collaborative learning, approaches to group work and to journal writing. Guidelines for tutoring, including a discussion of ethics and of what the tutee may expect from the tutor and vice versa, provides tutoring initiation into (or a reconsideration of) the actual tutoring process. Class projects stimulate thinking about teaching and learning. Lab applications guide the tutor's orientation to the materials and personnel of the specific program. Readings in this chapter focus on teaching styles as well as on one journal keeper's experience in tutoring; the last reading will help organize group work through the use of a "handbook" of group process strategies.

Chapter 2 gives tutors an overview of what they are likely to encounter during the first few weeks of tutoring; central to this is an understanding of the importance of evaluation and assessment—of oneself and of others. Two features of this chapter are the learning contract, to help tutors and tutees plan their work, and the case study, to help tutors evaluate the work of the entire period, both in process and after tutoring is over. Two peer-tutor case studies conclude the chapter.

Chapter 3 focuses on the handicapped. It attempts to give tutors background on learners with sight and hearing impairment, other physical limitations, and learning disabilities, and offers strategies for tutoring students with these problems. Class projects explore misconceptions about and experiences with the handicapped, encouraging students to do further research and develop learning aids specifically geared to helping such students learn. The reading is an autobiographical case study by a deaf teacher.

Chapter 4 analyzes the tutorial session. It discusses session planning, motivation, instruction, and reinforcement, and offers model strategies and sample tutoring techniques, concluding with a glossary of audiovisual hardware. Class projects and lab applications call on tutors to analyze their past learning experiences and their tutoring sessions and give them practice in planning, motivating, instructing, and reinforcing tutees. The readings include the classic, and very dramatic, device of Socratic questioning in "The Meno" and some very contemporary calculator games helpful in tutoring basic math skills and advance statistics.

Chapter 5 discusses tutoring in multicultural settings, emphasizing the need for cultural tolerance and understanding. It includes a general guide to tutoring second language learners, those whose native language is not English. Class projects and applications ask students to consider cultural differences in the context of local geographical and institutional conditions. Readings explore learning from three cultural perspectives, those of the Black American, the Mexican-American, and the Eskimo.

Chapter 6 looks at the all-important counseling aspect to tutoring. It presents theoretical models from current counseling and psychological theory and offers tutor-counseling approaches. A section on self-understanding should be of great value for tutoring a a profession. Class projects and applications encourage students to explore feelings about themselves and their tutees, provide extensive practice in specific counseling techniques, and then guide them in applying what they have learned in the tutorial. Readings include a selection by Carl Rogers and the transcript of a task-centered social work case-study developed at the University of Chicago.

Chapter 7 asks tutors to take what they have learned about counseling and apply it to problems they may be having in tutoring. This chapter offers roleplaying as one effective way of dealing with tutoring problems, explaining how and why roleplaying is so effective. The second half of the chapter is a glossary of potential problem areas—Tutor/Student, Teacher/Student, Tutor/Teacher, Student/Student—suggesting possible reasons for these conflicts and approaches to dealing with them. Using these problems as starting points, class projects ask students to roleplay tutoring conflicts in their class projects. In the readings section, Indian author R.K. Narayan writes of his own problems in school, a former peer-tutor explores conflicts with her tutee, and Ann Cornelisen writes about education of the poor in southern Italy.

In order to help students understand the complex factors that comprise the learning process, Chapter 8 is devoted to an analysis of current learning theory ranging from stimulus-response to information processing and other cognitive models, with especial focus on Jean Piaget's contribution to the psychology of learning. Class projects and applications encourage students to understand learning theory and to use it to inform tutoring practice. Readings explore aspects of cognitive learning theory as it applies to or is modified by field research and as it is used to develop a science of learning.

Chapter 9 provides a special focus on adult learners: it points to the special needs of those who have been returning to school or entering educational programs while assuming the responsibilities—and pressures—of work, family, and the maintenance of a home. The chapter emphasizes the challenges adults face and takes account of factors such as physiology and intellect, which may affect learning. Through class projects and applications, students deepen their knowledge of adult motivation, which includes understanding their educational options and the resources recently made available to them. The short story by Donald Barthelme is both satiric comedy and deadly serious as it questions the supposed differences between adults and children.

Chapter 10 is on evaluation. In this chapter, tutors consider how to evaluate their own and their students' progress during the period of tutoring. A form is included to show tutors how to do their own evaluation, and sample evaluation done by a peer tutor should serve as a practical guide to the evaluation process.

Marian Arkin would like to thank at LaGuardia Community College: Bert Eisenstadt for many years of comraderie, invaluable assistance, and countless ideas and suggestions; also Mark Prinz for administrative help; Enis Swarm, Florence Pasternack and Rosemarie Prinz for secretarial assistance; Doris Fassler, Leonard Vogt, and many other members of the English Department for their continued support of the writing center and peer-tutoring course. Roberta Matthews and Gil Muller for their help in writing the first peer-tutoring course and Daniel Lynch for his warm enthusiasm for peer tutoring at LaGuardia. Sarah Ocasio, Jim Misciewicz, Jeannie Pandolfo, Leida Torres, Elizabeth Woodruff, Keith Hanson, Barbara Carson, veteran tutors at the writing center whose unwavering commitment to tutoring has taught me much about the field, and to the College for granting me sabbatical leave without which this book could not have been written. Thanks also to all present and former peer tutors for their willingness to partake in the peer-tutoring experiment, John Roche of Rhode Island College for insights and conversation about tutoring writing, Arlene Robertson of RIC for secretarial help, and to Brown University for extending me the privilege of using its excellent library. Finally, many thanks to Brian Gallagher for his support, advice, copyediting, and creative insights and patience.

Barbara Shollar would like to thank those people at South Central Community College, New Haven, Connecticut, for their confidence in me and their faith in the program established there: Joseph Magyar, and Dorian Wilkes for her suggestions in the final version. My thanks to the community of the College of New Rochelle which has welcomed and nurtured the Learning Skills Center and its programs, and those who have done so much to make this book possible: to Tom Rocco, Associate Dean of the School of New Resources, for quiet and continued support; to the members of my peer-tutoring class at the New Rochelle campus of the School of New Resources, in which the need for this book became apparent. To Laura Ellis, Professor of Education at the Graduate School, for her reading of the final draft. To the Learning Skills Center's professional staff whose daily encouragement and helpfulness in providing materials and suggestions were no less important than their good will and cheering spirits; special thanks to Mary-ann Theising and Jim McGurk for attention to the math and science materials in the book. To the peer tutors in the Center whose valuable contributions and service have been a daily inspiration; special thanks to Kathy Blasius, who was the "first" tutor, and whose good humor and dedication have meant so much both to the program and to the book. And finally, to those friends, whose wonderful company I have had to spurn often in the last two years to be able to complete this book: Tom Venanzi, Barbara Cutney, Donna Mollica, Mark Maier.

A special thanks to Larry Badendyck and Cynthia Badendyck for their abiding faith and encouragement.

Both authors would like to thank all our reviewers: Gary Saretsky and Muriel Harris for their initial response to our proposal; Ken Bruffee and Thom Hawkins, for their ongoing involvement in the collaborative process. Their helpful criticism and suggestions had important and beneficial effects on the manuscript. Our appreciation to Tren Anderson and Harvey Weiner for their commitment to this project, and to Joan Matthews for her professionalism and unfailing patience. We are grateful to the staff of the Library of the College of New Rochelle, especially to Rosemary Lewis and Fred Smith, who were undaunted by a myriad of requests and our need for out-of-the-way references. Our dual authorship put a great burden on Charlotte Frede, and we owe a special debt to her for her grace under pressure. Her secretarial efficiency and generous spirit have often made the difference. We credit these and more who are not named for much of what is good in this book and reserve for ourselves whatever faults and errors still remain.

THE
TUTOR
BOOK

1 | TUTORING AND PEER TUTORING: AN INTRODUCTION

A small room with white walls. On one wall is a large colorful poster of Rome, the Eternal City. In the room are a desk and two chairs. The desk is cluttered with books, papers, pens, and several white styrofoam cups of coffee. A man and woman are seated at the table, talking earnestly.

RICK: I think Melville began *Moby Dick* with the lines, "Call me Ishmael," because he wanted to shock his readers.

SUSAN: Yeh, it was certainly a different way to begin a novel, if you consider when the book was written. It's so direct. I've always thought Hawthorne, for example, was so stiff in comparison.

RICK: I wonder if the name Ishmael is important; Melville must have used a biblical name for a reason.

SUSAN: Let's look it up! I'm sure we can find a copy of the Bible in the library.

RICK: Do you think it's going to be on the midterm?

These people could be any two friends studying together. They happen to be a tutor and tutee; but these terms do not change the fact that the dialogue is warm and informal and that learning seems to be taking place as they are sharing ideas and feelings. Although one of these people may know more than the other, neither party seems to be controlling the other. Learning seems to be happening as part of an evolving process. We call this process tutoring.

DEFINITIONS

When we refer to tutors, we speak of people who work outside a formal classroom structure, in a lab, a center, a dormroom, a library, even in a cafeteria. Their job is to support or supplement regular classroom instruction. In this book we are addressing two types of tutor: the professional tutor and the peer tutor.

Professional Tutors are like teachers: they are more advanced educationally than the people they tutor. They may be graduate students or may have achieved the same educational level as a teacher, but they lack the rank and power (and in many cases, the prestige) of faculty.

1

Professional tutors are expected to be relatively expert in their fields. Yet, while they are hired to pass on their expertise to others, much as faculty do, the setting in which they do so alters the traditional teacher-student relationship. Working in an informal atmosphere, singly or in small groups, they tend to place greater emphasis on process than product and to be more aware of the student as an individual than an instructor might. Further, their position outside the academic hierarchy means that they can more easily be the student's advocate. A positive experience with a tutor may give the student more confidence with which to approach faculty members.

Peer tutors are their tutees' fellow students. Therefore, peer tutors combine the roles of student and teacher, learning and tutoring at the same time; they may even be in a peer-tutoring course, in which they combine these two roles while learning to tutor. Peer tutors will probably have less expertise in the subject they tutor than professional tutors do, and most likely they will have had little or no experience tutoring. Nonetheless, the individualized and personal attention they give their tutees can compensate for their inexperience.

The fact that peer tutors are both their tutees' instructors and their fellow students changes the nature of the tutoring relationship. Peer tutors are tutoring as much to help themselves as to help others. Often they have recently taken the course they are tutoring and have had difficulties similar to those their tutees have, and so they can empathize with tutees more closely than either professional tutors or teachers, whose memories of the initial obstacles to learning may have faded with time. Peer tutors are likely to be more patient and to better understand student mistakes because they have recently grappled with the material they tutor, and they have novel, and even zany, methods of approaching it. Not yet entrenched in their disciplines, they are usually more receptive to, and less judgmental of, their tutees' unorthodox perspectives.

As the above suggests, the most important aspect in their self-definition and relation to tutees is that peer tutors have the same educational status as the people they tutor: they are their peers. And, in a culture in which peers (and the media) often supersede parents and teachers as authoritative sources of knowledge, peer status can offer tutors the chance to be immensely influential with their tutees, in both the development of skills and the shaping of values.

Teachers are members of the college faculty. Their many years of study prepare them to assume ultimate responsibility for instruction, curriculum, and student evaluation. Because of the demands their departments and their colleges make on teachers (students usually must learn certain material within a certain length of time, according to certain standards), and because they have attained such a high degree of specialization, some teachers emphasize the end product of learning rather than the learning process—forgetting that the students' knowledge is neither complete nor automatic. Also, their position of authority tends to make them seem remote and inaccessible to the student, even if they are not personally aloof; thus it may be difficult for students to make their learning needs known to teachers.

Photograph by Joseph Menna. Courtesy of LaGuardia Community College, Media Resources Center.

Tutees are those who are tutored. If they are doing independent study or working on instructional modules (see chapter 4), they will rely on the teacher (directly, or through the syllabus and class assignments) to define the boundaries of the discipline and to establish objectives for the course. They come to the tutor to gain clarity about those objectives, to get help in defining what they need, and to garner support with which to achieve their academic goals. Sometimes students on their own initiative ask for tutoring. Sometimes teachers refer students individually to tutors and require them to attend tutoring sessions for additional work or to meet special course requirements.

These definitions point to people who only recently have begun to play an important role in institutions of higher learning. As we will show, together professional tutors, peer tutors, teachers, and tutees comprise a new model for learning.

CLASS PROJECT 1

Before reading the next section, take some time to record your answers to the following questions:

a. In what ways do you expect the tutee to benefit from tutoring?

b. Why are you a tutor or why do you want to be a tutor? And what are the advantages or possible disadvantages of tutoring?

WHY TUTOR?

The Benefits to the Tutor

Most of the available documentation about how tutoring helps the tutor (particularly in regard to academic gains) pertains to elementary and sometimes high school students—and until recently referred primarily to older students in higher grades "teaching" younger students in lower grades (*cross-age tutoring*). However, anyone who has tutored or has been part of a college tutoring program knows that tutors gain substantially from tutoring.

Intellectual Scope and Depth Studies have shown that tutors learn the subject matter they tutor to an even greater degree than the students they tutor. It should be evident why this is so. In order to tutor, you must learn the material well enough to answer any questions the student might have. To do that, you will probably have to learn it from a number of vantage points. Merely memorizing concepts will prove insufficient. This continuous process of studying, tutoring, and studying will provide you with a truly solid mastery of the subject.

Further, to find the right way to reach a student, you will have to think about your subject thoroughly. In finding inventive ways to illuminate a topic, you might discover aspects of the subject that you never knew existed. The more confident you feel about your subject, the more you will be able to take creative leaps with it. For example, when tutoring subject-verb agreement, you may begin to think about the psychological or aesthetic ramifications of "person." "What is a subject?" you might ponder, "And, indeed, what is its relationship to the verb?" You will pass from rote learning to creative thought, from the level that recites concepts to the level that analyzes and recreates them. This degree of intellectual competence is reached by few people. Traditional education encourages distance between the learner and the teacher, and as long as students see themselves in subservient roles, independent thought is difficult for them. However, when the learner is also the instructor—as is specifically the case in peer-tutoring—independent thought is not only possible, but likely.

Skills Acquisition and Reinforcement By tutoring you practice skills and refine native abilities: you gain and use specific techniques that make your reading, writing, speaking, and counseling more effective. For instance, tutoring reinforces your ability to communicate clearly, logically, and creatively. It is not enough to *know* a subject well in order to tutor it well. Sometimes the most brilliant scholars make terrible tutors. If you don't *communicate* your subject well, you will soon be told directly, or by your students' annoyance or absence. Moreover, the tutor cannot (as many teachers can) rely solely on lecture to transmit knowledge. The one-to-one relationship demands that there be an intimate dialogue between tutor and tutee.

Maturity Tutoring encourages maturity, not only pedagogic but personal. In assuming the responsibility for a student, you transcend your own problems and involvements. You find you want to "be there" for your tutees, whether or not you like them or find them interesting. You become assertive when you feel passive, gentle when you feel angry. These attributes may, perhaps, sound saintly; but they are elements of adulthood, learned slowly but surely by those who perform service for others. Thus, the responsibility of tutoring often produces great character changes. The most obvious is self-confidence, the self-confidence that is gained from mastering a subject well enough to tutor it, and from transcending one's own insecurities enough to help someone else.

Psychological Insight The greatest benefit of tutoring is not the acquisition of academic knowledge, but knowledge of oneself and others. As we discuss in the chapters that follow, tutees are people with learning problems in a particular area or in a number of areas. Intellect and emotion are interrelated. Often students let emotional problems interfere with their studies, just as difficulties with their studies may result in emotional problems. Being sensitive to your tutees' emotional needs should give you insight into your own. If you are a peer tutor, you, too, are a learner and have probably exhibited behavior similar to that of your tutee when you were having trouble learning something. Understanding which behavior aids and which hinders learning is a hard-won and valuable lesson.

Career Development Many people think that tutoring is only helpful to those wishing to pursue teaching careers. That is a very limited view. Certainly, one learns to teach by tutoring, but, as must be obvious by now, tutoring involves much more. It allows you the opportunity to develop intellectually, psychologically, and personally, while giving you a firm sense of maturity, self-confidence, and authority. You will develop the ability to get along with others and the skills of mediation and negotiation. Even if you do not wind up working in the field you tutor, you will probably find that you feel more comfortable about working in a professional setting as a result of the tutoring experience.

The Benefits to the Tutee

A great part of the reward of tutoring comes from the real service you perform for others. For those times when your interest flags or you are discouraged, remember how important tutors are to their tutees. Indeed, your individual attention and support help your tutees learn better, and can make them feel better about school, about learning, and, generally, about themselves.

Improved Learning With the flexibility that individual instruction offers, students in tutoring can set their own learning goals and achieve them at their own pace. Peer tutoring provides them with someone close to their own level, and thus someone with whom they can be open; a peer tutor is a more accessible role model than a teacher.

Improved Attitude toward School and Learning If students improve as a result of being tutored, they will certainly feel more a part of the school and more excited about learning than before. But even if tutees don't improve substantially (learning takes place at a different rate for everyone), the individualized attention will give them the chance to be heard, to control their learning environment, and to pursue knowledge actively. An experience such as this must change the way they relate to learning in general. They will realize that if they actively seek to learn, they will learn more and find it more enjoyable.

Improved Self-Image As we shall discuss throughout the book, students with learning problems often have little self-confidence and still less self-esteem. Your personal and academic support of students, in effect, addresses both problems. Further, students who begin to see themselves progressing as a result of their own efforts gain the self-respect and pride that will fuel their personal and academic growth.

CLASS PROJECT 2

In groups, review your responses to Class Project 1. How do they correspond to or differ from the material discussed above? How do they correspond to and differ from the responses of members of your group or class?

COLLABORATIVE LEARNING

Those of you who are *peer* tutors or in a tutoring class or program may be part of an educational experiment called collaborative learning; to understand the concept of collaborative learning you need to look at it in the context of traditional education.

If your education has been traditional, your instruction has been carried out entirely in classrooms. In these classrooms the teacher usually lectured at the front, while the students, facing forward in rows and scribbling frantically to catch the teacher's words, stopped only when someone asked a question or made a comment. It was at times comforting to know that there was a person "up there" imbued with all knowledge, and that if you kept your eyes and ears open information would flow from the front back to you.

You probably enjoyed it immensely when your teachers used their creative energies to rivet your attention to their witty and dynamic lectures. At times, though, you were bored, puzzled, or distracted, and blamed it on yourself ("I must be dumb.") or on the teacher ("She's so boring."). Classes with the dramatic teacher, however, had several things in common with the less exciting classes. Although you may not have noticed it, in both situations the teacher did most of the talking and you the listening; and in both, you rarely spoke to your classmates—and then only in a whisper, outside of the classroom, or when the teacher left the room. In both classes the teacher stood at

Colloquium

Drawing by W. Steig; © 1980 The New Yorker Magazine, Inc.

the front of the room facing you and your fellow students. Now, if all students are placed in a block, all facing the same person, as in these classes, the person must seem more important than anyone else in the room. Students in the room generally gain or lose value based on their relationship with the class leader—the teacher. In short, most traditional teaching is hierarchical: the line between teachers and students does not merely indicate differing educational levels, but where the authority and power lie as well.

Educational theorists and learning psychologists have long been skeptical about the efficacy of the traditional classroom, at the very least questioning whether it was the optimal approach for all students. And a good number of these educators, who otherwise may have very divergent ideas, would also argue that, in fact, no learning can take place when students are passive and when there is little interaction among them. Certainly, there have been students who thrive on having one authority figure controlling their education on any given subject. Yet the traditional classroom structure does not serve most students well. It is, in fact, detrimental to many students' intellectual and emotional development. It encourages dependency on authority, fosters a competitive, even threatening atmosphere, and makes students bored and depressed about learning. And, most important, for an *increasing number of students, it does not seem to be working.* If students do pass their courses, mustering whatever skill and information they can to do so, they fail to sustain what they learned with any consistency.

Solutions to this problem are many and have evolved gradually. Some of these emerged during the social ferment of the sixties when other values and structures in the society at large were being questioned as well. In the classroom, teachers began practicing a new democracy by breaking the class into small groups and having students work with each other. Forced to establish their own goals and to set their own pace, students began to assume greater responsibility for their learning. And so collaborative learning came into being.

Collaborative learning means learning *with* others, not side by side, but *with*. This kind of group experience involves a commitment to peers, with each person contributing to the whole, compensating for or correcting the weaknesses or deficiencies of others. Such a model implies a communitarian ideal, and is directly antithetical to the competitive model on which traditional education has been based. The teacher in a collaborative experience is a facilitator, setting up the structure, introducing the material, providing a general idea of group expectations, and, perhaps, guiding discussion. Ideally, as a collaborative group becomes more and more autonomous, the teacher becomes less and less necessary.

Collaborative learning attempts to restructure the traditional classroom in several ways. First, in rejecting the traditional hierarchical structures, it emphasizes the learner's responsibility for learning. Then it provides a nurturing, supportive community within which learning can take place free of authoritarian restrictions. Finally, it abolishes the line between learner and teacher, allowing all people to be seen as learners and teachers, and the learning process to be viewed as a collaborative effort.

It is easy to see how a tutoring program or laboratory could become a collaborative learning experience and how the collaborative learning model within the lab could be used to extend learning beyond the classroom itself. At the very least, collaborative learning and tutoring are complementary, both part of an important social effort to humanize learning. Tutoring recognizes the difficulties of learning and the individual's own idiosyncratic methods of acquiring knowledge, and it tries to provide the support that will nurture that individual. Collaborative learning stresses the group's—and the individual's—contribution to a developing community.

CLASS PROJECT 3

1. One of the authors recalls with pleasure a traditional class: The teacher wore a formless tweed hat which he would flamboyantly toss across the room as he entered, so that it often landed and swung precariously from the knob of the radiator. Lecturing about Victorian literature and the Victorian sensibility, his interpretations were wild, often suggestive, and his bravado inspired class members to violate decorum, talking freely and spontaneously—so involved

were they in the subject matter. It proved to be a liberating experience, one which freed many people in the class to write imaginatively and well about the course material.

By yourself, think about an experience you have had in a traditional setting which helped you realize your potential. Try to remember what made the experience and the teacher so good. After you abstract key elements, write a brief scenario to share with your group. You and another tutor may enact the scenario; see if you can recapture the original experience.

2. Form groups of five to seven students. Share a learning experience you have had that you feel may have been a collaborative one. Consider how old you were, who was involved, where it occurred (inside or outside of school), and whether it was a positive or negative experience. Discuss any general conclusions you can make about collaborative learning based on your collective experience.

TUTOR PREPARATION

This part of the chapter will focus on two widely used approaches in tutor preparation: group work and journal keeping. We believe these methods are central to collaborative learning and especially effective in helping tutors develop interpersonal skills and personal insights.

Group Work

A collection of individuals is not necessarily a group; however, people can become a group, that is, a coherent unit, by working together to achieve common goals. As we have already mentioned, group work has definite advantages for learning. As a member of a group studying and learning about tutoring, you have people with whom you can compare your thoughts; if it is an effective group, individuals will take responsibility for the learning of their fellow group members. They will ask for clarification, give feedback, suggest ways of revising ideas, and help each other to think clearly and precisely. Thus, each group member benefits from the insights and perspectives of the others. Ideally members of your group should feel free to express their ideas and, more, to take chances without fear of humiliation.

Some of you may be in classes, so that groups are a *part* of the class; in collaborative-learning classes these groups *are* the class. Whether you are in a class or a training program, your teacher or supervisor may initially set standards, but the group (or groups) will work toward developing its own criteria. Your goal as a group member should be a dual one: to assume not only greater responsibility for your own learning, but for that of the group as well. Many of the exercises in this text have been designed to help you practice the skills you need to reach both these goals.

Some Models and/or Techniques for Group Work

As educators (and psychologists) have begun using groups a great deal, they have devised a number of group structures which facilitate the group's smooth functioning. The structures described below have proved particularly effective both for tutor training and for group tutoring:

Paraphrase Each student must paraphrase what the preceding student said before saying what he or she wants to say.

Fishbowl There is an outside and an inside circle. The inside circle discusses an issue (or roleplays it) and the outside circle observes. If members of the outside circle want to step into the inside circle, they may, but only for a while. The outside circle then comments on the inside circle's discussion while the inside circle listens in silence. This exercise focuses on the *content* of the issue and is related to the *task orientation* of the group (what the group needs to accomplish).

Observer-Critic This method is structured like the fishbowl, except the outside circle critiques the behavior (as opposed to the content) of the inside circle. Such a method emphasizes *group maintenance* (how the group develops or sustains itself as a group).

Peer Teacher Each member of the group is responsible for teaching a prepared lesson to the class (also called *microteaching*).

Recorder Each group has a recorder (rotating or permanent) whose job it is to take minutes at each group meeting and report on group decisions to the class as a whole.

Peer Critique Students in the group are responsible for giving written evaluations of each other's work—and they must then critique these critiques.

Steering Committee Two or more members of the group act as leaders of the group each session. It is their responsibility to summarize and evaluate the group's activities during the session and to make recommendations for future work.

CLASS PROJECT 4

1. Form groups of five to seven. Using one or more of the techniques noted above, each of you should describe a significant group experience in which you have participated. Some questions you might want to consider are: Who was involved? How long did it go on? Did it have a purpose? Was the purpose different from what actually happened?

Then evaluate your group's effectiveness by answering the following questions:

a. Did you learn something?

b. How did you feel in the group?

c. How did others react to you?

d. How was this meeting different from classes using a traditional structure?

2. Describe one of your traditionally structured classes according to questions a–c in exercise 1.

3. Write a paragraph in which you brainstorm about the cartoon on p. 7. Whom do the group members remind you of? What do you think their group sessions are like? Would you like to join such a group? Why? Share your paragraph with the members of your group. If possible, roleplay some scenarios.

The Tutor's Journal

When you were younger you may have received a diary as a gift. The dated pages gave you space to record your daily experiences. It may have had a lock; if it didn't you probably hid it. That was because this journal had become the repository of your innermost feelings—hopes, wishes, fears, likes, dislikes, and dreams. You were not only using the journal to record daily events, but to examine your thoughts and feelings about these events.

Your childhood journal, then, was selective only in so far as it focused on things that were very important to you at the time. Some people use journals, however, to record one particular area of their lives. Ship captains keep logs of their voyages, writers keep journals of their ideas and doctors keep diaries of the treatments they prescribe to their patients. These people use their journals to improve themselves professionally by examining their relationship to their work—their successes and failures and their hopes and dreams.

Journals have long acted as devices for self-teaching, as they give people a tangible record with which to analyze themselves. Psychologists, in fact, recognize this form of "self-analysis" and introspection as a valuable tool for understanding oneself. For the act of verbalizing experiences and reactions to them demands that the writer think through the details of what happened and sort them out—that is, separate them into meaningful categories. Once a person has put something into words it becomes easier to understand it—and if it is a problem, perhaps a solution can be found. In addition, a record protects us from the fallibility of memory and allows us to gain a certain objectivity about exactly what happened. From this record, we may be able to discern over time certain themes or patterns. Author Joan Didion, for example, in her notes on "Keeping a Diary," says the entries help her "remember what it was to be me."

Your tutor's journal, then, should give you a chance to explore your experience as a tutor. Writing about your class or group tutoring activities will give you a permanent record of information, procedures, and techniques you will need later. Examining your activities will better enable you to understand them.

Some people experience difficulty, at first, in keeping a journal. Some do not know what to write about; others have trouble writing about their feelings;

October 17th

Ronald came back! I was sure after last week's session that he wouldn't – he was so negative about school and didn't believe tutoring could help. But he walked into the center with a big smile on his face and an 82 on the math quiz. I felt as good (if not better) than he did. We spent most of the session talking about what helped him do well on the test (practice, understanding proportions, taking the timed test) and what we should concentrate on for future work. I thought simple fractions would be better than decimals but he

Excerpt from a Math Tutor's Journal.

some write too much and never feel they are really getting anywhere. The following guidelines should help you to begin your tutor's journal:

1. Get a new notebook. It need not be specifically designed for journal writing, but it should be used only as a journal.
2. Carry your journal with you at all times at first, so that you can write down things as they occur to you.
3. Put aside a special time of the day for journal writing and allow at least

one half-hour for it. Then, although you may write in your journal at other times, you are assured that you will be writing at last once a day.

4. Write every day that you are in class or in your lab, even if nothing significant seems to happen. Often the important things do not seem so at first and can be lost if not recorded. (Writing regularly will also keep you from getting rusty.)

5. Do not worry about length. There is no correct length and long entries are not necessarily better than incisive, meaty ones.

6. Don't edit or censor what you write. Journal entries are not normally graded and grammar should not be a primary consideration. What you censor may be just what you need to learn about your feelings.

7. Don't worry about what to write. Write about anything and everything that pertains to your tutoring experience.

8. Relax. Journal writing should never be a chore, although at first it may feel somewhat awkward. Once you get into it, it can be great fun.

In addition, you might read selections from Thom Hawkins' journal to see how someone else has used this form (p. 29). Here are some suggestions about what to include in your journal:*

- feelings or thoughts, before, during, and after a session, class, or group meeting
- description of student (age, sex, major, academic background, educational history, etc.)
- students' opinions or feelings about their courses, teachers, etc.
- bits of dialogue between you and the tutee
- diagnoses of students' needs
- decisions on how you plan to meet those needs
- problems that occurred and were or were not solved
- any approaches or techniques you used or learned from senior tutors and teachers
- effects of these techniques on tutees
- your struggles and successes as a tutor
- your attitude toward what you are learning about tutoring
- your attitudes toward your tutees
- political issues or philosophical implications raised as a result of your tutoring

*The material on this list was generated primarily by Bert Eisenstadt of the LaGuardia Writing Center.

LAB APPLICATION

Make arrangements to observe some experienced tutors at work (or, if available, watch videotapes of tutorials).

a. Describe one session in your journal, using no evaluative words and expressing no feelings.

b. Describe the same session hypothetically, from the tutee's point of view. (Use the first person "I.") Tell how the tutee must have felt during the session.

c. Write up the same session from a supervisor's point of view. Try to imagine how the supervisor would evaluate the tutor.

d. Finally, describe the session from your own point of view.

CLASS PROJECT 5

1. Write a journal entry describing how you felt about the above exercises and what they taught you about journal writing.

2. Bring a journal entry you admire into class—one of your own, a friend's, or one written by a professional—and analyze what is good about it (that is, what it teaches you).

3. Describe in your journal your feelings before and after your first teaching or tutoring experience.

ABOUT NEW YORK

A Diarist and the City, From Apple to Zest

By WILLIAM E. FARRELL

Edward Robb Ellis lives contentedly with his bibliomania in the space people normally allow for their bookshelves. The rest of his Chelsea apartment is given over to his books—more than 8,000 of them lining shelves, resting on chairs, tables and sofas, stacked waist-high all over the living room, dominating the kitchen, the hallway and the bedroom, forming aisles between rooms.

He sits in a chair almost obscured by stacks of books and points to some underlinings in the Encyclopaedia Britannica's entry on Samuel Pepys, the British diarist whose private journals illuminate life in 17th-century England. "It was secret; it was full; it was honest," the entry says.

"That's what I aim for, that's what I hope for," Mr. Ellis says of the diary he started as a 16-year-old boy in Kewanee, Ill., to fend off boredom during a Christmas vacation. That was on Dec. 27, 1927, and the diary, now in its 54th year, is about 15 million words long and growing.

•

The prodigious journal has made the latest edition of the Guinness Book of World Records as "longest diary," bumping the previous titleholder, T. C. Baskerville of Charlton-cum-Hardy, Manchester, England, whose record of his life totals a mere 3.4 million words.

In the beginning, says Mr. Ellis, a lively man who has just entered the details of his 70th birthday party in his diary, "I was an immature jerk, my language was insufferable and I was posing."

"It took me a long time to learn not to try to impress others but to express myself," he says. "I'm still going strong and I've become increasingly honest. Now, I'm sure I'm 99 percent honest."

For 35 years, Mr. Ellis was a newsman, working in New Orleans, Oklahoma City, Peoria, Chicago and finally in New York, where he was a feature writer for The World-Telegram. He has written several well-reviewed books, including a study of suicide, a work on the Great Depression and a history of the place he loves best, called "The Epic of New York City."

•

"The day I got here to try out for The World-Telegram, I said, 'Damn, I should have been born in New York,'" he says. And any criticism of the city, in which he has lived since the late 1940's, only unleashes a counterattack of superlatives from him.

That affection has prompted Mr. Ellis in the last few years to work on an encyclopedia of the city, an ambitious effort to place New York from A to Z between the covers of one large volume. So far, he has 18,000 notations and there is much work to be done.

But it is his diary, he feels, that will provide historians with material on what it was like to live in America during the middle and late years of the 20th century. Most of the work is stored at the Archive of Contemporary History at the University of Wyoming in Laramie. Gene M. Gressley, the archive's director, says Mr. Ellis is "the Pepys of 20th-century America."

Mr. Ellis is currently working on ground rules for access to his diaries in order to protect those mentioned in them.

"The thing had several titles," he says. "The first was 'My Saga,' then 'Gawking Through Life,' as corny as you can get, then 'Briefly, I Tarry,' cribbed from A. E. Housman, and now it's just 'The Ellis Diary.'"

•

He bemoans an age that has neglected letter writing and insists that everyone should keep a diary for their own benefit and for the use of historians.

"I've turned many people on to writing diaries," he says. "Do it the same time every day and physically in the same spot. A diary is therapy—it's a daily confrontation with yourself. It's been second nature for me for half a century.

If I couldn't write my diary, I'd spiral down into a depression."

The Ellis obsession is such that he has arranged for some close friends to take dictation from him on his death bed, "not because I'm an important person, but because it will be fascinating."

He looks a little surprised when asked if a dull day means a brief and perfunctory entry. He says he averages three typewritten pages a day and "a really important day" will yield as many as 15 typed pages.

•

"I am totally curious about everything but professional football," he says, and this zeal impels him to inveterate note-taking so that the quickly forgotten one-liner heard at a party will find its way into the Ellis Diary. "Some of my friends are a little afraid of me," he says.

Bits, pieces, minutiae, the commonplace all go into the journal because "someday they'll be of interest," he says. "I always include the price of things, the names and addresses of restaurants. I write routine stuff because I never know what will interest the historians, and it's often the obvious stuff that gets lost."

He advocates the creation of an institution called the American Diary Repository because "the journals of obscure people are valuable, for they mirror the mood of a given era."

•

"The world is going mad at an accelerating rate and television is the Typhoid Mary of this madness," he says, "and I try to show it with minutiae."

He opens an old gift box stuffed with items for the New York City encyclopedia under the letter B. All around him are books and clippings about the city.

"I never work in libraries," he says. "Because I underline, I can't use library books." The box starts him off again on the city's virtues and the need for a one-volume work that will contain its complexity.

The conversation veers back to the diary and Mr. Ellis exhorts an interviewer to "start a diary, establish the habit."

"Tomorrow I'll write in my diary how we sat here," he says.

THE ETHICS OF TUTORING

Tutoring is a responsibility, and, although there is no Hippocratic oath, such as doctors take when they enter the medical profession, there are certain guidelines that will help tutors do their jobs effectively. Although these may vary somewhat from program to program, those we have developed rely on the experience of tutors in our own centers and on the ethical standards developed by organizations of related professions, such as teaching and counseling. Many of these rules are obvious—some may even seem petty. The temptation to discount any one or all of them might be great, and occasionally you will give in to this temptation. Yet there are important reasons—psychological, moral, and even political—for following these guidelines. You will soon find that tutoring requires a delicate balance; you must try to straddle the line between teacher and student with grace, dignity, and intelligence.

TUTORING GUIDELINES

Institutional

Determine how your tutoring program or the student's teacher feels about your "going over" student work before it is handed in. Many teachers want to be sure they are looking at the student's own work and insist on reading or grading papers before anyone else has reviewed them. (This may be especially true of writing faculty.) Others feel just as strongly that collaborative learning is a method to be practiced at all times, and they urge students to work on their assignments with others.

Do not comment negatively to students on teachers' grading policies, their teaching, or their personality. You will hear many things about teachers from your tutees, and you may know some of these teachers and have your own opinion of them. But remember that your students are giving you only one point of view, and their viewpoint may be influenced negatively by learning difficulties. Most important, students have to live with their teachers for the term. Your role is to help students get through the course with a minimum amount of pain and a maximum amount of learning—and to do that you must help students understand their teachers' judgments and attitudes.

Evaluate students' work in terms of the progress they have made in the tutorial rather than in terms of a grade. Students may not get the grade you think they deserve, and if they don't they might lose confidence in your ability to gauge standards. In addition, they might try to use your opinion as a lever to win a higher grade from their teacher (if your estimation is higher than the teacher's). At any rate, if you and the teacher openly disagree about a grade, conflict between the teacher and you, and perhaps the tutoring program as well, is likely to result. In any case, you diminish your effectiveness as a tutor. Part of the value of your role is that you are, most likely, removed from the grading process and thus from the negative feelings grades often evoke in students.

Instructional

Guide your tutee toward doing his or her own work. Get the student as actively involved in the learning process as possible. Do not do work for a student (for example, write a paper, solve a problem).

Be honest with students when you don't know an answer. If you're unsure of an answer, ask another tutor or look it up: after all, you can't know everything. Don't be afraid or ashamed to say, "I don't know." In admitting that you don't know, you are showing the tutee that it is okay not to know; in fact, you've got to admit what it is that you don't know before you can begin to learn it.

Find out what you know. Whether you use the assessment material in the pamphlets accompanying this text or the diagnostic materials available in your program for this purpose, you will be able to learn what additional academic work you need for your tutoring.* A discussion with your supervisor might also help you define the goals for mastering the subject matter you tutor.

Always explain to tutees what you are doing and why, and gain their approval, when appropriate. In general, this guideline is based on the notion that students in an academic setting expect, and deserve, a rational explanation for whatever the institution involves them in, so that they can give their "informed consent."

Personal

Always call the student, program supervisor, or the center if you will be late or have to miss an appointment. Students do not ask for help easily, and if you are late or absent it is all too easy for them to interpret this as lack of caring. Even if a student tends to be late, *you* must be there on time; this will enhance his or her confidence in you as someone worthy of trust.

Honor the confidentiality of the tutorial relationship. Trust is at the heart of a tutoring relationship, and if your students feel they can trust you they will be more apt to want to learn from you. Even a harmless remark about a tutee or other tutees or tutors can be misinterpreted as a betrayal of trust. If you feel students will benefit from your revealing what you know to their teacher or counselor, do this only with the students' permission.

Know when and how to refer a student for professional guidance. It is important to establish a warm, friendly rapport with your tutees. Subsequent chapters will focus on the development of counseling skills and on your role as a tutor-counselor. But if the students' problems are at all serious—that is, if they seem to be interfering radically and consistently with learning—do not attempt to deal with the problem yourself. Learn about the kind of professional help available at school or elsewhere, locally; learn the school's procedures for referral; discuss such matters with your instructor or the lab or program supervisor.

The Writing Tutor by Marian Arkin and Barbara Shollar, *The Math Tutor* by Peter Rosnick, *Tutoring ESL Students* by Marian Arkin, and *Tutoring Reading and Academic Survival Skills* by Barbara Shollar.

WHAT YOU CAN EXPECT FROM YOUR TUTEE

In a sense, ethical standards you establish are one key to what your tutee can expect from you; therefore it may be beneficial to explain these standards to your tutee at some point during your initial sessions. You may also want to guide your tutees to an understanding of what they can bring to their sessions so that tutoring will be more productive for them.

1. Your tutees should bring with them relevant materials: text, class notes, syllabus, and written assignments. Tutees should also be prepared to provide any other information that will be helpful in defining their problems or needs (due dates, upcoming examinations, conflicts).
2. Your tutee should tell you if something the two of you are working on will be handed in to the teacher.
3. Tutees should extend you the same courtesy you give them of calling if they are to be late for or must cancel an appointment. (Policy in some schools dictates that tutors will not be paid unless their tutee shows, and if that is the case, you should make your tutee aware of it.) Similarly, if your tutee no longer wants tutoring (with you, or at all), you should be able to expect that he or she will inform you.

CLASS PROJECT 6

As a class or group, discuss the ethical questions laid out in the previous section. What are the psychological, moral, and practical reasons for them (in addition to the explanations we offer) that might be relevant? Discuss anything you would like to include in these guidelines or any items that you feel should be omitted.

LAB APPLICATION

Locate the most popular texts in your field and learn the audiovisual teaching aids in your center, in your tutoring department, or at the media center or library. Allow yourself time to browse and to become familiar with the instructional materials you might use in tutoring.

READING 1

The great British novelist Charles Dickens (1812–1870) wrote many works which protested the unjust conditions in Victorian Eng-

land brought about by the new technology and rapid industrialization of the countryside. The writer cast an equally scornful eye on many of the social institutions which dehumanized the English people: debtor's prisons, chancery (the courts), charities, and schools. Yet even in his sharpest and most withering satire, as in Hard Times, he still communicated the vitality and complexity of human beings and the drama of human experience. In creating Thomas Gradgrind, Dickens has created a "monster" teacher, an exaggeration of all the worst qualities a teacher can have: authoritarianism, bigotry, impatience, insensitivity. Instead of nurturing intelligence and imagination, Gradgrind stifles it.

READING QUESTIONS

1. Why did Dickens name his character Gradgrind? Why is Gradgrind so insistent on Facts? And what of the description of the physical environment—how does it relate to Dickens' purpose?

2. What are the ideal teacher and the ideal student as defined by Mr. Gradgrind and Mr. M'Choakumchild? How do these seem to contrast with Dickens' ideals? the ideals of collaborative learning? the ideals you have developed in your discussions so far?

1 | HARD TIMES

Charles Dickens

THE ONE THING NEEDFUL

"Now, what I want, is Facts. Teach these boys and girls nothing but Facts. Facts alone are wanted in life. Plant nothing else, and root out everything else. You can only form the minds of reasoning animals upon Facts: nothing else will ever be of any service to them. This is the principle on which I bring up my own children, and this is the principle on which I bring up these children. Stick to Facts, sir!"

The scene was a plain, bare, monotonous vault of a schoolroom, and the speaker's square forefinger emphasized his observations by underscoring every sentence with a line on the schoolmaster's sleeve. The emphasis was helped by the speaker's square wall of a forehead, which had his eyebrows for its base, while his eyes found commodious cellarage in two dark caves, overshadowed by the wall. The emphasis was helped by the speaker's mouth, which was wide, thin, and hard set. The emphasis was helped by the speaker's voice, which was inflexible, dry, and dictatorial. The emphasis was helped by the speaker's hair, which bristled on the skirts of his bald head, a plantation of firs to keep the wind from its shining surface, all covered with knobs, like the crust of a plum pie, as if the head had scarcely warehouse-room for the hard facts stored inside. The speaker's obstinate carriage, square coat, square legs, square shoulders,—nay, his very neckcloth, trained to take him by the throat with an unaccommodating grasp, like a stubborn fact, as it was,—all helped the emphasis.

"In this life we want nothing but Facts, sir; nothing but Facts!"

The speaker, and the schoolmaster, and the third grown person present, all backed a little, and swept with their eyes the inclined plane of little vessels then and there arranged in order, ready to have imperial gallons of facts poured into them until they were full to the brim.

MURDERING THE INNOCENTS

Thomas Gradgrind, sir. A man of realities. A man of facts and calculations. A man who proceeds upon the principle that two and two are four, and nothing over, and who is not to be talked into allowing for anything over. Thomas Gradgrind, sir — peremptorily Thomas—Thomas Gradgrind. With a rule and a pair of scales, and the multiplication table always in his pocket, sir, ready to weigh and measure any parcel of human nature, and tell you exactly what it comes to. It is a mere question of figures, a case of simple arithmatic. You might hope to get some other nonsensical belief into the head of George Gradgrind, or Augustus Gradgrind, or John Gradgrind, or Joseph Gradgrind (all supposititious, non-existent persons), but into the head of Thomas Gradgrind — no, sir!

In such terms Mr. Gradgrind always mentally introduced himself, whether to his private circle of acquaintance, or to the public in general. In such terms, no doubt, substituting the words "boys and girls" for "sir," Thomas Gradgrind now presented Thomas Gradgrind to the little pitchers before him, who were to be filled so full of facts.

Indeed, as he eagerly sparkled at them from the cellarage before mentioned, he seemed a kind of cannon loaded to the muzzle with facts, and prepared to blow them clean out of the regions of childhood at one discharge. He seemed a galvanizing apparatus, too, charged with a grim mechanical substitute for the tender young imaginations that were to be stormed away.

"Girl number twenty," said Mr. Gradgrind, squarely pointing with his square forefinger, "I don't know that girl. Who is that girl?"

"Sissy Jupe, sir," explained number twenty, blushing, standing up, and curtsying.

"Sissy is not a name," said Mr. Gradgrind. "Don't call yourself Sissy. Call yourself Cecilia."

"It's father as calls me Sissy, sir." returned the young girl in a trembling voice, and with another curtsy.

"Then he has no business to do it," said Mr. Gradgrind. "Tell him he mustn't. Cecilia Jupe. Let me see. What is your father?"

"He belongs to the horse-riding, if you please, sir."

Mr. Gradgrind frowned, and waved off the objectionable calling with his hand.

"We don't want to know anything about that here. You mustn't tell us about that here. Your father breaks horses, don't he?"

"If you please, sir, when they can get any to break, they do break horses in the ring, sir."

"You mustn't tell us about the ring here. Very well, then. Describe your father as a horse-breaker. He doctors sick horses, I dare say?"

"Oh yes, sir."

"Very well, then. He is a veterinary surgeon, a farrier, and horsebreaker. Give me your definition of a horse."

(Sissy Jupe thrown into the greatest alarm by this demand.)

"Girl number twenty unable to define a horse!" said Mr. Gradgrind, for the general behoof of all the little pitchers. "Girl number twenty possessed of no facts in reference to one of the commonest of animals! Some boy's definition of a horse. Bitzer, yours."

The square finger, moving here and there, lighted suddenly on Bitzer, perhaps, because he chanced to sit in the same ray of sunlight which, darting in at one of the bare windows of the intensely whitewashed room, irradiated Sissy. For, the boys and girls sat on the face of the inclined plane in two compact bodies, divided up the centre by a narrow interval; and Sissy, being at the corner of a row on the sunny side, came in for the beginning of a sunbeam, of which Bitzer, being at the corner of a row on the other side, a few rows in advance, caught the end. But, whereas the girl was so dark-eyed and dark-haired that she seemed to receive a deeper and more lustrous color from the sun when it shone upon her, the boy was so light-eyed and light-haired that the selfsame rays appeared to draw out of him what little color he ever possessed. His cold eyes would hardly have been eyes, but for the short ends of lashes which, by bringing them into immediate contrast with something paler than themselves, expressed their form. His short-cropped hair might have been a mere continuation of the sandy freckles on his forehead and face. His skin was so unwholesomely deficient in the natural tinge, that he looked as though, if he were cut, he would bleed white.

"Bitzer," said Thomas Gradgrind, "your definition of a horse."

"Quadruped. Graminivorous. Forty teeth, namely, twenty-four grinders, four eye-teeth, and twelve incisive. Sheds coat in the spring; in marshy countries, sheds hoofs too. Hoofs hard, but requiring to be shod with iron. Age known by marks in mouth." Thus (and much more) Bitzer.

"Now, girl number twenty," said Mr. Gradgrind, "you know what a horse is."

She curtsied again, and would have blushed deeper, if she could have blushed deeper than she had blushed all this time. Bitzer, after rapidly blinking at Thomas Gradgrind with both eyes at once, and so catching the light upon his quivering ends of lashes that they looked like the antennae of busy insects, put his knuckles to his freckled forehead, and sat down again.

The third gentleman now stepped forth. A mighty man at cutting and drying he was; a government officer; in his way (and in most other people's too) a professed pugilist; always in training, always with a system to force down the general throat like a bolus, always to be heard of at the bar of his little Public Office, ready to fight all England. To continue in fistic phraseology, he had a genius for coming up to the scratch, wherever and whatever it was, and proving himself an ugly customer. He would go in and damage any subject whatever with his right, follow up with his left, stop, exchange, counter, bore his opponent (he always fought All England) to the ropes, and fall upon him neatly. He was certain to knock the wind out of common sense, and render that unlucky adversary deaf to the call of time. And he had it in charge from high authority to bring about the great Public Office Millennium, when Commissioners should reign upon earth.

"Very well," said this gentlemen, briskly smiling, and folding his arms. "That's a horse. Now, let me ask you girls and boys, Would you paper a room with representations of horses?"

After a pause, one-half of the children cried in chorus, "Yes, sir!" Upon which the other half, seeing in the gentleman's face that Yes was wrong, cried out in chorus, "No, sir!" — as the custom is in these examinations.

"Of course, No. Why wouldn't you?"

A pause. One corpulent slow boy, with a wheezy manner of breathing, ventured the answer, Because he wouldn't paper a room at all, but would paint it.

"You *must* paper it," said the gentleman, rather warmly.

"You must paper it," said Thomas Gradgrind, "whether you like it or not. Don't tell *us* you wouldn't paper it. What do you mean, boy?"

"I'll explain to you, then," said the gentleman, after another and a dismal pause, "why you wouldn't paper a room with representations of horses. Do you ever see horses walking up and down the sides of rooms in reality—in fact? Do you?"

"Yes, sir!" from one-half. "No, sir!" from the other.

"Of course, no," said the gentleman, with an indignant look at the wrong half. "Why, then, you are not to see anywhere what you don't see in fact; you are not to have anywhere what you don't have in fact. What is called Taste is only another name for Fact."

Thomas Gradgrind nodded his approbation.

"This is a new principle, a discovery, a great discovery," said the gentleman. "Now, I'll try you again. Suppose you were going to carpet a room. Would you use a carpet having a representation of flowers upon it?"

There being a general conviction by this time that "No, sir!" was always the right answer to this gentleman, the chorus of No was very strong. Only a few feeble stragglers said Yes; among them Sissy Jupe.

"Girl number twenty," said the gentleman, smiling in the calm strength of knowledge.

Sissy blushed and stood up.

"So you would carpet your room—or your husband's room, if you were a grown woman, and had a husband—with representations of flowers, would you?" said the gentleman. "Why would you?"

"If you please, sir, I am very fond of flowers," returned the girl.

"And is that why you would put tables and chairs upon them, and have people walking over them with heavy boots?"

"It wouldn't hurt them, sir. They wouldn't crush and wither if you please, sir. They would be the pictures of what was very pretty and pleasant, and I would fancy—"

"Ay, ay, ay! But you mustn't fancy," cried the gentleman, quite elated by coming so happily to this point. "That's it! You are never to fancy."

"You are not, Cecilia Jupe," Thomas Gradgrind solemnly repeated, "to do anything of that kind."

"Fact, fact, fact!" said the gentleman. And "Fact, fact, fact!" repeated Thomas Gradgrind.

"You are to be in all things regulated and governed," said the gentleman, "by fact. We hope to have, before long, a board of fact, composed of commissioners of fact, who will force the people to be a people of fact, and of nothing but fact. You must discard the word Fancy altogether. You have nothing to do with it. You are not to have, in any object of use or ornament, what would be a contradiction in fact. You don't walk upon flowers in fact; you cannot be allowed to walk upon flowers in carpets. You don't find that foreign birds and butterflies come and perch upon your crockery; you cannot be permitted to paint foreign birds and butterflies upon your crockery. You never meet with quadrupeds going up and down walls; you must not have quadrupeds represented upon walls. You must use," said the gentleman, "for all these purposes, combinations and modifications (in primary colors) of mathematical figures which are susceptible of proof and demonstration. This is the new discovery. This is fact. This is taste."

The girl curtsied, and sat down. She was very young, and she looked as if she were frightened by the matter-of-fact prospect the world afforded.

"Now, if Mr. M'Choakumchild," said the gentleman, "will proceed to give his first lesson here, Mr. Gradgrind, I shall be happy, at your request, to observe his mode of procedure."

Mr. Gradgrind was much obliged. "Mr. M'Choakumchild, we only wait for you."

So, Mr. M'Choakumchild began in his best manner. He, and some one hundred and forty other schoolmasters, had been lately turned at the same time, in the same factory, on the same principles, like so many pianoforte legs. He had been put through an immense variety of paces, and had answered volumes of head-breaking questions. Orthography, etymology, syntax, and prosody, biography, astronomy, geography, and general cosmography, the sciences of compound proportion, algebra, land surveying and levelling, vocal music, and drawing from models, were all at the ends of his ten chilled fingers. He had worked his stony way into her Majesty's most Honorable Privy Council's Schedule B, and had taken the bloom off the higher branches of mathematics and physical science, French, German, Latin, and Greek. He knew all about all the

Water Sheds of all the world (whatever they are), and all the histories of all the peoples, and all the names of all the rivers and mountains, and all the productions, manners, and customs of all the countries, and all their boundaries and bearings on the two and thirty points of the compass. Ah, rather overdone, M'Choakumchild! If he had only learnt a little less, how infinitely better he might have taught much more!

He went to work, in this preparatory lesson, not unlike Morgiana in the Forty Thieves: looking into all the vessels ranged before him, one after another, to see what they contained. Say, good M'Choakumchild. When, from thy boiling store, thou shalt fill each jar brimful by and by, dost thou think that thou wilt always kill outright the robber Fancy lurking within—or sometimes only maim him and distort him?

READING 2

The excerpt you are about to read is from a textbook designed to teach students to write autobiography. As you will see, the book is based on premises similar to those expressed in this book, primarily that the class is a community in which ideas, and feelings about ideas, are shared.

READING QUESTIONS

1. What difference do you think it makes that this book was written at a time of great social ferment, when America was engaged in the war in Vietnam and students were protesting on campuses and in the streets? What aspects of today's society could arouse students and educators to seek changes in public institutions?

2. How can the classroom be used best as a place for learning?

3. Do you agree with the writers' psychological assessment of the "costumed" young woman? Might her disguise have any other social or political meaning?

4. What gives a teacher the right to be an authority?

5. What are a teacher's responsibilities to his or her students, department, and college?

6. What is the student's responsibility to the teacher, program, and college?

2 | AUTOBIOGRAPHY AND THE CLASSROOM

Roger Porter and Howard Wolf

Let us turn now to some remarks about education underlying much of this book. To begin with, this chapter (and indeed the entire book) is addressed to both the teacher and the student. We have deliberately avoided making a distinction in audience, because the book is based partly on the assumption that the course will work best when there is a sense of shared experience in the classroom, where the boundary between teacher and student is less rigid then usual. Our remarks in this chapter may seem to switch back and forth between the two audiences. but they are really meant for both.

We assume that a student's presentation of his own experience and the discussion of this experience in the classroom are as important as the texts we have chosen. We have thought of autobiography in this broad sense and even believe that the experience of the class as a group is a subject suitable for discussion and analysis. In its own way a class is a community, and there is no reason why students cannot write about their experience in that community just as they might write about life in a hometown or in any living group.

Although teachers of composition have always asked students to write about their personal experience, the assignments have generally been limited to "topics of interest" to the student. Teachers often ask, for instance, What does college mean to you? but not often enough, How do you feel about being in college? And even when the second question is asked, many teachers either do not expect, or are unprepared for, responses and feelings that do not fit into the context of what is "appropriate to express in a classroom." Even "enlightened" teachers can impose their own constraints on a class. This may be especially true when a student raises issues that are controversial and threatening to the life style or intellectual and emotional presuppositions of the teacher. And students themselves can support these constraints by refraining from introducing controversial issues and feelings.

Most students and teachers have been unaware of the classroom as a medium that has a decisive influence upon how we feel and act. Unless we can see the classroom as a place not for mere ritualistic learning but where significant emotional as well as intellectual events can occur, we are likely to continue promoting many of the attitudes and assumptions that have made so many of our campuses embittered and embattled. Before the classroom can become such a place where what happens within and between people means something to the members of the group as an event in itself, there will have to be a change in the concept of a class, not unlike changes that have taken place in contemporary theater.

The traditional classroom, like the traditional theater, put the student in a seat and asked him to observe a performance enacted on a stage at some distance. However, the classroom should not merely be an assigned place for meetings, but rather an arena in which all members are participants, conscious of choosing and creating roles in scenarios or from scripts of human development, insight, and learning. Like much of contemporary theater, classes could well be made "experiences-in-the-round," with even greater access to the stage, student participation in the play, and increased awareness on the part of the teacher that his best lines may arise spontaneously from the drama of the class. Although the teacher would also be a director, we should now think of him as a new, flexible director—capable of presenting classics but encouraging his cast to put themselves into the play and even to write their own dramas.

Whatever our attitudes toward education may be, it is difficult to deny that we bring ourselves to class in a profound sense. In not realizing this, teachers have often overlooked what the students may be experiencing in the classroom environment. Teachers too often forget that if they assume the role of absolute authority, they will necessarily evoke in students feelings that relate to their earliest experiences with authority in the home, the early school years, and the society at large. If the teacher assumes an authoritarian role, the students will expect him to be judgmental, to demand "right" answers, and to insist on students' passivity. Such expectations will make it difficult for a student to assert himself without fear of reprisal and will force him to play a passive role as a way of avoiding imagined judgment.

A crucial distinction must be made between authority and authoritarianism. The former represents articulated experience, knowledge, and insight. The latter represents their counterfeits: age masquerading as maturity, information as understand-ing, technique as originality. Authoritarianism is forced to demand the respect that authority draws naturally to itself. The former, like all demands, is likely to be met with hostility; the latter, like all authenticity, with emulation. Our universities—our schools at every level—are rife with authoritarianism, all but devoid of authority.[1]

This does not mean that the teacher should abandon or disavow his expertise or experi-ence, merely that he should create an atmosphere in class in which everyone is encour-aged to offer his own perspective on an issue, knowing that it will be respected and examined on its own terms. In this atmosphere everyone can begin to take respon-sibility for his own thought and education.

We have found in our experience that many students are passive and afraid to risk self-assertion, choosing, as it were, to conceal themselves behind a veil of noncommit-ment. Often a teacher's comments and responses will be taken not simply as one expe-rienced person's point of view but as gospel, and this may result, however inadvert-ently, in an awesome and overpowering condemnation of the student. Authoritarianism in the classroom probably means that much controversy goes underground; if it does, an opportunity is missed to help the student become aware of his varied—often oppos-ing—thoughts and feelings, and thus of his complexity as a person. If we neglect some of these issues, teacher and student may even come to see themselves as persecutor and persecuted, as the following classroom encounter reveals.

One of the authors of this book went into class to teach Hawthorne's short story "The Minister's Black Veil." The night before he had seen a film called *Far From Vietnam* and couldn't separate his feelings about the story from his response to the film. Had he been truer to his concept of teaching, he would have discussed the extent to which anyone, even a teacher of literature, can legitimately claim to read a text with "objective detachment." Could he have approached Hawthorne on that day without having the war in Vietnam somewhere in his mind? He might even have discussed whether it was possible for a teacher to separate literary analysis from his own life experience, his own moral and political values, or a particular moment in history. But he felt that such openness would betray "professional" standards; instead, he launched a formal analysis of the story.

When a student objected to the gloom and depression in Hawthorne, he began to attack her defensive blindness, her inclination to see art as merely entertaining and uplifting, and her desire to tame and domesticate harsh experience. He invoked as much modern history as came to mind and asked, Is that actuality or mere gloom? When the class ended, the student seemed frightened. He wondered if she would come back for the next class; she did, but in disguise. She was heavily powdered, her face almost masklike, and wearing a wig; she was, for a moment, unrecognizable. Had she assumed a false self to protect a wounded one? Had she chosen a kind of nonbeing as a way of not being hurt anymore? He taught a subdued class and afterward asked the girl to come to his office. There he apologized for turning his rage about the war against her. She accepted the apology, perhaps too readily, as if it were best to deny that there had ever been an upsetting experience.

In the following class, without making reference to the girl's disguise, he asked the group to speak about what had happened. There was a general discussion of the relation between subject matter and one's feelings toward it and about the extent to which one's personal feelings are admissable in the classroom. It was the best class of the semester. The girl continued to attend, undisguised, and was more willing to partic-ipate than before. However painful it was for her, she had begun to emerge as a person (as opposed to just being a "student"). The class had achieved, at least for awhile, a strong sense of community.

This young woman's experience suggests that self-evaluation is possible and, fi-

[1]Martin Duberman, "An Experiment in Education" *Daedalus* 97 (1968), 321-322.

nally, comfortable in a classroom if the teacher and the group are committed to creating an atmosphere of trust in which what one feels and thinks is respected in and of itself, and not merely subject to a teacher's approval or disapproval.

To illustrate further this deep and often unstated relationship between student and teacher, we would like to cite an account of a dream submitted to one of the authors in a course dealing with the literature of personal crisis, where an attempt was made to relate critical experiences of the members of the class, as expressed in their auto-biographical prose, to the literature of crisis in poetry, fiction, and drama. Keep in mind that we are trying to override traditional divisions between what students feel and what they think the teacher wants them to feel, between the self-image one offers for approval to others and the self-image one knows in moments of truth to be his own. This dream is one instance of an often unexamined dimension of the classroom:

> Since I couldn't think of any experience which seemed relevant to mental crises which I would want discussed, I decided instead to relate a dream which I feel is pertinent to this class. First, however, I feel a little background must be given. I was a student in one of ———'s classes last year and I had a hang-up about speaking in class. I was very interested in the discussion and always attended class, but I often hesitated to say what was on my mind, no matter how determined I was that I would speak. Also, lack of class participation was one of ———'s pet peeves, so it made the situation doubly tense. It seemed whenever I did speak I was rebuffed or a reply was made that slightly embarrassed me, thus adding to the dilemma. Enough history. This semester when I tried to register for ———'s class, I was closed out. This necessitated going to him personally and obtaining a class card. At this time, I had a dream which seems to capture my fears. I dreamt that I was the only girl in ———'s class and that during one session I was sitting on his desk carrying on an intimate discussion with him for the benefit of the whole class. I don't know what the discussion was about or any other details, but why was I sitting on the desk, expecially since ——— never sits at one but rather in a regular chair? I'm sure there is a significance in its being a predominantly male class. These things bother me—besides the obvious fact that I was carrying on a conversation with———, which in reality is something I have difficulty doing. I think it would be interesting to hear someone else's view of this apparently simple dream.

This dream, however brief, contains material that we could discuss at length—such as the unexpressed erotic components in the classroom—but what we want to emphasize here are this student's feeling of having been "rebuffed" and her appeal at the end "to hear someone else's view of this apparently simple dream." Her fear of being "closed out," as well as her desire to have her emotions shared and validated by the class, typify the feeling of many undergraduates, and certainly a great many women. Once students become aware that their feelings and crises may be shared and understood, it becomes easier for individuals to speak directly about their conflicts.

Two other examples, based on our experience, further suggest the ways in which we bring ourselves to class with apprehension and why it is important to reduce this apprehension. One of our students repeatedly handed in blank papers during class exercises, even when those exercises were not being graded. It became clear that judgment of any kind was intolerable to her. Her "blankness" was a way of saying, I will not put myself in a position where judgment is possible. She was able to support this fiction of safety, even while knowing it would lead to failure.

A friend of ours often dreams that he must pass a Latin exam if he is to get his M.A. degree. He already has an M.A. and has never studied Latin. This suggests that judgment in an educational setting can be internalized in a way that has little direct relation to a particular concrete reality, even to an experience of success.

These examples indicate the need for new approaches to teaching and learning, approaches that will help us all recover our humanness by gaining access to resources in the self that we often deny and close off to others. In this sense our book is an attempt to deal with the essentially modern problem of fragmentation and isolation. Most critics of modern culture agree that we do not easily express our inner life in its full emotional and intellectual wholeness, that the world we move through (including our institutions of higher education) does not reflect and support our deepest personal needs. Our lives have become splintered, and we must try to reconstitute ourselves by establishing a unity within the self and a meaningful connection between self and other.

In writing this book we have tried to find ways of moving toward an integration of the mind and the senses. Harold Taylor, a noted American educator, points to this integration: "The intellect is not a separate faculty. It is an activity of the *whole* organism, an activity which begins in the senses with direct experience of facts, events, and ideas, and it involves the emotions."[2] We hope that teachers and students will reject the notions that learning and human development are disconnected and that content and its recipient are unrelated. Although progressive educators have held to an integrative position for a long while, there is not much evidence that higher education has been responsive to the need for students to claim knowledge as their own or to impress themselves upon the material as much as some teachers want to imprint knowledge upon them. If we insist on maintaining that our ability to reason or analyze is separated from our emotional life, or that the classroom and the intellect are categorically distinct from all other aspects of our being, we may prevent each other from seeing how our values have developed and our aspirations formed. We may never understand ourselves in relation to whatever we are studying.

Even though most teachers in American colleges and universities do not, in any obvious sense, mean to make learning a frightening experience, the following excerpt from George Orwell's "Such, Such Were the Joys . . . "an autobiographical account of his early boarding-school days in England—illustrates a connection between his education in 1910 and our sense of the present situation of much American education.

> Very early it was impressed upon me that I had no chance of a decent future unless I won a scholarship at a public school. . . . Indeed, it was universally taken for granted at Crossgates that unless you went to a "good" public school (and only about fifteen came under this heading) you were ruined for life. It is not easy to convey to a grown-up person the sense of strain, of nerving oneself for some terrible, all-deciding combat, as the date of the examination crept nearer—eleven years old, twelve years old, then thirteen, the fatal year itself! Over a period of two years, I do not think there was ever a day when "the exam," as I called it, was quite out of my waking thoughts. In my prayers it figured invariably: and whenever I got the bigger portion of a wishbone, or picked up a horseshoe, or bowed seven times to a new moon, or succeeded in passing through a wishing-gate without touching the sides, then the wish I earned by doing so went on "the exam" as a matter of course. And yet curiously enough I was also tormented by an almost irresistible impulse not to work. . . I would go through periods of idleness and stupidity when I would sink deeper and deeper into disgrace and even achieve a sort of feeble defiance, fully conscious of my guilt and yet unable or unwilling—I could not be sure which—to do any better.

Orwell went on to pass "the exam," as he did many courageous things in his life—such as fight on the side of the Loyalists during the Spanish Civil War of 1936–39—but he never forgot the authoritarianism of his teachers at Crossgate: "Part of the reason for the ugliness of adults in a child's eyes is that the child is usually looking upwards, and few faces are at their best when seen from below."[3] Much of the usefulness of our book will depend on the ability of its readers to make education something other than an

---

[2]*Art and the Intellect* (New York: Museum of Modern Art, 1960), pp. 12–13.

[3]*A Collection of Essays* (New York: Doubleday, 1954), pp. 20–21, 52–53.

experience of "looking upwards" for the student. *Sharing vision* and *looking within* have been our aims all along.

Perhaps it would be best to start this course with each member of the class, including the teacher, discussing and writing about some version of the following questions: What are your expectations about this course? What have been the high and low points of your previous education? How might a course in reading and writing autobiography recapture and even move beyond those high points? In what ways do you think that writing about your present and past selves can be relevant to your education? To speak about your previous education may be the way to direct your present educational experience in new channels. To reduce the distance between the class and life does not mean that we deny the past (of either an individual, a culture, or a tradition), but rather that we acknowledge the continuities of what we have been and might become. Perhaps at the end of the semester another set of responses can be written with this additional question in mind: Have I changed and if so, how? A comparison of these arbitrary beginning and end points of self-investigation might replace "the exam."

READING 3

Thom Hawkins, Director of the Writing Center at the University of California at Berkeley, was a graduate student when he first decided to tutor a young black man named Benjamin and to keep a journal of that experience. The following is excerpted from his journal in which we see him at first "stumbling about" and then gradually developing security, competence, and expertise. While Hawkins rewrote and edited the journal to educate the reader and clarify the narrative, his final product does preserve the journal's chronological order and concern with process. Since the journal is about an adult tutee (and tutor), you may want to reread this after you have read chapter 9 on adult learners.

READING QUESTIONS

1. Aside from academic details, what does Hawkins record about Benjamin and his life, and why?

2. How does Hawkins feel about Benjamin? How does he convey it to you? How does Hawkins feel about his ability to tutor Benjamin?

3. Hawkins was tutoring outside a school structure and consequently had neither professional colleagues nor peer tutors to turn to. How and in what ways do you think this might have influenced his journal keeping?

4. What does *Benjamin* teach you about keeping your own journal?

5. Hawkins suggests several important guidelines for tutors. Some of these are implied, some are explicit. What are they?

6. Compare Hawkins to Gradgrind. What are the similarities and differences between the two? (Include any differences you note between teaching and tutoring.)

---

3 | BENJAMIN: READING AND BEYOND

Thom Hawkins

STUMBLING ABOUT

Friday, September 18, 1970

This first meeting will be short. I want chiefly to understand what is motivating Ben and to hear him read.

He sees me stumbling down the sidewalk trying to find his house number, and, opening the door, signals to me. We shake hands warmly, and he takes me inside. They have the lower flat in a duplex that has been condemned to make way for a new city parking lot. All the ambiguities of poverty are here, such as a giant color tv in the living room and a washboard in the kitchen. Ben quips, "The old way's da bes way. Who need a washin machine anyway." But his shirts are yellow and his wife is exhausted. Althea is the same age as her husband (nineteen years old) but seems wiser and older—perhaps she has fewer illusions. He sports a moustache and sideburns, and there's a jagged two-inch scar on his forehead, partially concealed by a mild Afro hairdo. His strong black features are animated by flashing eyes and a quick smile.

The children, Ben Jr. (two years old) and Paul (one year old) are asleep, so we sit down at the coffee table in the living room, putting the kitchen between us and the boys' open door. There's an impressive sofa, new and sheathed in plastic, with an ornately framed painting of a black conquistador covering most of the wall above it. We speak generally about why Ben wants to read. "Now, man, there ain't* no way I can gi

---

*On contractions like "don't," "didn't," "won't," etc., Ben customarily drops the final consonant, ending the word with a nasal. His dialect, however, is anything but consistent. While he may say "little" in one phrase, he'll say "lil" in the next. In one breath he'll say "nothin," but a second later it comes out "nuffin." He can be very ethnic or he can be very "proper."

I've not tried consciously to standardize his speech to any known model of what black dialect is but, rather, have tuned my ear solely to Ben's music. What I've transcribed is, therefore, as idiosyncratic as it is ethnic. In some cases, the reader will find phonetic approximations, while in others, the words are merely shortened, as in those instances where it would confuse the sense of a word unnecessarily to spell it phonetically.

Ben grew up around friends and relatives recently immigrated from the South, and his speech reflects a rural influence at least as much as it does the slang of the urban ghetto.

a job wifout bein able to read an write. It take me so long to fill out an apple-cation that by the time I'm done, the Man, he find hiself another boy."

Although he considers literacy the key to job success, it is plain at the outset that reading has become a matter of pride to him as well. "Well, I'm a revolutionary you know, like I doan take no shit from Mr. Charley. If someone on my back I'm gonna tell him where to gi off. But I doan think I'm a militant. Noway I'm gonna pick up a gun. I believe in God an love—let them others do the hatin. Me an Althea, we been readin *Malcolm X* together. Wow, that cat, he got it down—I mean he *really* down." (Althea seems to have no major problems with reading and writing.)

Ben was able to buy most of the furniture on the salary from his first job. Two years ago he was making $2.50 an hour, but it lasted only six months (the job was temporary), and he has never found work since at more than $2.00 an hour. At first, he accepted the low wages as being inevitable for a high school dropout, but he also came to realize that something else was involved—his color.

He had received training at the Job Skills Center to be a short order cook, and the center had placed him in a position. The work was in a newly opened restaurant, and business was slow at first, so Ben didn't complain about the salary ($1.80 an hour). He soon proved to be a good cook, both reliable and industrious. The restaurant prospered quickly, and as he watched the daily receipts pile up, he thought he would be justified in asking for a raise, since he felt he had demonstrated his competency. After repeatedly approaching the owner in a polite way, only to be turned down flat each time, he one day found himself telling his white employer, "I'm a man too an you got no right to treat me this way." The reply was that if he didn't like it there, he could go somewhere else and find a job. Never consciously anti-white before, Ben was turned by this experience toward a more "revolutionary" attitude about his place in society.

He now feels that he must learn to read and write because he has to prove that he's "jis as much a man as any white-cat, an more." He wants a job that will offer a chance to advance and reward him for good service.

Ben is in the process of self-discovery and has great ambitions. He looks beyond the present to a prosperous occupation in some skilled trade and hopes that someday he can go to college and become a social worker. Such a headful of dreams!

"Well, great," I think, "but how do I get him down to earth long enough to just read the newspaper and fill out applications?"

After he's talked about himself for a while, I ask him to read aloud a passage from a fourth grade-level adult reader. He has difficulty with it and has to read the paragraph twice to answer my questions about content. He is obviously not beyond fourth grade level in terms of most skills, although my instinct tells me that he may be able to work above that level in certain areas. For instance, he can syllabicate very well and is saturated with the familiar media vocabulary, including words like ecology, pollution, and recession. He frequently tries more difficult material on his own, such as the stories of famous black Americans published by *Classic Comics*. I can't help feeling that he knows more than he's letting on.

Replying to my question about reading orally, he tells me, "I can read to myself, but, man, it feel kinna funny. I doan feel like I really done read something less I do it out loud." Since my interest at this point is diagnostic, I offer no solution but prepare to leave (thirty minutes have passed). But first I show him some reading materials which he can either purchase or read now and pay for later. He gives me a dime for one issue of *News For You* (Syracuse, N.Y.: New Readers Press.), a weekly adult news tabloid attractively designed for beginning readers. It's published in two editions, and Ben takes the A edition, written for third and fourth grade skills level. The B edition is for the fourth to fifth grade level. The paper does an exemplary job of accurate reporting and gives better coverage to stories and features about minorities than most regular news services offer.

Ben takes one book on credit, a fifty-page, fourth-grade-level adult reader about blacks in American history. I have reservations about how Ben will react to the book because it implies that the most successful blacks were those who were the best Christians and looked most like white people. Ben, however, is enthusiastic about it and eagerly plans to read several of the one-page chapters before our next meeting. I figure he should make his own critical judgments. We are to see each other in about a week to begin regular lessons. I've asked him to write a paragraph about anything he likes for next time.

* * *

Wednesday, November 11

No reading lesson today. Ben called me to say he and Althea couldn't make heads or tails out of this "budget thing" so we're going to devote today's lesson to just that. I brought an outline of a budget and two pages of ideas (see below). I wrote them up in sort of a revolutionary mood, lacing conventional suggestions with rather militant ones (like how to outwit the utility companies). We read over the ideas (a reading lesson after all?) and filled in the budget. There was much discussion of each item, and it took a good hour.

Benjamin was expecting a phone call. He's hopeful of getting on at Macy's in a janitorial position one day a week for four dollars an hour. He considers this prospect "Outta sight, man!"

I left a map of the San Francisco State campus with Ben, because we had been talking about getting him out of the house to study. The new Graduate Library has 1500 student carrells. There he could study punctuation without feeling the least bit self-conscious that the guy in the carrell next to him was studying physics. He's also interested in looking around the campus to see his black brothers who are in the college. I suggest he not be too concerned with studying on his first visit, but give himself a chance to get acquainted with the layout of the campus first.

This budget primer deals with a situation common to persons like Benjamin—feast or famine. Unlike the publicized cases we hear about in the press, the struggle away from poverty is often less than spectacular. It's pushing and pulling, slipping and sliding. The road backward is too, too easy. When you're down you have to know how to get back up. These suggestions are meant to help bridge the gap between the worst and the best until the worst is long forgotten. They are about some, but not all, of the real problems of existing on the borderlines of poverty. If they seem mundane to the reader, he should just remember that most of these pointers were a revelation to Ben and Althea. This list was kept pinned to their kitchen wall, and whenever money troubles threatened, Ben referred to it. He later claimed it had helped him out of several jams. I also like to think it was an important step toward improving his reading ability.

Budget for Freedom

You're looking for trouble if you spend more than you make.

Always have money for food and rent. You cannot survive without food and shelter.

Your budget is balanced when your expenses do not go over your earnings. A balanced budget is one that is working for you.

Always figure expenses (costs) on the high side. Then, if you're off, you'll be ahead.

Don't be upset if all your spending doesn't exactly match your budget. Many budget items are only estimates or, in other words, what you expect to spend.

What really counts is the total amount you spend. You may go over on some items, under on others, but never let the total amount you spend in a month go over your total income.

Don't try to save on health items at the cost of quality. Good health means good food, proper medical care, sanitary living conditions, and proper clothing for bad weather.

Doctor's bills can usually be paid by monthly installments (with no interest) of five, ten, or even one dollar—just so long as you pay something on a regular basis. Some doctors like to be told what you will be paying each month. They usually go along with you.

Always leave something extra each month for unexpected, out-of-pocket (cash) expenses. For example, television or appliance repairs, and drugs or prescriptions.

If you buy on credit, make sure you know what your monthly payments are and how much you can pay each month from your budget.

Never miss an installment payment. Late payments always carry an extra charge, and you get poor credit ratings. Once you get a bad credit rating, it may take as long as five years to change it.

Utilities (gas, electricity, water, garbage) can usually be put off for a month in emergencies, but they will threaten to cut off service after you've missed two months. The law, however, doesn't allow them to do this. There are public health codes which say that all garbage must be picked up, and that homes must have running water and heat. If the heat, lights, or water are ever turned off, you are protected by law if you break the seals and turn them on again yourself. You'll be billed for what you use, anyway, since the meters will still be working. Nobody loses anything, and you can pay up when you're able. Don't, however, damage property. Break only wire seals, not padlocks (pick those).

You can't do anything if your phone is disconnected. Once you get into trouble with the phone company, it takes a huge deposit if you ever want service again.

If your garbage service should be cut off, find one of those large industrial containers and dump your garbage there at night. But don't trespass. Use the ones that sit in public streets; these are often found around construction sites. Be cool about it. Or you could get some friends together and rotate weekly trips to the dump.

Of course, any bad debts with utility companies will lower your credit rating and require large deposits when you want service restored.

Some bills, like water and garbage, are not due every month. These are paid every two months in this area. Know when to expect your bills.

Rent is the biggest item in your budget, and if you get behind once, it takes a long time to catch up. The landlord has a legal right to evict you. It's not fair, but that's the way it is.

A sound rule for budgets is:

If you go over on one item, make it good somewhere else. For example, if you spend $110 for food instead of $100 this month, it could be balanced by not spending five dollars on clothes and taking five dollars from miscellany. Or, perhaps, the PG&E bill was down a couple of dollars, and you earned a few extra bucks doing an odd job. Use your imagination.

If you spend less one month, put it away for next month—you may need it.

It takes time to pay by cash. Mail checks and you save time as well as having a visual record (easy to see) of what you spend. You can easily compare your checkbook record with your budget to see if you've got your money under control. It will cost you two or three dollars a month for stamps and checks, but you'll save at least that much by having better control of your money. You'll always know, at a glance, exactly where you stand.

Make sure you know how to use your checking account. Keep a record of each check and go over the statements you receive from the bank. Always know what your balance is and never let it get below five dollars. That leaves room for small mistakes and the monthly service charge.

When your earnings get larger, don't spend more until you have thought it over carefully. Decide if you want to start saving, and what you want to save for. Some people save money just to have it for emergencies, others because it makes them feel good or because they want to buy something and pay cash for it rather than bear the burden of interest charges.

As you master your budget (which means it works for you) and your earnings increase, you will find yourself able to live better without getting into money trouble. Even a millionaire can go over his budget. Seeing your income and expenses written down keeps you from thinking you have more than you really do. Dollars aren't balloons—they don't ever get bigger. These days, they keep getting smaller.

The more you earn the more taxes you have to pay.

* * *

BEN THE READER

Thursday, April 15

It's working! Ben did the first three lessons in the workbook without a single error. He's proud. Also got his first compliment on the job today. The boss likes his work. Ben couldn't be happier.

I've taken to preparing one page (typed, double-spaced) reading sheets for Ben. I call them flyers, and they always tie in directly with something we've talked about. This requires that I watch for material in newspapers, magazines, and books that I'm reading and rewrite it scaled to Ben's vocabulary. For the most part, just one or two paragraphs are involved, and I can prepare a flyer in about fifteen to twenty minutes. For instance, today I have part of an article by a San Quentin inmate . . . detailing the misery and degradation of prison life. This is in response to Ben's comment Monday night, "Hey, prison's not so bad. At least you get three square meals an a roof over your head."

Only teacher-selected and teacher-developed materials could respond adequately to that attitude. I know I can't find a cure-all workbook or text, so the next best thing is to respond to my student's interests with readings that are tailor-made. It's a remedial teacher's responsibility to adapt materials to his student's needs.

* * *

Thursday, April 29

From time to time, depending on how flush he is, Ben pays me a dollar or two towards materials. Althea is bringing in a little extra by taking care of a friend's child while the woman is at work. She seems to be adjusting well to her role as housewife-mother and generally appears happy.

Ben's trying to tutor his older brother Jess one night a week, but is becoming disgusted. "He not very dependable, Tom. He missed our lesson again last night."

A lot of discussion about language tonight. Ben thinks the clichés of street language ("Wow, cool man." "Hey, those are heavy vibes.") often degenerate into nothing but excuses for sloppy thinking. He wants his language to be more precise, with fewer meaningless phrases. We discussed the languages of the world, using quotes from the play, "A Word In Your Ear" by Lister Sinclair. It is a very fine way to introduce students to linguistics and dramatizes the infinite adaptability of language to the user's cultural needs.

We examine black dialect more closely, noting that it gets much of its beauty and power from words and phases which have multiple meanings. The black slave had to become expert at saying things his master wanted to hear but which had completely different connotations to his brothers. "Big prayer meetin tonight," could mean a break for freedom on the Underground Railway. Similar examples abound in the language of today.

I drop a few hints tonight to start Ben thinking about his future, especially about getting that high school diploma. But he's all hung up about going to Divinity School, maybe. He's interested in the Muslims. Feels they show him the common, decent respect he deserves as a man and admires the high status in which they place women and motherhood. But he's more than a little concerned about their policies of separation, and can't see anything good coming from isolation. According to Muslim law, he would have to give up his lessons with me because one is not to fraternize with the White Devils. Well, he's searching, and he knows he can't do anything without more schooling of some kind. I'm satisfied just so long as he's thinking about his future, not just leaving it to chance.

I've a new paperback to give Ben tonight. *On City Streets* is an anthology of urban poetry selected by Nancy Larrick. The poems are short, easy reading, with messages no less relevant, although not as strident as *Inner City Mother Goose*. They are concerned, in the main, with more lasting human values. Ben reads two aloud, in what is becoming his special style for oral poetry—low keyed and full of expression. Very effective.

IMPRESSIONS: We kicked off tonight's lesson with blackboard drill on *th* and *wh* words. It's obvious now that this is one of Ben's biggest stumbling blocks. He can't distinguish then from when, where from there, etc. Clearly, this problem results from lack of sight vocabulary in the little, one syllable connecting words that we all take for granted. The *wh, th* confusion is just one of many similar cases. Had for her, this for his, your for are; all typical of the many words he miscalls. Ben is a good example of the person who has learned to overrely on phonic analysis, at the expense of sight vocabulary. He has neglected to pay attention to whole words and sees only imperfect letter-sound relationships. You don't learn words, you learn sounds, he's been told. A living casualty of the attitude, prevalent with some teachers and theorists since the fifties, that you learn to read through either phonics instruction or the look-see (sight vocabulary) method, but not by any combination of the two.

It is a fact that although more skills and rules have been forgotten by students than were ever remembered, values and attitudes persist. Acquisition of skills requires very little time when the learner is highly motivated and is often accomplished without the aid of a teacher. But the skills will come if the student has a teacher who is alert and sensitive, introducing the right skill at the right moment. This approach can not be be taken as a license for teacher-unpreparedness, yet far less harm is done by missing an opportunity to teach a skill than by pressuring a student into learning something he's not ready for. Chances are another opportunity will present itself in the near future, if the student really wants to know. The big danger is that a teacher is going to push too hard on a kid who has emotional barriers that make learning difficult, and that the pressure will turn him off.

Admittedly, however, some need to be pushed. In *Summerhill: For and Against* [(New York: Hart, 1970), pp. 195–202], Sylvia Ashton Warner has chided A. S. Neil for not leading his Summerhill charges into reading sooner. She feels he missed countless opportunities to turn children's individual interests into reading instructions.

Perhaps I've missed many perfect opportunities to make a point or teach a skill to Ben, but this has been an informal tutorial. I went into it cold, and I've learned at least as much as my pupil. He's used me as a resource, and I've often been surprised to find I had previously untapped knowledge about something he wanted to know. This is why I feel nearly anyone can tutor remedial reading with no special training. The only essential qualification is that the tutor read above the level of his student and enjoy helping others.

READING 4

The following selection is a guide you can use to observe the dynamic interactions involved in group processes. The categories outlined are commonly used for analyzing group behavior; we would stress two group functions in particular: task orientation and group maintenance. The first is the capacity a group has for accomplishing the task, the ability to do the work. The second has to do with what members do to keep the group going. We hope that this guide will help you to become more aware of your own responsibility for these functions, particularly for the different ways in which you contribute to each of these important group goals.

Whether you choose to make use of the guide occasionally or to follow it extensively, it should help you gain insight into the way your group works. Before engaging in a class project or discussing a reading, you might select one process category from the guide on which to focus your appraisal of the group's activity. Two groups should work together—one observes while the other does the task. After the activity is completed, the observer group discusses the process for 15 minutes, while the task group listens. Then the task group responds to the observation-analysis for 10 minutes. (It is helpful to keep to the time limits, and someone should be designated to anticipate the ending of each section for both groups.)

READING QUESTIONS

1. What do you think an awareness of group process, or activities which focus on group process, might contribute to collaborative learning?

2. Some critics of the group-dynamics movement argue that scrutinizing human behavior in the way recommended by this article is destructive.

Discuss the issue in your own group, and bring a record of your exchange to the class.

3. If you used the guide as a resource, was it helpful? Were you able to separate process from content?

4 | WHAT TO LOOK FOR IN GROUPS

Philip G. Hansen

In all human interactions there are two major ingredients—content and process. The first deals with the subject matter or the task upon which the group is working. In most interactions, the focus of attention of all persons is on the content. The second ingredient, process, is concerned with what is happening between and to group members while the group is working. Group process, or dynamics, deals with such items as morale, feeling tone, atmosphere, influence, participation, styles of influence, leadership struggles, conflict, competition, cooperation, etc. In most interactions, very little attention is paid to process, even when it is the major cause of ineffective group action. Sensitivity to group process will better enable one to diagnose group problems early and deal with them more effectively. Since these processes are present in all groups, awareness of them will enhance a person's worth to a group and enable him to be a more effective group participant.

Below are some observation guidelines to help one process analyze group behavior.

PARTICIPATION

One indication of involvement is verbal participation. Look for differences in the amount of participation among members.

1. Who are the high participators?
2. Who are the low participators?
3. Do you see any shift in participation, *e.g.,* highs become quiet; lows suddenly become talkative. Do you see any possible reason for this in the group's interaction?
4. How are the silent people treated? How is their silence interpreted? Consent? Disagreement? Disinterest? Fear? etc.
5. Who talks to whom? Do you see any reason for this in the group's interactions?
6. Who keeps the ball rolling? Why? Do you see any reason for this in the group's interactions?

INFLUENCE

Influence and participation are not the same. Some people may speak very little, yet they capture the attention of the whole group. Others may talk a lot but are generally not listened to by other members.

7. Which members are high in influence? That is, when they talk others seem to listen.
8. Which members are low in influence? Others do not listen to or follow them. Is there any shifting in influence? Who shifts?
9. Do you see any rivalry in the group? Is there a struggle for leadership? What effect does it have on other group members?

STYLES OF INFLUENCE

Influence can take many forms. It can be positive or negative; it can enlist the support or cooperation of others or alienate them. *How* a person attempts to influence another may be the crucial factor in determining how open or closed the other will be toward being influenced. Items 10 through 13 are suggestive of four styles that frequently emerge in groups.

10. Autocratic: Does anyone attempt to impose his will or values on other group members or try to push them to support his decisions? Who evaluates or passes judgment on other group members? Do any members block action when it is not moving in the direction they desire? Who pushes to "get the group organized"?
11. Peacemaker: Who eagerly supports other group members' decisions? Does anyone consistently try to avoid conflict or unpleasant feelings from being expressed by pouring oil on the troubled waters? Is any member typically deferential toward other group members—gives them power? Do any members appear to avoid giving negative feedback, *i.e.*, who will level only when they have positive feedback to give?
12. Laissez faire: Are any group members getting attention by their apparent lack of involvement in the group? Does any group member go along with group decisions without seeming to commit himself one way or the other? Who seems to be withdrawn and uninvolved; who does not initiate activity, participates mechanically and only in response to another member's question?
13. Democratic: Does anyone try to include everyone in a group decision or discussion? Who expresses his feelings and opinions openly and directly without evaluating or judging others? Who appears to be open to feedback and criticisms from others? When feelings run high and tension mounts, which members attempt to deal with the conflict in a problem-solving way?

DECISION-MAKING PROCEDURES

Many kinds of decisions are made in groups without considering the effects of these decisions on other members. Some people try to impose their own decisions on the group, while others want all members to participate or share in the decisions that are made.

14. Does anyone make a decision and carry it out without checking with other group members (self-authorized)? For example, he decides on the topic to be discussed and immediately begins to talk about it. What effect does this have on the other group members?
15. Does the group drift from topic to topic? Who topic-jumps? Do you see any reason for this in the group's interactions?
16. Who supports other members' suggestions or decisions? Does this support result in the two members deciding the topic or activity for the group (handclasp)? How does this effect other group members?

17. Is there any evidence of a majority pushing a decision through over other members' objections? Do they call for a vote (majority support)?
18. Is there any attempt to get all members participating in a decision (consensus)? What effect does this seem to have on the group?.
19. Does anyone make any contributions which do not receive any kind of response or recognition (plop)? What effect does this have on the members?

TASK FUNCTIONS

These functions illustrate behaviors that are concerned with getting the job done or accomplishing the task that the group has before them.

20. Does anyone ask for or make suggestions as to the best way to proceed or to solve a problem?
21. Does anyone attempt to summarize what has been covered or what has been going on in the group?
22. Is there any giving or asking for facts, ideas, opinions, feelings, feedback, or searching for alternatives?
23. Who keeps the group on target? Who prevents topic-jumping or going off on tangents?

MAINTENANCE FUNCTIONS

These functions are important to the morale of the group. They maintain good and harmonious working relationships among the members and create a group atmosphere which enables each member to contribute maximally. They insure smooth and effective teamwork within the group.

24. Who helps others get into the discussion (gate openers)?
25. Who cuts off others or interrupts them (gate closers)?
26. How well are members getting their ideas across? Are some members preoccupied and not listening? Are there any attempts by group members to help others clarify their ideas?
27. How are ideas rejected? How do members react when their ideas are not accepted? Do members attempt to support others when they reject their ideas?

GROUP ATMOSPHERE

Something about the way a group works creates an atmosphere which in turn is revealed in a general impression. In addition, people may differ in the kind of atmosphere they like in a group. Insight can be gained into the atmosphere characteristic of a group by finding words which describe the general impressions held by group members.

28. Who seems to prefer a friendly congenial atmosphere? Is there any attempt to suppress conflict or unpleasant feelings?
29. Who seems to prefer an atmosphere of conflict and disagreement? Do any members provoke or annoy others?

30. Do people seem involved and interested? Is the atmosphere one of work, play satisfaction, taking flight, sluggishness, etc?

MEMBERSHIP

A major concern for group members is the degree of acceptance or inclusion in the group. Different patterns of interaction may develop in the group which give clues to the degree and kind of membership.

31. Is there any sub-grouping? Sometimes two or three members may consistently agree and support each other or consistently disagree and oppose one another.
32. Do some people seem to be "outside" the group? Do some members seem to be "in"? How are those "outside" treated?
33. Do some members move in and out of the group, *e.g.* lean forward or backward in their chairs or move their chairs in and out? Under what conditions do they come in or move out?

FEELINGS

During any group discussion, feelings are frequently generated by the interactions between members. These feelings, however, are seldom talked about. Observers may have to make guesses based on tone of voice, facial expressions, gestures, and many other forms of nonverbal cues.

34. What signs of feelings do you observe in group members: anger, irritation, frustration, warmth, affection, excitement, boredom, defensiveness, competitiveness, etc.?
35. Do you see any attempts by group members to block the expression of feelings, particularly negative feelings? How is this done? Does anyone do this consistently?

NORMS

Standards or ground rules may develop in a group that control the behavior of its members. Norms usually express the beliefs or desires of the majority of the group members as to what behaviors *should* or *should not* take place in the group. These norms may be clear to all members (explicit), known or sensed by only a few (implicit), or operating completely below the level of awareness of any group members. Some norms facilitate group progress and some hinder it.

36. Are certain areas avoided in the group (*e.g.*, sex, religion, talk about present feelings in group, discussing the leader's behavior, etc.)? Who seems to reinforce this avoidance? How do they do it?
37. Are group members overly nice or polite to each other? Are only positive feelings expressed? Do members agree with each other too readily? What happens when members disagree?
38. Do you see norms operating about participation or the kinds of questions that are allowed (*e.g.*, "If I talk, you must talk"; "If I tell my problems you have to tell your problems")? Do members feel free to probe each other about their feelings? Do questions tend to be restricted to intellectual topics or events outside of the group?

BIBLIOGRAPHY

Abercrombie, M. L. Johnson. *Aims and Techniques of Group Teaching*. 2nd ed. London: Society for Research in Higher Education, 1970.

Beck, Paula, Thom Hawkins, and Marcia Silver. "Training and Using Peer Tutors." *College English*, 40 (December, 1978), 432–449.

Bloom, Sophie. *Peer and Cross-Age Tutoring in the Schools*. Washington, D.C.: U.S. Government Printing Office, 1976.

Boyer, Ernest. "Literacy and Education: Opportunity for Articulation." Keynote address, 94th Annual Convention of the Middle States Association of Colleges and Schools, Philadelphia. 11–13 Dec., 1980.

Bruffee, Kenneth A. "Collaborative Learning: Some Practical Models." *College English*, 34 (February, 1973), 634–643.

Bruffee, Kenneth A. *A Short Course in Writing: Practical Rhetoric for Composition Courses, Writing Workshops and Tutor Training Programs*. 2nd. ed. Cambridge, Mass.: Winthrop Pub. Inc., 1980.

Bruffee, Kenneth A. Unpublished Paper on Group Work. n.d.

Bruner, J. S. "The Nature and Uses of Immaturity." *American Psychologist,* 27 (1972), 687–705.

Dillner, Martha. *Tutoring by Students: Who Benefits*? Research Bulletin. Gainesville, Florida: Florida Educational Research and Development Council, 1972.

Elliot, Arthur. "Student Tutoring Benefits Everyone." *Phi Delta Kappan*, April, 1973, pp. 535–538.

Freire, Paulo. *Education for Critical Consciousness*. New York: Seabury Press, 1973.

Hawkins, Thom A. *Group Inquiry Techniques for Teaching Writing*. Urbana, Ill.: ERIC/NCTE, 1976.

Hawkins, Thom A. "Training Peer Tutors in the Art of Teaching." *College English*, 37 (March, 1976), 440–449.

Hill, W. Fawcett. *Learning Thru Discussion: Guide for Leaders and Members of Discussion Groups*. Introd. Herbert A. Thelen. Beverly Hills: Sage Publications, 1969.

Hoover, Regina M. "Experiments in Peer Teaching." *College Composition and Communication*, 23 (1972), 421–425.

Luft, Joseph. *Group Processes: An Introduction to Group Dynamics*. 2nd ed. Palo Alto: Mayfield Pub. Co., 1970.

Mason, Edwin. *Collaborative Learning*. Foreword by Ronald Gross. New York: Agathon Press, 1972.

Norton, Theodore Mills, and Bertell Ollman, eds. *Studies in Socialist Pedagogy*. New York: Monthly Review Press, 1978.

Pincus, Fred L. "The False Promises of Community Colleges." *Harvard Educational Review*, 50 (August, 1980), 332–361.

Rogers, Carl. *Freedom to Learn*. Columbus, Ohio: Charles E. Merrill, 1979.

Schmuck, Richard Allan and Patricia A. Schmuck. *Group Processes in the Classroom*. 2nd ed. Dubuque, Iowa: W. C. Brown, 1975.

Schoolboys of Barbiana. *Letter to a Teacher*. New York: Random House, 1971.

Shor, Ira. *Critical Teaching and Everyday Life*. Boston: South End Press, 1980.

Stevick, Earl W. *Memory, Meaning and Method*. Rowley, Mass.: Newbury House, 1976.

Volkan, Vamick D. and David R. Hawkins. "The Learning Group." *American Journal of Psychiatry*, 128 (March, 1972), 111–116.

$\mathcal{2}$ | *BEGINNING TO TUTOR*

Beginning to tutor may seem frightening at first. After all, you may think: "I'm still a student; what do I know?" You may have a lurking fear that you either will— or won't— be seen as an authority figure. If you are seen as an authority your tutees may expect perfection from you and you may not be able to live up to these expectations; if your tutees see you as a peer they may not respect you. Relax! Some of these anxieties reflect your lack of experience, and soon enough you will gain tutoring experience. At this point, the best way to allay your anxiety about tutoring is to *prepare* for tutoring by familiarizing yourself with the tutoring program at your school—its physical location, environment, and the mechanics of its administration—and by reviewing what actually goes on in tutoring sessions.

PREPARING FOR THE TUTORING SESSION

The Physical Environment

The situations in which tutoring takes place vary according to the personality and size of the school, its academic needs and standards, its budget, and its administrative concerns. You may tutor in a sophisticated learning center, equipped with computers, projection equipment, and a comprehensive library, and staffed by a host of tutors. At the other extreme, your school may have no learning center, as such, and you may arrange instead to meet your tutees in the library, in the student lounge, at the dorm, or even at home. Or, perhaps, your center is a small, converted classroom, with tables, chairs, books donated by teachers and students, and blackboards. Whichever setting best describes where you tutor, it is your job to make the place comfortable, free from distraction, and conducive to work—tasks not always easily accomplished. A desk or table on which to spread out materials, adequate lighting, access to necessary materials are all *minimal* requirements for tutoring. If you will not be tutoring in a designated center, you will need to develop your own mobile learning unit and carry the tools of your trade with you: pens and pencils, calculator or other special equipment, paper—enough for exercises, examples, practice, and review—along with answers to quizzes or to problems you may be working on, proper text materials, assignment sheets, and any forms your program requires. You can use a portable tutorial kit consisting of what you can stash in your briefcase and store in your head, to *create* an appropriate learning environment in whatever setting you find yourself.

The Mechanics of the Tutoring Program

The setting in which tutoring takes place will coincide with how the tutoring in your school is organized by the administration. Some labs have a very complicated administrative bureaucracy. Tutees may be registered and tested upon entering, and they may work at the lab on their own or with a tutor; tutoring may be either a class requirement or an instructional module; and sessions may be recorded in detail and filed in the center, or they may be sent to the tutee's teacher. Tutors may be involved in an elaborate learning program in which they are trained and monitored—in addition to their attending peer tutoring class. Some tutoring situations, on the other hand, are administratively casual and require little paper work.

As a tutor, your first responsibility will be to learn the mechanics of your particular tutorial situation. Find out such things as how tutees are referred for tutoring, how they are placed with tutors, what paperwork you will be expected to complete in regard to tutoring sessions, how important attendance is, and what you are to do if your tutee doesn't show up. Your lab may have other rules regarding tutoring, and you should learn these as well. Can you look at ungraded papers? Can you talk to your tutees' teachers? Can you "graduate" a tutee who doesn't really need your help? A most important question for many tutors, and one we deal with at length in chapter 10, is how they will be evaluated as tutors. It is quite possible you will be observed during the term by your lab director or peer-tutor instructor. You might have to hand in a tutoring log, an audio tape, or even a videotape of a tutoring session. The center's policy may be outlined in a booklet, pasted on a wall, or dictated at staff meetings; or you may learn it informally from your instructor, lab director, or fellow tutors. Be sure you have read and understood all directions pertaining to you.

The Tutorial Context

Preparing the environment in which you will be tutoring, and learning about the procedures you will have to follow, should give you a certain sense of security. The actual content of your tutoring sessions, however, especially that of your first session, cannot be easily predicted. It depends on a number of factors, especially on how broad your tutoring responsibilities are, whether you are seeing students on a drop-in or a regular basis, and whether or not you have received referral information from the student's teacher.

The scope of your responsibilities usually depends on the subject you tutor. Chemistry tutors, for instance, are more likely to have students from a single (or limited number of) chemistry courses—courses which they have probably taken, perhaps with the same instructor as their tutees. Therefore, these tutors will have an easier time predicting what they will be working on from session to session than will writing tutors, for example, who often lack first-hand knowledge of the course their students are taking (such as history or astronomy). Another variable determining the content of your tutoring session is the number of times you work with a tutee. Some courses or faculty members may require that students attend the lab on a regular basis. In such instances, you'll have time to get a good idea of students' capabilities and to use this information to determine the extent and nature of their problems. Then you can plan a term program for the students based on your assessment and any feedback from teachers. In contrast, when your students drop in for one tutoring session, you cannot plan in advance. The former situation allows you to select or develop materials such as handouts and exercises or illustrations of technical terms. With drop-in students, you will have to depend on your creative resources and/or the center's materials. (One way to prepare for drop-ins, then, is to get to know what books and materials your center has.)*

Since teachers are experienced diagnosticians, their referrals can be a great help when you are preparing for your first few sessions. Some labs have a form on which there are spaces for teachers to specify exactly what they want their students to be doing during the tutoring session. But even if no such form is available to you, you can use a corrected class paper or test as a diagnostic tool to show you in what areas the student needs work. For teachers tend to circle, underline, and note in margins items that students should work on.

If your student brings no referral form, paper, or test, rest assured; your first session can be a planning session. In fact, even if you have received instructions from the teacher, your plan for the term should be based, in part, on the tutee's conception of his or her needs. In other words, the tutee must concur with the teacher's or the tutor's plan. In any case, the first session can be one in which you and your tutee go over school work and agree on a plan that the two of you feel comfortable with.

The term preparation, then, is broad. It involves being skilled in the subject you tutor and being equipped with necessary materials. All this preparatory work will help you gain a sense of control and readiness; it is also an important way of giving your tutees confidence in you by letting them know that *you* know how to help them.

CLASS PROJECT 1

1. Form a fishbowl group configuration, with two tutors in the inside circle and four to five in the outside circle.

a. Those of you in the inside circle should choose a topic in your tutoring area (for example, sentence structure or the Civil War). List in order what a student ought to know to master this topic. (For sentence structure, list subject, verbs, clause construction; for the history of the Civil War, list causes, events, and effects of the war.) Then indicate how you would begin to tutor the student and why you have chosen this plan.

---

*While experience will make you more adept with drop-in students or occasional tutoring, the model presented in this text emphasizes a systematic procedure that usually requires a minimum of several sessions. The model is designed to encourage your tutee to return; on the other hand, you can isolate and transfer elements from it to apply to a short-term situation, thereby cutting down the waste of time and the number of mistakes that often result from trial and error.

Those of you in the outside circle should then critique the inside circle's tutoring plan, including the steps group members took to make it.

b. As a class, discuss the dynamics of the group or groups. What were the decision-making factors? Who had influence? What was the atmosphere? (See "What to Look for in Groups," p. 36.)

2. Bring in a paper or essay exam graded by a teacher. (It can be yours or a friend's.)

Work in pairs. First, based on the sample, each of you answer the following questions in writing:

a. What will your first reaction to the student be?

b. What do you think you should work on first? second? third?

Then exchange the graded sample with your partner and answer the same questions for the paper he or she has brought in.

Share your plans with each other, analyzing similarities and differences about beginning tutoring. What has this exercise taught you? Share your conclusions with the class.

LAB APPLICATIONS

1. Observe an experienced (senior) tutor and note in your journal how this tutor has prepared for tutoring.

2. If you work in a center in which files have been maintained, you may be able to find some of your tutee's past work. You should review this work carefully to discover the kinds of problems the student has been having and to determine his or her strengths and weaknesses.

3. At this point you should check the materials in your center (books, exercises, audiovisual materials) so that you know what you might use to teach certain skills or concepts.

THE INITIAL INTERVIEWS

Although each student you tutor is unique and will come to you with particular needs and abilities, you will find that, in general, beginning tutorial sessions have much in common and, within limits, will require similar approaches, no matter which subject you tutor. The following section offers you a general outline of these first sessions.

Getting to Know Your Tutee

Begin the session with an interview; introducing yourself and conversing will help you and your tutee get to know one another. The most natural things to talk about may be school-related matters, such as those pertaining to an academic major, the kinds of courses you and your tutee are taking, experiences with teachers, and extracurricular activities and responsibilities. Sharing this similar information with your tutee will provide the two of you with common ground, which is the basis for a warm relationship and is an important motive for learning together. One word of warning, however. While as "helper" it is your responsibility to draw the shy student out, you must, at the same time, be sensitive to your student's privacy. Some students do not want a personal relationship with you and that is their right. Thus you must develop the ability to discern what kind of relationship will best serve the ultimate goal of the session, which is student learning.

Defining the Student's Problem

Use questioning as a way to get students to explain their problems (for example, the assignment or a teacher's negative evaluation) in their own words. Good questioning techniques stimulate the student to talk. Ask open-ended questions—those which ask *why*, *how*, and *what*—rather than closed questions such as those which ask *who* and *when*, or which only elicit *yes/no* responses. Conducting an interview in this way takes time but will surely repay you for your efforts, because students will have to think about their answers and what they say will probably be more honest and accurate. (See chapter 4 for a more detailed examination of the questioning process.)

Getting tutees to talk about their problems will not only focus the session on the tutee (where it belongs) but will also offer you clues on where to begin your tutoring. For instance, suppose your tutee brings you a paper with major problems in organization. At first glance, it might seem sensible to start off the session by working on reorganizing the paragraphs and sentences. However, if you take time to read over the paper and discuss the student's major assertions, you may realize that the student has little concept of thesis; the student cannot understand the purpose of organization without understanding what he or she wants to say. Or you may have a student who is having trouble understanding the post-Freudian psychologist Helene Deutsch; a discussion with this student may reveal that the tutee has forgotten much of the original Freudian theory. The student's real trouble is not in understanding Deutsch but in understanding how Deutsch's work is similar to and different from Freud's. You should begin this tutoring session, then, with a brush-up on Freud.

Good questioning techniques should help reveal the level and scope of the problem as well. If a student says, "I just don't know what the readings in this course are about," he or she may be pointing to a number of different problems. Here is a list of possible interpretations and how they might be classified:

TUTEE STATEMENT	PROBLEM/SOURCE
a. "I'm having trouble reading because the print is too small."	Visual
b. "I can't read the book because it's too hard."	Reading Comprehension
c. "I'm not understanding because I don't know what the chapter is getting at."	Study Skills
d. "Some of the ideas in this course are really hard."	Content

TUTEE STATEMENT (*cont.*)	PROBLEM/SOURCE(*cont.*)
e. "I can't read the book because it doesn't make sense."	Reading Comprehension or Learning Disability (Difficulty processing the written word)
f. "I'm not interested enough in the course to do the reading."	Motivation/Attitude

Can you think of any others? Of course, a number of the items on the list could be contributing to the problem, but gaining insight into the chief source of the problem will help you and the tutee decide what the remedy should be.

Making the Plan

A visual problem can probably be remedied by an eye examination and glasses. You will have done your job well if you diagnosed accurately and helped your tutee to get this aid.

If the tutee's chief problem is reading comprehension, the tutorial plan might include studying difficult or technical vocabulary and reviewing the text to understand the main ideas. The student who doesn't know "what the chapter is getting at" may understand the words and content but be having trouble seeing relationships or implications. The same student probably has trouble remembering what was read and therefore cannot use the reading as a resource for writing an essay or for in-class discussions. In other words, the student doesn't know how to take notes that will help to organize and relate ideas. Along with discussing course content, it would be wise to help the student learn underlining and notetaking skills. If you are a reading tutor, you will probably work in a lab with specialized testing and teaching materials that focus on further development of these skills. Strategies to use with these tutees will depend on the severity of their problem, the nature of your tutoring responsibilities, and the availability ·of a reading program in your school.

If a student has read carefully and has taken copious notes but still cannot understand the ideas in a book or lecture, the course content may be too advanced for him or her. The tutee may not have learned or not have understood less complex material necessary for an understanding of the new material. In tutoring this student you might have to review the material from the previous course.

Learning disabilities are difficult to diagnose, and too little is known about either their origin or effects for the term to be very useful. However, since learning disabilities reveal themselves in persistent reading, spelling, and other word problems, a reading or writing tutor, especially, should be aware of them. You should, however, never diagnose something as a learning disability yourself—and certainly never apply the term to your tutee—but instead should speak to your instructor or lab director about getting the student tested if tutoring seems to have no effect. (A student may also come to you with an already diagnosed learning disability. Ask the student how you can be of help.) Your plan with someone you suspect is learning disabled should focus on one element at a time, use several senses to reinforce learning, and in general consistently apply the standards for good tutoring that are defined and discussed in your course or program and throughout this book. (See chapter 3 for further discussion of learning disabilities.)

Finally, your student may not be sufficiently motivated to put in the time or energy necessary to do well in this course. Simply talking about the problem might solve it by revealing possible insecurities and anxieties behind the student's negative attitude or by showing the student how interesting and relevant the subject can be. (See chapter 4 for discussion on motivation.)

Once you have defined the overall problem and the various components of it you can get down to a specific task or exercise. If the student is particularly anxious about an immediate problem (a test or upcoming paper), you might want to begin by working on that and waiting until the end of the session to talk about the long-range goals. Even though you may make your plan at the beginning or end of the initial session, you should be careful to keep an open mind and ear to elements that were not a part of your tutee's original description of his or her tutoring needs, and be ready to revise any assessments you have made.

Making a Learning Contract

Once you have had the chance to talk and work with each other for a while, you should be prepared to discuss where you will go from there. A contract— whether informal or formal, written or unwritten—can provide a good basis for your future work. What is a contract? A contract is an agreement between you and the tutee about what the tutee's goals are and how they will be achieved. This kind of contract is not usually written out, but it may be. In any case, it should be *expressed*.

A learning contract allows you to set either long- or short-term objectives. For instance, you may both decide that the tutee's problem with organization is partly the result of not beginning to write early enough and thus having to hand in as a final draft what is, in effect, a first draft; your short-term objective may involve the tutee's presenting you with a first draft a specified number of days prior to the assignment due date so that organization of the final draft can be discussed. The long-term objective may be to produce a series of such drafts for a consecutive number of papers. Additional elements of the contract might include the tutee's agreement to read some chapters on transitional phrases and other devices that contribute to good organization, to do various exercises in the lab relevant to organizational patterns, to develop outlining skills, and even to sketch different organizational structures, using the same quantity of material, as a way of gaining insight into the general concept of organization. All this may be summarized in the learning contract. (See Fig. 2.1; Fig. 2.2 shows a learning contract used in still another discipline.)

Why is a contract valuable? It allows both you and the tutee to clarify your goals and the tasks needed to accomplish them. The contract reflects the balance between *goal setting*, which can help people want to learn, and specific *tasks*, manageable units by which goals are achieved. Tasks offer variety, providing for practice and reinforcement, showing the different ways in which one concept can be approached. Later you will see how tasks can contribute to goal-setting in a counseling situation (p. 184). If tasks are paced over an appropriate period of time they can be incorporated into the student's schedule in a realistic way. Altogether, the contract serves as a *model* for learning, including various factors critical to academic success, such as time

LEARNING CONTRACT

NAME *Frank Caruso*   SEMESTER *Fall* YEAR *82*

DISCIPLINE *English*

RELEVANT COURSE (IF ANY) *Freshman Comp*

GOALS (OBJECTIVES) *to organize an essay*

TASKS	DEADLINES	COMMENTS
1. Read Ch. 5, p. 80 of *Writing Practice*.	For next tutoring session	On Unity
2. Read Ch. 3, p. 38 of *Writing Practice*	For next tutoring session	On transitions
3. Do lab exercise on outlining	For two tutoring sessions hence (Oct. 20)	
4. Bring in rough outline of first draft	Oct. 20	
5. Write a first draft.	Oct. 30	One month before final draft is due

Frank Caruso
SIGNATURE OF STUDENT

Mina Baron
SIGNATURE OF TUTOR

Figure 2.1 Learning Contract for Writing. A contract permits you and the tutee to discover and analyze the components needed to reach a particular goal. It also helps to set priorities for both of you.

management, task orientation, problem solving, practice and reinforcement, and application in a variety of contexts. The tutees, in making the contract and agreeing to it, have taken responsibility for their learning, and in this way the contract helps them learn how to learn. While students can feel proud in moving toward autonomous learning, they also have the safety and security of

LEARNING CONTRACT

NAME *Jenny Ryan*   SEMESTER *Sp.*   YEAR *82*

DISCIPLINE *Chemistry*

RELEVANT COURSE (IF ANY) *Chem 22X*

GOALS (OBJECTIVES) *to understand alkene chemistry*

TASKS	DEADLINES	COMMENTS
1. Outline Principles of Chem., Chap. 15. List questions to ask.	Before class lecture	
2. Add new vocabulary and reaction names to notebook glossary.		
3. Put reactions and examples on index cards for file.	↓	
4. Begin homework problems (based on self-study)	Before tutoring session	
5. Review class notes, self-study questions	Immediately after last alkene lecture	
6. Complete problem sets		
7. Do self-test	After last alkene lecture; before additional tutoring session	

Jenny Ryan
SIGNATURE OF STUDENT

Jim Laird
SIGNATURE OF TUTOR

Figure 2.2 Learning Contract for Alkene Chemistry. A contract helps your student gain clarity about how much work is involved in learning difficult subject matter.

these guidelines, as well as your support in providing the all-important feedback regarding their progress in reaching their goals. From another point of view, the contract helps both of you define what you can expect from tutoring. Keep in mind, however, that no contract is inviolable. It can and must be modified to suit the student's changing needs.

CLASS PROJECT 2

Below is a format for a learning contract, which you may use for this exercise. (This contract may be duplicated for lab or tutorial use.)

a. Form into groups; one student may volunteer to propose a personal learning goal (for example, learning to play a Mozart piano concerto). The group should then collaborate to break this objective into the tasks that will enable the student to accomplish it, specifying length of time, helpers necessary, and so on.

b. Have one member of each group act as observer-critic, identifying and critiquing the behavior of members of the group, and of the group as a whole, using a category drawn from "What to Look For in Groups," p. 36 in chapter 1.

LAB APPLICATIONS

1. Find out about the tutee's course by asking the tutee for a syllabus as well as any particular assignment and keep these on file. Also, be prepared to ask your tutee to clarify the assignment with the instructor and make sure the tutee understands everything the teacher expects from him or her (such as, What is the length of the paper? What, if any, reading and research is required? Does a presentation emphasize summary or analysis? What format is demanded? How does the reading relate to the lab session of the course?

2. Use the learning contract developed in your own program or center, or reproduce the one we have provided here, and develop a learning contract with your tutee based on the information you gathered.

```
                        Learning Contract

   Name_____Semester_____Year_____

   Discipline_____

   Specific Course (if relevant)_____

   Learning Goal(s)_____
   _____

   Tasks                    |  Deadlines      |  Comments
```

Ending the Tutorial Session

Needless to say, how you end each session is as important as how you begin it. It is the last impression your tutees will have of tutoring for awhile, and it will influence how they process what went on during the session as well as their attitudes when and if they return.

Keep to the time limit whenever possible. This lets the tutee know that the limit is administratively imposed, and that you cannot alter it at will. If you find you have trouble maintaining the limit, either because you or your tutee tend to get too involved, ask your receptionist or another tutor to remind you that time is up. If things are going particularly well and you have another hour free you might have to ask your supervisor for permission to continue the session; but let your tutee know this cannot happen on a regular basis. Once you have drawn attention to the fact that the session is coming to an end (about five minutes before the actual end) summarize what went on—or, better yet, encourage your tutee to summarize. This will give him or her a feeling of accomplishment, of time well spent, and will reinforce the instruction as well.

Next, plan with your tutee what you will be doing next session. This will allow the student to anticipate the next session, an important source of his or her motivation to return. Where applicable, give homework, as a way of keeping the tutoring experience fresh for the tutee by further reinforcing the material and by providing continuity from session to session.

First-Session Problems

Despite your skill and preparation, you cannot prevent or anticipate certain difficulties that may arise during the initial stages of tutoring. Some situations will not be within your control, reflecting attitudes or circumstances beyond the scope of tutoring. Other problems may take special handling. Shyness, hostility, resistance, and apparent indifference are the most common obstacles to effective tutoring—and they may be exactly what they seem, or they may be masks and facades of other feelings that are more difficult to acknowledge. How you deal with them depends, in part, on your personality and what sort of a match you and your tutee make, and on your own willingness to see the tutee's behavior as an effort to communicate rather than as a personal attack. (See chapter 6 for a detailed discussion and practice in tutor-counseling skills and chapter 7 for problem tutoring-situations.)

CLASS PROJECT 3

Break into groups: each one should focus on one of the following tutee statements, and develop a scenario or way to solve the problem.

I don't need to worry about this course. This teacher'd pass anybody who walks through the door . . . . Sure that's right. Everybody in the school knows that. That's why I took her.

Mmm . . . I don't know . . . . Uh, uh . . . I can't remember . . . .
I don't know . . . .

Listen, I'm used to takin' things easy. Teachers see me in a
wheelchair—they feel so sorry for me, they automatically pass me.

What makes you think you're so much smarter'n me? You just
took this course last term, anyway. You're just one step ahead a' me,
anyhow!

I do this before and alway I fail. What the point of doing again and
again?

THE TUTORIAL RELATIONSHIP: ROLES, EXPECTATIONS, AND MODELS

The tutorial relationship puts both you and the tutee into roles (the parts you
play) and along with any role comes expectations of how you will fulfill the
role; in fact, sometimes expectations, one's own and those of others, control
how one fulfills a role. An interesting series of studies in psychology may
illustrate the point. These studies focus on the pedagogic effects of what is
called "experimeter bias." Experimenter bias has to do with the ways in which
the presence of the experimenter and, by inference, his or her expectations,
prove to be a variable affecting the outcome of a test or experiment. Interested
in the effects of such expectation, psychologist Robert Rosenthal and his
colleagues told teachers that certain children were very bright and other
children normal: these labels were totally unrelated to the actual intelligence
of the children in the group. What happened in this experiment says a lot
about how we are affected by what people think of us. The so-called bright
children improved their IQ test scores, and to a far greater degree than those
children who had been identified as normal or average. These findings suggest
that the children did better because their teachers *expected* them to do so,
perhaps even giving them the kind of attention, nurture, and stimulation that
resulted in the unusual improvement of the students' performance. The implications for you as a tutor are obvious. What you expect your tutees to be
able to do, and the degree of your confidence in their capacity to do it, may
affect your ability to provide the necessary stimulation and personal attention
that condition their performance.

What about your tutees' expectations of you? They may feel warm toward
you because you too are a student: they will probably believe that you are
competent—and that your competence will help them learn. Studies have
shown that when people who need help are told (1) that the helping person
can give them the help they need, and (2) exactly how the helping person will
go about helping them, they improve to a greater degree than those who are

not prepared in this way. You can use this "role-expectancy structuring," then, to establish your credibility as a tutor, help build your tutee's confidence and trust, and thus increase your power to affect and influence the tutee's work. Structure your tutee's expectancy by showing your tutee how you plan to help and why that plan should succeed. Also, let the student know that you are qualified to tutor this subject. Of course, structuring is only effective when the expectations can realistically be fulfilled. For example, if you can actually tutor problem solving in chemistry so that the student learns something, then it is appropriate to set up these expectations.

In effect, your role as a tutor makes you a model. The word "model" in this context does not mean that you have to be an ideal or perfect creature: instead, it suggests that you are providing an example which students may follow to improve their academic performance. Since people learn by imitating the behavior of others, your tutees can shape their academic behavior from the model you provide. "Modeling" may be explicitly encouraged, "This is how I do it," or it may occur more or less unconsciously through the gradual development of certain learning habits (for example, underlining the verb and circling the subject of each sentence). Your tutees may then develop these habits outside the tutorial session to improve their performance in the classroom.

LAB APPLICATIONS

1. Before your initial interview with a tutee, discuss, with your lab supervisor or your instructor, the idea of "structuring" your tutorial session. If possible, have the supervisor, a senior tutor, or other staff member introduce you to your tutee—"framing" the relationship by noting that you are an excellent student, one who is very good in the subject and who will be able to help the tutee—while indicating perhaps that you are receiving training and supervision that will contribute positively to the quality of your tutoring.

2. As a term project, you, or a group of students, may want to consider making a videotape of an initial interview. If possible, actual tutors and tutees should be used, although class members may act out both parts. This tape may serve other tutees as an introduction to the lab and its services and serve as an example of what the tutee can expect in the tutoring situation.

BEGINNING TO EVALUATE

It may seem very early to talk about evaluation, but you have in fact already begun to evaluate in the earliest stages of your tutoring. If, for example, you looked at your tutees' files you were beginning to evaluate your tutees before you met them. Next, when you defined your tutees' problems, you were making diagnoses, and these initial assessments are also part of the evaluation procedure. When you made a contract you were writing a plan, and that, too, was a decision about what was needed, what would work, and what was possible given time limits and other individual circumstances. Exercises and review, whether in the form of pretests and post-tests, or conducted in a less formal way, are evaluative procedures; the student's performance in coursework constitutes a basis for evaluation as well.

Evaluation of your tutee, and of your own performance as tutor, is an ongoing *process* and intrinsic to tutoring.* As we suggested in chapter 1, your journal can serve as a record of your own learning process and can therefore be a tool for self-evaluation when you review what you have written. Still another way to trace the growth and development of what you and your student have learned is through a case study.

The Case Study

A very useful term project is to write a case study of your tutorial relationship with a tutee. A case study is a formal report of some person, activity, or institution which the writer considers exemplary of an idea or concept. What all case studies have in common is the scientifically objective way the material is presented: the writer gathers and presents pertinent data, analyzes important elements, draws conclusions, and recommends future action. Often the case study is organized in a standardized way, with information categorized or classified under predetermined headings.

The case study, then, is characterized by its effort to achieve impartiality—through tone, through the use of data and further explanation to support the writer's claims, and through a complete and thorough presentation of the case. Because of its precision, depth, and scope it is a valuable learning model: by concentrating on one person, one corporation, or one law suit, the case study offers a way to demonstrate all that one has learned. Put another way, a case study establishes a perspective from which all the writer has learned can be brought to bear on a particular instance. For this reason case studies are widely used in education, social work, the helping professions, and the social sciences in general. In many businesses and law schools, the case-study method is the primary teaching method.

Comparing your case study with your journal may help you understand the nature of both of these evaluative tools better. You make your journal entries chronologically but do not control the order of what you write; your journal, then, is a vehicle for your response to the immediate occasion and goes wherever your thoughts take you. Sometimes your journal notes may be no more than brief and undeveloped references: reminders, book titles, and sketches may also find their way into your journal. Your journal will be less selective then your case study, although it may have an underlying theme or a topic that defines its entries. Finally, the journal is, by comparison, more subjective and its subjectivity permits you to include the wide range of emotional responses you will have—anger, frustration, and pleasure, to name only the most obvious ones.

---

*Chapter 10 contains a complete examination of the evaluative process.

Because it is related directly to your life and work, your journal is a document that can stand on its own, valued for its immediacy, its rich descriptions, its charged feelings. It may also be seen as a counterpart to your case study. Your journal focuses on your *emotional* growth and your subjective responses to tutees. Your case study, in contrast, will focus on your *professional* growth and learning, and offer an objective assessment of your tutees' performance. The journal, in fact, may be an adjunct to the case study, and the first stage in beginning to write up the more formal summary document.

You can draw material for your case study from the random jottings in your journal. But the case study will not merely be a rearrangement of the material in your journal, although it may be that in part; hopefully in reformulating and selecting information, you will see patterns or relationships you have not previously noticed, and be able to reach conclusions not formerly possible.

To write your case study, select a student you have tutored four or more times. Your choice will depend partly on your relationship with the tutee, on the available notes in your journal, and on what you feel others can learn from your description and analysis. You may use the outline below as the format of your case study, although the emphasis given to each section will vary according to the type of tutoring course you're taking, or the program you're in. You may also want to use the outline to guide interviews with your tutee. Since you will gather information and develop ideas over a period of time, be sure to keep records and store your data in your journal.

Case-Study Guide

1. Background Information
   A. The tutee
      Family composition
      Significant life experience
      Significant academic or learning history (general experiences with school or the relationship to the particular subject being tutored)
   B. Brief teaching history of tutor

II. Appearance and Behavior
   Physical appearance
   Affective behavior (relationship with others, ability to adapt to new situations, feelings about self and family)
   Expressive language ability (informal assessment of learner's ability to communicate)

III. Diagnosis
   A. What are your reasons for tutoring? Your tutee's problems? (Include academic, emotional, and social impediments to learning.)
   B. What are your own problems in tutoring this student—academic, emotional, and social, especially at the early stages of your relationship with him or her?

IV. Plan
   What early decisions did you make in order to solve your tutee's problems—academic and counseling? Describe an example of any techniques you hoped would be helpful.

V. Description and Analysis
  A. This may be a session-by-session description of your tutoring experiences *or* a summary of the general order, schedule, and routine you followed including where and how often and for how long you met and how you proceeded. Either selectively or cumulatively, discuss the techniques and strategies you used, the exercises you tried, what worked, what didn't, and why. Remember to consider strategies that you used to overcome psychological barriers as well as difficulties with writing, math, or other subject matter. Then indicate the ways in which you maintained interest and motivation, fostered the relationship, and paced and varied the instruction.
  B. Analysis of your own progress as a tutor. What were your problems? What did you do to overcome them? How well did you succeed?

VI. Evaluation/Recommendations
  A. How do you feel the tutee will do in the subject in semesters to come? What do you recommend that the tutee do to ensure his or her continued progress? Include any specific work he or she should do, and where (lab, independent study, group).
  B. How do you judge your ability as a tutor: How have you grown? What directions would you like to move in? What do you need or want to learn?

CLASS PROJECT 4

a. At home, read the tutorial case studies in this chapter and critique them, according to the form shown in Figure 2.3.

b. In class, break into groups of five to seven and share your critiques of one of the studies. Elect a group recorder to write down the consensus and then read aloud to the class.

In the general class discussion you should try to come to some conclusions about what makes a good case study, what the most difficult tasks of a case study are, and what you have learned from the case studies you will read in this chapter.

READINGS 5a AND 5b

The following two case studies were written by students in the authors' peer-tutoring classes. You will find them similar in that each tutor had to find a way to overcome her tutee's apparent antagonism, but different in the way each resolved her problems.

Case Study Critique

DESCRIBE

1. What was the diagnosis, the plan, the final evaluation?

2. What, in general, occurred between tutor and tutee?

(Describe what they worked on and any major areas of conflict, etc.)

EVALUATE

3. How do you feel the tutor handled the tutee?   (Name both strengths

and weaknesses, and be specific.)

4. How does this document work as a case study? What does one learn

about the stages the tutor and tutee went through during tutoring and what

the results were of tutoring?

5. What can be done to improve this case study?

Figure 2.3 This critique is based, in part, on Kenneth A. Bruffee's model for the writing peer critique. (See *A Short Course in Writing*, 2nd ed., Winthrop, 1980.) This may be reproduced for group use.

READING QUESTIONS

1. What does each case study include that isn't in our outline on p. 55. Are these additions worthwhile? Are there things missing from these studies that you need to know to assess whether or not the tutorials were successful?

2. How do Retamar's and Bresnick's experiences with their tutees in their first sessions compare with our suggestions about initial interviews? Do you feel that the tutors' expectations (and ours) may have had a negative influence?

3. In what ways do Bresnick and Retamar use biographical material about their tutees to elucidate their case studies? Is this a valuable procedure? Why?

4. What do you feel contributed to the changes in Maria's and Edward's behavior? Substantiate your opinions with statements or details from each case study.

5. What have you learned from each of these case studies that you can use in your own tutoring? for your own case studies?

5a | TUTORING MARIA: A CASE STUDY

Antonia Retamar
LaGuardia Community College

I have been a paraprofessional in the New York City School System since 1973. My job consists of helping the teacher in all of her daily duties, and giving individual attention and instruction to the children. I enjoy teaching. I have also always enjoyed writing and sharing experiences, and whatever knowledge I've acquired with others. I believe that teaching and learning involves a mutual sharing that should prove beneficial and enjoyable to all of the parties involved. I, as well as my school counselor, felt that the peer-tutoring course would be an ideal·one for me to take.

After my first few classes in the course I was really anxious to meet my tutee. Maria is in her freshman year at the College and her major is data processing. She is presently in an English 099 [noncredit] class but she intends to go on to a four-year college and therefore will need to take more English courses. She is an attractive, forty-year-old woman with short, shiny black hair, big black eyes, and smooth olive-colored skin. Maria is originally from Colombia, South America, has a teenaged daughter, and works in an office as a secretary. I obtained most of the above information about Maria from the form that she filled out in the Writing Center; however, I found out that she had a teenaged daughter through an essay that she wrote, in which she mentioned that one night, when she returned from school, her daughter had cleaned the kitchen. (Maria never directly spoke about her home or personal life during our sessions.)

My first session with Maria was nothing like what I had expected because my tutee did not want to chat socially, share experiences, or be friendly during our tutoring session. All that she wanted was to "get down to business" and review one of her essays. After reviewing the essay, I gave Maria an exercise to do on fragments. During the review, Maria questioned two of my corrections, but I remained calm; however, when Maria insisted upon verification of both corrections, I began to feel very insecure and intimidated. I was hoping that my tutee's doubts in me and my feelings of insecurity would diminish as time went on. By the time Maria and I had finished our work, the session was over.

I felt very disappointed about the entire session, because I had planned and hoped to use it to establish a friendly rapport between us. That evening, after tutoring was over, my classmates and I were filling out our session reports, and all of my classmates were talking about how nicely their sessions had gone and that they thought the foundation for a good rapport had been laid. I was the only one to report that my tutee had a down-to-business attitude.

Although I realized that if my tutee wanted a business-like relationship, I would have to adjust, I just could not stop trying to be friendly. I knew the purpose of the peer-tutoring program was to provide the student with a friendly, relaxed atmosphere, where two students could help each other improve their writing by sharing their experiences and knowledge on the subject, and I could not see how we could reach this point without establishing a good rapport first.

During one session, we reviewed parts of speech. It was difficult for me to explain to her how some words can function as more than one part of speech, depending on the sentence, because she wanted written proof and verification for everything that I told her. After that, I began taking from two to three hours to prepare for our sessions. It took a long time, because I tried to prepare for all of her possible questions and all of my necessary answers. For example, after seeing some of her essays, I found that Maria needed to practice proofreading her papers carefully before handing them in for grading; even though she had her grammar rules "down pat," Maria found self-correcting difficult. Since this seemed the result of thinking in Spanish first, I suggested she practice writing in English as much as possible. I explained that through practice in writing it would become easier for her to think in English, and as a result, to write with fewer errors. She did not reply and her facial expression did not change. I asked her what she thought about what I was suggesting. She simply replied, "Thank you."

We once discussed sentence structure and I easily understood how she could make errors in word order. She is a student who speaks English as a second language, and word order changes when a sentence is translated from one language to another. To prove my point, I used a technique and coding device that I had seen my senior tutor use with a student. I wrote a sentence on the board in Spanish and then I wrote the same sentence in English under it. I showed her how in translating from Spanish to English the word order must change in order for the sentence to make sense. This helped Maria to understand her word-order mistakes.

Maria never spoke to me in Spanish. Many times she stumbled over her words and paused to think of an appropriate word; sometimes she spoke incorrectly in English, but she never clarified it by telling me what she actually meant in Spanish. I had told her that I was Spanish speaking and that at any time she could feel free, as I sometimes did, to speak in Spanish. At times I converted to speaking Spanish, without letting her know that I suspected that she had not fully understood me in English. I think that it is possible that Maria felt that her speaking to me in Spanish would be too informal, and might in turn cause her to relax and "let her hair down." Apparently, she did not think that these actions were appropriate for this setting, so I did not pressure her.

Our work progressed: the academic part went pretty well. I was now asking Maria to do more writing during our sessions. Her proofreading and self-correcting were improving. But the interpersonal part got harder. On one occasion, Maria was revising one of her papers and I told her that she needed to make the E in European a capital letter. She said, "No, I am sorry but you are wrong, because I have written it like that and my teacher has not marked me wrong." I tried to remind her that all proper nouns were capitalized. She continued to present her argument so strongly that, much to my amazement, I actually started doubting my own knowledge on capitalization. I got the dictionary, showed her the word, and she accepted it, but only after she had looked it up in her own pocket dictionary. I felt like a zero. I could not believe that my feelings of insecurity had permitted me to doubt even my basic knowledge of English. I had many times thought of just coming right out and telling her all of my feelings, but I held back out of the fear of coming off as authoritarian, or even worse as a sensitive baby. At this moment, I started dealing with the feelings that had developed in me as a result of all our past sessions. I told Maria that I seriously thought that she should get another tutor, since after all of this time, she had never proven me wrong, but had never had faith in me either. I also told her that she made me feel both inadequate and insecure and that I did not like feeling that way. I admitted to her that it was partially my fault too, because I should have spoken up sooner and not let these feelings mushroom inside me. I let her know that my reason for not taking any action before this was the fear of hurting both her and any chance that our tutoring relationship might have once had. Her facial expression did not change and she offered no comments. The session was now over and she said good-bye and left.

Since there was only one more session left in the course, I felt sure that Maria would not return after all that I had told her. I mentioned the incident to both my peer-tutor professor, and the tutorial supervisor. They were very supportive, just as they had been throughout the entire course. I seriously think that I would not have been able to tolerate this situation at all if I had not had the shoulders of my classmates, the other tutors, my senior tutor, and my professor and supervisor. When the day of our last session together arrived, Maria was about a half hour late; since she had never been late I was sure that she would not come at all. All of a sudden, she appeared and apologized for being late. She said that she had gone to see an advisor about next quarter's classes but was unable to meet with him because there were too many people waiting, and she did not want to miss all of our last session together. I was very shocked to know that our sessions meant that much to her. She had her last paper with her, which had twelve errors, and she shocked me again, by looking sad about her paper. I asked her if she was nervous when she wrote the paper. She said that she had been. I had suspected this because all of the errors were ones that were not common for her to make. She proceeded to correct her paper with ease. When she finished, she got up, kissed my cheek, put her hand on my shoulder and thanked me for being such a good tutor and friend. She went on to say that I had really helped her to improve her writing. I was stunned! Never, even in my wildest dreams, did I imagine that Maria considered me a friend! She wished me success in my teaching career. After she had spoken I took a few seconds to "get myself together." I then wished her luck with her exam, and told her that I was sure that she would pass it. After I wished her success in all of her further studies, we said good-bye and she left.

I was shocked, happy, and touched, Many questions ran through my mind. I felt like laughing and crying. Did she just think that it was inappropriate to treat me as a person when I was her tutor? Did my words to her last week mean anything to her? Did she really mistrust and disbelieve me, or did she just want to be absolutely perfect and correct in order to be able to pass the exam? Those few moments at the end of our session changed many of my thoughts about her. She had really given me food for thought.

If I am ever a peer tutor again I think that I will try to figure many things out and deal with them in the beginning of the tutoring relationship, and not in the end. By speaking up earlier, I might have been able to save myself a lot of aggravation. It made me feel very good to know that Maria realized that my aim was to help her. I guess that she is just a formal person, and a perfectionist; these qualities will help her to pass her exam and I hope that my constant reminders to her to proofread her work carefully will be an additional aid to her at the time of the test.

I am glad that I had this experience. It has taught me a lot: for example, never to think that I know what someone else feels, and never to allow someone to put me in a position where I became so insecure and intimidated that I risk being ineffective. I know that these lessons will prove to be very useful throughout my teaching career, as well as in my everyday interactions with others.

5b | EDWARD

Renee Bresnick
School of New Resources
College of New Rochelle

Edward is a black man, apparently 38–40 years old. He is always prompt for a tutoring session. He is always neatly dressed, and carries his books and papers in a thin leather-type case such as you see business and professional men carrying on the commuter trains. I would suggest that school to him is his current job, a step up the ladder toward his goal as a social worker.

Edward is back in school after serving in the Marine Corps for almost 20 years. He enlisted in the Corps at the age of 16 because his family could not support him and he felt it was the only way he could learn a trade and support himself. I believe he was trained to be a mechanic of some kind. I do not know why Edward left the Marines short of the 20 years that is the basis for pension. I do know that he served two tours in Vietnam. I learned only after some time working with Edward that he is married and has two sons, around 12 and 14 years of age. Edward also told me that his wife's working has enabled him to return to school.

Edward is taking social work courses at the School to complete the work for his baccalaureate degree. He has already graduated from a community college and seemed a bit antagonistic to the whole idea of tutoring when we started. After all, he did very well at the Community College, why should this be necessary?

Indeed, Edward did well before coming to the college. He speaks well and was president of an organization within the college community. Before the end of the term, I learned that Edward would be attending an honors' dinner at the Community College. He had worked as a volunteer at the Alcoholic Rehabilitation facility at the County complex under Dr. O. B., the psychiatrist in charge of the program. Dr. B. was to receive a special award at this dinner. Since Edward had recommended that she be the recipient, he was asked to be there and may even have spoken. Edward was also among the students receiving a citation and pin for scholarship and service to the school at this same dinner. It was, therefore, a shock to his ego to learn that his skills were not up to the standard of the College.

As part of his courses in the social services area, Edward has been working in a public agency nearby. His special concern appears to be a teen-age boy. The youngster's parents are divorced; the youngster lives with his mother and her boyfriend. The mother drinks, is on methadone, and so forth. Sometimes the boy spends time at his grandmother's; she is a stablizing influence. The boy is torn between the two households. Edward is working within the social services agency to set the teenager on the right track. As a father, Edward understands the boy's need for constructive guidance. Edward is very serious and committed to his chosen career.

I do not know who intimidated whom more when Edward and I began working together. He was always polite, but I could feel an anger or resentment almost as an aura when we would meet. I sensed an attitude which implied that if his skills were not adequate for the College and I was there to help, then I might as well do the work. I immediately made it clear that I was there to advise and to guide and to point out and help with weaknesses, but that the *work must be his*. Now, I hoped, we could get down to work.

Within a few weeks, we both relaxed and I realized that this man was so serious about the goals he had set for himself, he had closed himself off to humor or light pleasantries. Now that our roles were established, everything was SERIOUS. The instructor had hurt his vanity by recommending that he be tutored. He now needed the reassurance that he could succeed; his self-image must not be charred. His demeanor relaxed once he understood that I was part of a support system; that I was there to assist in constructive ways and would in no way demolish the sense of worth he strove so hard to build.

In reviewing the writing he gave me, I immediately noted some errors with subject-verb agreement. However, these errors were not consistent. Edward understood them as soon as they were pointed out to him. Sometimes I would have him read the sentence aloud and he would immediately see his own mistake. No special exercises were needed. Edward also occasionally used words as he *heard* them, not as they actually are. While I always suggested that he freely use a dictionary, it could not have helped correct these non-existent words. He might not think to check them out if he *thought* they were correct anyway. Actually, I appreciated that he was trying to increase his vocabulary and urged him often to use a dictionary simply to check on a new or doubtful word. I also suggested that he use a simple book such as the one I have of synonyms and antonyms. However, I feel that his vocabulary over time will improve because he has been reading so much and his comprehension is good. In other words, this is a self-correcting problem that will gradually disappear.

Basically, however, Edward's problem has not been with subject-verb agreement, run-ons, fragments, etc. His assignments in his class, Experience, Learning and Identity (ELI), required a great deal of reading and writing, analyzing or forming judgments or conclusions. I know this initially threw Edward. I first saw a paper he had worked on for a sociology class and understood his problem. Edward, as other students elsewhere do, had gone through two years of college lifting paragraphs and sentences from the required reading, then spewing them back in no special order; this gave evidence to the instructor that the work had been read. It did not, however, demand a coherent synthesis of the material. When I read Edward's paper for Sociology, it was gibberish. Edward needed help in organizing and in using Edward, not just using the reading material, for his writing. This was the key to any written material for ELI.

Fortuntately, I had taken an ELI course. The approach and readings vary with each instructor; the goals, however, are the same. This background proved helpful because we could discuss an assignment, check the questions, and seek the solution. Gradually, the importance and value of the course became clear. Edward was impressed by the readings and increasingly able to respond for himself. His organization improved and, in fact, I was impressed by his natural ability to make transitions from one paragraph to the next.

We would go over his assignments. I would point out where the writing was disjointed and did not follow within a paragraph. We would discuss grammatical errors. He would correct, make notes, and take the work home to re-write. I gave him the AAP pamphlet, "How to Build Your Writing Skills," and I suggested that if he felt he needed further assistance in organization, to use the Learning Skills Center tapes. I also had copies made of an ad I saw in *Newsweek* headed, "How to Write Clearly," written by Edward T. Thompson, editor in chief of *Reader's Digest*, and gave one to him. (I kept one for myself.)

Edward's inner drive to succeed was an asset for him. By term's end, he was reporting excellent grades. He was pleased with himself and more open to constructive help. He showed me some of his social work writing. It, too, was clearer and more ordered and readable than the initial writing he had shown me so many weeks before. His initial antagonism was gone, as was the "chip-on-the-shoulder" attitude. He now feels he is achieving and doing well. His "job" is not in jeopardy. His organization has improved tremendously; his writing is cohesive; he uses fewer fragments; his vocabulary has improved. He has completed the term with confidence returned and ego intact.

BIBLIOGRAPHY

Bandura, A., D. Ross, Sheila A. Ross. "Vicarious Reinforcement and Imitative Learning." *Journal of Abnormal and Social Psychology*, 67 (1963), 601–607.

Berte, Neal R., ed. *Individualizing Education Through Contract Learning*. University, Alabama: Univ. of Alabama Press, 1975.

Bruner, J. S. "The Nature and Uses of Immaturity." *American Psychologist*, 27 (1972), 687–705.

Critchlow, Warren E. "Contract Counseling." Third Annual Symposium of SUNY Brockport and NYS College Skills Assn. Conference, Rochester, N.Y., 20–22, April, 1980.

Flanders, James P. "A Review of Research on Imitative Behavior." *Psychological Bulletin*, 69 (1968), 316–337.

Rosenthal, R. *Experimenter Effects in Behavioral Research*. New York: Appleton-Century-Crofts, 1966.

Rosenthal, Robert and Lenore Jacobson. "Teacher Expectancies: Determinants of Pupils' I.Q. Gains." *Psychological Reports*, 19 (1966), 115–118.

3 | *TUTORING HANDICAPPED STUDENTS*

CLASS PROJECT 1

Take the quiz below and read the following section to find the answers.

	True	False
1. People who have cerebral palsy are brain-damaged.	————	————
2. The deaf cannot speak.	————	————
3. People with learning disabilities are of less than average intelligence.	————	————
4. The blind cannot read.	————	————
5. People in wheelchairs need to be accompanied by helpers to open doors, take their notes, etc.	————	————
6. Talking louder helps a deaf person to understand better.	————	————

Figure 3.1 Perceptions of Handicapped Persons.

The handicapped are a special population you may work with as a tutor: the blind, the deaf, those confined to wheelchairs or affected by cerebral palsy, and persons with learning disabilities are all classified under the general rubric of handicapped.* Especially in a society such as ours, with its obsessive concern for cosmetic flawlessness, the handicapped continue to be subject to prejudice and discrimination. People often isolate handicapped people from the rest of society by ignorantly labelling them mentally retarded or intellectually deficient and incompetent; other people patronize the handicapped, ignoring the disability and pretending that it has no effects on the student and causes him or her no limitations. Such denial mechanisms are not restricted to the non-handicapped, however; handicapped people may exhibit these attitudes also.

The list of true/false statements in Figure 3.1 should reveal to you some of your own possible misconceptions: they are all false, yet many in our society would say that some or all of them are true. If you are working with a handicapped tutee, you will be exploring your own attitudes about handicaps through your journal. Use it to deal honestly with any reservations you may have about tutoring a handicapped student. If you have real difficulty in working with a particular person, you should acknowledge this and discuss it with your lab supervisor or peer tutor instructor. Try not to be intimidated. There is special equipment, as well as techniques and strategies, to help you tutor your handicapped students; but what they need most is care, patience, and your belief in them.

DEAF STUDENTS

Such students may be hard of hearing, deafened during the course of growing up, or deaf from birth. The presence of hearing aids is not a necessary clue to the degree of hearing loss, since aids are sometimes used by the severely deaf to pick up sound only, and by others with less hearing loss, to hear. Its presence should provide the clue, however, that noise, amplified by the hearing aid, will distract your tutee; be sure to work in a quiet setting. The degree to which a deaf person may speak (or "articulate," which is the technical term) is dependent on the damage to the vocal cords, the severity of the hearing loss, and, in the case of the profoundly deaf, the age at which hearing was lost. In addition, some deaf persons are reluctant to articulate with hearing persons because they have been told that it "sounds funny." Whether or not you are able to understand your deaf tutee's speech depends on the quality of the student's articulation: it may take several sessions before you have become accustomed to the deaf student's oral pattern so that you can understand the words, and, as in all your tutorial relationships, it will take some time before you and your tutee have relaxed enough for conversation to flow. Your tutee's ability to understand you will depend on any previous training in lipreading that he or she may have had, and, more importantly, on an inherent capacity to lipread, combined with aspects of your particular speech pattern. Do you

*Some representative organizations prefer the term "physically challenged." We have chosen to use *handicapped*, partially because our category is broader, including not only those with physical limitations but learning disabilities as well, partially because we want to confront the issues and problems arising from social perceptions of the learner as handicapped.

"articulate" clearly or are you a "mumbler," that is, one who swallows words? Do you have a foreign accent that will change the way your mouth looks when you form words? These characteristics, along with others, such as the presence of a moustache or beard, may affect or limit oral communication between you and your tutee.

Several other aspects of your oral communication with the deaf should be pointed out at this time:

- *The loudness of your voice in no way affects your tutee's ability to hear, under any circumstances.* It may even make it more difficult for your student to understand you. Amplification distorts your facial expressions and may diminish your tutee's ability to read your lips. Don't shout. In fact, if articulation works for your tutee, you may find that you gradually forget to sound your words. That's okay.
- *If your tutee lipreads that does not mean that he or she will catch every word you say.* The good lipreader is adept at picking up the key words and getting the *general* sense. Studies show, however, that the deaf capture only about 40% of the message, relying on context and nonverbal cues to confirm meaning. Such communication, then, is subject to misunderstanding. Always check to be sure your tutee knows exactly what you have said by asking the student to give you feedback, oral or written.

The best way to supplement lipreading is through "Total Communication," which is the combined use of the spoken and the signed word. Sign language, or rather, sign languages (there are several types) use hands to form letters or symbols. Those you should be aware of are the *manual alphabet* (Fig. 3.2), which is used to spell out words, and American Sign Language, which is composed of signs that usually symbolize whole words. Even though American Sign Language (ASL) is the standard, American English Sign Language (*AMESLAN*) is more widely used. It is an informal, often highly condensed version of English, and one might think of it as a special dialect, or variant.

Tutorial services for the deaf fall into three major categories. As a tutor, you may act as one or more of the following:

1. An assistant who provides tutees with oral training using special equipment, such as "visible speech,"—electronic visual displays used to guide deaf students in "matching" their pronunciation and pitch to the graphic representation of a hearing person's speech.
2. An oral interpreter, who accompanies students and translates the spoken word of lectures and of class discussions into sign language. Interpreter-tutors may be called on to assist tutees by taking notes, communicating orally with others, and acting as "presenters" in seminars, for speech assignments, or in oral examinations.
3. A subject tutor, who helps students to master writing skills or some other academic discipline. As a subject tutor, you may or may not know sign language: you may be joined by an interpreter to make up a communication triangle, or, if no interpreter is available, you will need to use articulation, natural gestures, and the written or typed word to make your meaning clear.

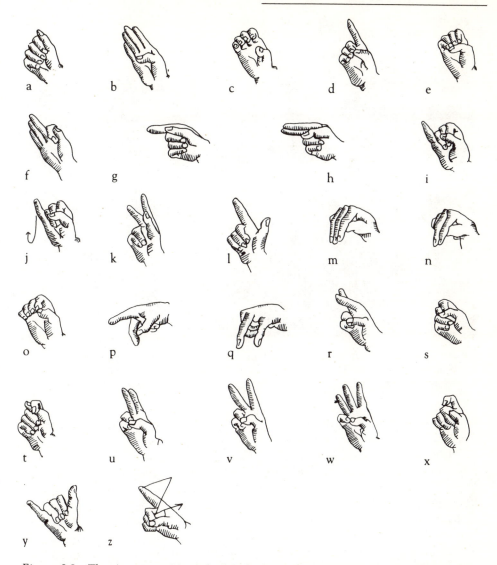

Figure 3.2 The American Manual Alphabet. Using only this letter and finger medium would make communication tedious; however, the alphabet is helpful, because the speaker may spell out specific, sometimes highly technical, words necessary for academic discussion and writing. It is also the easiest sign language to learn. (From *The College Student With A Disability: A Faculty Handbook,* The President's Committee on Employment of the Handicapped, Washington, D.C., 1980.)

In tutoring, it will be helpful to know language features that give deaf students the most trouble. As we discussed previously, lipreading relies on picking out key concepts: it does not permit easy recognition of small words or final endings. Thus, apparent errors in production such as missing plurals and omitted -*ing* endings, as well as other suffixes such as -*ment, -tion, -ness, -ly,* may indicate a lack of input rather than a problem in output. Further, "mistakes" in written English word order may not be apparent to a deaf student who is writing correct AMESLAN sentence structure. In the same light, idi-

Here a tutor reviews material with students, using sign language to correct errors in understanding and reinforce knowledge acquired in the classroom. (Photograph courtesy National Technical Institute for the Deaf at Rochester Institute of Technology.)

omatic expressions, part of our spoken and written language, are often foreign words and phrases to a deaf signer.

It is not surprising that the playful aspects of language, those which often rely on tone, pitch, and rhythm, cause great difficulty for nonhearing persons. Irony, sarcasm, understatement, or exaggeration—and the humor in them— frequently elude those who are concentrating on literal meaning. In fact, these verbal nuances may sometimes be the source of a real communication problem between a student and teacher, or tutor. You should not, however, avoid such verbal joking; instead, you should be sensitive to whether your tutees understand what you are saying and guide them toward understanding your way of communication as you learn to understand theirs.

When you tutor in content areas, you must consider that the nonhearing person may not have had the amount and diversity of input that a hearing person has had; they have lacked the opportunity to pick up knowledge casually, through conversation, by overhearing discussions, or listening to the media. And without aural reinforcement, reading can be a rather disembodied phenomenon. The deaf reader has greater difficulty connecting the written word with the reality to which it refers than the hearing person. Thus, relating the material to concrete situations will make sense of it for your tutee, and your animation of the material will bring it to life. As with all tutees, but critically so with the deaf, good nonverbal communication is essential. Make use of animated gestures, visual expressions, and tactile stimulation and you will find your tutee quick to pick up such cues and be responsive to them. Pats on the hand, arm or shoulder are normal expressions used to gain attention and are perhaps even more important as ways to convey your support.

CLASS PROJECT 2

1. As a term project, you may wish to learn the manual alphabet and/or sign language. Courses are often available through continuing education or general studies programs at local colleges; community or informal study groups may also post notices.

2. If you make a videotape (see chapter 2, *Lab Applications,* p. 53; chapter 4, pp. 88, 101, 108) consider how you might make it accessible to the deaf or hearing-impaired student, for example, by providing an interpreter or printed material.

3. As a term or group project, you may wish to research what is currently known about how the deaf acquire language, especially reading and writing skills.

VISUALLY HANDICAPPED STUDENTS

Visually handicapped students may have varying degrees of sight: some may learn to read print; but others are totally blind, or are only able to distinguish large shapes and forms, and must use a coding system called Braille to read and write. You may, therefore, find it helpful to learn something about this coding system.

Braille is an alphabet in which each letter or element of punctuation is represented by a different configuration of raised dots on a grid or cell two dots wide and three dots high (see Fig. 3.3). Braille writing is slow; the student uses a special slate (which comes in desk and pocket sizes) and a stylus to press through a pitted metal strip which holds the paper in place. (As the stylus hits the slate it causes a clicking sound that may be distracting at first.) Writing is done in reverse from right to left so that it can be "read" by touch when the paper is turned over.

Although Braille traditionally has been the blind person's most important link to the world of sight, its efficacy is extremely limited. For example, while braille materials in music, math, and science have been developed, they are incomplete. In addition, brailled books are extremely bulky and make for slow reading. Fortunately, phonographs and tape recorders are now more readily available and an extensive library of audio versions of books and other study materials has been created which supplement and may someday supplant Braille for the blind. However, at this point, Braille is still the major way that the blind communicate, and despite the drawbacks of Braille materials, many Brailled instruments permit blind students to carry on various academic activities without restriction: tape measures, slide rules, calculators and compasses are all available in Braille.

What equipment or techniques can you use to help your blind tutee? A large-type typewriter may remedy the problem of providing exercises or tests to

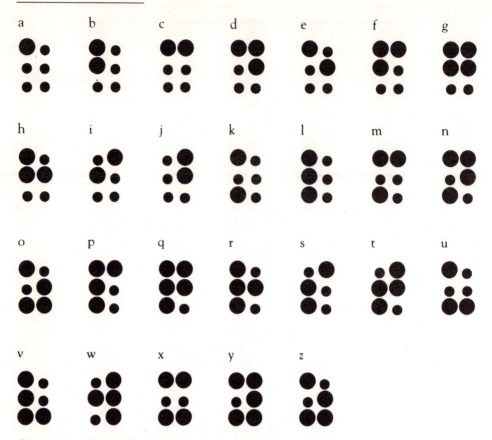

Figure 3.3 The Braille Alphabet. Braille is a system of raised dots for touch reading and writing by the blind. The entire system is derived from an arrangement of six dots referred to as the braille cell. Each arrangement of dots and each blank space occupy a cell. To aid in identifying the dot positions which comprise the various braille characters, [Inventor] Louis Braille numbered the dot positions of his cell 1–2–3 downward on the left, and 4–5–6 downward on the right. (From *Understanding Braille,* American Foundation for the Blind, 1969, p. 1.)

the tutee who is visually impaired but not completely blind. If such a typewriter is not available, you may substitute books and standardized tests printed in large-type formats for unusable teacher-made examinations, required textbooks, tutorial drills, and exercises. Of course, you should write in large, easy-to-see letters, and you should have access to a grey or green chalkboard and a supply of unglazed cream-colored paper and thick soft-leaded pencils. All these reflect more light, reduce glare, and thus increase visibility. If you work in a large, well-equipped learning laboratory you may have projection and magnifying machines available, both of which help a tutee with visual limitations by enlarging the visual image. (See chapter 4 for a discussion of audiovisual equipment.)

Obviously, the most valuable asset that you and your tutee have in common is oral communication, and this may be exploited in many ways. Be sure to help develop your tutee's listening skill, for listening is essential to the student's academic success. Do some reading aloud, checking to see if your

Talking Machine Center to Aid Blind Lawyers in Justice Dept.

WASHINGTON, Dec. 6 (UPI) — Blind Justice Department lawyers are now being provided with talking machines that convert print and computer data to automated voices.

On Wednesday Attorney General Benjamin R. Civiletti formally dedicated the department's Andrew Woods Sensory Assistance Center, which is equipped with $50,000 in electronic devices to allow sightless lawyers to fully research and prepare their cases.

Candice Aviles, the project's coordinator, said the facility included the first such equipment to be marketed.

She said that a blind department lawyer "can do research, read cases, look up statutes on his own. He doesn't need a reader."

The center was named after Andrew Woods, a blind civil rights lawyer in the department who helped design the center before he was stricken with cancer and died in February 1979.

Construction of the center was speeded under Daniel Meador, former assistant attorney general in charge of the Office for Improvements in the Administration of Justice, who became blind after being named to the post by former Attorney General Griffin Bell.

In a brief ceremony outside the center, Mr. Civiletti said the new machines provide "a hint of the future." The equipment scans typewriter print or computer impulses and produces audible words.

"Not only are they marvels of technology but most important," he said, "they will allow us more in the future to utilize the full talents of men and women who are visually handicapped whose talents are not being fully used now."

The equipment in the center, which is available for use by about 78 blind employees, including nearly a dozen lawyers, includes the following:

¶A "talking terminal," invented by Peter Maggs, a University of Illinois law professor, that hooks up to Juris, the Justice Department's computerized law library and speaks the material aloud at the push of a button.

¶An LED-110 Braille printer terminal, which provides the same access to legal research but prints out the material in high-quality braille.

¶The Kurzweil Reading Machine, invented by Raymond Kurzweil, president of Kurzweil Computer Products of Cambridge, Mass. It is programmed to read any of 200 typewriter faces.

As this article makes clear, equipment is a tool, compensating for human limitations and extending our capacity to master our environment.

---

tutee has gotten the main idea of the passage: to test or to reinforce recall, ask the student to define a term on the basis of its context ("How is it used here?") or, conversely, ask the tutee to name a process or concept the writer uses; have your tutee discuss the conclusions of the reading selection or predict what is to follow. Tutor your students to use their special skills during classroom lecture—taking advantage of the capacity of all humans to think faster than they talk—to review what has already been said or to evaluate the statements being made. Use a tape recorder to develop students' oral skills, and to record exercises as well as their responses to them. Also, visually handicapped students should be given practice in proofreading mechanics so that they know which words to use to specify punctuation and directions for printing; in that way tutees may also "write" an essay or answer exam questions on tape. (For example ". . . *Cap* Some students prefer term papers *comma* others would rather take final examinations *period.* . . .") A final way visually handicapped students can use their oral strengths productively is with the help of a specialized recorder known as a variable speech controller. Since this machine may slow down or accelerate the rate of speech without distorting pitch or tone, it can help students to "read" faster. While it may be used to develop all listeners' skills, it is especially valuable to students for whom listening is the primary method of acquiring knowledge.

All strategies for tutoring the visually handicapped should reflect an effort to compensate for their visual limitations. Try to be as concrete as possible by using a wide variety of verbal examples and actual structural models. For example, you can use pins and rubber bands to construct geometric designs and graphs on cork or geoboards; this will aid work in math or statistics, while magnets of different shapes can help you explain parts of speech and sentence structure. You can use miniatures, such as models of bridges or buildings to illustrate a variety of topics in math, art, engineering, or history. Using a model cathedral, for example, is a tactile way of teaching about the medieval spirit and its architecture. (You can probably get this at a local art department, architecture school, or souvenir shop.) Perhaps somewhat more accessible are embossed and relief maps, which allow students to trace trade routes or map the progress of a movement, like the Renaissance, through different parts of the world. Anatomical and skeletal models in biology, and molecular models in chemistry, can compensate for sensory deprivation while encouraging your tutee's active involvement in the learning process. In using these materials, you will also be giving your student verbal descriptions that explain differences in scale and size and suggest as well how these smaller parts fit into a larger context.

STUDENTS WITH OTHER PHYSICAL IMPAIRMENTS

With paraplegic and quadraplegic students your main concern will probably be physical access. For example, can they get to the tutoring session? With the quadraplegic, written exercises and responses will not be possible and alternative oral procedures will be necessary. Part of your tutorial function may involve acting as a notetaker and providing an outline of the material so that the student can study from it. Victims of cerebral palsy may also have difficulty writing, which the use of typewriter, recorder, and methods of oral dictation will remedy.

STUDENTS WITH LEARNING DISABILITIES

Some students seem to have a learning problem; although their senses are intact, their emotional adjustment normal, their intelligence average, or often, above average, these students have one or more of what are vaguely called learning disabilities. Little is known about this incapacity (or these incapacities), and researchers are still categorizing symptoms and hypothesizing about sources. Terms used to designate this problem include *aphasia*, difficulty in understanding spoken or written language; and *dyslexia*, disturbances in reading or writing. Some characteristic features of learning disabilities are shown in the chart (Fig. 3.4). Be aware, however, that these symptoms appear in the reading or writing of a wide range of people without learning disabilities and may have their roots in a variety of different sources. *Under no circumstances, therefore, should you label any student learning disabled.* If you think a student has a serious learning problem, discuss it promptly with your lab supervisor or your instructor.

Type/Problem	Example
letter or number substitutions	*him* for *his,* as in *him book*
word substitutions (often within the same category or designating a classifying element)	*dog* for *pet*; *daughter* for *mother*; *knife* for *sharp*
circumlocutions: functional definitions	*the thing that opens the door* for *key*
reversal/rotations	*pad* for *dad*; *peer* for *reap*; *93* for *63* or *39*; △ for ▽
relational words	*because, since, although* and prepositional words (*in, next, to, without*) avoided
size, scale, distance	cannot properly estimate
conservation	different arrangements are perceived as different quantities

Figure 3.4 Typical Features of Learning Disabilities. While this chart is meant to illustrate problems of learning disabled students, many of the types as well as examples may have their origins in other sources. Carelessness, dialect, previous educational background may also result in similar "errors."

In many cases, students—whether or not they themselves are aware of the disability—have learned to compensate for their learning disability and only some residual elements of it may remain. In some situations, the student may not need tutoring but *may* need to be given a test orally or to get more time to take tests. (Again, if you think this is the case, consult with your lab director or instructor.) If tutoring is considered appropriate, you should work in the same way as you do with other students while being particularly careful to structure and sequence the material. Break your material into its component parts, isolate the critical element, and, if necessary, use a boundary to define it (as in Figure 3.5), so that your tutee can perceive it as a unit. Be sure your tutee can identify the elements verbally, then visually, before asking him or her to reproduce it—first while looking at the example, and later without it. If students trace, copy, and repeat aloud what they write or read, they will get multisensory reinforcement. Repetition and drill are useful, but only after the student has understood the initial concept.

$$\frac{2}{4}$$

Figure 3.5 Bounded Figure. The example used here is less important than the rule drawn around it. The box helps to "frame" or isolate specific information and so makes learning more accessible to the learning disabled student.

two-fourths or one-half; expressed in fraction form

CLASS PROJECT 3

1. Discuss with your class experiences you have had with the handicapped. What were your reactions? Observations? If you feel comfortable, discuss someone you know who is handicapped. How has his or her handicap affected your relationship, your own routine?

2. At home, blindfold yourself for a minimum of two hours; in the journal or in an essay, record your experience, your responses, your conclusions regarding this deprivation.

3. As a term research project or for group discussion based on reading, learn the Federal legislation affecting college learners with handicaps. Explore the changes it has made and might make in your educational institution— whether physical, academic, or in terms of other student services. (Be sure to check school catalogues and handbooks and to interview persons in Student Services and the Physical Plant offices.)

LAB APPLICATIONS

1. As a term project, develop a tape-recorded or three-dimensional version of a standard test used in your lab or tutorial program to make it accessible to blind students or students with other physical impairments.

2. Using the session-planning chart in chapter 4 (p. 104), develop a session to meet the needs of a person with a given handicap.

3. Conduct a close examination of your lab layout and attempt to correct any hazards or obstacles to the handicapped (for example, wheelchair access).

READING 6

Howard Hofsteater was an unusual man. Profoundly deaf from nine months of age, he was, nonetheless, able to gain mastery of language. This self-study examines how he was able to do this, despite having no memory of hearing the English language. Not surprisingly, this unique document gained a wide reading and has won a place for itself in modern educational literature. It has stirred some controversy as well among those concerned with the special education of the deaf, for Hofsteater's case study is defending a particular strategy; and his autobiography is used as evidence to support it.

Hofsteater was graduated from Gallaudet College, Washington, D. C., the only four-year institution of higher education for the deaf in the world, and was a member of the faculty at the Illinois School for the Deaf, in Jacksonville, Illinois. He wrote the case study while he was a graduate student at the University of Illinois.

READING QUESTIONS

1. What method did Hofsteater's parents use to teach him language? How is it similar to ways hearing children are taught? How does it compare with the ways profoundly deaf children are normally taught?

2. Reread Hawkins' diary on the phonics method of teaching reading (p. 34). Compare his discussion to Hofsteater's (p. 79). What do both of these tell you about the limitations of any method or tutoring technique?

3. Hofsteater deplores the fact that his father did not keep a journal. Why? How does his statement about the sources of Hofsteater's information about himself affect your view of the validity of the case study? What does Hofsteater do to lend weight to his case?

4. What themes does Hofsteater want to underscore? What does he explicitly omit in his summary of section 2? Is this omission effective? In general, how effective is the document as a case study?

5. At the end, Hofsteater suggests the limitations of the case study method. What are they? What is his purpose in doing this?

6. How has this article influenced your view of the deaf? your view of human potential?

6 | AN EXPERIMENT IN PRESCHOOL EDUCATION
An Autobiographical Case Study

Howard T. Hofsteater

I

It has always been my belief that the exasperating problem of nonverbalism among deaf infants was quite adequately solved years ago by my parents when they set about giving me approximately the same language background as a normal hearing child possesses upon entering school.

To the best of my knowledge, the program for my education, as conceived and carried out by my parents, was so revolutionary—yet so simple—that it had never been attempted before then, nor since. Although it caused some controversial discussion at the time, no one else seems to have cared to duplicate the experiment on which my parents gambled my entire intellectual life.

At many different times I have been asked to write a detailed account of how I "learned to read," how I was "educated," how I was enabled to express myself freely in English long before the average deaf child possesses a single word in his vocabulary— let alone forms a concept of language as a means of communication. For years I have hesitated to do so, feeling that it would be far more seemly for someone else to write such a piece. But as time slithers by and the teaching profession is still baffled by the problem, I have at long last convinced myself that I should record the details of my so-called education, for the simple reason that this single case history might lead to further research and experimentation with happy results.

II

I was the only child born to Howard McPherson Hofsteater and Ollie Tracy, both deaf. He was 45 years of age and she 40 when I was born on November 22, 1909.

Dad lost his hearing at the age of two when his father, Eli Hofsteater, mislaid his spectacles and could not make out the labels on the bottles in the medicine chest with the horribly tragic result that he squirted carbolic acid into Dad's ears instead of the earache drops the doctor had prescribed.

Mother became deaf shortly before she was two years old when she crawled through an open kitchen door and plunged down the cellar stairs. Her brother, the late Rev. H. Lorraine Tracy, lost his hearing unnecessarily as the result of a protracted siege of catarrh when he was about ten years old.

Dad had two cousins who were deaf, and there was also a deaf cousin lurking in Mother's family background. All these factors taken together convinced my parents that there was a familial predisposition towards deafness on both sides, and for that reason they decided to forego the pleasures of parenthood. But when I insisted on being born, they accepted the event with good grace, nevertheless.

Both my parents were educated at the Iowa School for the Deaf in Council Bluffs where my mother taught for several years immediately after graduation. My father went on to Gallaudet College (1884-1887), but he left college after his sophomore year when Mr. Harry Simpson, the deaf founder of the Dakota Territorial School for the Deaf, prevailed upon him to accept a teaching position. That was a step Father bitterly regretted to the last, for he was a very proud and ambitious man, and it galled him no end to be forever explaining why he never was graduated from college. While at the Dakota school, Dad founded the school paper, the *Dakota Advocate*.

Shortly after my parents' marriage in 1893, they spent their next eleven years teaching at the North Carolina School in Morganton. While in North Carolina, my father started and edited the *Deaf Carolinian*. In 1907, they moved on to the Alabama School. In 1909 I was born, giving a new twist to their lives.

Stung by the embarrassments of having to explain why he did not finish college and by the feeling that he was not adequately educated, my father went heavily into independent historical study with the result that he became very familiar with ancient and modern history—a fact which had much influence on the nature of my reading.

In the meantime, my mother stuck to her program of adding bits here and there to her self-education as a primary grade teacher. She became an expert with retarded children. She acquired the reputation of being singularly able to salvage "hopelessly retarded children." Children who failed miserably in oral programs, children with mental deficiencies, children who arrived at school at embarrassingly late ages, were invariably turned over to my mother for instruction.

Our financial status was only moderate. In those days teachers were on a very low level of remuneration, but in spite of that, my parents managed to live quite comfortably and to afford the special expenses of my private education up to the age of nine.

To summarize—I was born into a determinedly academic and ambitious atmosphere, for which I am naturally thankful. My parents were unusually conscientious teachers, spending much of their spare time in devising new techniques of teaching. Our home was filled with good literature to which my parents added immeasurably when they were confronted by the special problem of raising a deaf infant.

III

Before a watchmaker's apprentice is introduced to the individual movements in a watch, he becomes thoroughly familiar with the watch as a completely integrated piece of machinery. Proceeding on the same line of thought, it seems advisable first of all to have a general, factual report on my progress from the time my deafness was discovered to the time I completed the elementary and secondary phases of my education.

I deplore my father's failure to keep a diary—outlining his philosophy of education and, at the same time, recording day-to-day occurrences. Such an account would have been invaluable as a case history study—far more detailed and accurate than this introspective essay which is based entirely on my own memory of events and of the things my parents and friends told me in regard to my preschool development. The idea of maintaining a daily record simply never occurred to Dad, for I am dead certain that he would have undertaken such a task with enduring, professional enthusiasm.

Let it be repeated that I was born on November 22, 1909—from a week to ten days overdue, and blue from head to foot. This anoxia was due to strangulation by the umbilical cord, and it still remains to be seen whether or not it affected my mind. Otherwise, there seems to have been nothing out of the ordinary in my development as a baby. My parents always stoutly maintained to me that up to the time I was eight or nine months old, they observed many indications of normal response to sound stimuli, ranging from loud noises to tapping a glass with a spoon, and so forth.

It was then that my father contracted pneumonia in both lungs and I a "heavy cold" as the result of his playing with me on a quilt spread out on the floor in a very drafty room. Oxygen tents had not been invented then, so it was necessary to keep all doors and windows open day and night in order that Dad might gasp his way through to recovery. In the meantime, Mother kept me as warmly bundled up as possible. In their desperate struggle to pull Dad through, neither Mother nor Dr. Sims considered my cold as being dangerous.

Dad and I recovered at about the same time. Immediately thereafter, my parents noticed that I no longer responded to any sound. I was taken at once to several ear specialists who confirmed my parents' worst fears. Our familial predisposition had struck again.

I do not know how long it took my parents to reach a decision as to how they were going to educate me—but once their plan was formulated, they stuck to it stubbornly in the face of considerable criticism, derision and abuse.

Visions of becoming a prosperous business man caused Dad to resign from the Alabama School in 1912 to enter into the printing and rubber-stamp business in Birmingham, Ala., with Osce Roberts—the father of Miss Maumee Roberts who was my private tutor in speech and lipreading for a period of two or three years.

We moved from our comfortable home in Talladega to the somewhat drab, crowded neighborhood of 50th Street in Birmingham. There were on that street a good many boys of approximately the same age as I, but much tougher. The appearance of a "new boy on the block" who was also "a deaf-and-dumb" freak made me legitimate prey. I got into many fights during the three years we lived there, but I must say that as soon as I learned the hard way how to defend myself, the harum-scarum life in the alleys back of 50th Street proved in the long run to be the most enjoyable and socially educative phase of my boyhood. I had no trouble at all in mixing with the 50th Street boys, with whom I conversed by means of "natural" signs.

When I was six or seven years old, Supt. F. H. Manning offered my parents their old jobs at the Alabama School. Father's dreams of becoming a bloated plutocrat having collapsed, my parents accepted with alacrity—so we moved back to the tranquil and scholarly atmosphere of old Talladega.

However genteel and cultured Talladega was—and still is—it had at that time the foulest, filthiest drinking water in the country. Half of the time between 1916 and 1920, it seems, Dad and I were in bed suffering from an incredible succession of infectious diseases. Generally it was dysentery, or something very close to it. I don't think I have ever gotten over the constant succession of lingering illnesses that beset me during that time. However, it must be conceded that my poor health must have spurred my reading progress, for that was practically the only way I could amuse myself and obtain vicariously the experience I needed.

When my parents were away at school, my care was entrusted to two deaf governesses, one after another. They had no influence whatsoever on my education. They functioned only to cater to my physical needs; however, they were required to converse with me only by spelling on the fingers.

Because of my frail health and because my parents really could not make up their minds what was best for me, I was kept out of school until I was nine years old and allowed to develop freely very much as John Dewey* would approve of, but, of course, under the firm, purposeful guidance of my parents. At that time, strong pressure was brought to bear down on my parents by the school authorities with the result that I was enrolled at the Alabama School for the Deaf in January, 1920.

I was placed in the fourth grade in the Oral Department. The following year I was shifted to the seventh grade. After one year in that class, the authorities moved me to the ninth grade. With that class I progressed through twelfth grade and graduation, which explains why I spent only 5½ years at the Alabama School and went on to Gallaudet College at the age of 14.

IV

When I was a college student back home for vacations, Dad, Mother, and I often discussed various phases of my early childhood. After I became a teacher, Mother (Dad died when I was only seventeen years old) and I went into the professional aspects of my early education pretty thoroughly at many different times. Time and again, I would run into people who knew me "back when" and would tell about seeing me talk with my fingers when I was a little boy and how it usually startled them. My relatives (most of them now gathered to their ancestors) also told me about many incidents. I mention all this by way of explaining how I am able to furnish so much information for the ensuing narrative. Miss Maumee Roberts, whom I have already mentioned, and Miss Eugenia Thornton—who was my beloved teacher for the last two years of my stay at the Alabama School—have also furnished valuable data.

As soon as my parents became convinced that I had irretrievably lost my hearing, they were confronted with the question of what next to do with me. They had before them these precedents established by other deaf parents of deaf children:—

(a) Employing signs for ordinary, practical purposes and leaving language development to properly constituted school authorities. This plan, of course, robs the child of early acquisition of a vocabulary and the concept of words used in proper relationship with others as the universally accepted mode of intercommunication.

(b) Using signs at first and slowly introducing words by means of the manual alphabet as the child grows up. The child then enters school with anywhere between 100 and 500 words in his vocabulary and has that much of a head start.

Neither of these alternatives appealed to my parents. They felt that they could do much better than that in the way of developing me during my early formative years.

Quite logically they argued that if a normal hearing child effortlessly acquires spoken language by hearing it and imitating it, a deaf child should be able to do exactly the same by seeing it used. They saw no psychological—nor physiological—difference between a baby's using his vocal cords, tongue, and lips to imitate spoken language and a baby's using his hands to imitate the movements of finger-spelled words. Furthermore, they maintained that since I had become totally deaf at so early an age that I might as well be considered congenitally deaf, sound would for me be forever only a

---

*John Dewey (1859-1952) Philosopher, educator, and activist and leader in public affairs, Dewey had an immense influence, especially on the so-called "progressive education" movement of the 1920's and 30's, an influence he disavowed when he felt his ideas were being distorted. Dewey did stress "learning by doing" and collaborative learning as essential to the full realization of a democratic society.

hazy, mental concept instead of the vivid thing it is to hearing people and to those who lose their sense of hearing at around ten years of age and to those with considerable residual hearing. Therefore, speech and speechreading would be an entirely foreign and artificial means of mental development for me. Carrying their line of reasoning still further, it occurred to them that, since they had committed themselves to some form of manual English, they might as well go the whole hog and use nothing but English through the medium of fingerspelling.

My parents' theories were in direct contradiction with the curious belief then prevailing and which persists to this very day in some quarters. Many people believed that it was dangerous for a child to learn language by any means other than hearing—or its makeshift equivalents—and that resorting to other methods would be "forcing the child" with disastrous aftereffects. I may be very much in the wrong, but I understand that some teachers are convinced that it is impossible for anyone to learn a word until he has previously learned the basic sounds thereof. The word, "airplane," is withheld from a first year pupil because he may not have mastered at that time the phonetics involved—a, r, pl, a, n—to say nothing about the mechanics of running them together in two syllables. This principle is adhered to in spite of the fact that an airplane is as much a part of the child's environment as a cow, a ball, a dog.

My parents then decided upon this course of action. They would (1) begin at once to talk casually and constantly to me on their fingers, just as hearing people do vocally to their babies—*whether or not I was paying any attention*; (2) talk to me just as naturally as hearing people do when attending to my physical needs, pausing only to emphasize key words tied to my bodily wants and interests; (3) use only fingerspelling between themselves when I was consciously present; and (4) in general, raise me as if I were a normal hearing baby with the sole exception of using the manual alphabet instead of speech.

So, instead of spelling only the world "milk" to me at feeding time, they said something like "Here is your milk—m-i-l-k," or "Howard, it's time for your milk—m-i-l-k," and so on. Apparently from all reliable accounts, the results were astoundingly quick.

Miss Eugenia Thornton, in her letter discussing my early education, writes, "The first vivid recollection I have of you was when you were very young. I am sure I saw you, before that time and many times when you were still a baby, but no other incident stands out clearly. You were lying in your crib. Your mother brought a bottle of milk to you. You reached for the bottle and at the same time spelled "m-k" several times, just as spontaneously and naturally as a hearing baby of the same age would have attempted to say "milk," and perhaps have said "mik." . . . This is not a story that I have heard about you but an occurrence that is clearly remembered."

Then followed *w, w-t, w-t-r, water; p, p-d, -dy, puddy* (custard pudding of which I was inordinately fond throughout my childhood), *c-t, cat; pa; ma; s-g-r, sugar; b-n, banana; a-pl, apple;* and so on. My parents are authorities for the foregoing information as regards the first few words I learned. While I was stumbling through the spelling of the words that appealed to me right off, the deluge of natural, everyday English continued unabated.

Anyone who knows the manual alphabet appreciates the fact that consonant letters are much more distinctly formed than the vowels. So I believe it was only natural for me to omit vowels at first. Miss Thornton compares this tendency of mine to "lisping" among hearing babies.

No one has ever been able to put his finger squarely on the subtle mental process by which a normal infant shifts from the vocabulary level to the beginnings of connected language. The nearest one can come to doing so is to speculate on the part suggestion for imitation plays. When Daddy leaves for work, Mama says fondly to Baby, "Tell Daddy good-bye," and waves her hand to Daddy. Daddy waves back. Mama takes hold of Baby's hand and waves it up and down. After Baby has been repeatedly told to do so, the miracles of spontaneous hand-waving and "Bye" and "Goo'-by" follow. In general, the same thing happened to me.

Once that mysterious transition is made, development of connected language and thought (the two are inseperable) becomes swiftly cumulative and is limited only by the quality and quantity of the child's experiences and the nature of his environment.

My parents assured me time and again they never had to resort to formal teaching procedures to get me started in free, idiomatic language. I used more and more every-day English because I saw it used all the time and because I wanted to participate. Dad and Mother repeatedly emphasized to me this point:—never did they physically force me to look at their fingers when they were talking to me; nor did they insist on my "copying" consciously or memorizing words or phrases or expressions. They, of course, helped me along when I struck out on my own to imitate.

The idea that whenever they manipulated their fingers in my direction would in some way affect my well-being must have percolated through somehow, for I developed at a rather early age the faculty of *concentrated visual attention*—subject, of course, to my fluctuating desire to listen.

Another interesting thing is this:—I learned the proper sequence of the letters in the alphabet some time after I could spell many words. That is in keeping with good, modern psychology.

I have a suspicion that even my parents were surprised by the extent and rapidity of the language "osmosis" their experiment precipitated. While it gratified and encour-aged them, it caused distress among many of my parents' friends and fellow-teachers. They were frankly alarmed, and some of them urged my parents to "cease and desist." And when Dad and Mother serenely went ahead as usual, some people went so far as to accuse them of trying artificially to produce a mental prodigy to satisfy their vanity, and to predict for me either a very early mental breakdown or a career as a Franken-steinian horror. I imagine my parents' feelings were hurt very much and often during that period, but they were convinced they were on the right track.

While I played more or less with the babies in our Talladega neighborhood, my reaction to companionship must have been only middling fair, for my parents never said much about that phase. If I had had brothers and sisters, within a close age range, my story might have taken a different direction. It was really not until we moved to 50th Street in Birmingham that I learned to enjoy the company of others of my own age and size. Upon my return to Talladega, my frequent illnesses and growing fond-ness for books kept me from mixing a great deal with hearing boys of my age. How-ever, I did have a few cronies, all of whom quickly learned to spell on their fingers—and to read fingerspelling. I learned many colloquialisms and Southern expressions from them.

I was naturally introduced to picture books at about the same time as I began to manipulate building blocks intelligently. I became familiar with the printed symbols for various letters through informal play with the blocks. My parents saw to it that I could identify each block with its equivalent on my fingers. At the same time, so my parents said, I was fascinated by the gaudy picture books published at that time. They were huge affairs printed in a lavish medley of colors on pages of indestructible linen. The initials, A-B-C, etc., were sunbursts; so were the illustrations.

My parents began to tell me stories shortly before we moved to Birmingham, and I quickly slid into the phase in which a child insists on a bedtime story as well as stories at various times of the day.

When I asked for a story, Dad or Mother would always drop everything else to gratify me, and my appetite for stories became a great drain on their time and energy. I was pretty badly spoiled in that connection. They would ask me what story I wanted and, unless Dad had brought home a new book, I would ask for one of my old favorites for a repeat just as all children do. Then they would get the book and, with me comfortably snuggled in their laps, "spell aloud" the story. They would hold their hands pretty close to the pages and spell.

At this point, I am afraid it devolves on me to explain a peculiar phenomenon to people who are not thoroughly familiar with the ins-and-outs of the psychology of the bona-fide deaf. It is not necessary for one who is adept in fingerspelling or signs to look directly at the hands of the person talking. He catches the fingerspelling or signs on the outer edge of the cone of his vision while centering his attention on something else. That is why many deaf people have the disconcerting habit of looking straight into the eyes or at the face of the person to whom they are listening, not at his fingers.

With this explanation in mind, one can see how easy it was for me to center my attention on the illustrations and text and, at the same time, get the words as Dad or Mother spelled them out. Spelling out the words close to the pages also had the effect of keeping my attention on the printed pages. This factor probably had something to do with speeding up my reading readiness.

I was about four and a half years or so old when I received such a shock that I can remember every detail of the event. I asked Mother one day to read me the story of Silver Paw—which I knew by heart and which always caused me to cry. It was a very sad story about a puppy that got lost. I got impatient with the rate at which Mother was spelling it out and turned a page before she had finished it. She stopped spelling, but I kept right on and sobbed and bawled through to the end. The next day when I asked for another story, she flatly refused, telling me to go read it myself. I was very much hurt, but I did retire into a nook and read the story. That evening when Dad came home, I rushed to him and asked him to read me a story, only to be rebuffed likewise. That was how I was abruptly weaned away from having stories read to me.

Several interesting points come to light in the foregoing account of how I learned to read.

It was only to be expected that I skipped entirely the "oral reading" phase of the standard learning process. It would have been silly for me to spell out the words, too, while my parents were spelling the stories to me. It would have slowed down the reading so much as to make it tedious and uninteresting. I could follow the story and the spelling at a more rapid and natural speed.

It was very easy for me to stop my parents at any time for explanations or for them to pause and ask me if I knew the meanings of words they were pretty sure were new to me.

I have a theory that, in addition to the concepts I was establishing all along through ordinary conversation and observation, this fast reading contributed a great deal to my unconscious acceptance of the fact that words can have different contextual meanings.

Another important point in regard to my reading is that I dearly loved to dramatize the stories I read. I learned to pretend in a big way from my association with the children on 50th Street. We pretended we were Indians, played cops and robbers and so forth. "Bang!" and we'd fall down dead, and so on. We had quite a lot of fun, although it must have been tiresome at times for my parents.

I recall that, after I got through Little Red Riding Hood, Jack and the Beanstalk, Puss-in-Boots, The Three Bears and the like, I went on to fairyland. I loved the Brownie stories. Thornton Burgess' endless series of humanized animal stories held my interest for quite a while. Aesop's Fables, the Riverside and the Eclectic series of adapted tales, The Raindrop, Greek, Roman and Teutonic myths, and tales of ancient times and heroes led me on and on to the classics. In between, I read a good many stories about Indians, wilderness scouts, the Pilgrims, George Washington, pirates, cowboys, knights, and Boy Scout adventurers. In my imagination, I shot it out with Zane Grey's badmen. Sherlock Holmes was a prime favorite for a long time. My father spent a great deal of time looking through publishers' catalogs and ordering books he thought I would enjoy. And, too, there was the Carnegie Public Library just across the street from the Alabama School.

The following facts and implications stand out clearly in this case history study:

(1) It is possible to *spell* on one's fingers to a deaf baby and gradually to attract sufficient attention from it for educational purposes.

(2) It is possible for a deaf baby to *identify* important letters and words formed on the hands and later on, to imitate them.

(3) Sound is by no means the *sine qua non* of the very foundation of a deaf infant's acculturation.

(4) It is easier for a deaf infant to identify and understand something he can see very clearly than something he has to guess at.

(5) It is possible for a congenitally and totally deaf child to achieve through spelling approximately the same amount of "language absorption" that a normal hearing child does, and at the same pace—other factors being equal.

(6) The process used by my parents was exactly like that followed by most educated parents of hearing children expect that fingerspelling was substituted for hearing and speech.

(7) It is during the formative, preschool years of a child's life—hearing or deaf— that he should be started on language.

One can with good reason infer from this narrative two things in regard to reading:—(a) It is easier for a deaf child trained exclusively by the manual alphabet to get started in reading than his hearing counterpart because of the elimination of all phonetic difficulties; (b) that would not be true of a deaf child whose sole method of communication during his preschool life was that of signs alone.

It occurs to one that hearing parents of deaf children could very easily make use of the manual alphabet to get their babies off to a flying start and wait until they are about three years old before attempting to introduce them to the alien world of sound. The important thing is to establish a free and easy means of intercommunication between the deaf child and his intimates from the very beginning—not only for the sake of exchange of ideas but also for the sake of alerting as early as possible the deaf child's mind. One can even logically argue that it is easier to introduce speech and lipreading to a deaf child who already has some language than to one who has absolutely no language concepts.

Approximately the same observation was made by Dr. Harris L. Taylor in his article, "The Missing Mind," in the May, 1937, issue of the *American Annals of the Deaf.* To quote him,

> "I would recall some deaf children of intelligent deaf parents; these children came to school with a mental development far greater than that of other deaf children with approximately equal ability. It was true that these deaf children of deaf parents were developed through the sign language, but it was equally true that they excelled in oral school work. Their school progress was more rapid on account of their development. If so much could be done through the sign language, why could not more be done by using English from the beginning?"

Another inference that could be made is that the deaf child who is trained by a medley of signs and finger-spelled words is in a much better position, both mentally and linguistically, to begin school work than one who starts from scratch. *If the signs and words are uniformly used in the same grammatical order as spoken language, the child is vastly that much better prepared.*

VII

The story of how my parents endowed me, a totally deaf child, with practically the same language background that the average normal hearing child enjoys before entering school is of special interest only to myself and to the few who have wondered how it was done. It does establish a few facts, and it does open the way for some discussion. But since (a) it was written from a subjective point of view, and (b) it is an isolated case, it cannot be taken seriously by the profession.

However, if one were to make out a list of at least fifty (one hundred or more would be better) congenitally deaf people with unusually good command of English and—

(1) Inquire very closely into the means by which they were enabled to conquer their language handicaps.
(2) Prepare a detailed study of each case, presenting all relevant data available.
(3) Get as much corroborative evidence for each case history as possible.
(4) Point out similarities and differences.
(5) Analyze, draw conclusions and offer constructive recommendations.

then the findings of such a study would carry considerable weight, especially if it were undertaken under the scientific guidance of a responsible educational institute—for example, the Department of Special Education of the University of Illinois. It is my opinion that a research project along that line will more likely than not uncover some highly interesting and significant data on the language problem of the deaf.

BIBLIOGRAPHY

Bishop, M. E., ed. *Mainstreaming: Practical Ideas for Educating Hearing-Impaired Students*. Washington, D.C.: A.G. Bell Association for the Deaf, 1979.

Gray, Rusty. "Serving Adults with Presumed Learning Disabilities—Some Considerations." *Journal of Developmental and Remedial Education,* 4, (Winter, 1981) 3-5, 33.

Johnson, Doris and Helmer Mykledust. *Learning Disabilities; Educational Principles and Practices*. New York: Grune and Stratton, 1967.

Kirk, Samuel A. *Educating Exceptional Children*. 2nd ed. Boston: Houghton Mifflin Co., 1972.

Klevins, Chester, ed. *Materials and Methods in Continuing Education*. Los Angeles: Klevens Publications Inc., 1978.

Ohlson, E. La Monte. *Identification of Specific Learning Disabilities*. Champaign, Ill.: Research Press Company, 1978.

Silver, Wayne, Coleen Fix, and George Tarpley. *A Little Help From Friends*. Miami, Fla.: Miami Dade Community College, n.d. (videotape)

4 | *THE TUTORIAL SESSION*

THE ROLE OF PLANNING

Why Plan?

Most of you have begun to tutor already and are, we hope, not finding it as intimidating as you might have feared. You *do* know something (your mind didn't go blank during the session), your tutees like you (you think)—at least they promised to return. But the questions you are probably having the most trouble answering are: Did your tutees learn anything? Are your sessions interesting, instructional, memorable? What, in fact, constitutes a good tutoring session? These are excellent questions, which need to be asked continually by all tutors who really care about their tutees. For as we have seen in the previous chapters, tutors do not merely impart knowledge to students. They use their skill, nerve, talent, intelligence, and sensitivity to create an environment in which people can learn.

Experienced tutors do not need to prepare much, because they can rely on their "intuition"—refined by many preparations and tutoring sessions—to tell them what needs to be done in a given session. But if you are a beginner, you may not easily be able to recognize what you ought to do to meet your tutees' learning needs. In the beginning, then, you should plan your sessions as carefully as possible. This chapter is dedicated to making the planning time more productive and efficient.

How Much to Plan

Clearly, the amount of preparation you do will depend on your tutorial program. If you tutor primarily on a drop-in basis, you will not have much time to plan; but you can prepare in a general way by sitting in on tutoring sessions and by plotting out sample sessions. If, on the other hand, you will be seeing the same tutees on a regular basis, you will be able to make a general map of what your tutorials with this student will consist of. However, these plans are always provisional, since the final shape of your tutorials must reflect your tutees' needs and desires as well as your own.

Courtesy Mark Dandelske

CLASS PROJECT 1

1. Form groups of five to seven to discuss what you believe are the ingredients of a model session. Two members of each group act as a steering committee (see p. 10) to summarize what goes on and to generalize on the ingredients of a model session.

2. Write a short essay called "A Model Class" in which you describe the best lesson you have observed or attended. Then compare those things that make a good class with the components of a good tutoring session (as defined by you, the group, and in the section that follows). You might want to devote a group session to reading these essays aloud.

3. Interview a senior tutor and find out how his or her sessions are planned. Record your interview in your journal.

In your journal:

a. Make a list of all the things you do before your tutoring session that you could call planning.

b. Make a list of all the things you are not doing in your sessions that you feel you should be doing.

How to Plan

As we will discuss at greater length in chapter 8, in any given tutoring session, students pass through a variety of stages in order to learn the material. To understand the material, they must code it so they are able to produce it at will; they must be able to show they have understood what they learned and then that they can generalize the material and show they are able to transfer their learning to other areas. Your tutoring session, therefore, must include ways in which the student can demonstrate that these goals have been accomplished. Below is an overview of things you can do before, during, and after your tutoring sessions to help make these sessions as effective as possible.

Before Tutoring

If possible, review the student's folder. Look for diagnostics, referral forms from the teacher, past session reports from former tutors, and any material your tutee may have completed during previous tutoring sessions. (If your tutee has no folder or has never been tutored before, ask him or her to bring in any papers or tests that might pertain to the subject being tutored.)

Gather your materials before the session. Your session may call for exercises, tests, books, slide shows, etc. Be sure you know what is available and how to get it.

(We have discussed pre-tutoring techniques at length in chapter 2. Review the section if you have any questions.)

While Tutoring

Together with your tutee, plan the session. See what the tutee wants to accomplish and how that correlates with what you think needs to be accomplished. Come to a compromise, a plan that satisfies both of you. See chapter 2 on how to make a learning contract.

Motivate your student. So that he or she will be interested at the beginning and throughout the session, you will need to develop strategies and techniques for exciting and maintaining your tutee's curiosity.

Find out what your tutee remembers about the subject. Encouraging students to go back a step and show mastery of the area directly preceding an area of study not only motivates them for the coming session by showing them they are capable of learning the new material, but it also assures you that students are ready to learn it. Such review and recall also, of course, reinforces your previous sessions.

Guide the student through the instruction. This is best done by using techniques that keep students interested and attentive, that help students retain what is tutored, and that enable students to transfer the learning so that they can apply it to a variety of circumstances.

Check frequently for learning. Ask the student to perform orally and in writing. Use these performances to evaluate the tutee's work and to give him or her *feedback.*

After Tutoring

If possible, give your tutee some kind of work to do at home. You can examine this work during the next session or the student can check it on his or her own. Homework serves as a good way to reinforce what students have learned during the session, and to prepare them for the next session.

Make notes of what went on during the session, either in a tutor log or a session report. This will help you with your planning for the next session. If you have any report to write to the tutee's teacher, this is the time to do that, not later when you may have tutored other students or let your own work intervene.

Evaluate your session by comparing your plan with what actually happened during the session. Analyze why some strategies and techniques worked and others didn't. (Use your journal for this analysis.) See how close you came to meeting your goals. (You will then be able to use this material in your case study.)

LAB APPLICATION

Plan your next session using the suggestions above and analyze whether planning really did improve your session.

COMPONENTS OF A GOOD SESSION

Motivation

Motivation is most important at the start of the session, for it prepares the way for everything that is to follow. It is the "turn on" and, like any system run on energy, unless the switch is on, nothing else can happen. Often we do not give enough time or attention to motivating our students because we are so eager to get to the instruction. (This is especially true if we have a lot of material to cover.) So we rush into the session, leaving our students staring past us, or doodling, or yawning, or thinking about the cafeteria. Motivating a tutee means spending time in every session making certain the tutee wants to learn what you have to tutor. However motivation does not only get your tutee going; it also affects the entire session. The nature and degree of motivational material you use depends on your students and how much interest and enthusiasm they bring with them. What makes for good learning generally makes for good tutoring—and what makes for good tutoring are those things which interest and challenge a student. Whatever achieves these things can be called motivating. Remember, however, that techniques and strategies can only work if, and as much as, your students will let them. Your students must take responsibility for supplying the deepest kinds of motivation, the kinds that determine why they are in school in the first place, why they do their homework, and why they care about ideas at all. (See chapter 6 for further discussion on this topic.)

LAB APPLICATION

Observe a tutoring session or view a videotape of one and pick out three motivational techniques your fellow tutors use.

Instruction

This is the heart of your tutorial session—the substance of what your tutees need to learn. It is sometimes the hardest thing to accomplish because while tutors can often present material well, tutees do not always learn. Nonetheless, *your* responsibility in developing a good session will be to find the material and use the strategies and techniques that you think will be most effective with your tutees.

Relevance is a particularly important instructional consideration. Tutees must understand how the material relates to their own world view or their incentive for learning it will be low. It is relatively easy for students to see how schoolwork will be potentially useful—they will learn how to do simple math problems or how to write a business letter; however, more abstract material (a work of literature, an historical event) may not seem intrinsically important to them, and if the students' teachers have not already attended to this matter, it will be your job to help them to see how the subject is relevant to their personal lives or careers. For example, most good literature deals with very basic philosophic questions about good and evil, life and death, and love. See if you can get your tutees to see how they, or someone they know, are wrestling with questions similar to those of the characters in the story or play they are reading. *Romeo and Juliet*, for example, is about parental opposition to a love relationship between young people. Few college students have not dealt with or seen friends deal with that problem.

Substance is another issue in instruction. Do not let your tutees' weaknesses in some areas lead you to oversimplify material. Varying the level of material, or occasionally using simpler language, should still permit you to challenge your students and ensure that you are giving them something to think about.

Interaction between you and your tutees is an essential component of tutorial instruction. Not only does it keep students involved in the session but it improves their chances of retaining the material. Most of the strategies and techniques we discuss in this chapter emphasize the active response on the part of the tutee.

Reinforcement

Reinforcement in tutoring refers to the strengthening process that tightens and bolsters the learning that has taken place during your session. Reinforcement techniques are utilized to help tutees retain what they learn from you. Most everything you do during a session, while serving a motivational or instructional purpose, will probably also be reinforcing other material learned during the session.

As the last statement implies, the components of a session are synergistic; that is, no one of them works independently. Their interaction is what makes a good session. We have outlined them here as the underlying principles of tutoring, the criteria against which you can measure the choices you will make in regard to what and how you tutor.

We make some broad distinctions in this chapter. We divide ways to motivate, instruct, and reinforce into strategies, techniques, and motivational devices. We don't pretend that these categories are really anything more than arbitrary; if pressed, we might say that strategies are a *series* of activities or approaches which tend to structure an entire session. They are more general and more formal than techniques, which are more idiosyncratic, singular, and likely to be used in combination with other techniques or incorporated into strategies. Needless to say, you can use the methods we describe in any part of the session. The final criteria has to be what works.

MAKING A GOOD SESSION

Motivational Devices

Media As we will discuss later in the chapter, the use of media is a natural motivational technique because different media actively appeal to one or more of the five senses. The primary asset of instructional media is that many of these materials have been designed by experts as alternatives to traditional teaching material (as tutoring is an alternative to traditional teaching methods). Because some students are not interested initially by books or traditional lectures, educational media use themes and motifs from the contemporary popular domain, which may include familiar as well as exotic settings, to incite students' interest.

Games and Simulations Similar in appeal to media is the game or simulation, which can motivate students by using the challenge and involvement inherent in the gameplaying process to teach them concepts and processes. Although games and simulations have been used informally for a long time, especially to educate children, they have only recently been given status by educators as a sound method to teach and to tutor students of any age.

All learning should be enjoyable, but gaming, because it is associated with leisure time and childhood—when all time was leisure time—helps to knock down the unfortunate barrier between learning and fun. Games relate directly to the world outside of education, where winning and losing are everyday occurrences (a fact which carries with it all the positive and negative aspects of the competitive system in which we live). Therefore, the gaming process has a practical application beyond the classroom, something students intuit and find exciting. Some examples of games you might be familiar with are: spelling bees, scrabble, math rummy, and Fact. (See p. 114 for other sample games.)

While simulations can be games, they also may be total environments in which people test-drive simulated vehicles or, like astronauts and other experimental subjects, live under certain carefully controlled conditions where the effects are carefully monitored. Labs required in certain chemistry and biology courses might be considered simulations; and in cases where conditions cannot be simulated in the lab, computer programs, which can handle more complex and extensive data, are created to show the effects of different factors, (for example, a program which shows changes in the ecology of a coral reef when variables are systematically varied). Simulations are very exciting because they are real and unreal at the same time, and like games, involve the participants emotionally as well as intellectually; those developed for computers often have the advantage of using an "interactive" approach (requiring an active response from the person running the program) and having beautiful, visually exciting, graphics.

Roleplaying Roleplaying is considered a special kind of simulated activity, because students pretend to be someone or something they are not in order to learn something. Many kinds of learning involve dramatic situations, or can be put into dramatic terms (*e.g.*, understanding a passage in a book, discovering feelings about a political issue, finding a composition topic). If they can be dramatized, they can be roleplayed—that is, you and the tutee can each choose a part and act it out. Roleplaying can be very exciting, for it involves its participants actively in what is happening. (See chapter 7 for a full discussion of roleplaying as it relates to tutor preparation.)

Classwork or Tests One of the main reasons students will come for tutoring is that they have done badly in classwork. Discussing a test or paper and what students can do to improve it is a good way to interest them in the instruction that is to follow. If the students have been improving since tutoring began, reviewing past papers will surely bolster their confidence while providing them with an incentive to continue in tutoring.

CLASS PROJECT 2

1. Within your groups, you have five minutes to plan and ten minutes to motivate a group member in a subject or area you know particularly well and about which he or she knows little. Your "tutee" will rate you on a scale of one to ten, with ten awarded for the best motivation; rate yourself on how well you think you motivated the student. The group should discuss the demonstration.

2. Bring in a game with which you are unfamiliar and play it with one or more members of your group. Jot down your feelings as you play it: boredom, excitement, frustration, challenge. Use these feelings as the basis for a discussion of why the game would or would not motivate learning. Share your conclusions with the class.

3. Invent a game you can use to tutor. Form a fishbowl group: you play your game with a group member while the larger group watches and, later, comments on the success or failure of your game as a motivational technique and offers concrete suggestions to improve the game. Discuss the results and share your conclusions with the class.

LAB APPLICATION

Try out at least one of the above motivational techniques on a tutee and record the results in your journal.

Some Model Tutoring Strategies

Once you begin tutoring you may be surprised by how many choices you will have about how to present new material to your tutee. Your tutoring strategy should depend, to a great extent, on the subject matter, who you are (what your abilities are), your tutee's interests and experiences, *and* the nature of your relationship with your tutee. As is implicit in the model strategies below, tutoring is a partnership, and in a partnership each partner must agree to his or her role. When you choose a teaching strategy you are not only choosing a role for yourself, but one for your tutee as well. Therefore, you must be sensitive to whether the role you give your tutee is an appropriate one.

Questioning Teachers and tutors use questioning to find out whether a student has understood them and/or the reading matter, and to determine what the student thinks or feels about a given topic. The purpose of questioning is to get students actively involved in their learning by eliciting responses from them instead of giving them information. Questions can be direct and to the point (Did you read chapter 2?) or more indirect (What did you think of Chekov's *The Sea Gull*?). They can be about ideas (Why was Bonaparte so popular?) or feelings (How did you feel about Napoléon's final fate? Do you care about French history?). Good questioning usually proceeds from the concrete situation (Why did the Allies land on Normandy Beach?) to the more abstract problem (Why were the Jews such a threat to Hitler?); for once students understand less complicated material they will be ready to tackle more complex ideas.

Questioning can be difficult at first because the process is a spontaneous one (tutor questions emerge from students' answers). You cannot control a questioning session. On the other hand, if you know your subject area well beforehand, you will find the lack of control less threatening, and, at times, rather exciting (because of the spontaneous nature of what is going on between you and the tutee). To offset the unpredictability, you may find it helpful to plot out key questions. Also, you should ask different kinds of questions: depending on your discipline, opinion and feeling, interpretive and analytical questions are in order. Use different question formats as well: true-false, multiple-choice, short-answer questions (who? what? when?) as well as longer and more complex questions (how? and why?) which deal with content. Be certain to reformulate questions when students don't seem to understand. And by all means wait after asking a question to give the student sufficient time to answer.

The Socratic Method The Socratic Method, a very specialized form of questioning, is named after the dialogues between the philosopher Socrates and his numerous disciples; these were preserved and recorded by Plato in the fifth century B.C. In these dialogues, Socrates and student interacted on the basis of a series of questions leading to the student's discovery of certain pre-determined truths. The Socratic method is seen as a "showing" rather than "telling" strategy because tutors never directly interpret the material but lead their tutees to interpret the material themselves as a result of well-focused questions. (See "Meno," p. 109.)

The Socratic Method is difficult, however, for, as with any question process, you cannot prewrite the tutee's responses (although certain key questions can be and, in some cases, should be written beforehand). The dialogues must evolve as a result of what is taking place between you and your tutee. Therefore, you must always be prepared for the discussion to stray from the topic, and you must be able to bring it back to the topic. Also, you must be sure to stop the discussion periodically for a summary of what has been taking place. For example, using Socratic dialogue to ascertain what is human, you might prepare general questions based on natural and philosophic speculation, (*e.g.*, "What immediate differences do you notice between people and animals? What similarities?") Your first summary might sound like this: "O.K. Here's where we are: Humans think. They are primates. They have ten fingers and ten toes." Then you would go on to another series of questions and summary, all leading to your ultimate definition (*e.g.*, "A human is someone capable of reason and intellectual control").

The Discovery Method In the discovery method, you set up problems for tutees to solve. By solving these problems, students can learn many things about the nature of a given subject. (Simulation and roleplay, therefore, also lend themselves to this method.) In getting deeply involved in the subject, your tutees will be able to explore their feelings about it, and you should encourage them to do so, for it will help them to understand how what they learn relates to them personally.

For example, a social science or history tutor studying modern American society with his or her tutee might pose the following problem in order to get the tutee to understand the role of women in the first half of the twentieth century. "It is 1903. You, Mrs. Thelma Gray, are a forty-year-old woman with two children, ages six and eight. Your husband loses his job as a worker in the Gilbert clock factory in Connecticut. What will you do? Suppose the same thing happens to your daughter's husband thirty-five years later? How will her options differ from yours? How will her options differ from her brother's, who is two years younger than she?" The tutee will then either work alone or with you to come up with written or oral answers to the problem.

Let's take another example. After a session on different kinds of budgeting systems, you might pose the following question: "How do you find out what budgeting system you should use to save enough money to go to Europe this summer, given that you make $20,000 and have two loans, one for $30,000 @ 15% interest, one for $15,000 @ 12% interest, and a house mortgage for $60,000 @ 10% interest?"

The purpose of the discovery method is to encourage tutees to become actively involved in learning by thinking through a problem carefully, comparing options and, once finding the best solution, backing up what they believe so they can justify it to others. Tutees who solve Mrs. Gray's problem will discover for themselves how much more limited women's options were in 1903 than in 1938, and note the change thirty-five years made in women's and men's roles. Tutees who discover the appropriate budgetary system will experience what budgeting is like.

Discovery is also an excellent reinforcement method, for it actively involves students' highest learning functions and thus promotes great interest and retention. As with any tutoring method, however, be certain that the problem is relevant, as problem-solving demands a great deal of work on the tutee's part—and the tutee must be very motivated to do it. Also, be certain your questions are open to a variety of "right" answers. Discovery questions are even less directive than Socratic ones.

Drill Drills are a series of questions in which you control the response and in which there is only one right answer. *Mechanical* drills are the most elementary kind of drill work. Tutees do not even need to understand the question to respond correctly to mechanical drills (*e.g.*, "Conjugate the verb 'to go.' I will say the subject; you say the verb: I——, You——". etc. "Do the two times multiplication table. Two times two is _____; two times three is _____," etc.). They need only memorize the correct response. As drills get more complex, more and more understanding of the material is necessary and the student is allowed greater freedom to express this understanding (*e.g.*, "Conjugate 'to go' and add an adverb—as in *I go slowly, you go slowly*.").

The Alternation Method In the alternation method, you and the tutee change roles. In order to tutor, the tutee must master the material and, in tutoring it, he or she will often get a deeper understanding of it than would otherwise have been possible.

Application All material in a tutoring session should relate to the overall goals of a course of study. Things are rarely ever learned in isolation. When you use an application strategy, you are ensuring that your tutees can apply what they are learning to previous and future work (*e.g.*, After tutoring the subject of figurative language, you might say, "Now that you've learned what a metaphor is, let's go back to Amy Lowell's 'Patterns' and see if we can find examples of metaphors there"). Thus, you are not only teaching something new; you are reinforcing what the student has already learned.

Self-Instructed Learning Sometimes your tutees can learn a part or all of a lesson better by themselves than they can from you, either because they need the additional time and space to review it or because being alone allows them to concentrate and lessens their anxiety. If you find your tutees are not responding to other tutoring techniques, it might be useful to send them off to learn the material on their own.

They might write a paper, review class notes, read their textbook, or they might work on a *learning module* (a small, instructional unit dealing with a single concept) especially developed for *self-paced learning*, that is, learning designed to meet the particular needs of the individual learner. Based on the premise that everyone learns in a different way and at a different rate, different kinds of self-paced learning carefully describe and limit the instructional objectives in each learning module. Following are two samples of self-paced learning currently available:

1. *Programmed Instruction* The work of behavioral psychologists such as B.F. Skinner influenced the development of programmed learning; in programmed learning, students advance through learning at carefully mapped intervals and are reinforced immediately. Therefore, they master one small area before going on to the next. Programmed instruction is used as the format for certain texts and is also widely used with computers.
2. *Audio-Tutorial* In audio-tutorial (slide-tape, filmstrip-tape, workbook-tape), audio-tape supplements other kinds of written and visual aids for

PLATO Computer-Based Education. A student uses a computer to extend her vocabulary; programmed learning permits her to test herself and her knowledge of antonyms. In the process, she is also acquiring the fourth R, computer literacy. (Courtesy Control Data Corporation.)

each unit studied, thus literally doubling or tripling the instruction the student receives: audio, visual, literal. Responses are built into some audio programs as well, so that students can practice or test their learning. For example, an audio-tutorial slide-tape program on propaganda might contain units on advertising, newspapers, politics. The advertising unit may be divided into tv, radio, billboards, and flyers. After the lesson on tv propaganda, the following directions might appear on the screen and, at the same time, be read by the narrator: "Stop the machine and answer the following questions: Why is tv such a good medium for propaganda? What does *covert message* mean? What is an *overt message*? Give an example of a tv ad you have seen that contains covert propaganda. Then turn the machine back on." After the tutee answers the questions, he or she turns on the slide-tape machine again, and the answers appear on the screen (and are repeated by the narrator). Audio devices are often housed in learning carrels where students can enjoy privacy.

Although self-instructed learning can be a welcome change of pace for students, and can be useful when budgetary constraints put heavy demands on tutors, it is highly doubtful it will ever replace the human tutor, who can offer warmth, support, and concern, as well as the necessary information, to students. Such programs can only be used efficiently when they are part of a larger effort which can give the appropriate guidance and feedback.

CLASS PROJECT 3

Break into groups of two and develop a session using one of the model strategies described above.

1. One person from each pair should tutor the other, surrounded by a circle of four to five observers. The observers should write down strong and weak aspects of the approach.

2. Without discussion, the pair should switch roles, and repeat the process using the same tutoring strategy.

3. The discussion that follows should try to answer the following questions:

> What strategy was the tutor using?
> Was it an appropriate strategy for the subject matter?
> For the tutee? For the tutor?
> What was good about the session?
> What went wrong with it?
> Which tutor was successful and why?
> Is this an approach you would use in your tutoring?
> Why? Why not?

LAB APPLICATIONS

1. a. Everyone in the class should locate a self-paced learning program in a subject he or she does not know and try it. See how far each of you can get before you need to call a fellow tutor for help.

b. In your log, describe how you felt about instructing yourself.

2. Try a tutoring strategy with your tutee. Use the criteria in the above Class Project 3.3 to assess your effectiveness. Again, record your analysis in your journal. If possible, videotape the session and show it to your group or class for additional evaluation.

Sample Tutoring Techniques

A tutoring technique is anything you try, no matter how unorthodox or bizarre, that can help you tutor your student. In employing one or more of the above strategies, you will probably use dozens of techniques to make it work. And the techniques which you use will inevitably be different from those which are used by other tutors who employ the same strategy. Techniques are usually quite personal and not always transferable from tutor to tutor. The following techniques, however, are repeatedly mentioned in tutoring manuals and tutor-training workshops because they consistently work well for tutors.

Silence Silence is an excellent way of getting your tutee to play a more active role in the tutoring session. Count to ten—at least to seven—before

"I find this acid rain gives a nice little fillip to it."

Drawing by Joe Mirachi; © 1981 The New Yorker Magazine, Inc.

answering a question. Give tutees enough time to gather their thoughts so they can answer your questions (or their own) or comment on the subject matter. Allow time after a student answers a question, so that the student can reflect further before you ask another one. Rushing in to fill empty spaces, which new tutors do at times out of anxiety or frustration, will only close down the lines of communication and make the tutoring a one-way process.

Paraphrase To paraphrase is to put the students' comments or questions into other words, to show them you have understood what they're trying to say, and to give them confidence that they are being heard. If, for example, a student is trying to define a math principle, and has managed to get out a jumbled but overall accurate definition, your rephrasing will either help make it clearer or demonstrate that the tutee is not communicating accurately. A tutoring dialogue using paraphrase, in history, might go like this:

TUTOR: Why were the English so anxious to hold on to South Africa?
TUTEE: Well, there weren't that many Boers. The English were certain they could win.
TUTOR: Are you saying that the English wanted to hold onto South Africa because they knew they could win?

TUTEE: No. There were other reasons, of course. Economic reasons. South Africa was, and is, very wealthy.

In that way the tutor was able to clarify where the tutee was missing information without actually giving the student the answer.

Lecture Lecturing, or telling a tutee information, has lost favor of late, because it doesn't involve the student actively enough in the learning process. It is, however, effective in introducing new information that must be presented in an ordered and systematic way, quickly and succinctly. Lecturing is best used in *tutoring* (as opposed to teaching) in combination with the other, more process-oriented techniques or methods listed. Beware of lecturing too much —perhaps five minutes should be your limit. And when you do lecture, encourage your tutee to ask questions and to interrupt whenever necessary.

Demonstration "Demonstration is to show as lecture is to tell," says the tutor demonstrating what an analogy is. In this sense, demonstration *can* be verbal, but normally, we think of it as an activity in which someone performs something to show how it is done. Demonstrations are often used in labs to help students who are about to do some procedure for the first time (dissect a frog, correct fragment errors). However, demonstrations can also help students grasp an abstract idea—if you also describe how *you* go about understanding it and give them a sense of your *process*. For example, in showing tutees how symbols work in a film, you might demonstrate how you figured out the importance of the color red in Nicholas Roeg's *Don't Look Now*. Take the student with you as you replay the reel (literally, or verbally) and gather your clues. Demonstrate how you put all your evidence together to come to a conclusion.

Tutee Demonstration Tutees can demonstrate techniques too, and one of the best ways to help them develop confidence is to ask them to share their techniques with you. For example, one tutee may have found an excellent way to remember the terms of the Treaty of Versailles or another to understand subject-verb agreement. These students may not realize, however, that they have come to a creative understanding of how to learn by themselves and that they are capable of self-teaching. Your asking them *how* they learned something or *how* they study for their tests can help you find out what techniques they have developed on their own. On the other hand, tutee demonstrations can reveal learning problems, instances in which self-teaching is not working. You may find out that your tutee consistently takes an incorrect step in solving a certain kind of homework problem. Only by finding out how your tutees work can you reinforce their positive behavior and help them eliminate their negative habits.

Boardwork and Diagramming People often need to see things visualized before they can understand them. That is why using the blackboard is such a popular demonstration technique. The board gives you a large area in which to dramatize your information in big white or multi-colored letters or diagrams that students can then take home as a mental picture. Notations, key words, formulas are particularly helpful to deaf tutees. Letting your tutee do some of

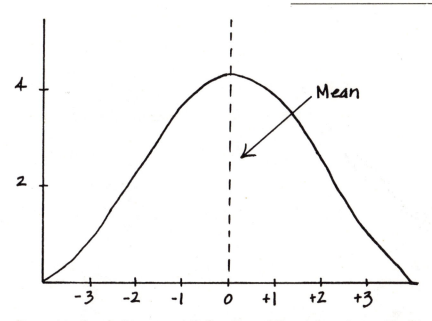

Figure 4.1 Sample Diagram—A Bell or Normal Distribution Curve, which shows how a random sample would be arranged according to the number of times something occurs in relation to the total number of possible occurrences.

the boardwork is a good practice as well, for it involves students actively (literally forces them out of their seats) and lets you check on their understanding of what is being discussed. Not all such work need be done on the board, however. Paper and a pencil, or crayons, are all you need for diagramming.

Referral Sometimes you won't know an answer, especially in your beginning sessions. Try not to feel that this disqualifies you from tutoring the student. No one can know everything, and everyone has a right to learn. Being a new tutor means that you have the background and ability to tutor but don't have all the information at your fingertips. Your attitude about your apprenticeship, however, is very important! You do not want to lose your tutee's confidence. You must show your tutee that it is perfectly natural for someone to ask for help. The important thing is to know when and how to ask. For example, you may have trouble remembering a certain math rule. Don't guess. Tell your tutee, "I'm not sure I remember the rule and I don't want to give you misinformation. But I'm sure one of the other tutors can tell you." If you are convinced it is okay not to know everything, you will convince your tutee.

Look It Up You won't always have to ask another tutor for an answer (or there won't always be another tutor available to answer your question). If your tutee is using a textbook, your answer will very often be found there. You can, in fact, also make this a lesson in study skills by showing the tutee how to retrieve information.

In an informal learning setting, diagramming lends structure and coherence to the material under discussion. (Photograph by Anne Helena Dolen. Courtesy of Anne Helena Dolen and the College of New Rochelle.)

The Strange, Unusual, Funny, and Emotional People tend to remember better if when they learn something it is associated with an event, person, picture, or saying that can be linked with a strong emotion. If you can tell a story or draw an evocative picture to help illustrate new material, students will much more easily learn it. This process is sometimes called *coding*. For example, the relationship between an independent and dependent clause can be likened to the relationship between a mother and a small child. Children cannot be allowed to walk by themselves; they are dependent. This image helps students remember the concept of subordination. A coding device that has helped numerous school children learn the displacement of water theory is the image of Archimedes jumping out of the bathtub and running naked down the street yelling, "Eureka."

Summarizing We tend to think of summarizing as an activity reserved for the end of the session but the session can and should be stopped a number of times along the way so that tutees can summarize what they have learned thus far. Summarizing can be done in a number of ways. Tutees can summarize orally, in writing, or with the use of diagrams or pictures, if appropriate. You may ask them to keep a log or notebook in which they can summarize on their own. Then you can begin your next session using the summary of this past material as groundwork for the new material. Make it clear to your tutee, however, that summarizing in the session does not necessarily imply an end; conversely, it is a review of recent material which is preparation for learning new, related material.

The Test Tests are excellent reinforcement devices as well as good ways to gauge whether your student has learned the material. There are various kinds of tests, including essay, sentence completion or fill-in, true-false, matching, and multiple choice. Each of these requires a different degree and kind of expertise from the student. To answer a true-false question, for example, students need only pick one of two choices; their chance of getting a correct answer is one in two, regardless of what they know. To answer an essay question, though, students must usually understand the context of the question and be able to develop an answer.

Your criteria for choosing or developing a test should be based on what you want to know about your student's mastery, how well the test material is presented (it should be clearly written and interesting), and how long it will take for your student to complete it. You might want an all-session test, or a ten-minute quiz, depending on how much material you want to cover. Since your tutees are probably used to viewing tests as ways to grade them, you should take care to present your test as a nonpunitive device, really a way of helping them to evaluate their own abilities. It can also be used to give students practice in taking actual exams; while it does subject them to some tension, it may also help them to improve their performance on the real thing.

CLASS PROJECT 4

1. a. Break into pairs and write a tutoring dialogue (see Paraphrase, p. 97) in which you use two or more of the techniques presented above.

   b. Roleplay your dialogues while the class critiques your session using the following checklist:
   What techniques was the tutor using?
   Were they appropriate for the subject matter? for the tutee? For the tutor?
   What went wrong with them?
   Are these techniques which you will use when you tutor? Why? Why not?

2. a. Isolate a problem your tutee is having in understanding some aspect of the subject area you're tutoring. Break into groups of five to seven; share your problem and see if the group can discover a strategy or technique to solve that problem.

   b. If possible, have two group members act as observer critics to note some aspect of group dynamics. (See p. 35.)

3. One or more of you may wish to develop a videotape of various tutoring techniques. This would, of course, make an excellent audio visual supplement, used to reinforce lecture, roleplay, and in-class discussion.

The Session Planning Chart

All that you have learned in this chapter so far can be put into schematic form—and the Session Planning Chart illustrates one way that this can be done. Although you may never use such an elaborate device to plan an actual session, you can use the chart to create sample lessons, applying what you have learned in this chapter and during the term. In that way you can practice tutoring on your own, preparing alternative ways to deal with tutee problems. Also, filling out the chart should help familiarize you with the stages of the tutoring session.

The chart on p. 103 was used to help a tutor plan a session on writing. The tutor was experienced and, therefore, was able to fill out the chart in a detailed way; for not only did he know what techniques would motivate, instruct, and reinforce the student's learning, but he knew what his goal should be at each phase of the lesson. At this stage of your training, you are not expected to know as much as an experienced tutor would know, but your goal should be to recognize the components of a good session and to plan one yourself on something you know well.

CLASS PROJECT 5

1. Pick a topic you enjoy and know well and plan a session using the blank chart. Your topic may be more broad or narrow than the sample shown, depending on the subject matter, the students you're tutoring, and the problems they're having.

2. Break into groups. One of you should tutor a second student using the session plan you have developed (*i.e.*, microteach). The other members of the group should check on whether you have reached your goals at each phase and whether your methods, materials, and techniques were appropriate.

3. Plan an actual tutoring session to use with your tutee.
   a. Break into groups of five to seven and critique each other's plans using the following criteria:
      Are the strategies appropriate at each phase?
      Are the materials/techniques likely to work?
      What are the best qualities of this plan?
      What would you do to improve this plan?
   b. Rewrite the plan based on the critiques.
   c. After you have actually tutored the session (see the Lab Application below), meet with the same group members and read them your log analysis of the session.
   d. After all analyses have been discussed, group members should come up with at least three things they have learned about session planning.

LAB APPLICATION

Tutor the session planned above and analyze how it went in your log.

SESSION PLANNING CHART

Note: Fill in #3 first for, as you will see, only then can you plan the rest of your session.

OVERALL GOAL: To help Linda write paper on how language is manipulative

Session Phase:	Strategy	Materials, Techniques
Motivation	a. Read and discuss essays about the subject b. Read and discuss examples of manipulative language	Center for Humanities slide-tape show on language Orwell: "Politics and the English Language" Sunday newspaper or magazine
Check for Prior Learning	Review Linda's former essays to see if she followed proper essay form. If not: Instruct Linda on proper essay form.	Former essay by Linda Example of essay written in proper essay form
Instruction (New Learning)	a. Help Linda find topic of new essay. b. Help Linda find thesis of new essay.	1) Free writing (subject: language) 2) Brainstorming (subject: particular topic found in free writing).
Check for Learning	Chat with Linda about the material already generated; have Linda take notes and read back those notes. Ascertain whether Linda knows what she wants to say in essay.	1) Results of free writing 2) Results of brainstorming
Reinforcement of Material in Lesson	Ask student to write a summary and/or a general outline (list) of what she plans to write about.	Outline model: draft of paper and an outline of it.

SESSION PLANNING CHART

Note: Fill in #3 first for, as you will see, only then can you plan the rest of your session. (This chart may be duplicated for lab or tutorial use.)

OVERALL GOAL:

Session Phase:	STRATEGY	MATERIALS, TECHNIQUES
1. Motivation		
2. Check for prior learning		
3. Instruction (New Learning)		
4. Check for Learning		
5. Reinforcement of Material in Lesson		

AUDIOVISUAL AIDS:
A GLOSSARY OF HARDWARE

Audiovisual materials are used for a number of purposes in a lesson. As we suggested earlier, you can use them for motivation, instruction, or reinforcement. They are commonly used in self-instructed learning, but they can also be valuable supplements to your tutoring, especially since audiovisual aids have been developed for every type of educational audience and for many subjects. Hundreds of companies produce great quantities of new filmstrips, videotapes, slide-tapes, audiotapes, yearly. Some of them are quite good; some are not. They must, like a textbook, be carefully reviewed before use and evaluated for level of efficacy. The machines on which you use these materials do not have to be troublesome if, like the materials, you study them beforehand, know how to use them, and know when they are available. Below is a description of audiovisual machines commonly found in skills centers, labs, and libraries.

Record Player Most everyone has a record player, so it is not usually thought of as an educational machine. Yet a variety of things can be learned on records (*e.g.,* music, language) and the machine is familiar and easy to use.

Tape Recorder Tapes are smaller and more durable than records; they are also more portable than records and easier to store. Their real advantage, however, is that they are easy and inexpensive to use, so easy you can tape your own educational material or use the tape to record work you do with your tutee during a session. Your tutee can then play the tape back while driving to or from school or while studying at home.

Videotape Player Most people watch tv; some are addicted to it, in fact. Tv's popularity makes it an extremely effective teaching device, which is why, lately, a number of companies have prepared educational tapes using video technology. Videotaped instruction usually comes in modular units of a given subject. As with the tape recorder (although not as easily), you can use video to record students' activities. Being videotaped forces students out of the role of spectator and into the role of actor, and, like many actors, the thought of seeing themselves on camera helps to motivate them to perform well. Also, by storing action, video allows tutees to critique the process by which they came to a certain conclusion. For example, if you are tutoring interviewing techniques for a social work class, you can conduct a sample interview. When you play it back for the tutee, both of you will be able to isolate positive and negative statements or responses. If your tutoring group is learning about sex roles in the 1900s, you can roleplay Mrs. Thelma Gray's problem and her options (see p. 93). Do be aware that some students get very nervous when being taped and this could impede their learning: you should avoid taping someone who doesn't want to be taped.

Slide-tape and Filmstrip-tape Projectors Less expensive than video but offering some of video's advantages are the slide-tape and filmstrip-tape programs in which a narrator teaches a concept to the accompaniment of slides or filmstrips that illustrate what he or she is saying. (See Fig 4.2 and p. 94 for discussion of audio-tutorial.) Usually, reinforcement devices, like self-tests or exercises, will be included in the program after segments of instruction.

Overhead and Opaque Projectors The overhead projector is used with transparencies—a transparent plastic sheet onto which can be transferred typed material or on which one can write. The lamp from the machine projects the material onto the wall, enlarged several times so that it will be easy to read. (See Fig. 4.3.) This and the opaque projector, which is used in a similar fashion with printed material instead of a transparency, are excellent for use with groups, for students can all read the same material together.

Computers Once your school goes "on line," that is plugs into a computer, your tutoring program can avail itself of computer-assisted instruction. Some colleges buy commercially-prepared instructional programs; however, in many institutions faculty and tutors prepare their own software (which is the term used for computer material). You can currently use computers to present new material and to drill students on material they have previously learned to reinforce it. The computer is so versatile that it may also be used as a research or problem-solving tool. Since computer-assisted instruction is still in its infancy, educators have not yet gauged which kinds of materials are most appropriate to computer learning. Nor have they yet ascertained whether or not computers provide more efficient or effective means of learning than other,

Figure 4.2 Filmstrip-Tape Projector. This equipment is for students who want to work on their own and get the reinforcement of sight and sound along with printed material. (Courtesy Charles Beseler Company.)

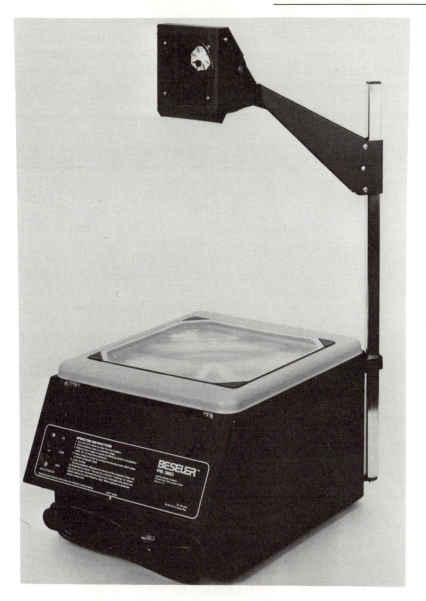

Figure 4.3 Overhead Projector. While facing your tutee, you can present visual material at your own pace. By means of multiple transparency overlays, you can create superimpositions. With the addition of a roll and marking pencil, you can even turn the projector into an "electric blackboard." (Courtesy Charles Beseler Company.)

more traditional methods. Although some students find computers very exciting, others find the new technology intimidating. Therefore you probably should get some experience with computer-assisted instruction to see how to best use it with your tutee.

Teaching machines will never take the place of people. We will always need people to explain difficult concepts, to check for learning, to rephrase material, and to answer questions; and it is most important that we not use machines to the exclusion of other types of teaching. For, like all approaches in this chapter, they are only some of the many devices you can try, with the hope that one or more of these will be the way in which your tutee learns the material.

CLASS PROJECT 6

1. Present a self-prepared 15-minute module to the class or group using one of the machines listed above. Be certain to show your classmates how to use the machine.

2. Research the audiovisual (AV) resources—tapes, slides, video—in your library or media center and:

a. present a module to the group that you feel is effective, and be prepared to justify your choice.

b. Do the same (as above) with an AV module that you do not like.

LAB APPLICATION

Write a session plan incorporating one of the machines listed in this chapter and use it with your tutee. Record the results in your log.

READING 7

In the Socratic Dialogues, Plato (427?–347 B.C.) recorded the teachings of his mentor Socrates (469–399 B.C.) in dialogue form. This dialogue probably took place shortly before Socrates chose to take hemlock rather than respond to charges of treason by the Athenian government.

In the passage below Socrates teaches the slave boy to understand an elementary concept of geometry by asking him a series of carefully controlled questions. Since Socrates knew exactly where he wanted the questioning to go he was able to elicit after a time the correct answer, without ever once telling it to the slave. We might also say that Socrates is using demonstration for, while teaching the slave, he is showing Meno, the slave's master, how to discover truth and acquire knowledge.

READING QUESTIONS

1. What, specifically, has the boy learned? What role does the slave boy's status play in this process?

2. Socrates argues for confusion. That is he purposely creates a situation in which the boy, using a common-sense approach, comes up with the wrong answer. Do you think this is of any value as a strategy? Can you cite instances in your own learning in which you experienced productive confusion?

3. Is Socrates' claim that he "simply ask[s] [the boy] questions without teaching him" correct? If not, what is happening? What does he mean?

4. What role do the diagrams play in Socrates procedure?

5. Plato is concerned to show the notion of pre-existing or absolute truth. Does the dialogue convince you? How is Socrates' interchange with the slave boy "proof" of absolute truth? Would you consider another teaching method more effective? Why?

7 | *From* MENO

Plato

MENO. I see, Socrates. But what do you mean when you say that we don't learn anything, but that what we call learning is recollection? Can you teach me that it is so?

SOCRATES. I have just said that you're a rascal, and now you ask me if I can teach you, when I say there is no such thing as teaching, only recollection. Evidently you want to catch me contradicting myself straight away.

MENO. No, honestly, Socrates, I wasn't thinking of that. It was just habit. If you can in any way make clear to me that what you say is true, please do.

SOCRATES. It isn't an easy thing, but still I should like to do what I can since you ask me. I see you have a large number of retainers here. Call one of them, anyone you like, and I will use him to demonstrate it to you.

MENO. Certainly. (*To a slave-boy.*) Come here.

SOCRATES. He is a Greek and speaks our language?

MENO. Indeed yes—born and bred in the house.

SOCRATES. Listen carefully then, and see whether it seems to you that he is learning from me or simply being reminded.

MENO. I will.

SOCRATES. Now boy, you know that a square is a figure like this? (*Socrates begins to draw figures in the sand at his feet. He points to the square ABCD.*)

BOY. Yes.

SOCRATES. It has all four sides equal?

BOY. Yes.

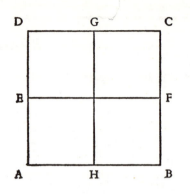

SOCRATES. And these lines which go through the middle of it are also equal? (The lines EF, GH.)

BOY. Yes.

SOCRATES. Such a figure could be either larger or smaller, could it not?

BOY. Yes.

SOCRATES. Now if this side is two feet long, and this side the same, how many feet will the whole be? Put it this way. If it were two feet in this direction and only one in that, must not the area be two feet taken once?

BOY. Yes.

SOCRATES. But since it is two feet this way also, does it not become twice two feet?

BOY. Yes.

SOCRATES. And how many feet is twice two? Work it out and tell me.

BOY. Four.

SOCRATES. Now could one draw another figure double the size of this, but similar, that is, with all its sides equal like this one?

BOY. Yes.

SOCRATES. How may feet will its area be?

BOY. Eight.

SOCRATES. Now then, try to tell me how long each of its sides will be. The present figure has a side of two feet. What will be the side of the double–sized one?

BOY. It will be double, Socrates, obviously.

SOCRATES. You see, Meno, that I am not teaching him anything, only asking. Now he thinks he knows the length of the side of the eight–feet square.

MENO. Yes.

SOCRATES. But does he?

MENO. Certainly not.

SOCRATES. He thinks it is twice the length of the other.

MENO. Yes.

SOCRATES. Now watch how he recollects things in order—the proper way to recollect. You say that the side of double length produces the double-sized figure? Like this I mean, not long this way and short that. It must be equal on all sides like the first figure, only twice its size, that is eight feet. Think a moment whether you still expect to get it from doubling the side.

BOY. Yes, I do.

SOCRATES. Well now, shall we have a line double the length of this (AB) if we add another the same length at this end (BJ)?

BOY. Yes.

SOCRATES. It is on this line then, according to you, that we shall make the eight–feet square, by taking four of the same length?

BOY. Yes.

SOCRATES. Let us draw in four equal lines (*i.e., counting AJ, and adding JK, KL, and LA made complete by drawing in its second half LD*), using the first as a base. Does this not give us what you call the eight–feet figure?

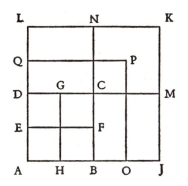

BOY. Certainly.

SOCRATES. But does it contain these four squares, each equal to the original four–feet one?

(*Socrates has drawn in the lines* CM, CN *to complete the squares that he wishes to point out.*)

BOY. Yes.

SOCRATES. How big is it then? Won't it be four times as big?

BOY. Of course.

SOCRATES. And is four times the same as twice?

BOY. Of course not.

SOCRATES. So doubling the side has given us not a double but a fourfold figure?

BOY. True.

SOCRATES. And four times four are sixteen, are they not?

BOY. Yes.

SOCRATES. Then how big is the side of the eight–feet figure? This one has given us four times the original area, hasn't it?

BOY. Yes.

SOCRATES. And a side half the length gave us a square of four feet?

BOY. Yes.

SOCRATES. Good. And isn't a square of eight feet double this one and half that?

BOY. Yes.

SOCRATES. Will it not have a side greater than this one but less than that?

BOY. I think it will.

SOCRATES. Right. Always answer what you think. Now tell me: was not this side two feet long, and this one four?

BOY. Yes.

SOCRATES. Then the side of the eight–feet figure must be longer than two feet but shorter than four?

BOY. It must.

SOCRATES. Try to say how long you think it is.

BOY. Three feet.

SOCRATES. If so, shall we add half of this bit (BO, *half of* BJ) and make it three feet? Here are two, and this is one, and on this side similarly we have two plus one; and here is the figure you want.

(*Socrates completes the square* AOPQ.)

BOY. Yes.

SOCRATES. If it is three feet this way and three that, will the whole area be three times three feet?

BOY. It looks like it.

SOCRATES. And that is how many?

BOY. Nine.

SOCRATES. Whereas the square double our first square had to be how many?

BOY. Eight.

SOCRATES. But we haven't yet got the square of eight feet even from a three–feet side?

BOY. No.

SOCRATES. Then what length will give it? Try to tell us exactly. If you don't want to count it up, just show us on the diagram.

BOY. It's no use, Socrates, I just don't know.

SOCRATES. Observe, Meno, the stage he has reached on the path of recollection. At the beginning he did not know the side of the square of eight feet. Nor indeed does he know it now, but then he thought he knew it and answered boldly, as was appropriate—he felt no perplexity. Now however he does feel perplexed. Not only does he not know the answer; he doesn't even think he knows.

MENO. Quite true.

SOCRATES. Isn't he in a better position now in relation to what he didn't know?

MENO. I admit that too.

SOCRATES. So in perplexing him and numbing him like the sting–ray, have we done him any harm?

MENO. I think not.

SOCRATES. In fact we have helped him to some extent towards finding out the right answer, for now not only is he ignorant of it but he will be quite glad to look for it. Up to now, he thought he could speak well and fluently, on many occasions and before large audiences, on the subject of a square double the size of a given square, maintaining that it must have a side double the length.

MENO. No doubt.

SOCRATES. Do you suppose then that he would have attempted to look for, or learn, what he thought he knew (though he did not), before he was thrown into perplexity, became aware of his ignorance, and felt a desire to know?

MENO. No.

SOCRATES. Then the numbing process was good for him?

MENO. I agree.

SOCRATES. Now notice what, starting from this state of perplexity, he will discover by seeking the truth in company with me, though I simply ask him questions without teaching him. Be ready to catch me if I give him any instruction or explanation instead of simply interrogating him on his own opinions.

(Socrates here rubs out the previous figures and starts again.)

Tell me, boy, is not this our square of four feet? (ABCD.) You understand?

BOY. Yes.

SOCRATES. Now we can add another equal to it like this? (BCEF.)

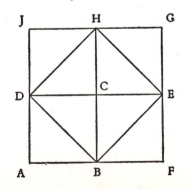

BOY. Yes.

SOCRATES. And a third here, equal to each of the others? (CEGH.)

BOY. Yes.

SOCRATES. And then we can fill in this one in the corner? (DCHJ.)

BOY. Yes.

SOCRATES. Then here we have four equal squares?

BOY. Yes.

SOCRATES. And how many times the size of the first square is the whole?

BOY. Four times.

SOCRATES. And we want one double the size. You remember?

BOY. Yes.

SOCRATES. Now does this line going from corner to corner cut each of these squares in half?

BOY. Yes.

SOCRATES. And these are four equal lines enclosing this area? (BEHD.)

BOY. They are.

SOCRATES. Now think. How big is this area?

BOY. I don't understand.

SOCRATES. Here are four squares. Has not each line cut off the inner half of each of them?

BOY. Yes.

SOCRATES. And how many such halves are there in this figure? (BEHD.)

BOY. Four.

SOCRATES. And how many in this one? (ABCD.)

BOY. Two.

SOCRATES. And what is the relation of four to two?

BOY. Double.

SOCRATES. How big is this figure then?

BOY. Eight feet.

SOCRATES. On what base?

BOY. This one.

SOCRATES. The line which goes from corner to corner of the square of four feet?

BOY. Yes.

SOCRATES. The technical name for it is 'diagonal'; so if we use that name, it is your personal opinion that the square on the diagonal of the original square is double its area.

BOY. That is so, Socrates.

SOCRATES. What do you think, Meno? Has he answered with any opinions that were not his own?

MENO. No, they were all his.

SOCRATES. Yet he did not know, as we agreed a few minutes ago.

MENO. True.

SOCRATES. But these opinions were somewhere in him, were they not?

MENO. Yes.

SOCRATES. So a man who does not know has in himself true opinions on a subject without having knowledge.

MENO. It would appear so.

SOCRATES. At present these opinions, being newly aroused, have a dream-like quality. But if the same questions are put to him on many occasions and in different ways, you can see that in the end he will have a knowledge on the subject as accurate as anybody's.

MENO. Probably.

SOCRATES. This knowledge will not come from teaching but from questioning. He will recover it for himself.

MENO. Yes.

SOCRATES. And the spontaneous recovery of knowledge that is in him is recollection, isn't it?

MENO. Yes.

SOCRATES. Either then he has at some time acquired the knowledge which he now has, or he has always possessed it. If he always possessed it, he must always have known; if on the other hand he acquired it at some previous time, it cannot have been in this life, unless somebody has taught him geometry. He will behave in the same way with all geometrical knowledge, and every other subject. Has anyone taught him all these? You ought to know, especially as he has been brought up in your household.

MENO. Yes, I know that no one ever taught him.

SOCRATES. And has he these opinions, or hasn't he?

MENO. It seems we can't deny it.

SOCRATES. Then if he did not acquire them in this life, isn't it immediately clear that he possessed and had learned them during some other period?

MENO. It seems so.

SOCRATES. When he was not in human shape?

MENO. Yes.

READINGS 8a, 8b, AND 8c

As we have indicated, a degree of controversy surrounds the use of games in education; and specifically, there has been controversy over the use of calculators. Some mathematics educators fear that students will become over-reliant on them, without having mastered basic computational skills or the concepts underlying numerical manipulation. One of your jobs as a math or science tutor will be to check that your tutee has this essential knowledge before plunging into extensive use of the calculator; we think some of the games included below will help you determine your tutees' basic arithmetic knowledge.

At another stage of tutoring, the challenge will be to find or invent games that (1) can show students how to make optimal use of their calculator, that is creative and efficient use, to avoid the tedious mathematical work that the calculator can do for them, and (2) can show students how calculators can help them recognize and gauge what they do know. Obviously you are also drawing on the electronic-game craze that has captivated people of all ages. Calculators are thus wonderful motivational devices as well as tools for learning and reinforcement.

READING QUESTIONS

1. Since "Numerical Intuition," specifically *insists* that the player(s) do *no* calculations nor any thinking, why and at what stage of tutoring do you think this would be a good game to play?

2. How might you use the computational games to tutor basic computational skills? algebraic skills? programming skills (or the use of the calculator for programming)? Which examples in the second selection would be most appropriate for each of these objectives?

3. Why and for what sort of student might #1 in the second selection be a motivational game?

4. To vary games 1 and 2 from *The Calculator Game Book* you might choose to vary the denominator rather than the numerator (for example, 1/101, 1/102, 1/103, 1/104). This is of interest because the progression here is rooted in the same mathematical concept which yields the relativistic mass formula, used to explain why nothing can change faster than the speed of light. What other similar games could you invent or develop using higher forms of mathematics (fractions, decimals, operations on polynomials, and high-order equations) with one or more of these formats?

5. For what course or courses might you use "Reluctance" and/or "Conjugal Reluctance"? What are the basic objectives of such statistical games? How might you further develop the games and for what purposes (in order to tutor what statistical concepts)?

8a | CALCULATOR SATURNALIA

Gordon Pask, Ranulph Glanville, and Mike Robinson

NUMERICAL INTUITION

The Game

Requirements   1 or 2 players, 1 calculator.

Object   To answer mathematical questions instantly, and *without* doing any calculation or thinking.

Two-Player Version   Player A selects a function (multiplication or division) and two numbers from the number chart. (See p. 116.)
Player A then asks the questions as he enters it into the calculator.
e.g. '18 times 77 ='
Player B answers with the first number that comes into his head.
e.g. '1493'
Player B must answer immediately, without hesitation.
Write down the difference between the correct answer from the calculator and Player B's guess. (In each case subtract the smaller number from the larger.)
e.g. 1493 (Player B's guess) minus 1386 (correct answer) = 107.
Repeat this ten times for each player, then add the differences. The player with the smallest score wins.

Complex Two-Player Version   As in the simple version, except that the player who answers also gives an estimate of his error.

Calculate the error as follows:

(i) calculate the difference between the guess and the answer by subtracting the smaller from the larger.

(ii) divide the difference by the answer and multiply by 100. This gives the % error.

e.g.   18 × 77   = ?

guess	1493
answer	1386
difference	107

$$\frac{107 \times 100}{1386} = 7.7\%$$

One-Player Version   As in the two-player version except that the player both selects the question and answers it.

As the player selects the numbers he should enter them into the calculator, and then immediately (as he presses the = key) give the answer.

Scoring   Points are awarded on the following basis.

% error		points
0	– 0.09	100
0.1	– 0.49	80
0.5	– 0.99	40
1	– 1.99	20
2	– 4.99	10
5	– 9.99	2

If the player who gives the answer has also correctly estimated the error, the number of points is squared. The estimate is accounted 'correct' if it falls within the same category, see table above, as the actual error.

e.g.   18 × 77   = ?

guess	1493 with 9% error
actual error	7.7%
points (2 × 2) = 4	

As in the simple game, each player asks and answers 10 questions.

The winner is the player with most points.

Number Chart

53	47	981	111	5980	136	122	17	59
26	40	238	405	7739	351	432	11	69
97	34	470	328	5811	691	964	24	48
66	23	380	277	7452	371	118	84	89
30	17	648	979	9215	338	416	42	43
62	67	368	390	3447	229	921	91	18
54	19	596	938	8517	885	977	15	60
67	76	406	664	3328	873	798	70	44
27	72	873	798	8641	895	418	96	13
26	18	982	476	7474	714	556	63	77
81	19	699	777	8558	863	430	70	84
33	61	388	793	5544	995	638	14	22

Commentary The important thing is not to do any conscious thinking.
Keep the mind a blank and let the subconscious do the work.

With practice most people can get into the 2–5% error band, and some can do much better.

8b | THE CALCULATOR GAME BOOK
FOR KIDS OF ALL AGES

Arlene Hartman

1. 101 REVISITED

[Use your calculator to do the first three conversions (change the fractions to decimals to 7 places)]; remember to try to predict the last six on the list before using your calculator to check your predictions.

    1/101 =
    2/101 =
    3/101 =
    4/101 =
    5/101 =
    6/101 =
    7/101 =
    8/101 =
    9/101 =

It may be a little difficult to see the repeating pattern in these because the calculator "runs out of room." However, you can probably figure out what it will be. If so, try the:

Brain-stretcher! Can you write the answers for these with a vinculum?*

2. IS IT 11 OR 9?

Notice how the numbers around 10, 100, etc. are special? . . . . See what happens with 11 as a denominator.

    1/11 =
    2/11 =
    3/11 =
    4/11 =
    5/11 =
    6/11 =
    7/11 =
    8/11 =
    9/11 =

Why do you suppose this trick has the title it does?

Brain-stretcher! Can you write these answers with a vinculum?

*The vinculum is a bar drawn over two or more algebraic terms to indicate that it can be treated as a single term.

3. GAUSS' "GIMMICK"*

Find the sum of the first 100 counting (natural) numbers on your calculator: $1 + 2 + 3 + \ldots + 100$.

Gauss, [Karl Friedrich] [(1777-1855)] generally regarded as one of the top three mathematicians of all time, found a short way to do this problem in his head. The story is told that this problem was actually given to his class one day. He startled the instructor by writing the sum almost immediately. His career as a mathematician was launched that day. Below is his "gimmick".

$$
\begin{array}{rcccccc}
1 + & 2 + & 3 + \ldots + & 50 \\
+ 100 + & 99 + & 98 + \ldots + & 51 \\
\hline
101 + & 101 + & 101 + \ldots + & 101
\end{array}
$$

Notice that by pairing the numbers as he did, he got pairs for which the sum would always be 101. There would be 50 such pairs. Therefore, the sum could be found by multiplying 101×50, or 5,050. . . .

* * *

Brain-stretcher! Find the sum of the first 200 counting numbers by using a process similar to Gauss' "gimmick." Check your answer on your calculator.

4. FIBONACCI FOLLIES†

Write the first ten numbers of a Fibonacci sequence pattern. That is, select two random numbers for the first and second in your sequence. The third number must be the sum of the first two; the fourth, the sum of the second and the third; the fifth, the sum of the third and fourth; etc.

Find the series sum.

Now multiply the seventh number by 11. What do you observe? Check another series to see if it happens again.

*Gauss' work in mathematics was extremely varied. It included pure theory as well as applied mathematics: number theory (including the first systematic discussion of complex numbers containing the $\sqrt{-1}$); calculation of the orbit of Ceres by methods modified but still used with computers; "Intrinsic Surface Theory" derived from his study of the shape of the earth; and a non-Euclidean geometry which was published posthumously. Working in collaboration with the physicist Wilhelm Weber, Gauss established a worldwide series of observations and did studies which resulted in the bell curve which is used in modern statistics and which became the basis of electric telegraphy.

†Leonardo Fibonacci (circa 1170– ?) Perhaps the most prominent of the mathematicians of the Middle Ages, Fibonacci was brought from his native Italy by his merchant father to what is now Bejaia, Algeria to study mathematics with an Arab master. With his book he introduced Europe to the Hindu–Arabic system of notation (0, 1, 2, 3, 4 . . . . . . +, −, ×, ÷), the concept of place values, and gave practical examples. He is the man responsible for our use of the base–10 number system.

The famous Fibonacci sequence is the first recursive sequence (a sequence that refers to itself and can be generated by a formula) known to Europe. In 1753, Robert Simson found that the ratio between succeeding numbers approaches the golden sequence, $\dfrac{1 + \sqrt{5}}{2}$, and soon afterward, scientists began to find evidence of this sequence in nature, as in the spiral of sunflower heads, pine cones, and the spiral of snail shells.

5. PARTRIDGE IN A PEAR TREE

This trick is especially good to use around the holiday season. You may remember some of the song "Partridge in a Pear Tree."

"On the first day of Christmas my true love gave to me
A partridge in a pear tree.
On the second day of Christmas my true love gave to me
Two turtle doves and a partridge in a pear tree."

The question is, what is the *total* number of gifts received during the twelve days? Be careful—this is a tricky one.

6. THE ODDS ARE IN YOUR FAVOR

Ask a friend to select any odd number. Warn him not to make it too great for his own sake! (Suggest a number not greater than 59.) Then have your friend add all the odd numbers up to the one picked. Suppose the number picked is 37. Then your friend does $1 + 3 + 5 + \ldots + 37$ on the calculator, writing the answer, but hiding it from you.

When your friend gives you the calculator:

1. Add 1 to the original greatest odd number used (38).
2. Divide by 2 (19).
3. Multiply that result by itself (361).

You can tell your friend that the sum is 361. (If you have two calculators available, you can do your calculations while your friend is still hard at work adding!)
Brain-stretcher! Can you explain or prove why this works.

7. MORE ODDS IN YOUR FAVOR

This trick is similar to #6, except this time you find the sum of all counting numbers up to a designated odd number $(1 + 2 + 3 \ldots)$. Again, let your friend select the "top" odd number and begin adding on one calculator. Suppose your friend chooses 43. Meanwhile, you do the following on another calculator:

1. Add 1 to the "top" number (44).
2. Divide by 2 (22).
3. Multiply the result by itself (484).
4. Multiply that by 2 (968).
5. Subtract the result of step 2 from the result of step 4 (946).

That result (946) should be the sum of $(1 + 2 + 3 + \ldots + 43)$.

8. THE GOLDEN RATIO

The ancient geometers and architects had a ratio for the length of a rectangle to its width for which the most attractive demensions of a building were used. This value, called the Golden Ratio, is approximately 1.6180.

If the length of a building were to be 247.2 meters, what should its height (width of the "front" rectangle) be to get maximum eye appeal?

You may want to do some additional reading on the Golden Ratio, including its many occurrences in nature. One example, the starfish, is shown below. Note the ratio 8/5 = 1.6, which is quite close.

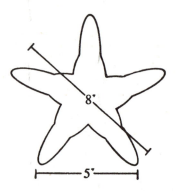

The starfish is an example of an organism, the dimensions of which match the golden ratio developed by the Greeks. (Courtesy *The Calculator Game Book For Kids of All Ages.*)

8c | CALCULATOR SATURNALIA

Gordon Pask, Ranulph Glanville, and Mike Robinson

RELUCTANCE

The Game

Requirements   Any number of players, each with a calculator, general area maps (if accuracy is required), paper and pen.

Object   To examine personal mobility.

Description   RELUCTANCE to travel and actual distance are used to highlight personal views of journeys. These views are extended to give ideas of mobility and to emphasize personal distances.

The calculator is used to help the player(s) reflect on their own ways of thinking. There is no 'winner' (though a 'competitive' form is suggested in the next game, CONJUGAL RELUCTANCE).

Method   Each player decides upon 10 places the player goes quite often, which can be described by types: e.g. Home, Work, Shops, various Friends, Theatres, Pubs,

Reluctance, from *Calculator Saturnalia*. (Courtesy Random House, Inc.)

Restaurants, etc.; places which have actual locations and areas. You do not have to quote precisely what these are, provided the places have personal significance.

List the places with columns beside them, as shown in the example below.

The columns are used for scoring and headed by a fixed place such as Home or Work (but any common central points will do, for example, your Town House or your Country Estate!).

	Points	Miles	Hours	Rm	Rh	Ratio	Rm/Rh
Office (Work)							
Home							
Local Shop							
City Pub							
Theatre							
Laundry							
Jane's House							
Marjorie's House							
Restaurant X							
Restaurant Y							

First fill in the 'Points' column with numbers, from 0 to 5. On the scale, number 0 represents a place you hardly go to at all, i.e. a place you are unwilling to visit, and 5 represents a place you are very willing to visit. The distance travelled is irrelevant here, since what you are describing by point numbers is 'bother'. It is a purely personal, subjective index.

When you have done this, *and not before*, fill the next pair of columns with distance travelled in Miles† (either from a map or as objectively estimated as you can manage) and the time taken in Hours (again either measured or as objectively estimated as you can manage). Multiply each of these by the points in the first column which represents bother, to obtain a RELUCTANCE factor in terms of distance (Rm) and time (Rh). The higher the number, the less reluctant you are to travel on that particular journey. Divide the reluctance measured in time (Rh) into the reluctance measured in distance (Rm) to get the reluctance ratio, Rm/Rh.

These figures crystallize and have been found to give realism to people's attitudes. Using this standard technique you can examine your own RELUCTANCE to travel (the results may surprise you) and compare your own view and other people's view.

The ratio between the RELUCTANCES in Miles and Hours reveals the nature of the journey. In general, the higher the ratio the faster the trip. But why is that actually so? Are there other factors that affect this ratio, for instance, pleasantness of trip, routine, desire to reach the other end?

The results from the game are a mirror, no doubt distorting . . ., through which you can examine your own attitudes. However, some generally agreed properties exist. If the points in the different columns of the points table are all added together and each total is then divided by the number of places (i.e. 12) as in the table below this gives a mean or average score. The higher the mean 'bother' score, the more easily you travel.

Mean scores, obtained in the same way, for the Miles and Hours columns, show mobility, and ability to leave your 'neighbourhood'. The mean RELUCTANCES show how much you feel home-bound, and the mean ratio shows your rate of travel. These mean scores can be compared, between people, to give a general view of mobility. Does your husband get around too much?

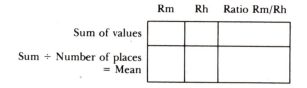

	Rm	Rh	Ratio Rm/Rh
Sum of values			
Sum ÷ Number of places = Mean			

Using the results so far, note the RELUCTANCE order (using both distance, Rm, and time, Rh) of the places, putting those with the least RELUCTANCE (i.e. the highest scores) first, followed by those that are lower in a table like that above. This is called 'ranking'. Is there much of a difference between the distance and time RELUCTANCE ranks?

The game becomes a powerful and interesting diagnostic tool if it is replayed using another fixed place (such as Work if at first you used Home) as a starting point, in order to see the different roles that places take on, depending on where you are, by comparing the results of the two plays. Thus, you have two batches of data, as shown opposite.

You may find that whilst it is easy to go to Work from Home going back Home is not so easy. Indeed, if you always go to the Pub (for instance) after Work, you never need to go *straight* Home.

†Or, by agreement, kilometres.

	Your numerical value			Your rank value		
	Rm	Rh	Ratio Rm/Rh	Rm	Rh	Ratio Rm/Rh
Office (Work)						
Home						
Local Shop						
City Pub						
Theatre						
Laundry						
Jane's House						
Marjorie's House						
Restaurant X						
Restaurant Y						

From Home	Points	Miles	Hours	Rm	Rh	Ratio Rm/Rh
Office (Work)						
Home						
Local Shop						
City Pub						
Theatre						
Laundry						
Jane's House						
Marjorie's House						
Restaurant X						
Restaurant Y						

From Work						
Office (Work)						
Home						
Local Shop						
City Pub						
Theatre						
Laundry						
Jane's House						
Marjorie's House						
Restaurant X						
Restaurant Y						

CONJUGAL RELUCTANCE

The Game

Requirements Any number of players, each with a calculator, general area maps (if accuracy is required), paper and pen.

Object To test one's understanding of how others view journeys.

Description A competitive version of RELUCTANCE is played to highlight the comparison of the actual ranks in which players order the places visited and the ranks that the other players assume they would have.

Method The game is played initially just as is the normal version of RELUCTANCE, but the players must all agree to use the same 12 places. This does not mean to say that the location will all be the same: different families probably use different launderettes, but go to the launderette anyway.

The difference between RELUCTANCE and CONJUGAL RELUCTANCE is the way that the second part is played. In CONJUGAL RELUCTANCE, each player places his initial table at the disposal of each other player.

Here are two filled-out examples.

SAMPLE PLAY 1

	Husband								Wife							
	Points	Miles†	Hours†	Rm	Rh	Ratio/Rm/Rh	Rm rank	Rh rank	Points	Miles†	Hours§	Rm	Rh	Ratio/Rm/Rh	Rm rank	Rh rank
	5	23	1.3	115	6.5	17.7	1	1	2	3.5†	0.7	7	1.4	5	5	5
Kid's School	1	2	0.4	2	0.4	5	6	|7	5	2	0.4	10	2	5	4	2=
Infant's Play Group	0	0.7	0.2	0	0	1	10=	10=	5	0.7	0.4	3.5	2	1.75	6	2=
Evening Classes	0	3.2	0.3	0	0	1	10=	10=	3	4.5†	0.3	13.5	0.9	15	3	7
Local Pub	5	0.1	0.1	0.5	0.5	1	8	6	1	0.1	0.1	0.1	0.1	1	10	10
City Pub	1	23	1.3	23	1.3	17.7	4	4	0	23	1.3	0	0	1	11=	11=
Cinema	3	4.5	0.4	13.5	1.2	11.25	5	5	4	4.5	0.4	18	1.6	11.25	2	4
Local Shop	1	0.1	0.1	0.1	0.1	1	9	9	4	0.3	0.3	1.2	1.2	1	8	6
City Shop	2	19	1.4	38	2.8	13.6	2	2	5	19	2.1	95	1	9	1	
Launderette	0	0.1	0.1	0	0	1	10=	10=	5	0.1	0.1	0.5	0.5	1	9	9
Sid & Mary's	4	7	0.4	28	1.6	17.5	3	3	0	7	0.4	0	0	1	11=	11=
Harry & Jane's			0.2	0.6	0.2	3	7	8	4	0.6	0.2	2.4	0.8	3	7	8
Total	23	83.3	6.2	220.7	14.6	90.7b			38	65.3	6.7	151.2	21.0	55		
Average	1.92	6.94	0.52	18.39	1.22	7.56			3.17	5.44	0.56	12.6	1.75	4.58		

Note that husband's and wife's work and evening classes happen at different places.

† Note certain differences in places visited and journey times existing between husband and wife.

The players now choose a common alternative starting point, for instance Work, and secretly fill out a simple form in which they rank each other player's RELUCTANCE to travel to the various locations from this new starting point. A table such as the following one will be filled out by each player for each other player.

For other player named	Supposed rank order of Rm	Supposed rank order of Rh	Actual rank order of Rm	Actual rank order of Rh	Difference between supposed and actual Rm	Difference between supposed and actual Rh
Home						
Work						
Kid's School						
Infant's Play Group						
Evening Classes						
Local Pub						
City Pub						
Local Shop						
City Shop						
Cinema						
Launderette						
Sid & Mary's						
Harry & Jane's						
Total						
Average						

Finally each player works through the full table, to calculate his actual RELUC-TANCE. When he has ranked his places the other players compare the differences between their supposed rankings, and the actual ones, and record these differences.

Commentary The total difference in each case may be used to show which players have better understandings of the others (the lower the difference the better the understanding) and the winner is the player who has matched the other players' understandings most accurately.

However, what is usually rather more interesting than this measure (which may, after all, be inaccurate in at least two respects, namely the places chosen, and the actual point scale used in the game,) is to discuss why differences between your guessed ranking and actual rankings occur. You can, of course, do this by yourself, too: just fill in the supposition form before you actually work through the large form. The procedure of this game just gets you to work through some implications of distance and

SAMPLE PLAY 2

	Husband								Wife's Suppositions			
	Points	Miles	Hours	Rm	Rh	Ratio/Rm/Rh	Rm Rank	Rh Rank	Supposed rank order of Rm	Supposed rank order of Rh	Difference between supposed and actual Rm	Difference between supposed and actual Rh
Home Work	2	23	1.3	46	2.6	17.7	4	4	1	1	3	3
Kid's School	0	25	1.4	0	0	1	9=	9=	8	10	1	1
Infant's Play Group	0	23	1.3	0	0	1	9=	9=	10	11	1	2
Evening Classes	0	21	1.1	0	0	1	9=	9=	7	5	2	4
Local Pub	1	23	1.3	23	1.3	17.7	5=	5=	6	6	1	1
City Pub	4	0.2	0.1	0.8	0.4	2	8	8	4=	3	4	5
Cinema	3	21	1.4	63	4.2	15	2	2	2	4	0	2
Local Shop	1	23	1.3	23	1.3	17.7	5=	5=	11	8	6	3
City Shop	4	0.6	0.2	2.4	0.8	3	7	7	3	2	4	5
Launderette	0	23	1.3	0	0	1	9=	9=	12	12	3	3
Sid & Mary's	3	18	1.2	54	3.6	15	3	3	4=	7	1	4
Harry & Jane's	4	24	1.4	96	5.6	17.1	1	1	9	9	8	8
Total	22	224.8	13.3	308.2	19.8	109.2					34	41
Average	1.83	18.73	1.11	25.68	1.65	9.1					2.83	3.42

A Husband's response from work, and his Wife's suppositions about this.

mobility in a coherent manner, so that you reach some clear-cut picture at the end. This is not necessarily a completely accurate picture of how you do it yourself, however.

BIBLIOGRAPHY

Abt, Clark C. *Serious Games*. New York: Viking Press, 1970.

Flanders, Ned. *Analyzing Teaching Behavior*. Reading, Mass.: Addison-Wesley, 1970.

Gagné, Robert M. *Essentials of Learning for Instruction*. Principles of Educational Psychology Series. Eds. William and Carol Rohmer. Hinsdale, Ill.: Dryden Press, 1974.

Hyman, Ronald Terry. *Ways of Teaching*. New York: Lippincott, 1970.

Roberts, Robin. *New Roads: Tutoring Today*. [Palo Alto, Calif.]: n.p., 1977.

Rockart, John Fralick and Michael S. Scott Morton. *Computers and the Learning Process in Higher Education*. Carnegie Commission on Higher Education Sponsored Research Studies. New York: McGraw-Hill Book Company, 1975.

Russell, James D. *Modular Instruction*. Minneapolis, Burgess Publishing Co., 1974.

Salisbury, Lee. "Role-Playing—Rehearsal for Language Change." *TESOL Quarterly*, 4, no. 4, pp. 331–336.

Skinner, B. F. *The Technology of Teaching*. The Century Psychology Series. Englewood Cliffs, N. J.: Prentice-Hall, 1968.

Wallen, James Bagford. *Strategies for Teaching*. Metuchen, N.J.: Scarecrow Press, 1979.

5 | *TUTORING IN MULTICULTURAL SETTINGS*

CULTURAL UNDERSTANDING

All of us are born into a cultural group, a group whose identity is shaped by a distinct code of values. We are taught cultural values from birth, either explicitly, as rules and regulations, or implicitly, via social codes and attitudes. In a large, multicultural society such as ours, formal education serves to introduce those from minority cultures to the value system of the larger social grouping. Often the socialization process results in students' giving up some of the values of their culture and adopting the value system of the dominant culture, although acculturation rarely occurs without immense anxiety over the conflicting sets of values. Cultural conflict is, in fact, one of the major problem areas of college students because it is in college that they are exposed to values that differ greatly from those that they had, until then, accepted as absolute.

Although you cannot resolve your tutees' conflicts over culture and, indeed, should not try, you should be aware that cultural values will play as important a part in your tutees' lives as they do in yours, and will therefore play a part in your tutoring sessions. Attitudes about life (such as the role of the family, of government, of sex, of religion), will determine how your tutees feel about the subjects which they are studying in school and how much you can help them to learn those subjects. In addition, conventions of address, greetings, eating, dress, ways of being polite or friendly, and attitudes towards time or authority all shape behavior and will affect your sessions. For example, if your tutee's culture is particularly respectful of parental authority, the student may have trouble understanding (or may even be offended by) a novel in which authority toward parents is challenged. On the other hand, someone from a culture in which children are raised collectively may be puzzled by the same novel, because, in this case, parents are not the major sources of authority in this person's culture. Another student may insist on calling you Mr., Miss, or Mrs., even though you've asked your tutees to use your first name; this may be so because this student has been socialized to see school as a formal situation. Another student may come to tutoring sessions late because the cultural norms concerning time in this student's culture are different from those in your culture. In sum, cultural differences are likely to affect learning and tutoring. Hawkins' journal of his experiences tutoring Ben and the student case-studies you read in chapter 2 attest to this.

Ideally, you should be tolerant of cultural differences. When tutoring, try to avoid judging a tutee's behavior until you understand the reason for it. Expect topics like religion, sex roles, politics, to be extremely volatile because they are value-laden, and be prepared to accept your tutee's point of view on these subjects despite your own biases. However, as idealistic as you are, you cannot expect that you will always behave selflessly. Clashes because of cultural differences will occur in the tutorial setting as they do in society outside the college environment. In fact, the nature of the tutorial makes clashes inevitable.

As a tutor you have knowledge and, therefore, a certain kind of authority. (See chapter 1 for a full discussion of this issue.) Much as you may want to promote a *peer* relationship, your tutees will inevitably invest you with some degree of power. If students are members of a racial minority, black or Latin, for example, some of them may be tempted to see you as part of the white power structure from which they are excluded, and by whom they are often judged inferior. In doing this, they are stereotyping you, assuming that because some people in white culture are racists, you too are a racist. If some tutees feel this way, they will naturally be very resistant to working with you; and you, on the other hand, will probably find it difficult to work with these students. Or, you may be a minority tutor assigned some white tutees who think nonwhites inferior. Because these tutees devalue you, they may feel the tutorial is worthless.

How you respond to your tutees' prejudices will depend, in part, on the nature of your own acculturation. If you have grown up in a cultural ghetto, be it white, black, Latin, Chinese, it may be hard for you to understand and accept people from other cultures, especially if they regard you with suspicion; certainly, it will take time, effort, and a gread deal of desire.

To complicate matters, tutoring, contingent as it is on one-to-one and small-group settings, demands openness and trust. Openness, and trust, of course, only exist between people who respect each other. And mutual respect is exactly what prejudice and cultural stereotyping undermine. That so many tutorials are immensely successful, and are successful because of the closeness that grows between tutor and tutee, provides evidence that people can surmount cultural barriers if they want to enough.

CLASS PROJECT 1

1. As a class, list all the cultural groups in your college. Then form into groups, each group picking a culture and listing the cultural attributes of this community for the following areas: dress code, time, forms of address, or other categories you develop. Then each group member should gather actual data on these cultural attributes through interviews and research; take a week or two for this research and when you meet again, compare your findings with your original conceptions. Discuss the implications of your findings with the entire class.

2. As a research paper, some of you may be interested in a demographic or historical study of migration patterns as a way of developing insight into the

populations within your institution; students interested in anthropology, sociology, or social psychology may pursue studies of how local cultural groups have changed over the years. Be sure to include interviews with individual students or agencies as reference sources.

SECOND-LANGUAGE LEARNERS

Language differences are, perhaps, the most difficult of all cultural barriers to overcome; it is natural, therefore, that many people with language or dialect problems go for tutoring. For in the intimacy of the tutorial they have a better chance to be heard and understood than in a large classroom.

The following material was designed to help you comprehend this student better. Although the pamphlet on tutoring students for whom English is a second language, which accompanies *The Tutor Book*, contains specific methods for tutoring them, and the Writing pamphlet contains background on Black English, this section strives to give you a more general understanding of those students whose native language is not English and who have come for tutoring.

Tutoring Second-Language Learners

The degree to which second-language learners will manifest academic problems will be relative to their expertise in English, to their mastery of reading and writing skills, and to the needs of the courses they are taking. Science or math majors, for example, could reasonably have few problems because of the universality of the sign system used in these courses. Students who completed high school in their native country will probably have an easier time mastering concepts that call for an understanding of material they already knew in their native language than students who attended grammar or high school in this country and learned the foundations of many subjects when they knew English only slightly. Also, those students who do not actively use English outside of class will have a harder time understanding and using what they are learning in the classroom than those who are continually reinforcing their knowledge of it.

Some second-language learners speak better than they write or vice versa. The first may be especially true of those who went to grade school in this country and who never learned to read and write in their native language, and only imperfectly in English. On the other hand, oral communication, more necessary and immediately relevant, is more practiced. Their lack of difficulty speaking and understanding English, and their lack of an accent, may disguise the problems which they are having in understanding and in writing English.

The reverse phenomenon may be more true of older students, especially those educated in the "foreign" language of English in their own country. Be sure, then, to assess these skills separately, distinguishing between reading and writing, and between understanding and speaking.

Limited fluency in English will be a source of great anxiety to your tutees. In effect, they have to learn two things in each class—the subject matter and English. They know that incomplete knowledge of English will surely impede their understanding of the subject matter and even inhibit their ability to keep up with the class; therefore, some may be overly anxious about how they did on tests, papers, etc. Others will try to protect themselves from their fear of failure—they may pretend they are indifferent to how they are doing in the class or they may become quickly frustrated or angry with the teacher or the college for not meeting their needs. (Sometimes, this anger is quite appropriate.) Some may feel depressed, even if doing well, because they feel so insecure.

Although it can be assumed that you always try to be sensitive to your students' vulnerabilities, you need to be especially supportive with a second-language learner. Be aware that some are daily facing a double blow to their egos—not easily understanding the subject matter of a particular class and having trouble with English in general. The resulting frustration can be immense—and much greater than many of them will reveal to you. *Praise* small areas of progress and *reinforce* new material whenever possible so your students can recognize what and how much they have learned.

If you know your tutee's native language you can put your knowledge to good use by analyzing those problems that come as a result of the idio-syncrasies of that language. For example, a French student may be having trouble understanding a written passage because the student doesn't know the difference between "still," "yet," and "again"—in French all three words are expressed by one word, *encore.* If you know and can tell a student the source of a problem, he or she can self-correct it. Also, if your tutee is having difficulty understanding your instruction, try explaining in his or her language. You may remember Retamar using similar techniques with her tutee (p. 59). If your knowledge of the language is imperfect, this technique will help to bolster your student's confidence by giving the tutee a chance to be instructor, while at the same time diminishing your tutee's anxiety about oral expression.

Some second-language learners resist working on their English language skills. Although this would, obviously, be a key way for them to do better, not learning English provides them with an excuse for failure. As we will discuss further in the chapter on adult learners, it is also a symptom of a natural and overwhelming fear that if they become fluent in English they will lose their native language, their culture, in fact, even their family. And to some extent, they are right, especially if their family has not mastered English. (See Richard Rodriguez' "Going Home Again," p. 136.) Consequently, they may be especially passive or uninterested during sessions; they may be unwilling to do the extra work they need to do to master the subject matter (for example, homework or extra sessions); and they may be easily distracted. In other words, they may *seem* not to take their sessions seriously. One way for you to help alleviate their fear—as we have said—is to use their language; another is to talk or have them write about their native culture. And if you incorporate this cultural material in your sessions (in developing a topic for a research assignment or by using relevant examples, let's say) your student may become more motivated and more involved in the course or discipline. Talk about your culture too, because such sharing is a good way to promote a warm, trusting relationship between you and your tutees.

Another sort of strategy involves forming either same-language or hetero-geneous pairs or groups of second-language learners. In these groups students can share their language-based problems, emotional and academic, and in that way see that their problems aren't unique to them or even to their own language group. A second-language learner tutoring group will help decrease alienation by giving your tutees a forum in which to bring their culture and by encouraging collaborative learning.

Your second-language learner may be having trouble reading English. Often what is diagnosed as a writing or cognitive problem is really a reading problem. For second-language learners, difficulties with reading come from limited vocabulary and/or unfamiliarity with syntax. Your tutee will probably read more slowly and, at times, with little comprehension. Poor reading will affect all your tutee's schoolwork, making it difficult for the student to understand the textbook and/or the requirements of assignments and tests.

If you are not specifically a reading tutor, refer your student to the reading program (if one exists) in your college for testing and additional tutoring. Nonetheless, you can also be of help. If the tutee reads with difficulty because he or she has to look up many words, you and your tutee may go over key passages in the course textbook together, and practice important words that might come up in class or on a test. If your tutee is in a science program you could review the highly specialized vocabulary used in these courses.

Problems with reading will probably affect your tutees' performance on out-of-class assignments or in-class essay exams. Be certain to go over assignments with your tutees to make sure they understand what is expected of them. You might also ask your lab director to ask teachers of second-language learners to be especially careful to explain directions on in-class exam questions. If you give your tutees material to read during the session, allow them extra time to read it; also urge *them* to allow themselves extra time to do assigned reading for class. Consider using or having them use reading material that is simpler than their regular texts but also has the virtue of reinforcing the required material.

Second-language learners may try to hide the fact that they don't understand you very well. Often they are embarrassed that their English isn't more fluent and they are too proud to admit it. Second-language learners may also hide their difficulty understanding you because they feel it would be impolite to question you or to interrupt you continually for clarification. The latter may be especially true if you are working with the student in a group; the tutee may not want to draw attention to him- or herself, or to stop group progress.

To start with, don't add to problems of understanding by conducting the tutoring session in a noisy, distracting environment—find quiet space in the library, study hall, or in an empty classroom, if necessary. Then, be aware of your oral expression; speak slowly and clearly. Try not to use too many idioms or too much jargon. Idioms are the most difficult aspects of language to translate because they cannot be taken literally although they often are, (as when you give your second-language learner "a raincheck" on the tutorial and he or she proffers a hand to take it). You may need to use the special terms, or jargon of a particular discipline or special-interest group, (*feedback, communication process, paradigm* are some trendy examples), but even if you are careful to explain their meaning each time you use such words, the flow of your session will be seriously impeded. Of course, you don't want to patronize your tutees by speaking too simply and we do not suggest you eliminate idioms and jargon from your vocabulary—but that you use them with self-consciousness, sparingly and to good effect. Finally, back up oral instruction with some kind of visual reinforcement whenever possible. For example, drawing a map of Europe on the chalkboard (or on a sheet of paper) to describe the German troop movements that led up to World War II may help second-language learners "see" what you're explaining and make the job of comprehension somewhat easier for them.

To ensure that your tutees are comprehending, require active demonstrations from them, to show that they understand. Don't assume your tutees' silence means that they understand—or that they don't. They may not feel that they need to show you. On the other hand, nodding and saying "uh-huh" are no guarantees of comprehension either. And those are certainly not ways in which your tutees can practice *expressing* what they know. So elicit full and complete statements from them.

Having students write their responses to your questions is a way to ensure complete answers. Since writing is an important tool in learning to think, and

Courtesy Mark Dandelske

the major way students are judged in college, writing gives your tutees a good opportunity to practice an activity essential to their academic success.

In considering their responses be aware that your tutees might be reliant on a dictionary or thesaurus for much of their English vocabulary and will probably be using words awkwardly. Try to discover what they are saying by looking for synonyms or by figuring out what words mean in their context, and gently point out their correct usage. However, try not to make tutees too self-conscious about the way they use language by correcting every vocabulary or sentence error they make.

Second-language learners may be unwilling to express themselves in English because they are embarrassed about their pronunciation. As we said, this does not, necessarily, reflect on how well they understand the session. Since tutoring is one of the few times students can get regular one-to-one attention, it represents a unique opportunity for them to practice conversational English. Although you should not sacrifice the subject matter being tutored to improving your students' oral abilities, it should be obvious that second-language learners would do better in class if they spoke and understood English better. Aside from formal activities, such as weekly oral summaries of class notes or discussion of world affairs or school events, informal conversation with students on a regular basis will give them much-needed practice.

CLASS PROJECT 2

1. Sit in on an upper-level class (or with a group of native speakers) of a language foreign to you; discuss this experience with members of your class.
2. Complete a homework assignment in a foreign language of which you have some knowledge; share your frustrations with your class.

LAB APPLICATIONS

1. Try one of the approaches suggested in the section above with a tutee and report back to the class on how well it worked.
2. Ask a foreign student who has recently mastered English what the greatest obstacles were and how he or she overcame them.

READING 9

America has not been known for its cultural understanding and tolerance, as Langston Hughes (1902–1967), one of the first Afro-

*American writers to be widely read, has made clear in his many
stories and essays. Simple's Uncle Sam (1965) is a collection of
columns Hughes wrote for the black weekly, the* Chicago Defender,
*and other newspapers on aspects of American life as seen by an
average black citizen of Harlem. Hughes was one of the founders of
the Harlem Renaissance, a movement which brought together talented
artists to interpret the black experience for the world.*

READING QUESTIONS

1. What is the point of view in "Coffee Break"? How does Hughes convey his point of view?

2. How many of the names in this story do you recognize? How many do you actually know something about? How might your response relate to Rodriguez's point in "Going Home Again" that (academic) culture "can lose track of human societies and whole areas of human experience" (p. 140)? How relevant is this to your tutoring?

3. What argument(s) does Simple use to his boss about the people who represent Simple? In what ways might these be relevant to your tutoring situation?

4. Who decides when the coffee break is over? Why? What is Hughes' point here? Why does Hughes entitle his story "Coffee Break"?

5. Although Hughes argues against stereotypes in this story, he also uses them. Discuss this. (Is it a paradox or is it something which undermines the integrity of the story?)

9 | COFFEE BREAK

Langston Hughes

"My boss is white," said Simple.

"Most bosses are," I said.

"And being white and curious, my boss keeps asking me just what does THE Negro want. Yesterday he tackled me during the coffee break, talking about THE Negro. He always says 'THE Negro,' as if there was not 50-11 different kinds of Negroes in the U.S.A.," complained Simple. "My boss says, 'Now that you-all have got the Civil Rights Bill and the Supreme Court, Adam Powell in Congress, Ralph Bunche in the United Nations, and Leontyne Price singing in the Metropolitan Opera, plus Dr. Martin Luther King getting the Nobel Prize, what more do you want? I am asking you, just what does THE Negro want?'

" 'I am not THE Negro,' I says, 'I am *me*.'

" 'Well,' says my boss, 'you represent THE Negro.'

" 'I do not,' I says. 'I represent my own self.'

" 'Ralph Bunche represents you, then,' says my boss, 'and Thurgood Marshall and Martin Luther King. Do they not?'

" 'I am proud to be represented by such men, if you say they represent me,' I said. 'But all them men you name are *way* up there, and they do not drink beer in my bar. I have never seen a single one of them mens on Lenox Avenue in my natural life. So far as I know, they do not even live in Harlem. I cannot find them in the telephone book. They all got private numbers. But since you say they represent THE Negro, why do you not ask them what THE Negro wants?'

" 'I cannot get to them,' says my boss.

" 'Neither can I,' I says, 'so we both is in the same boat.'

" 'Well then, to come nearer home,' says my boss, 'Roy Wilkins fights your battles, also James Farmer.'

" 'They do not drink in my bar, neither,' I said.

" 'Don't Wilkins and Farmer live in Harlem?' he asked.

" 'Not to my knowledge,' I said. 'And I bet they have not been to the Apollo since Jackie Mabley cracked the first joke.'

" 'I do not know him,' said my boss, 'but I see Nipsey Russell and Bill Cosby on TV.'

" 'Jackie Mabley is no *him*,' I said. 'She is a *she*—better known as Moms.'

"Oh,' said my boss.

" 'And Moms Mabley has a story on one of her records about Little Cindy Ella and the magic slippers going to the Junior Prom at Ole Miss which tells all about what THE Negro wants."

" 'What's its conclusion?' asked my boss.

" 'When the clock strikes midnight, Little Cindy Ella is dancing with the President of the Ku Klux Klan, says Moms, but at the stroke of twelve, Cindy Ella turns back to her natural self, black, and her blond wig turns to a stocking cap—and her trial comes up next week.'

" 'A symbolic tale,' says my boss, 'meaning, I take it, that THE Negro is in jail. But you are not in jail.'

" 'That's what you think,' I said.

" 'Anyhow, you claim you are not THE Negro,' said my boss.

" 'I am not, I am *this* Negro.'

" 'Then what do *you* want?' asked my boss.

" 'To get out of jail,' I said.

" 'What jail?'

" 'The jail you got me in.'

" 'Me?' yells my boss. 'I have not got you in jail. Why, boy, I like you, I am a liberal. I voted for Kennedy. And this time for Johnson. I believe in integration. Now that you got it, though, what more do you want?'

" 'Reintegration,' I said.

" 'Meaning by that, what?'

" 'That you be integrated with *me*, not me with you.'

" 'Do you mean that I come and live in Harlem?' asked my boss. 'Never!'

" 'I live in Harlem,' I said.

" 'You are adjusted to it,' said my boss. 'But there is so much crime in Harlem.'

" 'There are no two-hundred-thousand-dollar bank robberies, though,' I said, 'of which there was three lately *elsewhere*—all done by white folks, and nary one in Harlem. The biggest and best crime is outside of Harlem. We never has no half-million-dollar jewelry robberies, no missing star sapphires. You better come uptown with me and reintegrate.'

" 'Negroes are the ones who want to be integrated,' said my boss.

" 'And white folks are the ones who do not want to be,' I said.

" 'Up to a point, we do,' said my boss.

" 'That is what THE Negro wants,' I said, 'to remove that *point.*'
" 'The coffee break is over,' said my boss."

READING 10

*In his autobiographical essay, Richard Rodriguez explores the
cultural contradictions implicit in his position as a Mexican-American getting his doctorate in Renaissance English Literature at University of California, Berkeley. Currently he is a writer and lecturer
who lives in San Francisco. The essay has been published in revised
form in* Hunger of Memory: The Education of Richard Rodriguez
(1981).

READING QUESTIONS

1. What are the implications of being a new American scholarship boy?

2. Must education separate people from their family and culture? Discuss the
   responsibility an educational institution has to nurturing traditional culture
   (and the possibilities of its doing so).

3. What do you think of Rodriguez's reasons for deciding not to teach a course
   on the Chicano novel in a community program. Is or isn't it a "slick,
   academic justification for evading social responsibility"? How does this relate
   to how Rodriguez feels about being "Chicano," that is, part of a readily
   identifiable culture group?

4. How do you think your initiation into academic culture has helped to assimi-
   late you to or alienate you from a community?

5. Compare this essay to Hofsteater's case study (p. 74). Consider purpose,
   tone, style, and point of view as well as content.

10 | GOING HOME AGAIN:
THE NEW AMERICAN
SCHOLARSHIP BOY

Richard Rodriguez

At each step, with every graduation from one level of education to the next, the refrain
from bystanders was strangely the same: "Your parents must be so proud of you." I
suppose that my parents were proud, although I suspect, too, that they felt more than

pride alone as they watched me advance through my education. They seemed to know that my education was separating us from one another, making it difficult to resume familiar intimacies. Mixed with the instincts of parental pride, a certain hurt also communicated itself—too private ever to be adequately expressed in words, but real nonetheless.

The autobiographical facts pertinent to this essay are simply stated in two sentences, though they exist in somewhat awkward juxtaposition to each other. I am the son of Mexican-American parents, who speak a blend of Spanish and English, but who read neither language easily. I am about to receive a Ph.D in English Renaissance literature. What sort of life—what tensions, feelings, conflicts—connects these two sentences? I look back and remember my life from the time I was seven or eight years old as one of constant movement away from a Spanish-speaking folk culture toward the world of the English-language classroom. As the years passed, I felt myself becoming less like my parents and less comfortable with the assumption of visiting relatives that I was still the Spanish-speaking child they remembered. By the time I began college, visits home became suffused with silent embarrassment: there seemed so little to share, however strong the ties of our affection. My parents would tell me what happened in their lives or in the lives of relatives; I would respond with news of my own. Polite questions would follow. Our conversations came to seem more like interviews.

A few months ago, my dissertation nearly complete, I came upon my father looking through my bookcase. He quietly fingered the volumes of Milton's tracts and Augustine's theology with that combination of reverence and distrust those who are not literate sometimes show for the written word. Silently, I watched him from the door of the room. However much he would have insisted that he was "proud" of his son for being able to master the texts, I knew, if pressed further, he would have admitted to complicated feelings about my success. When he looked across the room and suddenly saw me, his body tightened slightly with surprise, then we both smiled.

For many years I kept my uneasiness about becoming a success in education to myself. I did so in part because I wanted to avoid vague feelings that, if considered carefully, I would have no way of dealing with; and in part because I felt that no one else shared my reaction to the opportunity provided by education. When I began to rehearse my story of cultural dislocation publicly, however, I found my listeners willing to admit to similar feelings from their own pasts. Equally impressive was the fact that many among those I spoke with were *not* from nonwhite racial groups, which made me realize that one can grow up to enter the culture of the academy and find it a "foreign" culture for a variety of reasons, ranging from economic status to religious heritage. But why, I next wondered, was it that, though there were so many of us who came from childhood cultures alien to the academy's, we voiced our uneasiness to one another and to ourselves so infrequently? Why did it take *me* so long to acknowledge publicly the cultural costs I had paid to earn a Ph.D. in Renaissance English literature? Why, more precisely, am I writing these words only now when my connection to my past barely survives except as nostalgic memory?

Looking back, a person risks losing hold of the present while being confounded by the past. For the child who moves to an academic culture from a culture that dramatically lacks academic traditions, looking back can jeopardize the certainty he has about the desirability of this new academic culture. Richard Hoggart's description, in *The Uses of Literacy,* of the cultural pressures on such a student, whom Hoggart calls the "scholarship boy," helps make the point. The scholarship boy must give nearly unquestioning allegiance to academic culture, Hoggart argues, if he is to succeed at all, so different is the milieu of the classroom from the culture he leaves behind. For a time, the scholarship boy may try to balance his loyalty between his concretely experienced family life and the more abstract mental life of the classroom. In the end, though, he must choose between the two worlds: if he intends to succeed as a student, he must, literally and figuratively, separate himself from his family, with its gregarious life, and find a quiet place to be alone with his thoughts.

After a while, the kind of allegiance the young student might once have given his parents is transferred to the teacher, the new parent. Now without the support of the old ties and certainties of the family. he almost mechanically acquires the assumptions, practices, and style of the classroom milieu. For the loss he might otherwise feel, the scholarship boy substitutes an enormous enthusiasm for nearly everything having to do with school.

How readily I read my own past into the portrait of Hoggart's scholarship boy. Coming from a home in which mostly Spanish was spoken, for example, I had to decide to forget Spanish when I began my education. To succeed in the classroom, I needed psychologically to sever my ties with Spanish. Spanish represented an alternate culture as well as another language—and the basis of my deepest sense of relationship to my family. Although I recently taught myself to read Spanish, the language that I see on the printed page is not quite the language I heard in my youth. That other Spanish, the spoken Spanish of my family, I remember with nostalgia and guilt: guilt because I cannot explain to aunts and uncles why I do not answer their questions any longer in their own idiomatic language. Nor was I able to explain to teachers in graduate school, who regularly expected me to read and speak Spanish with ease, why my very ability to reach graduate school as a student of English literature in the first place required me to loosen my attachments to a language I spoke years earlier. Yet, having lost the ability to speak Spanish, I never forgot it so totally that I could not understand it. Hearing Spanish spoken on the street reminded me of the community I once felt a part of, and still cared deeply about. I never forgot Spanish so thoroughly, in other words, as to move outside the range of its nostalgic pull.

Such moments of guilt and nostalgia were, however, just that—momentary. They punctuated the history of my otherwise successful progress from *barrio* to classroom. Perhaps they even encouraged it. Whenever I felt my determination to succeed wavering, I tightened my hold on the conventions of academic life.

Spanish was one aspect of the problem, my parents another. They could raise deeper, more persistent doubts. They offered encouragement to my brothers and me in our work, but they also spoke, only half jokingly, about the way education was putting "big ideas" into our heads. When we would come home, for example, and challenge assumptions we earlier believed, they would be forced to defend their beliefs (which, given our new verbal skills, they did increasingly less well) or, more frequently, to submit to our logic with the disclaimer, "It's what we were taught in our time to believe. . . ." More important, after we began to leave home for college, they voiced regret about how "changed" we had become, how much further away from one another we had grown. They partly yearned for a return to the time before education assumed their children's primary loyalty. This yearning was renewed each time they saw their nieces and nephews (none of whom continued their education beyond high school, all of whom continued to speak fluent Spanish) living according to the conventions and assumptions of their parents' culture. If I was already troubled by the time I graduated from high school by that refrain of congratulations ("Your parents must be so proud. . . ."), I realize now how much more difficult and complicated was my progress into academic life for my parents, as they saw the cultural foundation of their family erode, than it was for me.

Yet my parents were willing to pay the price of alienation and continued to encourage me to become a scholarship boy because they perceived, as others of the lower classes had before them, the relation between education and social mobility. Lacking the former themselves made them acutely aware of its necessity as prerequisite for the latter. They sent their children off to school in the hopes of their acquiring something "better" beyond education. Notice the assumption here that education is something of a tool or license—a means to an end, which has been the traditional way the lower or working classes have viewed the value of education in the past. That education might alter children in more basic ways than providing them with skills, certificates of proficiency, and even upward mobility, may come as a surprise to some, but the financial cost is usually tolerated.

Complicating my own status as a scholarship boy in the last ten years was the rise, in the mid-1960s, of what was then called "The Third World Student Movement." Racial minority groups, led chiefly by black intellectuals, began to press for greater access to higher education. The assumption behind their criticism, like the assumption of white working-class families, was that [educational] opportunity was useful for economic and social advancement. The racial minority leaders went one step further, however, and it was this step that was probably most revolutionary. Minority students came to the campus feeling that they were representative of larger groups of people— that, indeed, they were advancing the conditions of entire societies by their matricula- tion. Actually, this assumption was not altogether new to me. Years before, educational success was something my parents urged me to strive for precisely because it would reflect favorably on *all* Mexican-Americans—specifically, my intellectual achievement would help deflate the stereotype of the "dumb Pancho." This early goal was only given greater currency by the rhetoric of the Third World spokesmen. But it was the fact that I felt myself suddenly much more a "public" Mexican-American, a representative of sorts, that was to prove so crucial for me during these years.

One college admission officer assured me one day that he recognized my impor- tance to his school precisely as deriving from the fact that, after graduation, I would surely be "going back to [my] community." More recently, teachers have urged me not to trouble over the fact that I am not "representative" of my culture, assuring me that I can serve as a "model" for those still in the *barrio* working toward academic careers. This is the line that I hear, too, when being interviewed for a faculty position. The interviewer almost invariably assumes that, because I am racially a Mexican-American, I can serve as a special counselor to minority students. The expectation is that I still retain the capacity for intimacy with "my people."

This new way of thinking about the possible uses of education is what has made the entrance of minority students into higher education so dramatic. When the minority group student was accepted into the academy, he came—in everyone's mind—as part of a "group." When I began college, I barely attracted attention except perhaps as a slightly exotic ("Are you from India?") brown-skinned student; by the time I graduated, my presence was annually noted by, among others, the college public relations office as "one of the fifty-two students with Spanish surnames enrolled this year." By having his presence announced to the campus in this way, the minority group student was unlike any other scholarship boy the campus had seen before. The minority group student now dramatized more publicly, if also in new ways, the issues of cultural dislocation that education forces, issues that are not solely racial in origin. When Richard Rodriguez *became* a Chicano, the dilemmas he earlier had as a scholarship boy were complicated but not decisively altered by the fact that he had assumed a group identity.

The assurance I heard that, somehow, I was being useful to my community by being a student was gratefully believed, because it gave me a way of dealing with the guilt and cynicism that each year came my way along with the scholarships, grants, and lately, job offers from schools which a few years earlier would have refused me admission as a student. Each year, in fact, it became harder to believe that my success had anything to do with my intellectual performance, and harder to resist the conclu- sion that it was due to my minority group status. When I drove to the airport, on my way to London as a Fulbright Fellow last year, leaving behind cousins of my age who were already hopelessly burdened by financial insecurity and dead-end jobs, momentary guilt could be relieved by the thought that somehow my trip was beneficial to persons other than myself. But, of course, if the thought was a way of dealing with the guilt, it was also the reason for the guilt. Sitting in a university library, I would notice a janitor of my own race and grow uneasy; I was, I knew, in a rough way a beneficiary of his condition. Guilt was accompanied by cynicism. The most dazzlingly talented minority students I know today refuse to believe that their success is wholly based on their own talent, or even that when they speak in a classroom anyone hears them as anything but *the* voice of their minority group. It is scarcely surprising, then, though initially it probably seemed puzzling, that so many of the angriest voices on the campus against the injustices of racism came from those not visibly its primary victims.

It became necessary to believe the rhetoric about the value of one's presence on campus simply as a way of living with one's "success." Among ourselves, however, minority group students often admitted to a shattering sense of loss—the feeling that, somehow, something was happening to us. Especially from students who had not yet become accustomed, as by that time I had, to the campus, I remember hearing confessions of extreme discomfort and isolation. Our close associations, the separate dining-room tables, and the special dormitories helped to relieve some of the pain, but only some of it.

Significant here was the development of the ethnic studies concept—black studies, Chicano studies, et cetera—and the related assumption held by minority group students in a number of departments that they could keep in touch with their old cultures by making these cultures the subject of their study. Here again one notices how different the minority student was from other comparable students: other scholarship boys—poor Jews and the sons of various immigrant cultures came to the academy singly, much more inclined to accept the courses and material they found. The ethnic studies concept was an indication that, for a multitude of reasons, the new racial minority group students were not willing to give up so easily their ties with their old cultures.

The importance of these new ethnic studies was that they introduced the academy to subject matter that generally deserved to be studied, and at the same time offered a staggering critique of the academy's tendency toward parochialism. Most minority group intellectuals never noted this tendency toward academic parochialism. They more often saw the reason for, say, the absence of a course on black literature in an English department as a case of simple racism. That it might instead be an instance of the fact that academic culture can lose track of human societies and whole areas of human experience was rarely raised. Never asking such a question, the minority group students never seemed to wonder either if as teachers their own courses might suffer the same cultural limitations other seminars and classes suffered. Consequently, in a peculiar way the new minority group critics of higher education came to justify the academy's assumptions. The possibility that academic culture could encourage one to grow out of touch with cultures beyond its conceptual horizon was never seriously considered.

Too often in the last ten years one heard minority group students repeat the joke, never very funny in the first place, about the racial minority academic who ended up sounding more "white" than white academics. Behind the scorn for such a figure was the belief that the new generation of minority group students would be able to avoid having to make similar kinds of cultural concessions. The pressures that might have led to such conformity went unexamined.

For the last few years my annoyance at hearing such jokes was doubtless related to the fact that I was increasingly beginning to sense that I was the "bleached" academic the minority group students found so laughable. I suppose I had always sensed that my cultural allegiance was undergoing subtle alterations as I was being educated. Only when I finished my course work in graduate school and went off to England for my dissertation year did I grasp how far I had traveled from my cultural origins. My year in England was actually my first opportunity to write and reflect upon the kind of material that I would spend my life producing. It was my first chance, too, to be free simultaneously of the distractions of course-work and of the insecurities of trying to find my niche in academic life. Sitting in the reading room of the British Museum, I no longer doubted that I had joined academic society. Ironically, this feeling of having finally arrived allowed me to look back to the community whence I came. That I was geographically farther away from my home than I had ever been lent a metaphorical resonance to the cultural distance I suddenly felt.

But the feeling was not pleasing. The reward of feeling a part of the world of the

British Museum was an odd one. Each morning I would arrive at the reading room and grow increasingly depressed by the silence and what the silence implied—that my life as a scholar would require self-absorption. Who, I wondered, would find my work helpful enough to want to read it? Was not my dissertation—whose title alone would puzzle my relatives—only my grandest exercise thus far in self-enclosure? The sight of the heads around me bent over their texts and papers, many so thoroughly engrossed that they wouldn't look up at the silent clock overhead for hours at a stretch, made me recall the remarkable noises of life in my family home. The tedious prose I was writing, a prose constantly qualified by footnotes, reminded me of the capacity for passionate statement those of the culture I was born into commanded—and which, could it be, I had now lost.

As I remembered it during those gray English afternoons, the past rushed forward to define more precisely my present condition. Remembering my youth, a time when I was not restricted to a chair but ran barefoot under a summer sun that tightened my skin with its white heat, made the fact that it was only my mind that "moved" each hour in the library painfully obvious.

I did need to figure out where I had lost touch with my past. I started to become alien to my family culture the day I became a scholarship boy. In the British Museum the realization seemed obvious. But later, returning to America, I returned to minority group students who were still speaking of their cultural ties to their past. How was I to tell them what I had learned about myself in England?

A short while ago, a group of enthusiastic Chicano undergraduates came to my office to ask me to teach a course to high school students in the *barrio* on the Chicano novel. This new literature, they assured me, has an important role to play in helping to shape the consciousness of a people currently without adequate representation in literature. Listening to them I was struck immediately with the cultural problems raised by their assumption. I told them that the novel is not capable of dealing with Chicano experience adequately, simply because most Chicanos are not literate, or are at least not yet comfortably so. This is not something Chicanos need to apologize for (though, I suppose, remembering my own childhood ambition to combat sterotypes of the Chicano as mental menial, it is not something easily admitted). Rather the genius and value of those Chicanos who do not read seem to me to be largely that their reliance on voice, the spoken word, has given them the capacity for intimate conversation that I, as someone who now relies heavily on the written word, can only envy. The second problem, I went on, is more in the nature of a technical one: the novel, in my opinion, is not a form capable of being true to the basic sense of communal life that typifies Chicano culture. What the novel as a literary form is best capable of representing is solitary existence set against a large social background. Chicano novelists, not coincidentally, nearly always fail to capture the breathtakingly rich family life of most Chicanos, and instead often describe only the individual Chicano in transit between Mexican and American cultures.

I said all of this to the Chicano students in my office, and could see that little of it made an impression. They seemed only frustrated by what they probably took to be a slick, academic justification for evading social responsibilities. After a time, they left me, sitting alone.

There is a danger of being misunderstood here. I am not suggesting that an academic cannot reestablish ties of any kind with his old culture. Indeed, he can have an impact on the culture of his childhood. But as an academic, one exists by definition in a culture separate from one's nonacademic roots and, therefore, any future ties one has with those who remain "behind" are complicated by one's new cultural perspective.

Paradoxically, the distance separating the academic from his nonacademic past can make his past seem, if not closer, then clearer. It is possible for the academic to understand the culture from which he came "better" than those who still live within it.

In my own experience, it has only been as I have come to appraise my past through categories and notions derived from the social sciences that I have been able to think of Chicano life in cultural terms at all. Characteristics I took for granted or noticed only in passing—the spontaneity, the passionate speech, the trust in concrete experience, the willingness to think communally rather than individually—these are all significant phenomena to me now as aspects of a total culture. (My parents have neither the time nor the inclination to think about their culture as a culture.) Able to conceptualize a sense of Chicano culture, I am now also more attracted to that culture than I was before. The temptation now is to try to preserve those traits of my old culture that have not yet, in effect, atrophied.

The racial self-consciousness of minority group students during the last few years evident in the ethnic costumes, the stylized gestures, and the idiomatic though often evasive devices for insisting on one's continuing membership in the community of the past, are also indications that the minority group student has gained a new appreciation of the culture of his origin precisely because of his earlier alienation from it. As a result, Chicano students sometimes become more Chicano than most Chicanos. I remember, for example, my father's surprise when, walking across my college campus one afternoon, we came upon two Chicano academics wearing serapes. He and my mother were also surprised—indeed offended—when they earlier heard student activists use the word "Chicano." For them the term was a private one, primarily descriptive of persons they knew. It suggested intimacy. Hearing the word shouted into a microphone by a stranger left them bewildered. What they could not understand was that the student activist finds it easier than they to use "Chicano" in a more public way, for his distance from their culture and his membership in academic culture permits a wider and more abstract view.

The Mexican-Americans who begin to call themselves Chicanos in this new way are actually forming a new version of what it means to be a Chicano. The culture that didn't see itself as a culture is suddenly prized and identified for being one. The price one pays for this new self-consciousness is the knowledge of just that—it is *new*—and this knowledge is not available to those who remain at home. So it is knowledge that separates as well as unites people. Wanting more desperately than ever to assert his ties with the newly visible culture, the minority group student is tempted to exploit those characteristics of that culture that might yet survive in him. But the self-consciousness never allows one to feel completely at ease with the old culture. Worse, the knowledge of the culture of the past often leaves one feeling strangely solitary. At home, I hear relatives speak and find myself analyzing too much of what they say. It is embarrassing being a cultural anthropologist in one's own family's kitchen. I keep feeling myself little more than a cultural voyeur. I often come away from family gatherings suspecting, in fact, that what conceptions of my culture I carry with me are no more than illusions. Because they were never there before, because no one back home shares them, I grow less and less to trust their reliability: too often they seem no more than mental bubbles floating before an academic's eye.

Many who have taught minority group students in the last decade testify to sensing characteristics of a childhood culture still very much alive in these students. Should the teacher make these students aware of these characteristics? Initially, most of us would probably answer negatively. Better to trust the unconscious survival of the past than the always problematical, sometimes even clownish, re-creations of it. But the cultural past cannot be assured of survival; perhaps many of its characteristics are lost simply because the student is never encouraged to look for them. Even those that do survive do so tenuously. As a teacher, one can only hope that the best qualities in his minority group students' cultural legacy aren't altogether snuffed out by academic education.

More easy to live with and distinguishable from self-conscious awareness of the past are the ways the past unconsciously survives—perhaps even yet survives in me. As it turns out, the issue becomes less acute with time. With each year, the chance that the student is unaware of his cultural legacy is diminished as the habit of academic reflectiveness grows stronger. Although the culture of the academy makes innocence about one's cultural past less likely, this same culture, and the conceptual tools it provides, increases the desire to want to write and speak about the past. The paradox persists.

Awaiting the scholarship boy who finally acknowledges the fact that his perceptions of reality have changed is the dilemma of action. The sentimental reaction to this knowledge entails merely a refusal to renew contract with one's nonacademic culture lest one contaminate it. The problem, however, with this sentimental solution is that it overlooks the way academic culture renders one capable of dealing with the transactions of mass society. Academic culture, with its habits of conceptualization and abstraction, allows those of us from other cultures to deal with each other in a mass society. In this sense academic culture does have a profound political impact. Although people intent upon social mobility think of education as a means to an end, education does become an end: its culture allows one to exist more easily in a society increasingly anonymous and impersonal. The truth is, the academic's distance from his own experience brings the capacity for communicating with bureaucracies and understanding one's position in society—a prerequisite for political action.

If the sentimental reaction to nonacademic culture is to fear changing it, the political response, typical especially of working-class and lately minority group leaders, is to see higher education solely in terms of its political and social possibilities. Its cultural consequences, in this view, are disregarded. At this time when we are so keenly aware of social and economic inequality, it might seem beside the point to warn those who are working to bring about equality that education alters culture as well as economic status. And yet, if there is one main criticism that I, as a minority group student, must make of minority group leaders in their past attacks on the "racism" of the academy, it is that they never distinguished between my right to higher education and the desirability of my actually entering the academy—which is another way of saying again that they never recognized that there were things I could lose by becoming a scholarship boy.

Certainly, the academy changes those from alien cultures more than it is changed by them. While minority groups had an impact on higher education, largely because of their advantage in coming as a group, within the last few years students such as myself, who finally ended up certified as academics, also ended up sounding very much like the academics we found when we came to the campus. I do not enjoy making such admissions. But perhaps now the time has come when questions about the cultural costs of education ought to be delayed no longer. Those of us who have been scholarship boys know in our bones that our education has exacted a large price in exchange for the large benefits it has conferred upon us. And what is sadder to consider, after we have paid that price, we go home and casually change the cultures that nurtured us. My parents today understand how they are "Chicanos" in a large and impersonal sense. The gains from such knowledge are clear. But so, too, are the reasons for regret.

READING 11

The following essay focuses on the cognitive strengths in one group. While the primary reason for including it here is its cross-cultural (anthropological) focus, it will also introduce you to some of the concepts to be discussed in chapters 8 and 9. You may wish to refer to the article again when reading those sections of the text.

READING QUESTIONS

1. How might you apply what you have learned from this essay to your tutoring? to tutoring an Eskimo student? any other student? tutoring Math? English? other fields?

2. What does this essay tell you about the Eskimo culture? What cultural factors—both Eskimo and Western—does Kleinfeld point to as influencing learning *or* learning performance?

11 | INTELLECTUAL STRENGTHS IN CULTURALLY DIFFERENT GROUPS: AN ESKIMO ILLUSTRATION

J. S. Kleinfeld
University of Alaska

THEORETICAL BASIS

Demands of Arctic Hunting

The ecological demands made by a particular environment together with a group's cultural adaptations to these demands may stimulate the development of particular types of cognitive abilities (Berry, 1971). For thousands of years the Eskimos' economy has been based on hunting in the Arctic. The Arctic, in contrast to urban areas or farmland, is an environment of extreme visual uniformity. As Laughlin (1970) describes it:

> The horizon is commonly flat with minor relief. There are no trees or forest canopy. The visual cues are often small, consisting of subtle changes in the colour of the ice, of small patches of snow which reveal wind direction and intensity, of water texture and slight indications of tidal changes and currents. The available cues are obscured and diminished by fog, snow, wind, rain glare, darkness, ice, and low level contrasts that camouflage the animals as well [p.9].

That Eskimos have made a highly successful adaptation to the demands of arctic hunting is evidenced by their ability not only to maintain the group but also to expand geographically. The Eskimos together with the closely related Aleuts inhabit the longest distance of any people in the world (Laughlin, 1970).

To hunt successfully in the visually uniform Arctic requires particular types of cognitive skills. The Eskimo hunter, for example, must be extremely sensitive to visual detail (Berry, 1971). In his ethnography of Eskimo hunting, Nelson (1969) emphasizes that the hunter must be able to detect slight cracks in the ice because a breaking icepack could set him adrift in the ocean. To find his way back to a few houses in the tundra, the hunter must attend to the angle and shape of small drifts of snow. If he is to survive should he venture out, the hunter must judge weather conditions by carefully observing subtle patterns of dark and light on clouds made by reflected water, ice, and land. For an urbanite, in contrast, attention to such visual detail may even be nonadaptive. The driver of a car, for example, needs to code a reddish hexagonal figure as a stop sign despite any individual peculiarities of color or shape. On the other hand, functional adaption for the Eskimo hunter requires that he code visual information on the basis of its uniqueness not that he categorize in terms of general form.

Not only awareness of figural detail but also the ability to memorize this detail and especially its spatial arrangement is crucial to successful navigation through the Arctic. As Nelson (1969) observes:

> On the flat and monotonous tundra or the jumbled piles of sea ice, the smallest unique features become important landmarks—an upturned rock, a cut in the river bank, an unusually large or strangely shaped ice pile. The Eskimos are extraordinarily skillful at observing such landmarks and remembering their spatial relationships [p.102].

Caucasians who have traveled with the Eskimo frequently remark upon their apparently extraordinary ability to find their way through what appears to be a featureless terrain by remembering visual configurations (Nelson, 1969; Carpenter, 1955). According to some reports, such memories persist for long periods of time. Elderly hunters have succeeded in guiding parties through terrain seen only in their youth (Carpenter, Varley, & Flaherty, 1959).

A number of other figural abilities may be critical to the Eskimo hunter. For example, he must be able to recognize rotated visual patterns since he may return to an area from a different direction. Spatial scanning is important in selecting a clear path for sled and dogs through terrain broken with rough ice piles. The hunter must be able to analyze or break down complex visual configurations, for example, determining if an ice boulder is composed of the rounded ice pieces on which it is safe to camp or the sharp pieces which may break apart under him. In short, to survive in the Arctic, the hunter must continually be aware of, be able to recall, and be able to evaluate figural information. Such environmental demands are rarely made of urban Caucasians and for them attention to figural detail could even be dysfunctional.

Languages as a Cultural Adaptation

In its adaptation to the demands of arctic hunting, the grammatical character of the Eskimo language appears to be a powerful intellectual tool for the processing of figural information (Berry, 1966). In Eskimo, localizers consisting of prefixes and suffixes specifying shape and location may be grammatically integral to the word that represents an object. As Gagné (1968) points out, the English sentence, "Please put this thing over there," could be translated into four different three-word sentences in Eskimo because both the shape of the object and also the shape of the surface on which it is to be placed must be specified through localizers. Moreover, contrasts between certain localizers used in such a three-word Eskimo sentence might also specify the directional position of the object on the surface. The English language, in contrast, would require several additional words to code the same amount of figural information. Since the use of such localizers is grammatically obligatory, the Eskimo language speaker may be more likely to attend to shape and location. Moreover, because such localizers permit economical coding of spatial information, the speaker of the Eskimo language may also find such information easier to remember than speakers of English.

Socialization Practices

Eskimo socialization practices also seem likely to foster a high level of figural abilities. Eskimo children are treated with great indulgence and child-rearing practices for both sexes emphasize independence and exploration (Briggs, 1970). A number of studies suggest that this type of child-rearing orientation leads to highly developed figural abilities. Within Western culture, development of such spatial skills as a high level of field independence* appears to be related to parental encouragement of independence as opposed to parental strictness and pressure toward conformity (Witkin, 1967). Within African groups, greater experience in exploring the environment also has been found to relate to a higher level of spatial ability (Munroe & Munroe, 1971; Nerlove, Munroe, & Munroe, 1971). Comparisons between cultures also suggest that members of cultures with more severe socialization tend to have a lower level of spatial skills (Berry, 1966).

Other aspects of Eskimo socialization may contribute to highly developed figural abilities. Traditionally, children learn more by carefully watching adults than by receiving verbal instruction. In addition, Eskimos tend to place great emphasis on observable information. Marshall (1933) compared the conversational topics of Eskimos versus whites living and hunting in the same area, and found that Eskimos' conversation centered much more frequently on geography. An Eskimo hunter, for example, might entertain the group by a detailed description of the forks of a minor river and his audience would interrupt to ask even more specific questions. Severe social sanctions as well as natural disasters befall Eskimos who fail to learn such figural information. Nelson (1969) observes that hunters who become lost are mercilessly ridiculed upon their return.

Genetic Influences

It seems possible that genetic factors also may help account for the high level of figural abilities noted among Eskimos. Comparisons of identical and fraternal twins suggest that spatial ability, at least among western groups, has a high degree of heritability (Thurstone, 1951; Osborne & Gregor, 1966). Moreover, sophisticated studies attempting to relate specific environmental factors to different mental abilities have found that the learning environment of the home accounts for a very small percentage of the variance in spatial skills in contrast to other abilities (Marjoribanks, 1972).

Since the penalty for navigational errors in the Arctic could easily be rapid death through freezing, natural selection may have resulted in a high level of figural skills in the Eskimo group. Those hunters who possessed a high level of figural abilities may have been more likely to survive and to have many offspring. The offspring of successful hunters could also have been better fed and thus more resistant to disease. Such natural selection processes may be of great importance in determining characteristics of a population such as the Eskimo, who have lived in the same environment for long periods of time, who have been sexually isolated for many generations, and who passed through winter periods of food scarcity which reduced population (Witkin, 1967; Laughlin, 1970).

Compensatory Influences

Compensation for difficulties in receiving information through verbal channels may also contribute to the development of Eskimos' figural abilities. Otitis media, an ear infection, has resulted in prevalent hearing loss among Eskimos. Moreover, many Eskimos have difficulty understanding information presented in English and may attempt to

---

*Field independence refers to the ability to distinguish a figure or shape from its surrounding environment (or field).

compensate by reliance on figural skills. An Eskimo student employed in our research institute, for example, was found to be memorizing the visual arrangement of folders in the files since he did not understand the filing system.

No studies have been done which attempt to determine to what extent language, socialization, genetic or other factors are related to the development of figural abilities in Eskimos. In contrast to the male superiority characteristic of Western groups (Berry, 1966; Kunce & Sturman, 1966; MacArthur, 1967; Feldman & Bock, 1970), the intriguing lack of sex differences in spatial abilities commonly found among Eskimos suggests that the high level of spatial abilities among Eskimos probably depends on general factors rather than on specific hunting experience. Clearly, Eskimo males would have more hunting experience than females.

ANECDOTAL ACCOUNTS

Anecdotal reports of high level performance on specific tasks are not generally considered strong evidence of the possession of a high level of a specific ability. However, frequent and consistent reports of high performance are at least suggestive. For example, the relationship between certain spatial abilities and mechanical aptitude is generally accepted, and descriptions of Eskimos' mechanical ability have become folklore of the Arctic (Foster, 1969; Hall, 1967). Carpenter (1955) reports that in several instances Eskimos were able to repair complicated pieces of machinery which trained white mechanics had failed to fix. Crisler (1958) remarks that Eskimos succeeded in repairing a radio that their party had been forced to abandon. Oil companies who have hired Eskimos to work in the Prudhoe Bay oil fields recently have reported, "We have found that the Eskimo has more innate ability to work around equipment than anyone else around the world (Democrats talk on oil, 1970)." While Eskimos' apparently high mechanical aptitude may result in part from their higher level finger dexterity (Alaska Department of Labor, 1969), skill in analyzing spatial relationships may also be involved.

Another commonly observed figural skill of Eskimos is an uncanny ability to comprehend rotated visual configurations. Carpenter (1955) notes that Eskimos often carve figures oriented in different directions without bothering to turn the tusk they are working on. Similarly, Eskimos may examine photographs in whatever direction they are received and hang pictures with little attempt to make them vertical. In an impromptu experiment, Carpenter (1955) drew twenty figures oriented in different directions on a single sheet of paper and asked a number of the Eskimos to point to the seal, walrus, and so forth. He reported that the Eskimos could identify the figures immediately while he had to turn the page around even though he himself had drawn them. Briggs (1970) similarly observes that Eskimo children had a disconcerting ability to read her private field notes as easily upside down as right side up.

Anecdotal reports also contain numerous descriptions of Eskimos' exceptional performance in tasks requiring memory for visual information. Many Caucasians have asked Eskimos to draw maps of the terrain and later found them to be extraordinarily accurate both in significant detail and in spatial arrangements (Briggs, 1970; King, 1848). Indeed, Marshall (1933) reports that an Eskimo woman "once sketched for me the first fifteen miles of the Alatna River, a stream which is nothing but bends in this lower portion, and she had them all plotted from memory almost as accurately as the instrumentally constructed Geological Survey map [p. 81]." Similarly, Carpenter (1955) found that maps of Southampton Island made by Eskimos in 1929 were almost identical to maps made years later by aerial photography.

Evidence of Eskimos' figural memory abilities is found in many other sources. Eskimos' drawings are notable for their precise detail (Ryan, 1965). Eskimos were able to describe birds in north Alaska and northeast Canada in sufficient detail for a naturalist to make a taxonomic identification of more than eighty species (Lantis, 1968). Highly developed abilities in visual memory may also underlie Eskimos' talent for mimicry, which visiting anthropologists, who are often the objects of the ridicule, have had frequent occasion to observe (Briggs, 1970, p. 129; King, 1848; Carpenter et al., 1959). In a survey of teachers in Alaskan Eskimo villages, Kleinfeld (1970) found that about 70 per cent of the responding teachers thought that their students showed unusual ability to observe and remember visual detail. These teachers mentioned that their students were quite good in tasks which required visual memory or spatial abilities such as geometry, map studies, handwriting, puzzles, repeating designs, and remembering the number and arrangements of objects.

Eskimos' inventive abilities, especially in tasks involving unconventional uses of concrete objects, have also become legendary. Lacking specialized repair shops, Eskimos have had to devise unusual solutions to practical problems (Nelson, 1969). Eskimos' divergent intellectual skills are indicated by such ingenuity as using pieces of frozen meat to construct a sled or using dental floss to replace the cross hairs of a telescopic sight. Interestingly, among Caucasians as well, highly developed figural abilities such as field independence appears to be associated with the ability to find unconventional solutions to problems (Harris, 1962). . . .

EMPIRICAL RESEARCH

Cross-Cultural Testing Problems

A number of studies have compared the figural abilities of Eskimos with those of other groups through psychological tests. In reviewing this research, the familiar problems of cross-cultural testing need to be recalled. Eskimos' performance on standardized tests may be lowered because of their unfamiliarity with test-taking conventions and because of cultural biases of the tests. Eskimos, for example, may find it difficult to view a trivial, pointless task such as copying a design or running through a finger maze as worthy of serious concentration and maximum effort. Cultural biases in figural tests are still present if more subtle than on verbal tasks. On a spatial test which used directional arrows, for example, Feldman and Bock (1970) report that about a third of their Eskimo subjects did not appear to understand the directions and scored at or near chance levels.

In addition to these familiar difficulties in cross-cultural research, three special problems may occur with the Eskimo which could result in test scores lower than ability levels. First, Eskimos, especially young males, have become increasingly antagonistic to any sort of testing and research, which they view as another form of white exploitation. Cooperation, if given at all, may be perfunctory, resulting in extremely low test scores (see Feldman & Bock, 1970). Second, in many figural tests, the score depends on speed of response. Eskimos, especially males, have been socialized into extreme caution before making judgments. The hunter is taught never to take risks, never to call out a hasty evaluation because the penalty can be swift death not only for himself but also for others who rely on his decision (Nelson, 1969). Error may result in humiliating social ridicule. Especially more traditional Eskimos tend to have a slow, cautious response style which may depress their scores on speeded figural tests (Preston, 1964). Power rather than speed tests may be better indicators of Eskimos' figural abilities. Third, some evidence that Eskimos' peak performance on figural tests occurs later than that of Western groups raises the possibility of a slower rate of cognitive maturation among Eskimos which would be consistent with their somewhat slower rate of physical maturation (Feldman & Bock, 1970). If this is the case, the usual age-matched comparison between Western and Eskimo children on figural tests may be misleading. . . .

Tests of Awareness of Figural Detail

Several tests have been given to Eskimos which require the ability to conceptualize figures in precise detail. In an exceptionally well-designed study, Berry (1966) gave a visual discrimination test involving awareness of small gaps in geometrical figures flashed on a screen to Canadian Eskimos, to the Temne of Sierra Leone, and also to Scots who served as a Western comparison group. He found that the Eskimos not only far surpassed the Temne but also the Scots as well. In another task which required accurate reproduction of simple geometrical forms which could easily be assimilated to the shape of associated objects, Berry (1969) again found that the Eskimo far surpassed both the Temne and the Scots.

The Goodenough Draw-A-Man Test which also requires detailed conceptualization of figures has been used in a number of investigations. Eskimos' performance on this test has been quite variable, however, possibly because extraneous factors appear to have substantial effects on test scores. Thus, in a very early 1930-1931 testing of isolated Eskimo children, unfamiliarity with the drawing materials was probably responsible for scores below test norms (Anderson & Eels, 1935). However, Marshall (1933) gave this test to a small group of Eskimo children living in close proximity to Westerners and found that young Eskimo children scored markedly above test norms while older children scored at appropriate norms. In a recent study of Eskimo children in a transitional town, Levensky (1970) found that young children scored slightly above test norms and that older children scored at appropriate norms. Vernon (1969) found that eleven year old Eskimo boys performed slightly below test norms, but he points out that this result may be partially attributable to an art teacher who trained students to make impressionistic rather than detailed drawings. Harris (1963), in contrast, found consistent superiority in Eskimo children's scores on the Draw-A-Man test. However, these tests were sent to Harris by village teachers who may not have included poorer drawings.

Tests of Figural Memory

Little research has been done in the area of memory for visual information. . . .

[An] indicator of Eskimos' visual memory abilities may be their scores on standardized spelling tests. These scores are often almost as high as the scores of white groups despite Eskimo children's lack of proficiency in other English skills (MacArthur, 1968). An intriguing possibility is that Eskimo students learn spelling words by memorizing the word's figural shape even when they do not know its meaning.

Tests of Spatial Abilities

Several types of spatial tests have been given to Eskimos. In general, where the Eskimos have had little education or little familiarity with Western institutions such as test-taking, they tend to match the performance of Western groups or score slightly lower. However, where their educational level is similar to that of the Western group, Eskimos score significantly higher in a number of instances. Moreover, on those types of spatial tests where Eskimos' performance is not substantially associated with education, Eskimos with very little education may surpass the performance of Western groups.

Studies of Eskimos' performance on tasks involving the reproduction of designs such as Kohs Blocks or the Block Design sub-test of the Wechsler Adult Intelligence Scale (WAIS) illustrate this pattern. Berry (1966) found that a traditional group of Eskimos scored significantly lower than the Scottish comparison group on this test while a transitional group, which averaged only three years of education, scored at the same level. Preston (1964) and Foster (1969) similarly report that Eskimos with less education than whites scored at about the same level as the test norms. Only Vernon

(1969) reports a slightly lower median performance of Eskimo boys on this test, and their schooling was often delayed or irregular. However, in two studies where Eskimo children had attended village schools for the same length of time as Western age-mates, they were found to score significantly higher than test norms (Forbes, 1971; Feldman, 1971).

On the Object Assembly sub-test of the WAIS, which shows little relationship to education among Alaska Natives (Foster, 1969), Eskimo or Alaska Native adults (a political rather than racial grouping which includes Indians) with little education have been found to surpass test norms (Preston, 1964; Foster, 1969). Indeed, Lantis (1968) reports that adolescent and young adult Eskimo males performed on a somewhat similar Block Assembly Test at the same level as Harvard undergraduates, whose nonverbal intelligence is probably substantially higher than that of the general population.

Eskimos' performance on maze tests also raises the possibility that Eskimos might surpass Westerners if education or familiarity with Western institutions were equalized. As a group, Eskimo adults performed slightly below test norms on Peter's Circular Mazes, but the subgroup of Eskimos with only a high school education performed substantially higher (Kunce, Rankin, & Clement, 1969). Vernon (1969), however, found that Eskimo boys' median performance on Porteus Mazes was lower than an English comparison group, but the Eskimo students frequently had delayed or irregular schooling.

On measures of field-independence, Eskimos' performance tends to be about the same as Western groups. Berry (1966) found no significant difference between Scots and either traditional or transitional groups of Eskimos on the Embedded Figures Tests. Vernon (1969) and MacArthur (1968) found that Eskimo students performed slightly lower than white students on Embedded Figures, but MacKinnon (1972) found no significant difference. On the Draw-A-Man test scored for field independence, Vernon (1969) found that the Eskimo males surpassed a white comparison group.

Only one spatial test requiring comprehension of rotated figures—a skill frequently mentioned in Eskimo anecdotal reports—has been given to Eskimos. Berry (1966) found that both traditional and transitional groups of Eskimos surpassed Scots' performance on Morrisby Shapes. The difference between the transitional Eskimo group and the urbanized Scots reached statistical significance.

In sum, available empirical research, while possibly biased by a tendency to report unexpected findings, gives some support to theoretical expectations and anecdotal accounts which suggest that Eskimos could have relatively high figural abilities. Despite a number of cross-cultural testing problems which would be expected to lead to scores indicating lower than actual ability level, Eskimos frequently perform significantly higher than Western groups on psychological tests measuring ability to conceptualize or remember visual detail and sometimes perform significantly higher on tests measuring spatial abilities.

Another interesting consideration is the Western figural tests tend to be based on the dominant figural experiences of Western cultural groups. Most tests, for example, require manipulation of idealized geometrical forms such as perfect hexagons. While such forms may be very familiar to Westerners who live in highly carpentered environments, the experiential world of village Eskimos is dominated as much by natural irregularities such as ice piles and twisting rivers as by Western importations. An intriguing possibility is that tests measuring abilities to process information concerning visual irregularities could reveal more pronounced figural strengths among Eskimos.

Occupational Implications

Since the precise nature of Eskimos' figural abilities has not yet been clearly identified, these abilities can not yet be related to specific occupational aptitudes. Only general implications can be speculated upon. Figural skills have been found to predict success in a number of technical school subjects (reviewed in Smith, 1964). Such abilities as perceptual accuracy are known to be important in clerical occupations. Spatial and visualization abilities have been found to predict pilot aptitude (reviewed in Hoffman et al, 1968), a skill in high demand in the Arctic where settled areas are linked primarily by plane. Thus, if Eskimos have a high level of figural abilities, they may have an advantage in the technical occupations, where, for a great many, initial entry into the Western occupational structure is likely to occur.

An intriguing speculation, however, is that Eskimos' figural skills could ultimately enable them to make significant contributions to advanced fields such as higher mathematics and physics. Smith (1964) reviews a number of lines of evidence which suggest that, after a certain minimum level of verbal ability is achieved, it is spatial abilities that are related to outstanding performance in such areas as advanced mathematics and physics. One has only to recall Einstein's (1954, p. 25) description of his mental processes as "visual and motion" with words not playing a role until a secondary stage. Smith (1964) reports that many spatially talented students who eventually became famous mathematicians or scientists were considered dull in school, where talent is judged primarily by verbal facility. After prolonged contact, when Eskimos' English competence has become higher, it is possible that their figural abilities could lead to significant technical achievements.

REFERENCES

Alaska Department of Education, Division of State-Operated Schools. Testing Results in Rural Schools, 1967–1971.

Alaska Department of Labor, Smaller Communities Program. *Alaska manpower resources: The Barrow Wainwright area,* 1969.

Anderson, H. D. & Eels, W. C. *Alaska Natives: A survey of their sociological and educational status.* California: Stanford University Press, 1935.

Bar-Yam, M. *The interaction of instructional strategies with students' characteristics.* Cambridge: Center for Research and Development of Educational Differences, 1969.

Bereiter, C. The future of individual differences. *Harvard Educational Review,* 1969, 39 (2), 310–318.

Berry, J. W. Temne and Eskimo perceptual skills. *Journal of International Psychology,* 1966, 1, 207–299.

Berry, J. W. Ecology and socialization as factors in figural assimilation and the resolution of binocular rivalry. *International Journal of Psychology,* 1969, 4 (4), 271–280.

Berry, J. W. Ecological and cultural factors in spatial perceptual development. *Canada Journal of Behavioral Science,* 1971, 3 (4), 324–336.

Bloom, R. S. Testing cognitive ability and achievement. In N. L. Gage (Ed.), *Handbook of research on teaching.* Chicago: Rand McNally, 1963.

Bracht, G. H. Experimental factors related to aptitude-treatment interactions. *Review of Educational Research,* 1970, 40 (5), 626–645.

Bradley, P. A., Hoepfner, R., & Guilford, J. P. *A factor analysis of figural-memory abilities.* Reports from the psychological laboratory of the University of Southern California, 1969.

Briggs, J. L. *Never in anger: Portrait of an Eskimo family.* Cambridge: Harvard University Press, 1970.

Carpenter, E. S. Space concepts of the Aivilik Eskimos. *Explorations,* 1955, 131–145.

Carpenter, E. S., Varley, F., & Flaherty, R. *Eskimo.* Toronto: University of Toronto Press, 1959.

Carroll, J. B. Discussion of Dr. Cronbach's paper. Instructional methods and individual differences. In R. M. Gagné (Ed.), *Learning and individual differences.* Columbus: Charles Merrill Books, 1967.

Crisler, L. *Arctic Wilds,* New York: Harper & Row, 1958.

Cronbach, L. J. How can instruction be adapted to individual differences? In R. M. Gagné (Ed.), *Learning and individual differences*. Columbus: Charles Merrill Books, 1967.

Democrats talk on oil, *Anchorage Daily Times,* September 26, 1970.

Einstein, A. *Ideas and opinions.* New York: Crown Publishers, 1954.

Federal Field Committee for Development Planning in Alaska. *Alaska natives and the land.* Washington: U.S. Government Printing Office, 1968.

Feldman, C. F. Cognitive development in Eskimos. Paper presented at the meeting of the Society for Research in Cognitive Development, April 1971.

Feldman, C. F., & Bock, R. D. Cognitive studies among residents of Wainwright village, Alaska. *Arctic Anthropology,* 1970, 7 (1), 101–108.

Forbes, N. Effects of attitude and intelligence variables on the English language achievement of Alaska Eskimo. Unpublished master's thesis, San Jose State, 1971.

Foster, A. The use of psychological testing in rehabilitation planning for Alaska Native people, 1969. In *Rehabilitation Project Final Report.* Anchorage: Alaska Native Medical Center, 1969.

French, J. W., Ekstrom, R. B., & Price, L. A. *Manual for kit of reference tests for cognitive factors.* Princeton: Educational Testing Service, 1963.

Gagné, R. M. Spatial concepts in the Eskimo language. In V. F. Valentine and F. C. Vallee (Eds.), *Eskimo of the Canadian Arctic.* Toronto: McClelland and Stewart Limited, 1968.

Guilford, J. P. *The nature of human intelligence.* New York: McGraw-Hill, 1967.

Hall, E. *Manpower potential of our ethnic groups.* Seminar on Manpower Policy and Program. U. S. Department of Labor, 1967.

Harris, D. B. *Children's drawings as measures of intellectual maturity.* New York: Harcourt, Brace & World, 1963.

Harris, F. Personal communication. In H. A. Witkin, R. B. Dyk, H. F. Paterson, D. R. Goodenough, & S. A. Karp, *Psychological differentiation.* New York: John Wiley and Sons, 1962.

Hoffman, K. I., Guilford, J. P., Hoepfner, R., & Doherty, W. J. *A factor analysis of the figural-cognition and figural-evaluation abilities.* Reports from the psychological laboratory of the University of Southern California, 1968.

Jensen, A. R. How much can we boost IQ and scholastic achievement? *Harvard Educational Review,* 1969, 39 (1), 1–123.

King, A. R. *The school at Mopass: A problem in identity.* New York: Holt, Rinehart, and Winston, 1967.

King, R. On the intellectual character of the Esquimaux. *Journal of the Ethnological Society of London,* 1848, 1, 127–153.

Kleinfeld, J. *Cognitive strengths of Eskimos and implications for education.* Fairbanks: University of Alaska, Institute of Social, Economic and Government Research, 1970.

Kleinfeld, J. Visual memory in village Eskimo and urban Caucasian children. *Arctic,* 1971, 24 (2), 132–138.

Kunce, J., Rankin, L. S., & Clement, E. Maze performance and personal, social, and economic adjustment of Alaskan Natives, 1966. In *Rehabilitation Project Final Report.* Anchorage: Alaska Native Medical Center, 1969.

Kunce, J., & Sturman, J. Cultural impoverishment and intellectual deficits. Unpublished paper, Anchorage: Alaska Native Medical Center, 1966.

Lantis, M. A teacher's view of culture. In *A Positive Image for the Alaska Native Learner,* Anchorage: Bureau of Indian Affairs Area-Wide Education Workshop, 1968, 17–61.

Laughlin, W. S. The purpose of studying Eskimos and their population systems. *Arctic,* 1970, 23 (1), 3–13.

Lesser, G., Fifer, G., & Clark, D. H. Mental abilities of children in different social and cultural groups. In J. I. Rogers (Ed.), *School children in the urban slum.* New York: Hunter College, Project TRUE, 1965.

Levensky, K. The performance of American Indian children on the Draw-A-Man Test. In R. J. Havighurst (Ed.), *The national study of American Indian Education,* Vol. 1. Minneapolis: Center for Urban and Regional Affairs, Office of Community Programs, 1970.

MacArthur, R. S. Some differential abilities of northern Canadian Native youth. *International Journal of Psychology,* 1968, 3 (1), 43–51.

MacArthur, R. S. Sex differences in field dependence for the Eskimo. *International Journal of Psychology,* 1967, 2 (2), 139–140.

MacKinnon, A. A. *Eskimo and Caucasian: A discordant note on cognitive-perceptual abilities.* Unpublished. Saskatoon: Saskatchewan Department of Health, 1972.

Marjoribanks, K. Environment, social class, and mental abilities. *Journal of Educational Psychology,* 1972, 63 (2), 103–109.

Marshall, R. *Arctic village.* New York: Harrison Smith and Robert Haas, 1933.

Munroe, R. L., & Munroe, R. H. Effect of environmental experience on spatial ability in an East African society. *Journal of Social Psychology,* 1971, 83, 15–22.

Nelson, R. K. *Hunters of the northern ice.* Chicago: University of Chicago Press, 1969.

Nerlove, S. B., Munroe, R. H., & Munroe, R. L. Effect of environmental experience on spatial ability: A replication. *Journal of Social Psychology,* 1971, 84, 3–10.

Osborne, R. T., & Gregor, A. J. The heritability of visualization, perceptual speed and spatial orientation. *Perceptual and Motor Skills,* 1966, 23, 379–390.

Preston, C. E. Psychological testing with northwest coast Alaskan Eskimos. *Genetic Psychology Monographs,* 1964, 69, 323–419.

Ryan, T. Eskimo pencil drawings, a neglected art. *Canadian Art,* 1965, 22 (1), 30–35.

Shockley, W. Dysgenics, geneticity, raceology: Challenges to the intellectual responsibility of educators. *Phi Delta Kappan,* 1972, 53 (5), 297–307.

Smith, I. M. *Spatial ability.* San Diego: Robert Knapp, 1964.

Thurstone, L. C. Factor analysis. In M. H. Marx (Ed.), *Psychological theory: Contemporary readings,* New York: Macmillan, 1951, 276–284.

Vernon, P. E. *Intelligence and cultural environment.* London: Methuen and Company, 1969.

Witkin, H. A. A cognitive-style approach to cross-cultural research. *International Journal of Psychology,* 1967, 2 (4), 233–250.

BIBLIOGRAPHY

Celce-Murcia, Marianne and Lois McIntosh, eds. *Teaching English as a Second or Foreign Language.* Rowley, Mass.: Newbury House, 1979.

Karabel, Jerome and A. H. Halsey, eds. *Power and Ideology in Education.* New York: Oxford University Press, 1977.

Katz, Michael. *Class, Bureaucracy and Schools: The Illusion of Educational Change in America.* (Expanded Edition.) New York: Praeger Publishers, 1975.

Levine, Donald M. and Mary Jo Bane, eds. *The "Inequality" Controversy: Schooling and Distributive Justice.* New York: Basic Books, Inc., 1975.

Papalia, Anthony. *Learner-Centered Language Teaching: Methods and Materials.* Rowley, Mass.: Newbury House, 1976.

Paulston, Christina Bratt and Mary Newton Bruder. *Teaching English as a Second Language: Techniques and Procedures.* Cambridge, Mass.: Winthrop Publishing, Inc., 1976.

Pollard, W. Grosvenor III. "Implications of the Rank Concession Syndrome for Adult Education Programs: An Exploration in Social Roles and Program Effectiveness." *Adult Education,* 14 (Summer, 1974), 255–269.

Wattenmaker, Beverly S. and Virginia Wilson. *A Guidebook for Teaching English as a Second Language.* Boston: Allyn and Bacon, 1980.

6 | *TUTOR-COUNSELING*

DEALING WITH THE WHOLE STUDENT

Your tutee is someone with needs, goals, and desires, who has complex values and ideals, and who has a varying degree of competence in coping with the range of his or her academic and family responsibilities—in other words, someone very much like yourself, with strengths in some areas and weaknesses in others, with capabilities that vary with time, person, and place. Therefore, you must be sensitive to these aspects of the student as well as to the student's academic needs. In other words, you must always tutor a whole person. While you may be attending to areas of weakness—academic deficiencies or problems, you must not forget that academic problems occur within the context and fabric of a person's life. A tutee's learning is never just an intellectual accomplishment: it is as much, if not more, the product and the expression of interest, desire, attitude, and feeling, as it is one of intelligence; obstacles to learning are consequently emotional as well as intellectual. As a student "helper," you are bound to take affective aspects of learning into consideration, recognizing that transferring information or teaching a skill is only one part of tutoring. The following pages, then, will focus on some of the psychological factors relevant to learning as well as some of their practical implications. The insight you gain will be reinforced by practice exercises to help show you how to communicate caring in the most effective ways. We hope this chapter will allow you to move from tutoring to tutor-counseling.

MOTIVATION

Abraham Maslow's Hierarchy of Needs

Motivation is what makes someone want to do something. In chapter 4, we discussed motivation as it related to that phase in the session where you actively work at "turning your student on" to the material. However, when we speak of motivation in tutoring we are not only talking about motivation within a particular lesson but are referring to what makes a tutee seek tutoring in the first place, and what it is that makes the tutee remain in tutoring, despite disappointment, time conflicts, and so forth.

The most obvious reasons people are motivated to seek out tutoring are practical or instrumental ones—a good grade, a gift from a parent, a better job.

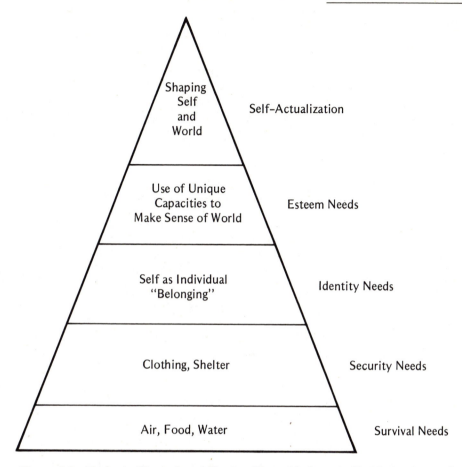

Figure 6.1 Maslow's Hierarchy of Needs. (From Maslow, A. H. *Motivation and Personality.* 2nd ed. New York: Harper & Row, 1970.)

But they can be motivated at a deeper level by real interest in the subject, by creative desires, by inspiration from a teacher or another role model. According to psychologist Abraham Maslow, motivation can be described in terms of a needs hierarchy. People first need physiological security, then a sense of identity, and then a sense of self-esteem, before they can even attempt to satisfy the highest need of all, self-actualization. Self-actualization is the ability to realize oneself fully; it is characterized by autonomy, integrity, and continual growth. Self-actualizing individuals are able to make commitments to themselves, to intimate relationships, and to the society in which they live. Often, needs unsatisfied at one of the lower levels, especially for self-esteem or identity, interfere with self-actualization.

Nonetheless, Maslow's hierarchy is schematic while in reality your tutee may have many motives for wanting to be tutored. He or she may really be interested in the subject you are tutoring *and* may also need a good grade to get into graduate school. Yet these motives may be sadly undermined by a lack of self-esteem, a feeling that he or she is not capable of mastering the subject matter. Thus, sensitivity to your tutee's motives can help you in a number of ways: If you isolate the tutee's *practical* motives for being in tutoring you will be able to relate tutoring to the accomplishment of these goals. If you become aware of *deeper* motives you may be able to draw on these at times when your tutee is frustrated or discouraged. If you are sensitive to some of the tutee's other needs, needs that are not directly related to the subject matter but present all the same during a tutoring session—physical needs, identity needs, needs for self-esteem and self-actualization—you may be able to meet those needs in simple ways: Your tutee may need to eat before beginning the session. Or the need may be more complex: Your tutee may need more reassurance than you are giving him or her. Later in the chapter, when we discuss some tutor-counseling methods, we will talk about how this range of needs can be met.

CLASS PROJECT 1

1. Analyze (in writing or in group discussion) your own motivations for being in this class. What do you want out of it? Are you getting everything that you hoped to get out of it?

2. a. Feelings can be important motivating factors.* The first part of this exercise asks you to explore these feelings in a systematic way through group work. Group members should discuss how they define the feelings in the list below and then explore situations in which they experience them.

cared for   proud
excited   challenged
confident   anxious
relaxed   peaceful

Discuss the material you have come up with. Can you isolate features that many group members have found concomitant with or necessary to a particular feeling? (For example, "I can only feel proud of a project when I have done all the work myself!") The group should identify a recorder who will take responsibility for writing out the conclusions.

b. For the second part of this project, form into groups of three, with one person to act as observer, and the other two to play the roles of tutor and tutee. The tutor should choose a feeling from the above list, and, without informing anyone else, attempt to elicit that feeling in the tutee during a simulated tutoring session. The observer should attempt to isolate elements that contributed to stimulating a certain feeling. In the discussion that follows the tutor should reveal the chosen feeling and compare what strategies, techniques, and statements he or she used, to those the observer noted. The tutee should then discuss how he or she actually felt. Be prepared to discuss any other conclusions you reach as a group, including how you think these feelings relate to Maslow's hierarchy of needs.

3. Interests, like feelings, constitute a form of motivation. Use this exercise to explore interests in a systematic way with groups (of five to seven

*This exercise has been adapted from Paul G. Friedman, *Inter-personal Communications: Innovations in Instruction*, Aspects of Learning Series (Washington, D.C: National Education Association, 1978), p. 81.

persons). Have each person in the group list his or her major hobby. Then each person should record the answers to the following questions before sharing them with other members of the group.

a. What got you interested? What keeps you interested? Include here persons, events, and any other relevant factors.

b. How long have you been involved in this activity—on a daily, weekly, or monthly basis?

c. Are there or have there been any obstacles to pursuing your interest? How have you overcome them? How did these obstacles make you feel?

d. How do you characterize yourself in relationship to the interest? What are you like when you are involved? What effects has your interest had on you socially, intellectually, and emotionally?

Toward the end of your discussion, record how people in the group responded to your interest (be as specific as possible) and reflect on how those responses made you feel.

Another task of the group might be to reflect on or to discuss what interested you in other people's statements or presentations.

LAB APPLICATIONS

1. Explore with your tutees their motives for taking the course or for attending tutoring. In your journal, record your efforts to uncover those motives and how you plan to use this knowledge.

2. Since this chapter focuses on reasons for certain kinds of behavior, you might find it helpful to record exchanges with your tutee as actual dialogue for later analysis.

3. Using what you learned in the class project about when and how people feel cared for, excited, confident, and so forth, attempt to elicit one or more of such positive feelings in your tutee. In your journal, record your strategies and whether or not you think they were effective.

---

1. _____ a. In the long run people get the respect they deserve in the world.

_____ b. Unfortunately, an individual's worth often passes unrecognized no matter how hard he or she tries.

2. _____ a. In the case of the well-prepared student there is rarely, if ever, such a thing as an unfair test.

_____ b. Many times exam questions tend to be so unrelated to course work that studying is really useless.

Figure 6.2 Internal-External Control Scale. Above are sample items from one of several different psychological scales used to assess a person's attitudes about influence and control. Other scales are the F Scale (Adorno et al, 1950) and the Machiavellianism Scale (Christie and Geis, 1970).

CLASS PROJECT 2

Before reading the next section, select the statement for each of the two items listed in Figure 6.2 above with which you most agree (either a or b). Although your responses can only be suggestive, consider how they relate to the discussion that follows.

Locus of Control

Locus of control is a concept that people have used to explore motivation. It refers to how people conceptualize or explain who or what determines why things happen. People having an *internal* locus of control will tend to see themselves as the determinant of events in their lives while people who are *external* will tend to attribute outcomes to external circumstances or agencies. For example, caught in a sudden downpour, the internal's response might be: "How stupid of me not to have taken my unbrella—the forecast said rain." In contrast, the external might make some off-hand comment about the unpredictability of the weather as well as the unreliability of the weather reporter, adding that whenever he or she does take raingear it never rains. "It's gotten so I don't bother listening to the radio in the morning anymore."

How might such responses, if *characteristic*, that is persistent and reflected in behavior, affect the student's learning? Students who, like our external person faced with the rain, feel that the results of their performance are beyond their control, are more disposed to leave things to chance, "forgetting" to bring necessary books and papers to the lab, answering randomly, working intermittently, and consequently, accomplishing less. In contrast, students with an internal sense of control will tend to take their work more seriously since they believe that only they are responsible for what they do; they will probably come on time, rarely miss a session, complete assignments, and the like.

Although an internal locus of control would seem more desirable than the external locus of control, it has its drawbacks too. First of all, people with an internal locus of control at times assign responsibility to talent and intelligence, or lack of it, *rather than to practice or effort*. If, for example, students claim that they are failing because they are stupid, they are really saying that no amount of effort will help them and that learning, by definition, is impossible. So, it is important for students to see not only that the potential for learning lies within themselves, but that effort can affect how and what they learn. (One experimental reading program, for example, achieved remarkable success, not by its radical techniques in teaching reading but by helping students believe that what they did rather than their innate ability was the critical factor.) Second, when some students with an internal locus of control do not do well, they tend to blame themselves, even when they aren't at fault. In other words, an internal locus of control can interfere with learning in those people who are prone to anxiety and guilt.

We might prefer to have an internal locus of control because it makes us feel good about ourselves to feel in control. But we have to be realistic as well. If the world in which we live does not affirm us, if in reality we have little or no control, we cannot hold ourselves responsible. Thus social and economic factors which affect access and opportunity will have a strong impact on the *actual* locus of control: persons who have suffered discrimination are more likely to feel that they have little control over certain aspects of their lives (which is true in actuality) and this may in turn affect their motivation and their attitude toward learning.

Motivational Tutoring Strategies

What are the practical implications of our knowledge of motivation?

Recognize new behavior, that is, notice and affirm your tutee's efforts and distinguish them from less positive behaviors. Attribute effects to their causes: "You see, you got that perfectly right—and that's *because* you reviewed the whole problem, found out what you knew, and what you needed to know, and then worked it out." (This is obviously also a good way to summarize what has been learned.) Another example: "You see the difference that writing a first draft makes—your first A this semester. Great!" Or, negatively, "I sure wish you did what you said you would: now we'll have to use the time on the outline, instead of working on the introduction." Help the tutee to see the effect of his or her behavior and to take responsibility for it.

Highlight discrepancies between what the tutee says and what the tutee does. People's behavior is often inconsistent with their attitudes. Sometimes pointing out the disparities will permit a learner to integrate action with perception: "Don't tell me you can't do that; you worked really hard on that other project." "You say you're stupid but that proposal you developed at work doesn't sound like something a dodo could do."

Inoculate the tutee against possible failure. As with inconsistencies between attitudes and behavior, people are sometimes uneven in their ability to perform. Help your learner deal with the possibility of failure; things do go wrong. Especially when anxiety is high and/or self-esteem is low it is appropriate to assign some effects to external causes. A situation which is defined as being environmentally induced is one which can be changed. Therefore, explanations which stress these elements can motivate the tutee to keep trying: "That test was a hard one: there was no way you could've known the answer to number 4 [external], but you'll catch up and be all set for the finals [internal]." Notice that even by assigning the problem to temporary or unstable external causes, the tutor does not erase the tutee's responsibility to work and improve. However, the value assigned to external variables is as important as is the value given to internal variables.

COUNSELING APPROACHES

Theories of personality also contribute to our understanding of human learning and you will find the educational and counseling applications that flow from them particularly useful while tutoring.

Rogerian Psychology

Nondirective Listening Dr. Carl Rogers first became known for client-centered nondirective therapy—an approach which encouraged clients (no longer referred to as patients) to assume responsibility for their own growth, to be assertive and to find their own authentic direction. For Rogers, the most important skill the counselor could master was listening.

There is a reciprocal relationship between understanding and listening: the better a listener you are, the more understanding you are likely to gain; the greater understanding you show, the likelier it is that you will hear "more"—both because you are more receptive and because the speaker, in your case, the tutee, feels freer to transmit important messages to you. Rogers believed it was critical to establish a nonjudgmental atmosphere in which confidence, trust, and ease was possible—and that these qualities would, in turn, nurture growth. In what Rogers called nondirective listening, you establish *empathy* with the speaker: you listen *with* the person—hearing what is said from his or her point of view—and come to an understanding of what the speaker means.

Reflecting From Rogers' point of view nondirective listening can only be conveyed through *feedback*, the series of responses—verbal and nonverbal—you make to the speaker. Paradoxically, then, your first responsibility as a listener is to communicate or "reflect" exactly what you have heard so that you and the speaker know that what you heard is what he or she meant to convey. If your tutee said: "I just can't seem to do those dosages for my pharmaceutical course," you might respond: "You're having a hard time working out the percentages" (which is how one determines dosages). While the original statement in this example may seem obvious, and the response superfluous, communication—making oneself understood and feeling understood—is usually both more difficult and complex. As a tutor-counselor, you will have to build on the basic message, and so you must be sure that you have a proper foundation. You do this by checking the original message and paraphrasing it. (As you may recall from chapter 4, paraphrase was listed as a powerful technique for reflecting student learning; here we are focusing on it as a response to your tutee's statements as expression rather than information.) Paraphrase in this context is a response to a person's emotional rather than academic needs.

When you listen with empathy you do not merely repeat the words of the speaker; you must also demonstrate that you understand the feeling or idea behind the statement or the facts. So when a student mumbles: "I didn't do the math assignment you gave me because I failed the test yesterday," you might say: "You were so discouraged by failing the test you didn't bother preparing." Or, "You thought it was pointless to work on the stuff when you'd already flunked the exam." And be sure to notice the tutee's nonverbal cues as well: getting the message also involves interpreting the grimace on a student's face, the shrug of someone's shoulders, the rising pitch of a voice.

CLASS PROJECT 3

Form into groups and practice nondirective listening and reflecting skills by acting out the passages below; do this in stages, or have one person in the group be responsible for each element:*
  a. first, identify the feeling(s)
  b. then, identify the problem
  c. then, note the nonverbal cues
  d. finally, paraphrase the whole message, indicating you have heard "between the lines."

(The actor may want to ease into the statement with some introductory material or to use additional gestures.) The observers should watch for these cues. If you have access to the proper equipment, you might like an audio- or videotape of this exercise; otherwise a student recorder should be responsible for keeping the responses for later discussion.

  Aw, man, (slapping paper down on desk) *I ain't never gonna get this right. It be so easy when I say it but when I gotta write it down* (tipping chair back on its legs while pushing away from desk with hands) *it's a whole other thing.*

  (Head bent with hair practically hiding student's face and left hand cramped over paper hurriedly writing corrections) *When I was taking the test I forgot to check the figures. It's perfectly obvious now, but meanwhile I lost all that credit.*

  I don't understand why we have to be responsible for knowing all these dates (whisking head from side to side). *Who cares if it was 1723 or 1727–or even 1827?*

  Look! (Holding out paper and beaming) *It worked! I can't believe that I didn't have one grammar mistake–not even a run-on.*

  (Whining) *But she asked for our opinion on this essay, and now,* (pitch rising, student moves up to edge of seat and looks away from tutor to comments on paper, posture now contorted) *she says it's not good enough.*

---

*The strategy for this exercise and the discussion in the section which follows has been adapted from the counseling theory of Dermod McDermott based on a workshop he gave for trainers of peer counselors at the College of New Rochelle in the Summer of 1980. See also his *Peer Consultation: The Art of Friends Helping Friends* (New York: Full Circle Associates, 1978).

Courtesy Mark Dandelske

(Crying and holding book clenched to chest) *It was an open book test but I could have had 10 of these* (holding book out at arms' length), *and it wouldn't've helped.*

At first I think I understand the reading–I work with computers all day long–but then (hesitates) *the language is so abstract and suddenly I'm lost.*

(Comes in looking distracted, carrying a big load of books which are dropped on the floor with a heavy thud) *I just don't know how I'm going to get through the course. I can't see how the teacher expects me to solve binomial equations when I've never even had basic algebra.*

Reflecting involves more than just clarifying and paraphrasing. We also hypothesize about what a statement means—not only what is "between the lines" but behind the message as well. Recall the earlier example of the student who failed the math exam and didn't do the tutoring assignment:

STUDENT: I didn't do my math because I failed the test.
TUTOR: You were so discouraged about failing the test you didn't bother preparing (*identification of feeling/paraphrase*). (*Adding*), Were

you so angry with yourself for failing that you had no energy left to do the homework?

Here the tutor-counselor forms a hypothesis. And by phrasing the hypothesis as a question, the tutor leaves the tutee free to disagree with it. In this way, reflecting not only makes tutees feel understood but can help them to understand the implications of what they say, and to examine their real motives. For they may be so upset or angry that they may not make the connection between their thoughts and their actions without the aid of your response.

To demonstrate and integrate the techniques and skills we have been discussing, let's review one of the statements in the last class project:

> Tutee (comes in looking distracted, carrying a big load of books which are dropped on the floor with a heavy thud): *I just don't know how I'm going to get through the course. I can't see how the teacher expects me to solve the binomial equations when I've never even had basic algebra.*

Possible responses would include the following components:

identification of tutee's feeling(s):	worry, frustration, resentment, anger, panic, desperation
identification of problem:	math concepts necessary for solution of chemistry problems (prerequisite)
paraphrase:	"You must be feeling overwhelmed; it's tricky trying to do the homework and get the math at the same time carrying a full-time load. And to top it off you're feeling angry that the teacher's not very sympathetic to your problem."

Now add a tentative interpretation:

Paraphrase plus hypothesis:	"I guess you think it's pretty unfair to be held responsible for something you didn't know you'd have to know."

The response might then be:

Tutee:	"You're not kidding. There are times I feel like a juggler tossing one too many oranges. But that's not really the teacher's fault—she doesn't even know that I don't have the math requirement. I guess I should have gotten a better idea about the course before I registered for it."

By way of hypothesis, you *might* have said: "You seem to blame your problems on other people all the time: it's not the teacher's fault you don't know the math." This response would have offered a psychological interpretation about *why* the person feels a certain way. With the preferred former response, however, you left your tutee free to explore his or her feelings and to claim responsibility—and in the process, to redeem the instructor in his or her *own* way.

CLASS PROJECT 4

1. On your own, record your responses to the following tutee statements, identifying the problem, the feeling, and paraphrasing the message. Then form into groups, and have two students play the roles of tutor and student, while the rest of you act as observers. One observer should focus on the tutee's nonverbal responses, another on those of the tutor. A third observer should focus on the reflections offered in response to the following statements. Those roleplaying the tutors are responsible for adding a hypothesis. "Tutees" should discuss whether or not they felt understood. Group work should focus on describing and evaluating the process. The recorder should be prepared to share the results of your discussion with the class.

> *We've only got a week to do this and I've got a test in chem. and a report in psych. both due on Wednesday—and you want me to do an outline and a first draft!*

> *I'll never get this: I was never good at formulas—even for my own kids' food. (Laughs.) And as soon as my kids started bringing home science work my husband took over the tutoring in our house.*

> *I thought philosophy would be an easy course—but he's asking us to talk about what we think and I don't like a course that's so personal.*

> *I took this course because I thought it would be related to my major, but you wouldn't know it was psych—this chapter is all about the eye; it's not helping me understand anything about people or society.*

> *All she said was to write about any topic in a philosophic way . . . . She said we should do reading . . . from the newspaper . . . . and books, too. Then philosophize . . . .*

2. Form into groups. Have two students talk for three minutes about another class. A third student should then reflect on what was said. After that, the students should express their feelings about the reflection. (Did the two students who first talked feel the third student reflected accurately? How did the third student feel about reflecting?) A fourth person may act as a recorder, providing a written *description* of the interchange. This description should also follow the guidelines for the reflecting *process* (Class Project 3), identifying feelings, problems and paraphrasing messages. The entire group should then be responsible for adding an hypothesis.

LAB APPLICATION

Return to some of the transcripts you have been keeping in your journal and analyse the dialogues according to the criteria developed so far in this chapter.

Transactional Analysis

Transactional analysis is founded on the assumption that within each person there are three possible ego states: Parent, Child, and Adult. Formulated by Eric Berne, the theory says that we act according to which of the three states controls our ego at any given time. The Parent can be the punitive adult who scolds and tells us what we should and shouldn't do; or the Parent can be overprotective, discouraging independent action on our part. Either way, guilt is an inevitable by-product. The Child is the irresponsible and insecure individual who either has little ability to put off gratification or wants to please adults and works hard at trying to avoid their displeasure. The Adult is the unified ego—realistic, mature, capable of balancing the other two ego states, all three of which are present in us. While some criticize this theory as an over-simplified view of human behavior, often tutors have found transactional analysis a helpful tool to understand their tutees' and their own actions.

As a tutor you are apt to assume the Parent state (probably because you've seen so many teachers and parents act like Parents) even though this state is a negative one in terms of your tutee's needs. For by acting the Parent, you may seem to encourage a Child response in your tutee and the dependency and passivity or the rebellion that go with it—none of which is conducive to learning. Because so many students have become conditioned to play the Child in school settings, you may find considerable pressure to play the Parental role. And your tutee may assume either a Child or (if an older student) Parent role regardless of your best intentions.

Expect that some of your tutees may experience discomfort about collaborative learning since it is based on an unauthoritarian model that might be new to them. Give them time to adjust, and don't be too critical of yourself if you sometimes get trapped into playing Parent. If the entrapment continues interfering with the tutorial session, tell your tutee what you think is going on and how you feel about it. And if both you and your tutee are aware of these states, you can work towards an Adult/Adult transaction, the most healthy and productive relationship of all because it reflects mutual respect and responsibility.

CLASS PROJECT 5

1. On your own, identify and analyze the transactions below. Then form into groups to discuss your answers. Finally, take turns roleplaying more constructive transactions, where appropriate, with the observers discussing the effectiveness of the new transactions (and replaying transactions where necessary). Have a recorder transcribe the transactions and conclusions you reach about them for class discussion.

TUTOR: You didn't do that right.

TUTEE: I'm sorry; I really wasn't listening.

TUTOR: Well, you shouldn't get distracted. We don't have all that much time.

TUTEE: Well, I don't care if I fail.
TUTOR: If you do, you'll just have wasted my time.
TUTEE: It's not "wasted"—you get paid to tutor.

TUTEE: Please do this example for me. I just don't have time and I need it for tomorrow.
TUTOR: Well, alright—just this once.

TUTOR: Why don't we go over your paper?
TUTEE: I didn't bring it with me.
TUTOR: Well, then, maybe, we can look at your next assignment.
TUTEE: I forgot my notebook.

2. In your group, share a transaction that took place between you and your tutee which troubled you. Have two other members of the group play more constructive, alternative transactions. The recorder for this exercise should summarize what your group learned from the discussion.

LAB APPLICATION

Review the transcripts in your journal. Analyze some of the dialogues to determine what sort of transaction took place. Be prepared to discuss one of these with your group.

Acceptance Parent–Child transactions very often reflect the feelings of worthlessness those participating in them might have. Dignity is one of the first things to go when someone is doing poorly academically, and tutors should be aware, at all times, of possible threats to a tutee's self-esteem. Bresnick's case study about Edward (p. 61) is sensitive to just this issue. While Edward is at first rebellious, he becomes more open to learning from his tutor after he realizes that he is accepted by her. Bresnick demonstrates that the alternatives to Parent-Child transactions are those in which there is mutual respect.

Lack of self-acceptance is also revealed, according to Berne's construct, in child-like expressions of incapacity, as when your trustee says, "I guess I'm just not good in languages." In such an instance, moreover, it is both easy and tempting to say "That's ridiculous," or "Don't be stupid." These comments, however well-intended, are nonetheless parental responses which invalidate your tutee's feeling. An adult transaction might try to locate a rational way to alleviate the despair: "Let's look at that test again and analyze why you did so badly." Another way to encourage adult responses is to involve your tutees actively in all steps of the decision-making process.

There are many ways of establishing acceptance. Earlier, we mentioned your tutee's nonverbal responses as cues to his or her feelings. But you, too, communicate nonverbally. For example, how you say things is important. *Pitch, tone,* and *pace* are as much a part of your response as words. A high pitch can communicate nervous concern and negate your effort to help your tutee work calmly; a sarcastic tone can imply you doubt the tutee can do the work. Mumbling or talking quickly may mean you don't care whether or not your tutee understands you. And if you talk so fast that your tutees do not get a chance to put in a word, you communicate the real message soon enough, which is (a parental) one of not really being interested in what they have to say. Also, you won't find out what your tutees do or don't know.

Other nonverbal responses include the way you look (or don't look) at the tutee, your smile, which not only reinforces a correct answer but encourages someone to continue an explanation, and your hand gestures, which may express annoyance or boredom (watch those twiddling pencils) or show support and understanding. And remember, sitting behind a desk may make you feel protected and powerful (a Parent) but it can make your tutee feel exposed and vulnerable (the Child).

Don't forget that your silence also speaks: it may be disapproving or it may be attentive. Silence is difficult to maintain and can be awkward in most social situations: in tutoring, however, there are good reasons for keeping quiet. Because tutees are often insecure about and/or unfamiliar with the material, they need time to think about what you've said and to formulate responses. Silences give speakers a time in which they can listen to themselves. Moreover, tutee silence often signals that creative work is going on beneath the surface. Students may be attending to the self-feedback that enables them to hear their own errors and correct themselves. Finally, giving tutees time to initiate interchanges will help them feel they have something worthwhile to say.

CLASS PROJECT 6

Write about a situation in which you did or did not feel accepted. If negative, analyze what could have been done by the other person(s) to make you feel more accepted. If positive, analyze what the person(s) did to make you feel accepted. Be prepared to discuss this in your group and to record your collective conclusions.

Reassurance Reassurance is a way of letting tutees know they have done good work and are capable of doing good work in the future. This affirmation will help them to be hopeful and therefore more motivated to live up to their own positive self-expectations.

When you give your tutees reassurance about the progress they're making, you give them feedback that helps to reduce their anxiety, which is often the major obstacle to their performing well. But to be able to deal with their anxiety, your tutees must be allowed to express their fears. Then, once their fears are out in the open, you can help your tutee to address them rationally, and to alleviate them to some extent. You can discuss the fact that many others are having difficulty, and that having problems with the subject is quite normal. You can even use your own experiences to show your tutees that they are not alone in what they are going through.

You may share your own past difficulties with the subject, as does the tutor in the following exchange:

> TUTEE: Look, I failed this course once already. I must be stupid or somethin'.
>
> TUTOR: You know, I actually flunked my first physics course. Boy, was I depressed, but my high school counselor made me take it again. And, I dunno, the second time it just clicked. But lemme tell you, man, I was scared goin' back into that teacher's classroom.
>
> TUTEE: Yeah . . . , you mean you really flunked the course. Gee, I know it sounds terrible, but that makes me feel a whole lot better.

You may also share personal experiences unrelated to school, in which you felt like a failure, or were frustrated and disappointed in yourself.

Reviewing your tutees' strengths on a regular basis will do wonders for their self-confidence. Share with them any favorable prognosis you have about their work so far and be optimistic about the probable improvement: this may give them the extra boost to succeed. In other ways stress the positive. Even talking about weaknesses can be done constructively, in terms of what can and should be done about them.

Validating your students' *potential* is probably the single most important means you have for reassuring your tutees. And since all of us have talents, capacities, or energies that we have not fully tapped into we need help sometimes, in "getting in touch" with the best qualities within ourselves; you as a tutor-counselor can help your tutees to recognize their worth. Such validation helps your tutees see their academic weaknesses in perspective, that is in relationship to their other abilities. Here is an example of what we've been discussing:

> TUTOR: You know, if you'd practice solving those problems out loud— maybe with your roommate or another partner from class—you could be really good at them.
>
> TUTEE: O, yeah, well, you know, I don't like to talk much. Besides, I don't know the work so well, and I'm behind and they wouldn't want to study with me.
>
> TUTOR: Gee, that's funny. If all those things are true, how come I like working with you?—You know, you ask very good questions and you're a good listener and that makes other people feel good about themselves.
>
> TUTEE: You think so? I didn't think people cared about that—my listening, I mean.

CLASS PROJECT 7

In your group write and/or roleplay a scenario in which your tutee is discouraged because of something happening in the course. Note ways the tutor is accepting and reassuring. Use "What to Look for in Groups" (p. 36) to guide your process activity.

LAB APPLICATION

Try to use accepting and reassuring techniques consciously with your tutee and note in your log any improvements in your relationship or problems that you may have using these techniques.

Confrontation Confrontation means facing something. For example, in tutoring, you will sometimes have to confront a student to motivate him or her by pointing out discrepancies between what a tutee said and did. You might say: "You claim you're no good in languages; how come you pulled a B in your last course?" The application of this skill can help tutees to see what they are doing well, or what they can do, better than they themselves might perceive. Yet confrontations often deal with "negative" or unpleasant aspects of behavior like your tutees' continual lateness or lack of interest in tutoring. Therefore, confronting the student may involve a hostile, seemingly aggressive exchange, and one which our society often considers somewhat unacceptable. No surprise, then, that we are often tempted to avoid confrontation wherever possible. You may remember in "Maria: A Case Study" the difficulty that Retamar had in facing up to Maria (p. 59). It was an excellent example of how difficult it is to confront, and Retamar is able to "confront" that issue in her own assessment. To a large extent, your ability to confront your tutee will depend on your own personal style and how comfortable you feel with the tutee.

Confrontation can be done in a number of ways. It can take place directly or indirectly. It can also be done with humor and by using paradox. Often it will involve an hypothesis, one that you can pose tentatively to check out with your tutee. Notice in the following example how the tutor is careful to point out contradictions and disparities, using these as a basis for the hypothesis:

TUTOR: I'm confused. First you said that you thought the instructor was right about the paper needing to be rewritten. Then you said that you shouldn't have to rewrite the paper. (*confrontation*) Are you suddenly becoming lazy? (*hypothesis*)

Here is another:

TUTEE: I just can't do these problems and I'll fail if I don't hand them in.
TUTOR: Well, you keep saying you don't want to fail the course and then you tell me that you never have time to study for the course. Which do you really mean?

In this last exchange a number of possibilities might evolve: the tutee may not be aware of the connection between possibly failing and not studying; the tutee may want to pass the course *and* not want to do the work necessary and so may "mean" both; the tutee may be avoiding having to deal with the equally unpleasant realities of either dropping or failing the course or giving up some other responsibilities or pleasures in order to complete the course successfully. In any of these possibilities, however, the tutor's willingness to "work through" the confrontation can help direct him or her toward productive thought and action.

CLASS PROJECT 8

1. Form into groups and discuss some confrontational situations you've been in, both as the person confronted and as the person confronting. Discuss the effects and whether or not they were positive and constructive.

2. Here are some confrontational statements. Someone in the group should assume the voice of the speaker while another group member replies. Other members may offer alternative solutions to the dialogue. One observer should be responsible for noting nonverbal responses, another for recording verbal ones. The group should reflect on the relationship between the verbal and nonverbal responses in the discussion that follows:

You say you really care about my studies and you like my going to school, but you're always saying how we never go out anymore.

It's really hard for me to talk about my feelings but I guess I want you to know that I really like you.

Yeah, I'm really interested. Mmmm . . . uh-huh . . . yes, honey . . . I'm sorry—what'd you say? . . . Of course, I am.

Boy, if that's friendship, I'd hate to see what you do with your enemies.

You always make me feel good. You praise me in public and in private. But I haven't gotten a merit increase in three years.

3. Discuss a situation with your group that you have not "confronted" and gather suggestions about how to confront it. (You may wish to develop a scenario and roleplay the confrontation.)

Afterwards, jot down your response to this discussion in your journal. How did it make you feel? Are you more or less willing to risk confrontation with the actual person or persons involved?

A WORD OF CAUTION ABOUT COUNSELING

All the theories we have been discussing presume that while your students may have certain problems that interfere with or stem from learning, they are normal problems which we all of us experience to some extent in different spheres of our lives. We have provided the information to give you insight into these normal processes, and practice in techniques which facilitate tutoring and learning. However, this chapter should not be used as a mandate to establish therapeutic treatment with your tutee. Further, there are some students who do suffer from severe emotional disturbances and you should not be misled into thinking that you are prepared to cope with such people. Indeed some psychological problems are so complex that you may do great harm if you attempt to treat them.

Your primary responsibility is as a tutor. In general, most of your discussion in the tutorial should center on academic work: if the student is so troubled, erratic, or anti-social that you and the tutee cannot work together, then you should be prepared to refer him or her to someone trained to do counseling. (Refer to the glossary on tutoring problems in chapter 7, and to the policies and procedures established in your tutorial program.)

SELF-UNDERSTANDING

Tutoring is an intimate interpersonal relationship and, as such, demands a great deal of honesty and self-awareness on the part of tutor and tutee.

The Role of Assertiveness

Perhaps the most challenging and difficult part of self-understanding will be the feelings of hurt, passivity, anger, and aggression that you will experience within the tutorial relationship. Many counselors talk of "owning" feelings. Partly this means acknowledging them to yourself. This self-awareness is not always so easy to come by; yet in the complex realm of emotion, sorting out exactly what you do feel is often a triumphantly cathartic experience and its own reward.

The danger in not being self-aware is that unacknowledged or even unexpressed feelings will take on an independent life, doing damage to yourself and others. For example, you may feel miffed or even hostile to a student, but if you express this by being sullen with your tutee when he or she has come to trust you and to expect your confidence, you are violating the tutor-counseling relationship. And when you remain distracted by or obsessed with some minor slight, you are probably diverting energies that could be better spent planning your tutorial session.

Owning your feelings also refers to the ways in which you express them to others. Too often *any* expression is seen as an act of aggression toward others rather than an assertion of the self. Yet it is important to be able to defend and protect yourself. The language you use can help you feel more comfortable in doing so. When you are angry, the difference between an assertion of anger and hostile aggression lies in the different ways you express your feelings. Let's say you feel disturbed by your tutee's chronic lateness. Your statement might be one of the following:

I feel angry with you because you're always coming late to sessions.

When you come late, I get angry.

You make me angry.

The last statement heaps blame and guilt onto the tutee, and may fan hostile responses in return. It makes that person responsible for your emotion and can engender a defensive reaction rather than a constructive resolution. The first statement is better because it allows you to use the skill you've gained in confronting your tutee to meet your own needs. However, it implies that you will remain angry for a while, even if the student tries to be more punctual. The second sentence is the best, because it makes your anger totally contingent on the tutee's *actions*. If the tutee comes to sessions on time, you clearly won't be angry anymore.

One final note: while owning your feelings may make you braver, more consistent, and timely in your responses, allowing you to make demands or refuse them, it offers no guarantee that you will get what you want or that things will be the way you would like them to be.

CLASS PROJECT 9

1. In your groups brainstorm school-related situations you find most easy and most difficult to assert yourself in. List these and then rank order them 10 units apart, 0 for most comfortable, 100 for most uncomfortable.*
   a. Share your conclusions with the class and see if, as a class, you can come up with a collective list of difficult situations.
   b. Write an essay or extended journal entry about what you learned about yourself in doing the first part of this exercise.
2. a. In your group, take turns acting out dramatic situations based on the following tasks:†
   1) refuse an object (*e.g.*, a book someone is throwing away)
   2) request something (*e.g.*, a special book-order at a bookstore)
   3) refuse an interaction (*e.g.*, call from a cable tv company)
   4) request an interaction (*e.g.*, asking a question of a lecturer)
   b. Discuss how well feelings were expressed in each dramatization.
3. Choose two members of each group to act out the following tasks in sequence. Refuse to lend ten dollars to:
   a. an acquaintance when you don't have it
   b. a friend when you don't have it

---

*This exercise is based on the Subjective Units of Disturbance (SUDS) Scale developed by J. Wolpe and A. A. Lazarus, *Behavior Therapy Techniques: A Guide to the Treatment of Neuroses* (New York: Pergamon Press, 1966), p. 125.

†This exercise and the one following are taken from John V. Flowers, "Simulation and Roleplaying Methods," in *Helping People Change: A Textbook of Methods*, eds. Arnold P. Goldstein and Frederick H. Kanfer (New York: Pergamon Press, 1975), pp. 159–194.

    c. an acquaintance when you do
    d. a friend when you do
Compare the outcomes with the entire class.

LAB APPLICATIONS

1. In your journal, describe a tutorial situation in which you have difficulty asserting yourself and what you are doing or plan to do about it.

2. In one of your sessions, try an assertive act that requires refusing to do something, or requesting something. (They should be in order of increasing difficulty for you.) Record and reflect on your efforts and their consequences in your journal.

Other Sources for Self-Discovery

Here are some other methods whereby you, the tutor, can understand your feelings about the tutoring process and thus be as honest and open as possible about your own actions and motivations.

Supervision Supervision is part of many helping professions. It is a systematic process by which someone with considerable experience guides someone who is in training. By being in this class or program, you are "in supervision," with your instructor or lab director acting as supervisor. Your log, your session notes, and your case study, as well as videotaped sessions, actual observations, roleplaying (and any other writings you or your supervisor have done about your tutoring) are all records which can help your supervisor understand you and can help you to understand yourself.

Videotaped Sessions Supervision may also involve actual observation of your tutoring and it may require videotaping your tutoring sessions. These videotaped sessions can serve as an important tool for self-discovery if you establish goals for yourself and decide what you'd like to focus on, what specific areas you'd like to improve. You might use one session, for instance, to see how well you're responding with and to non-verbal messages; another to see whether or not you followed your session plan, when and why you departed from it, and whether or not it turned out the way you expected it to. And don't worry if you get nervous in front of an observer or before the camera. It's a common feeling which tends to diminish with time.

Journal The journal, or log, can also be used as a means of self-analysis. (See chapter 1.) Work on being as honest as possible in the log. Do not be

Research shows that videotaping provides invaluable visual feedback to participants. The tape offers a record, and often, people "see" discrepancies between what they say and what they do. As a counseling or training tool, videotaping allows people to gain insight and understanding necessary to personal and professional development. (Photograph courtesy of Anne Helena Dolen and the College of New Rochelle.)

satisfied with easy answers. Probe beneath the surface to explore problems and analyze successes. Read back over previous sessions to evaluate your performance as a tutor.

Case Study The case study is organized in such a way as to offer you a place to analyze your tutoring ability and your feelings; it can serve as a true evaluation, something you can learn and change from rather than as a compendium of faults and failures. (See chapter 2.)

Self-Evaluation The final chapter of this book offers a summary form in which you can review and assess both what you've learned and how well you applied your knowledge.

Roleplaying This strategy very actively involves you in the process of your self-assessment. You've already used a variety of roleplaying techniques within your groups to become more comfortable with new techniques and skills. We'll be talking about and using it even more extensively in the following chapter as a tool for your training and growth, especially in handling and solving special problems.

Class or Tutor Meetings You should use group discussions with fellow tutors as a means of sharing feelings about being a tutor. If you are honest (and it might be difficult to admit fears of failure or insecurity) you will probably discover common problems and concerns. Learn from your colleagues; they are your best resources and guides. Get to know them outside of official meetings. Informal get-togethers can be a time for priceless feedback and validation.

CLASS PROJECT 10

1. Make a list of the personal qualities which are helping or hindering you from being a good tutor. What are you doing to change things? Either discuss this with your class and your supervisor or write about it in your log.

2. Discuss with your class group how well everyone is using the self-analysis mechanisms and what the major barriers are to self-understanding.

READING 12

Carl Rogers' theories on psychology, counseling, and education have had a profound effect on all three fields. He integrates these fields in his writing; counseling skills facilitate learning and learning techniques enhance personal growth, and both of these are grounded in a consistent theory of human personality. As we see in the following excerpt, Rogers refuses to separate formal education from the development of the whole person. In this reading (published in both Humanizing Education *and* Freedom to Learn) *Rogers outlines the role of the facilitator.*

READING QUESTIONS

1. What is "realness" and why may it be difficult to be "real"?

2. Rogers represents two views of human beings and two kinds of teachers. What are they? Which do you view as necessary to the educational process? Why?

3. What logical or experimental problems do you see in the "evidence" Rogers presents initially to support his thesis? What evidence is presented later in the text to support Rogers' arguments. What other (theoretical) evidence could be used to support Rogers' point of view? How?

4. Is there any contradiction between Rogers' stated philosophy and the attitudes he expresses toward teachers? How does this discrepancy affect your judgment of his ideas?

5. Rogers has been a controversial figure since *Counseling and Psychotherapy*, his first book, revolutionized American psychology when it was published in 1942. Who (types or categories rather than individuals) might be some of Rogers' opponents and what might they say?

---

12 | FREEDOM TO LEARN

Carl Rogers

QUALITIES WHICH FACILITATE LEARNING

What are these qualities, these attitudes, which facilitate learning? Let me describe them very briefly, drawing illustrations from the teaching field.

Realness in the Facilitator of Learning

Perhaps the most basic of these essential attitudes is realness or genuineness. When the facilitator is a real person, being what he is, entering into a relationship with the learner without presenting a front or a facade, he is much more likely to be effective. This means that the feelings which he is experiencing are available to him, available to his awareness, that he is able to live these feelings, be them, and able to communicate them if appropriate. It means that he comes into a direct personal encounter with the learner, meeting him on a person-to-person basis. It means that he is *being* himself, not denying himself.

Seen from this point of view it is suggested that the teacher can be a real person in his relationship with his students. He can be enthusiastic, he can be bored, he can be interested in students, he can be angry, he can be sensitive and sympathetic. Because he accepts these feelings as his own he has no need to impose them on his students. He can like or dislike a student product without implying that it is objectively good or bad or that the student is good or bad. He is simply expressing a feeling for the product, a feeling which exists within himself. Thus, he is a person to his students, not a faceless embodiment of a curricular requirement nor a sterile tube through which knowledge is passed from one generation to the next.

It is obvious that this attitudinal set, found to be effective in psychotherapy, is sharply in contrast with the tendency of most teachers to show themselves to their pupils simply as roles. It is quite customary for teachers rather consciously to put on a mask, the role, the facade, of being a teacher, and to wear this facade all day removing it only when they have left the school at night.

But not all teachers are like this. Take Sylvia Ashton-Warner, who took resistant, supposedly slow-learning primary school Maori children in New Zealand, and let them develop their own reading vocabulary. Each child could request one word—whatever word he wished—each day, and she would print it on a card and give it to him. "Kiss," "ghost," "bomb," "tiger," "fight," "love," "daddy"—these are samples. Soon they were building sentences, which they could also keep. "He'll get a licking." "Pussy's frightened." The children simply never forgot these self-initiated learnings. But it is not my purpose to tell you of her methods. I want instead to give you a glimpse of her attitude, of her passionate realness which must have been as evident to her tiny pupils as to her readers. An editor asked her some questions and she responded: "A few cool facts you asked me for . . . I don't know that there's a cool fact in me, or anything else cool for that matter, on this particular subject. I've got only hot long facts on the matter of Creative Teaching, scorching both the page and me" (Ashton-Warner, 1963, p. 26).

Here is no sterile facade. Here is a vital *person*, with convictions, with feelings. It is her transparent realness which was, I am sure, one of the elements that made her an exciting facilitator of learning. She doesn't fit into some neat educational formula. She is, and students grow by being in contact with someone who really and openly *is*.

Take another very different person, Barbara Shiel, whose exciting work in facilitating learning in sixth graders [was] described earlier [in the book]. She gave her pupils a great deal of responsible freedom, and I will mention some of the reactions of her students later. But here is an example of the way she shared herself with her pupils—not just sharing feelings of sweetness and light, but anger and frustration. She had made art materials freely available, and students often used these in creative ways, but the room frequently looked like a picture of chaos. Here is her report of her feelings and what she did with them.

> I find it maddening to live with the mess—with a capital M! No one seems to care except me. Finally, one day I told the children . . . that I am a neat, orderly person by nature and that the mess was driving me to distraction. Did they have a solution? It was suggested there were some volunteers who could clean up . . . I said it didn't seem fair to me to have the same people clean up all the time for others—but it would solve it for me. "Well, some people like to clean," they replied. So that's the way it is (Shiel, 1966).

I hope this example puts some lively meaning into the phrases I used earlier, that the facilitator "is able to live these feelings, be them, and able to communicate them if appropriate." I have chosen an example of negative feelings, because I think it is more difficult for most of us to visualize what this would mean. In this instance, Miss Shiel is taking the risk of being transparent in her angry frustrations about the mess. And what happens? The same thing which, in my experience, nearly always happens. These young people accept and respect her feelings, take them into account, and work out a novel solution which none of us, I believe, would have suggested. Miss Shiel wisely comments, "I used to get upset and feel guilty when I became angry. I finally realized the children could accept *my* feelings too. And it is important for them to know when they've 'pushed me.' I have my limits, too" (Shiel, 1966).

Just to show that positive feelings, when they are real, are equally effective, let me quote briefly a college student's reaction, in a different course:

> . . . Your sense of humor in the class was cheering; we all felt relaxed because you showed us your human self, not a mechanical teacher image. I feel as if I have more understanding and faith in my teachers now . . . . I feel closer to the students too. . . .

Another says:

> . . . You conducted the class on a personal level and therefore in my mind I was able to formulate a picture of you as a person and not as merely a walking textbook.

Another student in the same course:

> . . . It wasn't as if there was a teacher in the class, but rather someone whom we could trust and identify as a "sharer." You were so perceptive and sensitive to our thoughts, and this made it all the more "authentic" for me. It was an "authentic" *experience*, not just a class (Bull, 1966).

I trust I am making it clear that to be real is not always easy, nor is it achieved all at once, but it is basic to the person who wants to become that revolutionary individual, a facilitator of learning.

Prizing, Acceptance, Trust

There is another attitude which stands out in those who are successful in facilitating learning. I have observed this attitude. I have experienced it. Yet, it is hard to know what term to put to it so I shall use several. I think of it as prizing the learner, prizing his feelings, his opinions, his person. It is a caring for the learner, but a non-possessive caring. It is an acceptance of this other individual as a separate person, having worth in his own right. It is a basic trust—a belief that this other person is somehow fundamentally trustworthy. Whether we call it prizing, acceptance, trust, or by some other term, it shows up in a variety of observable ways. The facilitator who has a considerable degree of this attitude can be fully acceptant of the fear and hesitation of the student as he approaches a new problem as well as acceptant of the pupil's satisfaction in achievement. Such a teacher can accept the student's occasional apathy, his erratic desires to explore by-roads of knowledge, as well as his disciplined efforts to achieve major goals. He can accept personal feelings which both disturb and promote learning—rivalry with a sibling, hatred of authority, concern about personal adequacy. What we are describing is a prizing of the learner as an imperfect human being with many feelings, many potentialities. The facilitator's prizing or acceptance of the learner is an operational expression of his essential confidence and trust in the capacity of the human organism.

I would like to give some examples of this attitude from the classroom situation. Here any teacher statements would be properly suspect, since many of us would like to feel we hold such attitudes, and might have a biased perception of our qualities. But let me indicate how this attitude of prizing, of accepting, of trusting appears to the student who is fortunate enough to experience it.

Here is a statement from a college student in a class with Dr. Morey Appell:

> Your way of being with us is a revelation to me. In your class I feel important, mature, and capable of doing things on my own. I want to think for myself and this need cannot be accomplished through textbooks and lectures alone, but through living. I think you see me as a person with real feelings and needs, an individual. What I say and do are significant expressions from me, and you recognize this (Appell, 1959).

One of Miss Shiel's sixth graders' expresses much more briefly her misspelled appreciation of this attitude: "You are a wounderful teacher period!!!"

College students in a class with Dr. Patricia Bull describe not only these prizing, trusting attitudes, but the effect these have had on their other interactions.

> . . . I feel that I can say things to you that I can't say to other professors. . . . Never before have I been so aware of the other students or their personalities. I have never had so much interaction in a college classroom with my classmates. The climate of the classroom has had a very profound effect on me . . . the free atmosphere for discussion affected me . . . the general atmosphere of a particular session affected me. There have been many times when I have carried the discussion out of the class with me and thought about it for a long time.

> . . . I still feel close to you, as though there were some tacit understanding between us, almost a conspiracy. This adds to the in-class participation on my part because I feel that at least one person in the group will react, even when I am not sure of the others. It does not matter really whether your reaction is positive or negative, it just *IS*. Thank you.

> . . . I appreciate the respect and concern you have for others, including myself. . . . As a result of my experience in class, plus the influence of my readings, I sincerely believe that the student-centered teaching method does provide an ideal framework for learning; not just for the accumulation of facts, but more important, for

learning about ourselves in relation to others . . . When I think back to my shallow awareness in September compared to the depth of my insights now, I know that this course has offered me a learning experience of great value which I couldn't have acquired in any other way.

. . . Very few teachers would attempt this method because they would feel that they would lose the students' respect. On the contrary. You gained our respect, through your ability to speak to us on our level, instead of ten miles above us. With the complete lack of communication we see in this school, it was a wonderful experience to see people listening to each other and really communicating on an adult, intelligent level. More classes should afford us this experience (Bull, 1966).

As you might expect, college students are often suspicious that these seeming attitudes are phony. One of Dr. Bull's students writes:

. . . Rather than observe my classmates for the first few weeks, I concentrated my observations on you, Dr. Bull. I tried to figure out your motivations and purposes. I was convinced that you were a hypocrite. . . . I did change my opinion, however. You are not a hypocrite, by any means. . . . I do wish the course could continue. "Let each become all he is capable of being" . . . (Bull, 1966).

I am sure these examples are more than enough to show that the facilitator who cares, who prizes, who trusts the learner, creates a climate for learning so different from the ordinary classroom that any resemblance is "purely coincidental."

Empathic Understanding

A further element which establishes a climate for self-initiated, experiential learning is empathic understanding. When the teacher has the ability to understand the student's reactions from the inside, has a sensitive awareness of the way the process of education and learning seems *to the student*, then again the likelihood of significant learning is increased.

This kind of understanding is sharply different from the usual evaluative understanding, which follows the pattern of, "I understand what is wrong with you." When there is a sensitive empathy, however, the reaction in the learner follows something of this pattern, "At last someone understands how it feels and seems to be *me* without wanting to analyze me or judge me. Now I can blossom and grow and learn."

This attitude of standing in the other's shoes, of viewing the world through the student's eyes, is almost unheard of in the classroom. One could listen to thousands of ordinary classroom interactions without coming across one instance of clearly communicated, sensitively accurate, empathic understanding. But it has a tremendously releasing effect when it occurs.

Let me take an illustration from Virginia Axline, dealing with a second grade boy. Jay, age 7, has been aggressive, a trouble maker, slow of speech and learning. Because of his "cussing" he was taken to the principal, who paddled him, unknown to Miss Axline. During a free work period, he fashioned a man of clay, very carefully, down to a hat and a handkerchief in his pocket. "Who is that?" asked Miss Axline. "Dunno," replied Jay. "Maybe it is the principal. He has a handkerchief in his pocket like that." Jay glared at the clay figure. "Yes," he said. Then he began to tear the head off and looked up and smiled. Miss Axline said, "You sometimes feel like twisting his head off, don't you? You get so mad at him." Jay tore off one arm, another, then beat the figure to a pulp with his fists. Another boy, with the perception of the young, explained, "Jay is mad at Mr. X because he licked him this noon." "Then you must feel lots better now," Miss Axline commented. Jay grinned and began to rebuild Mr. X. (Adapted from Axline, 1944).

The other examples I have cited also indicate how deeply appreciative students feel when they are simply *understood*—not evaluated, not judged, simply understood from their *own* point of view, not the teacher's. If any teacher set himself the task of endeavoring to make one non-evaluative, acceptant, empathic response per day to a student's demonstrated or verbalized feeling, I believe he would discover the potency of this currently almost non-existent kind of understanding.

WHAT ARE THE BASES OF FACILITATIVE ATTITUDES?

A "Puzzlement"

It is natural that we do not always have the attitudes I have been describing. Some teachers raise the question, "But what if I am *not* feeling empathic, do *not*, at this moment, prize or accept or like my students. What then?" My response is that realness is the most important of the attitudes mentioned, and it is not accidental that this attitude was described first. So if one has little understanding of the student's inner world, and a dislike for his students or their behavior, it is almost certainly more constructive to be real than to be pseudo-empathic, or to put on a facade of caring.

But this is not nearly as simple as it sounds. To be genuine, or honest, or congruent, or real, means to be this way about *oneself*. I cannot be real about another, because I do not *know* what is real for him. I can only tell—if I wish to be truly honest—what is going on in me.

Let me take an example. Early in this chapter I reported Miss Shiel's feelings about the "mess" created by the art work. Essentially she said, "I find it maddening to live with the mess! I'm neat and orderly and it is driving me to distraction." But suppose her feelings had come out somewhat differently, in the disguised way which is much more common in classrooms at all levels. She might have said, "You are the messiest children I've ever seen! You don't care about tidiness or cleanliness. You are just terrible!" This is most definitely *not* an example of genuineness or realness, in the sense in which I am using these terms. There is a profound distinction between the two statements which I should like to spell out.

In the second statement she is telling nothing of herself, sharing none of her feelings. Doubtless the children will *sense* that she is angry, but because children are perceptively shrewd they may be uncertain as to whether she is angry at them, or has just come from an argument with the principal. It has none of the honesty of the first statement in which she tells of her *own* upsetness, of her *own* feeling of being driven to distraction.

Another aspect of the second statement is that it is all made up of judgments or evaluations, and like most judgments, they are all arguable. Are these children messy, or are they simply excited and involved in what they are doing? Are they *all* messy, or are some as disturbed by the chaos as she? Do they care nothing about tidiness, or is it simply that they don't care about it every day? If a group of visitors were coming would their attitude be different? Are they terrible, or simply children? I trust it is evident that when we make judgments they are almost never fully accurate, and hence cause resentment and anger as well as guilt and apprehension. Had she used the second statement the response of the class would have been entirely different.

I am going to some lengths to clarify this point because I have found from experience that to stress the value of being real, of *being* one's feelings, is taken by some as a license to pass judgments on others, to project on others all the feelings which one should be "owning." Nothing could be further from my meaning.

Actually the achievement of realness is most difficult, and even when one wishes to be truly genuine, it occurs but rarely. Certainly it is not simply a matter of the *words* used, and if one is feeling judgmental the use of a verbal formula which sounds like the sharing of feelings will not help. It is just another instance of a facade, of a lack of genuineness. Only slowly can we learn to be truly real. For first of all, one must be close to one's feelings, capable of being aware of them. Then one must be willing to take the risk of sharing them as they are, inside, not disguising them as judgments, or attributing them to other people. This is why I so admire Miss Shiel's sharing of her anger and frustration, without in any way disguising it.

A Trust in the Human Organism

It would be most unlikely that one could hold the three attitudes I have described, or could commit himself to being a facilitator of learning, unless he has come to have a profound trust in the human organism and its potentialities. If I distrust the human being then I *must* cram him with information of my own choosing, lest he go his own mistaken way. But if I trust the capacity of the human individual for developing his own potentiality, then I can provide him with many opportunities and permit him to choose his own way and his own direction in his learning.

It is clear, I believe, that the [four] teachers whose work was described in the preceding [sections] rely basically upon the tendency toward fulfilment, toward actualization, in their students. They are basing their work on the hypothesis that students who are in real contact with problems which are relevant to them wish to learn, want to grow, seek to discover, endeavor to master, desire to create, move toward self-discipline. The teacher is attempting to develop a quality of climate in the classroom, and a quality of personal relationship with his students, which will permit these natural tendencies to come to their fruition.

Living the Uncertainty of Discovery

I believe it should be said that this basically confident view of man, and the attitudes toward students which I have described, do not appear suddenly, in some miraculous manner, in the facilitator of learning. Instead, they come about through taking risks, through *acting* on tentative hypotheses. This is most obvious in the section describing Miss Shiel's work, where, acting on hypotheses of which she is unsure, risking herself uncertainly in new ways of relating to her students, she finds these new views confirmed by what happens in her class. . . . [And,] as for me . . . , I started my career with the firm view that individuals must be manipulated for their own good; I only came to the attitudes I have described, and the trust in the individual which is implicit in them, because I found that these attitudes were so much more potent in producing learning and constructive change. Hence, I believe that it is only by risking himself in these new ways that the teacher can *discover*, for himself, whether or not they are effective, whether or not they are for him.

I will then draw a conclusion, based on the experiences of the several facilitators and their students which have been included up to this point. When a facilitator creates, even to a modest degree, a classroom climate characterized by all that he can achieve of realness, prizing, and empathy; when he trusts the constructive tendency of the individual and the group; then he discovers that he has inaugurated an educational revolution. Learning of a different quality, proceeding at a different pace, with a greater degree of pervasiveness, occurs. Feelings—positive, negative, confused—become a part of the classroom experience. Learning becomes life, and a very vital life at that. The student is on his way, sometimes excitedly, sometimes reluctantly, to becoming a learning, changing being.

THE EVIDENCE

Already I can hear mutterings: "A very pretty picture—very touching. But where is the solid evidence? How do you know?" I would like to turn to this evidence. It is not overwhelming, but it is consistent. It is not perfect, but it is suggestive.

First of all, in the field of psychotherapy, Barrett-Lennard (1962) developed an instrument whereby he could measure these attitudinal qualities: genuineness or congruence, prizing or positive regard, empathy or understanding. This instrument was given to both client and therapist, so that we have the perception of the relationship both by the therapist and by the client whom he is trying to help. To state some of the findings very briefly it may be said that those clients who eventually showed more therapeutic change as measured by various instruments, perceived *more* of the qualities in their relationship with the therapist than did those who eventually showed less change. It is also significant that this difference in perceived relationships was evident as early as the fifth interview, and predicted later change or lack of change in therapy. Furthermore, it was found that the *client's* perception of the relationship, his experience of it, was a better predictor of ultimate outcome than was the perception of the relationship by the therapist. Barrett-Lennard's original study has been amplified and generally confirmed by other studies.

So we may say, cautiously, and with qualifications which would be too cumbersome for the present volume, that if, in therapy, the client perceives his therapist as real and genuine, as one who likes, prizes, and empathically understands him, self-learning and therapeutic change are facilitated.

Now another thread of evidence, this time related more closely to education. Emmerling (1961) found that when high school teachers were asked to identify the problems they regarded as most urgent, they could be divided into two groups. Those who regarded their most serious problems, for example, as "Helping children think for themselves and be independent"; "Getting students to participate"; "Learning new ways of helping students develop their maximum potential"; "Helping students express individual needs and interests" fell into what he called the "open" or "positively oriented" group. When Barrett-Lennard's Relationship Inventory was administered to the students of these teachers, it was found that they were perceived as significantly more real, more acceptant, more empathic than the other group of teachers whom I shall now describe.

The second category of teachers were those who tended to see their most urgent problems in negative terms, and in terms of student deficiencies and inabilities. For them the urgent problems were such as these: "Trying to teach children who don't even have the ability to follow directions"; "Teaching children who lack a desire to learn"; "Students who are not able to do the work required for their grade"; "Getting children to listen." It probably will be no surprise that when the students of these teachers filled out the Relationship Inventory they saw their teachers as exhibiting relatively little genuineness, acceptance, trust, or empathic understanding.

Hence we may say that the teacher whose orientation is toward releasing the student's potential exhibits a high degree of these attitudinal qualities which facilitate learning. The teacher whose orientation is toward shortcomings of his students exhibits much less of these qualities.

A small pilot study by Bills (1961, 1966) extends the significance of these findings. A group of eight teachers were selected, four of them rated as adequate and effective by their superiors, and also showing this more positive orientation to their problems. The other four were rated as inadequate teachers and also had a more negative orientation to their problems, as described above. The students of these teachers were then asked to fill out the Barrett-Lennard Relationship Inventory, giving their perception of their teacher's relationship to them. This made the students very happy. Those who saw their relationship with the teacher as good were happy to describe this relationship. Those who had an unfavorable relationship were pleased to have, for the first time, an opportunity to specify the ways in which the relationship was unsatisfactory.

The more effective teachers were rated higher in every attitude measured by the Inventory: they were seen as more real, as having a higher level of regard for their students, were less conditional or judgmental in their attitudes, showed more empathic understanding. Without going into the details of the study it may be illuminating to mention that the total scores summing up these attitudes vary sharply. For example, the relationships of a group of clients with their therapists, as perceived by the clients, received an average score of 108. The relationship with the four most adequate high school teachers, as seen by their students, received a score of 60. The relationship of the four less adequate teachers received a score of 34. The lowest rated teacher received an average score of 2 from her students on the Relationship Inventory.

This small study certainly suggests that the teacher regarded as effective displays in her attitudes those qualities I have described as facilitative of learning, while the inadequate teacher shows little of these qualities.

A more comprehensive study, by Macdonald and Zaret, studied the recorded interactions of nine teachers with their students. They found that both teacher and student behaviors could be reliably categorized. When teacher behaviors tended to be "open"—clarifying, stimulating, accepting, facilitating—the student responses tended to be "productive"—discovering, exploring, experimenting, synthesizing, deriving implications. When teacher behaviors tended to be "closed"—judging, directing, reproving, ignoring, probing, or priming—the student responses tended to be "reproductive"— parroting, guessing, acquiescing, reproducing facts, reasoning from given or remembered data. The pairing of these two sets of teacher-student behaviors were significantly related (Macdonald & Zaret, 1966). Though they are careful to qualify their findings, it would appear that teachers who are interested in process, and facilitative in their interactions, produce self-initiated and creative responses in their students. Teachers who are interested in evaluation of students produce passive, memorized, "eager to please" responses from their students. This evidence fits in with the thesis I have been presenting.

Approaching the problem from a different angle, Schmuck (1963) has shown that in classrooms where pupils perceive their teachers as understanding them, there is likely to be a more diffuse liking structure among the pupils. This means that where the teacher is empathic, there are not a few students strongly liked and a few strongly disliked, but liking and affection are more evenly diffused throughout the group. In a later study he has shown that among students who are highly involved in their classroom peer group, "significant relationships exist between actual liking status on the one hand and utilization of abilities, attitude toward self, and attitude toward school on the other hand" (1966, pp. 357–358). This seems to lend confirmation to the other evidence by indicating that in an understanding classroom climate where the teacher is more empathic, every student tends to feel liked by all the others, to have a more positive attitude toward himself and toward school. If he is highly involved with his peer group (and this appears probable in such a classroom climate), he also tends to utilize his abilities more fully in his school achievement.

But you may still ask, does the student actually *learn* more where these attitudes are present? Here an interesting study of third graders by Aspy (1965) helps to round out the suggestive evidence. He worked in six third-grade classes. The teachers tape-recorded two full weeks of their interaction with their students in the period devoted to the teaching of reading. These recordings were done two months apart so as to obtain an adequate sampling of the teacher's interactions with her pupils. Four-minute segments of these recordings were randomly selected for rating. Three raters, working independently and "blind," rated each segment for the degree of congruence or genuineness shown by the teacher, the degree of her prizing or unconditional positive regard, and the degree of her empathic understanding.

The Reading Achievement Tests (Stanford Achievement) were used as the criterion. Again, omitting some of the details of a carefully and rigorously controlled study, it may be said that the children in the three classes with the highest degree of the attitudes described above showed a significantly greater gain in reading achievement than those students in the three classes with a lesser degree of these qualities.

So we may say, with a certain degree of assurance, that the attitudes I have endeavored to describe are not only effective in facilitating a deeper learning and understanding of self in a relationship such as psychotherapy, but that these attitudes characterize teachers who are regarded as effective teachers, and that the students of these teachers learn more, even [from] a conventional curriculum, than do students of teachers who are lacking in these attitudes.

References

Appell, M. L. Selected student reactions to student-centered courses. Unpublished manuscript. Terre Haute, Indiana: State University of Ind., 1959.

Appell, M. L. Self-understanding for the guidance counselor. *Personnel & Guidance Journal,* October, 1963, 143–148.

Ashton-Warner, Sylvia. *Teacher.* New York: Simon and Schuster, 1963.

Aspy, D. N. A study of three facilitative conditions and their relationship to the achievement of third grade students. Unpublished doctoral dissertation, University of Kentucky, 1965.

Axline, Virginia M. Morale on the school front. *Journal of Educational Research,* 1944, 521–533.

Barrett-Lennard, G. T. Dimensions of therapist response as causal factors in therapeutic change. *Psychological Monographs,* 1962, 76 (Whole No. 562).

Bills, R. E. Personal correspondence. 1961, 1966.

Bull, Patricia. Student reactions, Fall, 1965. Unpublished manuscript. State University College, Cortland, New York, 1966.

Emmerling, F. C. A study of the relationships between personality characteristics of classroom teachers and pupil perceptions. Unpublished doctoral dissertation, Auburn University, Auburn, Alabama, 1961.

Jackson, P. W. The student's world. Unpublished manuscript. University of Chicago, 1966.

Macdonald, J. B. & Zaret, Esther. A study of openness in classroom interactions. Unpublished manuscript. Marquette University, 1966.

Moon, S. F. Teaching the self. *Improving College and University Teaching, 14,* Autumn, 1966, 213–229.

Rogers, C. R. *On becoming a person.* Boston: Houghton Mifflin, 1961.

Schmuck, R. Some relationships of peer liking patterns in the classroom to pupil attitudes and achievement. *The School Review,* 1963, *71,* 337–359.

Schmuck, R. Some aspects of classroom social climate. *Psychology in the Schools.* 1966, *3,* 59–65.

Shiel, Barbara J. Evaluation: A self-directed curriculum, 1965. Unpublished manuscript, 1966.

READING 13

Task-centered social work and counseling represents a reaction against long-term psychoanalytically oriented practice; more positively, it grows in part out of the work of such theorists as A. H. Maslow and Carl Rogers and others who respected the client's self-defined needs. The method stresses mutual definition of the problem by the counselor and the client with the client taking the lead. The practice is also strongly influenced by behaviorist theory in its focus on the specification of tasks, schedules, and structure.

The case-study below is a model of the task-centered approach: as such it stresses process and summary recording.

It consists of a series of actual interviews conducted between a counselor and a sixth-grader who is 11 years old. Although there are many differences between these interviews and your tutoring sessions, they share a common concern for psychological factors as they interfere with or aid learning.

READING QUESTIONS

1. What are the tasks and why did the caseworker and student decide to focus on the tasks they did? What can you learn from the task orientation (especially as indicated in the fourth interview) of the task-centered model that might be applied to your tutoring?

2. Do any of the techniques used in this model remind you of approaches discussed in this and earlier chapters? For instance, how does a learning "contract" fit with this casework?

3. How does the introduction of other persons in the interviews (Mrs. S., the mother, the stepfather) affect your perspective of the situation?

4. The central character in this case is an 11-year-old child. Do you think her problems are relevant to the traditional college-aged student? to the adult learner?

5. Can we tell how the caseworker feels about her client? Why or why not might the absence of a point of view be valuable to the reader? What might this aspect of the case-study method reflect about the educational goals of social work, counseling, or human services?

6. How does this case study differ from the ones you have looked at so far (Retamar and Bresnick on one hand, [p.58; p.61], Hofsteater's on the other [p.75])?

---

13 | TASK-CENTERED CASEWORK

William J. Reid
School of Social Welfare
SUNY at Albany

PUBLIC SCHOOL
MOTHER, FATHER, 6 SIBLINGS
BLACK, EMPLOYED FATHER

M.
Interview 1
2/16

M. 11 years, is a respondent, referred by her 6th grade teacher Mrs. S. for learning problems (i.e., she is not working up to her potential). M. said that she is having difficulty with math and social studies.

M. and I explored the nature of her difficulty in these subjects. It was determined that in both subject areas she feels that the teachers are moving too fast and that consequently she has difficulty in keeping up with the work. She has asked the math teacher to slow down, but she always speeds up again.

M. enjoys school, likes her work, takes her homework home and does it, is a good reader in her estimation, and gets assistance with her work regularly from her mother.

While M. acknowledged difficulty with math and social studies, the question of whether she wants or needs assistance with this, as well as whether there are any other problems we could work on was explored. She feels that she is capable of working on these subjects by herself and with her mother's assistance. Difficulty in studying and other possible blocks to learning were explored. She knows how to study and does not feel [that] there are any problems at home.

I suggested that it might be a problem, [that] of how much work she is expected to do, and how much she can get done. I suggested that we might talk with the teachers about this, and then, if indicated, some tutoring in math and social studies might help her to better keep up with her work. She feels that she knows how to work, but did discuss a problem in the classroom that is affecting her work. (A girl next to her keeps talking to her. M. has told the girl to keep quiet, but she doesn't.) She does not feel that she instigates the talking, and has talked with Mrs. S. about this before, and is going to ask to have her seat moved.

M. sees the problem with social studies as due to the talking and that she needs to do more work at home. She needs to work more at home on her math as well, but doesn't think that she needs tutoring.

Since she is concerned about doing better, because she is afraid that she might fail, which she has never done before, I suggested that we talk with Mrs. S. about what she sees M.'s problems to be, because maybe she sees something different than we do, and also talk with her about M.'s concern with failing. After that, we can decide whether we should see each other some more, find someone to help her with her work, or whether she is able to do it on her own. M. readily agreed to this.

Met with Mrs. S. following the first interview with M. Suggested that there was some difficulty in delineating a problem with M. that would necessitate my help, although referral for tutoring might be indicated. I suggested that M. and I felt that a meeting with the three of us might be beneficial, since M. is interested in doing well and is concerned about the possibility that she might fail. Mrs. S. feels that M. has a problem since she is not working up to potential and agreed to a joint interview. It was arranged for 2/17.

M.
Mrs. S.
Interview 2
2/17

M.'s school difficulties were discussed. Mrs. S. delineated a number of reasons why she felt that M. is not doing as well as she should be. Many of these, such as inattention in class, and in particular not listening to directions were not special to M., but to many of the children in the class. However, Mrs. S. suggested ways in which M. could improve in these areas and thinks that M. must take on the responsibility for herself, just as must the others in the class, and that if she improves in these areas of listening and following directions, her work will improve. Also, Mrs. S. thinks that if M. is doing all the work she says she is, her work would reflect this, and it does not.

A number of specific issues were raised and discussed which, as a result of this interaction, have a good possibility of being resolved. M.'s seeming lack of initiative in the reading room resulted from, at least partially, her reluctance to ask for assistance with a specific problem. M.'s concern with Mrs. S.'s anger was the reason for her not asking for help. She and Mrs. S. discussed this fear. I clarified that Mrs. S. was interested in helping her, even if she got annoyed. Later in the interview I discussed this situation further with M., i.e., whether it is better to get the help she needs and possibly have Mrs. S. get mad at her, or whether she should avoid the anger by not asking for help, and fall behind in her work, and then have Mrs. S. annoyed with her for not doing as well as she should. M. feels that it is better to ask for the assistance she needs and seems to be more willing to ask for it, regardless of whether Mrs. S. will briefly get angry with her.

The problem with the other girl talking to her was also discussed. Although Mrs. S. has moved M.'s seat several times, it was revealed that the same girl keeps moving her seat (switching with other students) to sit next to M. Although Mrs. S. thinks that at times M. may not be urging the other girl to leave her alone, she did agree that separating the two girls again would be beneficial.

I saw M.'s report card, and "the lack of effort reflects itself on her report card" according to Mrs. S. However, math is the only subject she is failing. She is doing fair to good in all the others, although her effort marks are low in some areas. Consequently, I was interested in exploring this matter with Mrs. S. and M. in order to clarify what the problem is and who sees it as a problem.

In comparison with the rest of the class, M. is average, but Mrs. S. feels that insofar as her potential is concerned, M. should be doing better. I asked how M. felt about this. She said she is doing better in Mrs. S.'s class then in her previous classes, but feels that she could be doing even better. Then explored with her what she felt we could do to help her do better in the classroom. She had no ideas. I acknowledged that she is getting help with work at home, but that maybe she needed additional help [from] someone in the school. This met with little positive response.

The response to my question of whether there are any problems in the classroom right now, or at home with her family that make it hard to study met with a positive response. The following follows the format of the first interview.

She has difficulty in studying at home because of her stepfather.

Her stepfather does not like her, although he likes her siblings. When she goes to study, he tells the other children to go into the room with her. When she informs him that she has to get her work done, he denies and ignores her concern with this. Because she can't get her work done at home, it creates a problem in school.

She tries to talk with him about this, but he will not listen to her. Her mother tries to help her with this, but has had only limited success. When she occasionally finds a quiet place to study he disturbs her, demanding that she do some chores. M. feels that her stepfather "does not like her much" and shows this in his words (telling her that he can't stand her) and his actions. Her real father takes time with her and likes her. She sees her own father daily, unbeknownst to her stepfather. Although all the children are from the same father, the stepfather likes the younger siblings better, and makes this evident through his words and actions. (He lets them play while making her work indoors, gives them money but not her.)

Her stepfather has been living with the family for about 5 months, and it seems that the family may have been living in his home with him for awhile before he moved in with them.

She likes her stepfather when he is not gruff with her. (This was elicited by Mrs. S. and I have some reservations about it.)

While acknowledging to us that M. had good reasons for not getting her work done at home, Mrs. S. interrupted at this point to discuss some of the classroom issues. After this interruption M. and I continued alone, proceeding along the lines of the first interview format as follows:

In transition from Mrs. S.'s discussion with her back to the first interview format [*sic*], I clarified with M. her feelings about Mrs. S. and what had been discussed concerning her asking for help in the classroom.

We proceeded to discuss what M. wants help with. She would like to do better in school. She does not think that she needs assistance on working to improve her classroom behavior. She feels that if the situation at home were better, "if they would stop bothering her," her school performance would improve. I would classify this as a problem of interpersonal conflict, resulting in a problem in role performance.

The target problem is to get the stepfather to understand that M. wants to do better in school and needs his cooperation in order for her to do this.

In exploring the task possibilities to improve school performance, we agreed that M. would work harder on her own in the areas that Mrs. S. talked about, and that doing this would help Mrs. S.'s attitude towards her. She and I would focus on ways of improving the situation with her stepfather with regard to her studying. One possibility which we have agreed on thus far is to speak with her stepfather and mother about this problem.

Agreement was made to see each other for approximately 8 times.

Our next step is to decide how best to go and speak with the stepfather and mother to see what can be done about this situation. She would not be upset about all of us talking together—she will feel better, and thinks that the situation might improve by doing this.

Set up an appointment to meet with her 2/22.

M.
Interview 3
2/22

At this time, the task decided upon in the last interview—to get M.'s stepfather (SF) to cooperate with her so that she can study at home—has been completed.

M. spoke with her SF the day after our last interview (2/18). She told him that I was coming to their home because of her school work. He asked if it was anything which concerned him. She said yes and explained her problem to him. Since then he has been keeping the other children out of the room when she is studying and has offered to help her with her school work.

M. is very pleased that the situation has improved. She does not feel that it is necessary for me to come to their home, and considers the problem resolved to her satisfaction. She feels that as a result of her talk with him, they are getting along better in general.

We discussed possible new tasks. She feels that she can handle her school and her home situation. M. is concerned about her failing grades in arithmetic and plans to see her arithmetic teacher on 2/23 to find out what she can do about it. The result of her discussion with her math teacher will determine whether there is a new task for us to work on.

In attempting to determine whether or not there are any other problems to be worked on, M. discussed both her school and home situation. She acknowledges problems in class, but feels that they are largely the result of Mrs. S.'s behavior and are shared by many of the other students. Academically M. feels she's doing all right, "good", (and her report card bears this out), and better than she has in the past. Following our discussion last week, she is trying to keep Mrs. S. off her back (with mixed results). She does not believe that she needs help in dealing with this. Her mother is taking an interest in what she is doing, i.e., she is coming to school Friday to discuss with Mrs. S. her not letting the children out to lunch on time, as well as discussing M.'s school work.

M. said that as a result of talking with her SF about school they are getting along better generally. I asked what she thought about his feelings towards her. She said that he still likes the other children better. I asked if she had talked with him about this, and she said yes. When she brought it up with him, he said that his feelings were his business. She seemed to accept this, and said usually she just didn't care about it.

M. then described the arguments her mother and SF have with regard to Mrs. S.'s behavior. (M. tells them what goes on in class and what she's done to bring on Mrs. S.'s wrath.) First one will defend Mrs. S. and the other M., and then they switch sides. M. related one incident in which she told her SF she was scared of Mrs. S. Her SF tried to get her to admit that she wasn't really scared of Mrs. S. He offered her $1, then $5 to say she wasn't scared. M. replied that she was scared and that "Money ain't gonna change my mind."

Related positive incidents as well. M.'s SF bought many boxes of girl scout cookies from her. M. was surprised at this, but glad. Her mother bought her a sixth grade math book to help her with her work.

By structuring the conversation, I was able to elicit the details of M.'s conversation with her SF and the consequences of it. In this way I was able to enhance her awareness of how well she had handled the situation. She admitted that she was scared at first, and had thought of alternative ways of getting through to her SF such as writing him a note or having her sister tell him. I conveyed that this feeling was natural. She continued, saying that she decided that "I got to be my own self and go ask him." I reinforced this self-awareness and encouraged her efforts in this situation and ones similar to this so as to strengthen her interactions of this type with other people when the need arises. She understood this and agreed that this was a good way to deal with problems.

I gave some direction in terms of ways she could continue to improve her relationship with [her] SF such as asking him for help if he seemed willing rather than only asking her mother, and explaining my reasons for this advice. She thought this was a useful suggestion.

While encouraging her success, I did convey to her that her SF might fall back into his old pattern. She replied that if this happens she will talk about it again with him or her mother.

In view of the fact that no new task could be agreed upon at this time, I suggested that we meet once more on 2/29 to determine whether there was a problem with math, and what we might do about it, as well as review the progress with her SF. If everything is satisfactory to her, and there is nothing for us to work on, I suggested that we terminate. While suggesting termination, I reinforced her coping capacities, and her good reality testing in terms of her ability to deal with her problems. Also told her that if at some later time she has a problem she needs help with she can contact me. She felt that this was acceptable and did not seem upset about terminating if there is nothing left for us to do at this time.

> M.
> *Interview 4*
> *3/1*

Termination had been discussed as a possibility for this session, pending a review of M.'s continued success with her stepfather and the results of her discussion with her math teacher.

Things are not going as well as last week when M. felt she had accomplished the task as a result of her talking about her problems of studying at home with her SF. He has fallen back into his old habits of disrupting her studying by sending the younger siblings into her room, or calling her out to wait on him or do the chores. She tried talking with him, but he now discounts the importance of her work.

M. was not able to see her math teacher last week and will do it this week.

Consequently, we considered the nature and validity of the task. While it is evident that the interpersonal conflict between M. and her SF is broadly based, his lack of cooperation with her studying is an important aspect of this and impinges on her role performance as a student.

Since this task is directed toward potentiating M.'s opportunities for studying, alternative possibilities for achieving this same end were discussed. These include the following and the reasons why they were rejected:

1. Staying after school to do her homework.
   School closes at 3:15.
2. Going to the YMCA where there are rooms in which to study.
   M. already tried this. [Her] SF called her there and told her to come home.
3. Studying at a friend's house.
   M. tried this. Unsuccessful for the same reason as #2.
4. Have a tutor come to her house to work with her.
   While this may have some possibility of success, it is at best a temporary solution.
5. Make a schedule of times for chores and homework.
   M. has tried this. Her SF refuses to stick to the schedule.
6. Refuse to respond to requests made by her SF during the time she is studying.
   She would probably get whipped for that.
7. Asking her sister (7 1/2 and the next oldest) to help her with some of the chores.
   M. has tried this, but sister refuses and her SF does not ask her sister to do the chores.
8. Termination.
   M. does not want it at this time.
9. I call the home and make an appointment for us all to discuss this problem. The focus of this meeting will be to enlist the SF's cooperation with M.'s studying.
   M. seems to be willing, though somewhat pessimistic about the results of this attempt.

Problems related to Mrs. S. were discussed briefly. She is somewhat concerned that Mrs. S. will carry through her threat to fail the entire class. Talking about the actual likelihood of this in terms of M.'s school performance and grades alleviated this fear as M. realized that Mrs. S. has no grounds on which to fail her. Failing math would, however, mean attending summer school

By structuring the interview around the task, M.'s discussion of her difficulties with her SF and her sister remained related to the task at hand. They were discussed in terms of the obstacles they presented to task achievement. Besides discussing [her] SF and [her] sister's current behavior and possible ways of changing these behaviors, we discussed alternative means of accomplishing the task of studying by circumventing the primary obstacles. While M. was open to direction, and mentioned some alternatives she has tried herself, her reasons for rejecting alternative ways to achieve the task were valid. I encouraged her attempts thus far, pointing out that although they were unsuccessful, she had assessed the situation and had taken it upon herself to try to rectify it.

By selectively responding to task-related remarks, and supporting efforts she made, I conveyed to her my belief in her capabilities and her capacity to seek means of coping with and improving her current situation, and enhancing her awareness of her capabilities, and her realistic impressions. These methods both implicitly and explicitly conveyed to M. that I would listen openly to the family interaction, solicit her responses and by and large validate them, and that I would not be "fooled" by her SF but seek to explore with the whole family possible obstacles to task completion.

The next step will be to call the family and arrange an appointment when M., SF, mother, sister, and I can meet to discuss this problem.

M., Mother, Stepfather,
2 siblings
Interview 5
3/7

Met with M. and her family to discuss M.'s school problem—that she is not working up to potential. I explored with the family their ideas on the nature of the problem. The focus shifted from the parents' (the stepfather in particular) ... making too many demands upon her so that M. is unable to study, to the possibility that due to the magnitude of work she is given, M. is reluctant to do it.

Parents expressed sincere concern about M. and her school difficulties. They consider her a bright youngster and are interested in helping her with her work. It was brought out that although M. talks about doing her work, and goes through the motions of preparing to study she often spends her time reading comic books instead, or coming to play with the other children, or letting them disturb her. While mother offers to help M., M. often does not take her up on this.

In exploring this problem with the family, M.'s attempts at studying were encouraged, but alternatives were suggested so that she could better succeed. The interview was structured around M. and the possible blocks to her studying at home. Awareness enhancement was directed toward M. and the family in the following ways. It was discussed that perhaps M. was resentful of the amount of work required of her, and the fact that her siblings did not have homework. Also discussed was the fact that M. didn't like all the work she was required to do and therefore didn't enjoy doing it. Also normal sibling rivalries were discussed. M.'s parents are aware that their two oldest daughters, M. and C., do not get along well. M. and L. are very close and share a bedroom, and C. and P. are close and they share a bedroom. This was done by the parents to alleviate some of the conflicts between the children. M.'s approaching puberty was also mentioned as a possible reason for her increased sensitivity toward slights and demands made upon her. Her parents individualize the children and are aware that M. is much more sensitive to criticism than C. and take this into account when relating to her. Other possible problems in the home were not evident as a result of the interview. My responses were made to increase M.'s awareness that perhaps as a result of her unhappiness with her school work, she was taking out some of her anger on her parents and siblings. M.'s parents offered direction that they would take with M.'s agreement. M. is to be excused from her chores for the next six weeks, except for making her bed and keeping her room neat. (The other chores were washing the dinner dishes and sweeping the floor.) Any additional errands would be given to the other children. M. and her mother would work on M.'s homework for about 45 minutes, after which M. would be permitted to go out to play with her siblings. They would all be called in after an hour, so that M. would not feel slighted. She would then do some more homework, either with her mother's assistance, or have her mother check over her work when she completed it. After she finished her homework, she could join the rest of the family in watching TV or whatever she felt like doing. This plan was acceptable to M. It was discussed in terms of being unable to change Mrs. S., and consequently as much as M. disliked it she would have to do her work, to keep Mrs. S. off her back. M.'s parents very aware of the problems in Mrs. S.'s class and do not blame M. for her difficulties in the classroom. While mother is more than willing to see Mrs. S. both she and M. agreed that this would have little effect on Mrs. S. and might only make things more difficult for M. M.'s self-awareness was encouraged, as was her parents' obvious concern for and regard for and interest in M. The plan evolved for M.'s studying was not punitive in nature, but rather that her efforts would be rewarded by liberal amounts of free time. Awareness enhancement also directed towards the idea that with her mother's assistance her work would go faster, and once she got the knack of doing it, it might not seem as onerous. It was brought out that the parents were interested in helping M., and understood the difficult situation [which] she is in. M. accepted this plan, and seemed more aware that some of her anger at her family was a result of school pressures and adolescence [rather] than because she was being singled out by them and picked on. (C. also has chores to do, for example.)

This new plan for homework is to be tried for six weeks. If this does not succeed, if her report card does not reflect her increased effort, and her mother can testify to the fact that she (M.) has been doing her work, alternative steps, such as removing her from Mrs. S.'s room, or transferring her back to her old school will be seriously considered. However, for the time being, M. will be given additional support in the home, and the aforementioned plan will be implemented. I made an appointment with M. to see her 3/13 to discuss with her how things are going.

M.
Interview 6
3/13

M. and I discussed the results thus far of the family interview of 3/7 in relation to her task of being able to improve her studying at home by having her stepfather cooperate. The study situation has improved substantially. Her mother and in particular her stepfather are now helping her with her homework, encouraging her in doing it, and rewarding her efforts with small sums of money every other week ($3). In addition M. expressed interest in having a parakeet. She and her stepfather read up on it, and for continued efforts in her studying she will receive a parakeet on March 24. She is finding it much less difficult to study at home now, and is pleased with the results.

In structuring the conversation around the task, and focusing on the results of the family interview, M. said that both her parents felt that since they had all gotten together to discuss the situation, they felt that the situation would improve. Awareness enhancement was directed toward increasing M.'s awareness of the change in her stepfather's behavior which she told me about, and its results on her behavior. For example, the stepfather is now being more considerate of M.'s feelings, by praising both older girls rather than just C. He and her mother are also acknowledging M. as an individual and the oldest girl by differentiating her privileges from the other children's. In terms of the results on her behavior, she is better able to relate to her stepfather, and can better differentiate when he is "fooling around" or "just playing" and when he is serious, particularly in terms of being [either] pleased or annoyed with her. I encouraged her efforts to relate to her stepfather and supported her continuing study efforts. We discussed possible obstacles which might eventuate, such as the stepfather being less considerate of her, or of M.'s becoming resentful of her work and taking out some of her anger on her family, and various means of dealing with this. I encouraged her clear perceptions of how she would do this.

We will meet again on 5/2 to evaluate the situation at that time. Having reminded M. of our decision to meet approximately 8 times, we decided that we should meet again once more with termination as a definite possibility at that meeting.

M.
Interview 7
4/4

Termination: [1] M.'s reaction to termination was positive. She has given thought to the idea of termination proposed in the last session. She discussed this with her mother who, by advising her to continue to see me if she felt a need to or discontinue if she did not, left the decision up to M. There seemed to be a small amount of ambivalence which was dissipated when I told her that should any problem arise she could contact me and we would get together. This was fine with her and she felt that at this time she no longer needs my help.

2. M. and I discussed the means she has learned to deal with her stepfather and Mrs. S. in terms of task accomplishment. By following some of Mrs. S's suggestions on classroom behavior, such as getting her pencil and paper out on time, getting her homework in, and changing her seat, as well as more subtle means of getting around Mrs. S., or avoiding her wrath, she feels that she is better able to cope with Mrs. S. Coping with her classroom situation is a continuing task.

In the process of increasing her role performance in school, a major task was to get her stepfather to cooperate with her so that she could study at home. In the process of achieving this task, she has developed better techniques for dealing with her stepfather. As a result of task accomplishment she is better able to relate to her stepfather in general. She is able now to differentiate when he is serious and when he is teasing her. Possible problems may arise if her stepfather becomes less considerate of her need to study and M.'s feelings of resentment about the amount of work she has. She feels that she will be able to talk these out with her parents. Problems still remain with regard to her relationship to her stepfather and her sister C. She feels that she can deal with these on her own. She thinks of herself as her mother's favorite and her stepfather's friend, and C. as stepfather's favorite and mother's friend. At present this conceptualization is acceptable to her.

    3. The agreed upon task, to increase M.'s role performance in the classroom has, according to M, been substantial. She believes this to be so because she can better deal with Mrs. S. Mrs. S., on the other hand, sees the task as partially accomplished. She is pleased with the results thus far, but believes that M. could improve her grades further. It is my opinion that M. is pleased with her increased ability to cope both with her stepfather (which was ancillary to task accomplishment in terms of getting him to cooperate with her studying at home, and which he now does) and Mrs. S. Improved grades, which are Mrs. S.'s major criteria for improvement, are of secondary importance to M. M.'s capacity to deal with her situation has been validated by her mother, who told M. that she would not need to come to school to see Mrs. S. because if M. could handle C. and her stepfather as she has been, she can certainly handle Mrs. S. M. agrees with this, and in my opinion, M. has made substantial task accomplishments.

BIBLIOGRAPHY

Adorno, T. W., et al. *Authoritarian Personality*. New York: W. W. Norton, 1969.

Ball, Samuel, ed. *Motivation in Education*. Educational Psychology Series. Ed. Allen J. Edwards. New York: Academic Press, 1977. (See esp. Gerard C. Fanelli, "Locus of Control," pp. 45–66.)

Barker, Larry L. *Listening Behavior*. Englewood Cliffs, N. J.: Prentice–Hall, 1971.

Berne, Eric. *Games People Play*. New York: Grove Press, 1964.

Brammer, Lawrence M. and Everett L. Shostrom. *Therapeutic Psychology*. 3rd ed. Englewood Cliffs, N.J.: Prentice-Hall, 1977.

Christie, Richard, et al. *Studies in Machiavellianism*. New York: Gordon Printing, 1970.

Curran, Charles S. *Counseling-Learning: A Whole-Person Model for Education*. New York: Grune and Stratton, Inc., 1972.

Friedman, Paul G. *Interpersonal Communication: Innovations in Instruction*. Aspects of Learning Series. Washington, D.C.: National Education Association, 1978.

Gazda, George M., Frank R. Asbury, Fred J. Balzer, et al. *Human Relations Development: A Manual for Educators*. 2nd ed. Boston: Allyn and Bacon, 1977.

Goldstein, Arnold P. and Frederick H. Kanfer, eds. *Helping People Change: A Textbook of Methods*. New York: Pergamon Press, Inc., 1975.

Maslow, A. H. *Motivation and Personality*. 2nd ed. New York: Harper & Row, 1970.

McDermott, Dermod. *Peer Consultation: The Art of Friends Helping Friends*. New York: Full Circle Associates, 1978.

Nichols, Ralph G. and Leonard A. Stevens. *Are You Listening?* New York: McGraw-Hill Book Co., Inc., 1957.

Rogers, Carl R. *Freedom to Learn*. Columbus, Ohio: Charles E. Merrill, 1979.

Rogers, Carl R. *On Becoming a Person*. Boston: Beacon Press, 1954.

Rotter, J. B. "Generalized Expectancies for Internal Versus External Control of Reinforcements." *Psychological Monographs*, 80, No. 10 (1966), 1–28.

Staub, Ervin, ed. *Personality: Basic Aspects and Current Research*. Englewood Cliffs, N.J.: Prentice-Hall, 1980. (See esp. Herbert Lefcourt, "Locus of Control and Coping with Life's Events," pp. 200–235.)

Stevick, Earl W. *Memory, Meaning and Method*. Boston: Newbury Press, 1976.

7 | *ROLEPLAYING TUTORING PROBLEMS*

In the previous chapter, you acquired tutor-counseling techniques. You learned how to respond to student needs and practiced ways that would cement a positive relationship between you and your tutee while nurturing your student's academic development. This chapter draws on what you learned in chapter 6 by focusing on specific tutoring problems and ways to handle them. The major method you will be using to practice dealing with problem situations will be roleplaying, because roleplaying problem situations will give you the opportunity to practice and extend your tutor-counseling capacity.

ROLEPLAYING

Roleplaying is an activity in which someone imitates someone else's behavior. (See chapter 1 for beginning discussion of roleplaying as a group device.) The purposes of doing so are wide-ranging: you may learn a skill by trying it out within the context of a roleplaying situation; you may learn a series of behaviors; you may learn how to change your own or a student's dysfunctional behavior; or you may learn to understand and handle problem situations like the ones described in the last section of this chapter.

Roleplaying was made popular by the psychologist Jacob Moreno, who used it as a method of giving the girls in a home for delinquents a chance to experience, if only in play, the kinds of problems they would encounter in the world outside their institution. It had, thus, at the outset, a functional purpose. However, Moreno soon recognized that roleplaying could give people a chance to experience and re-experience deep feelings, and so he developed what is known as psychodrama, literally, "theatre of the mind." Many psychologists today continue to use roleplaying and have extended its scope to help patients understand and resolve emotional problems.

Nevertheless, the original functional benefits of roleplaying have not been forgotten; indeed, a whole area of psychology, as well as education, business, and in fact, any group that is engaged in training, may use roleplaying as a way of changing behavior by reviewing the outcomes of dysfunctional behavior and by learning and practicing the skills necessary for new, more productive behaviors. As opposed to the practitioners of psychodrama and its affiliates, the primary goal of roleplaying in training is not to gain insight—it is to learn and to practice alternate behaviors.

You have been using roleplaying in this class to learn and practice tutoring skills, for example, how to show instead of tell, how to explain and rein-force difficult concepts, how to use boardwork effectively. Roleplaying has sensitized you to students' emotional needs, and has given you an arena in which to practice tutor-counseling techniques. It has also helped you to under-stand problem situations you are likely to encounter when tutoring. By taking on the roles of tutor and tutee, and by simulating the variety of situations in which you may be involved at some time in your tutoring career, you will not only be able to find out how prepared you are to handle these situations but you will be able to anticipate how you may respond emotionally to them and how the tutee may feel as well; you may even uncover attitudes you did not know you had, for example, your own problems with authority or your own insecurities about your expertise in a particular area, and thus you will be even more prepared when you confront them in actuality.

How Roleplaying Works

Roleplaying begins in childhood and is a major socialization device all through life; putting oneself in another's role (as children play mommy, daddy, fire-man, doctor) gives one the chance to practice *roletaking*, that is, the under-standing and internalization of the roles people expect one another to play. Roleplaying as a way to help you understand the tutoring process works in much the same way. Taking a particular tutoring role helps you learn personal and professional techniques necessary for actual tutoring—you get a chance to see what is expected of you and how well prepared you are to meet the expec-tations of that role. At the same time, playing the role of the tutee enables you to explore aspects of that position as well. Specifically, roleplaying does some or all of the following:

- helps you to identify your problems as a tutor
- helps you to isolate these problems, making it easier to deal with them
- helps you to see the consequences of your actions by getting feedback on them from fellow actors and observors
- helps you to develop creative problem-solving capabilities by providing you with alternate ways of resolving difficult situations
- helps you to see why you make certain decisions by giving you the opportunity to discuss roleplaying decisions with fellow participants and observors
- helps you to develop self-confidence by giving you both practice solving problems and feedback on your tutoring ability
- helps you to discover the imaginative resources within yourself
- increases your understanding of people's motivations through discussion about why people play the roles the way they do (and whether they would play them differently another time)
- helps you to identify your own goals and values by understanding why you act the way you do
- creates actual situations in which you can check the effectiveness of your methods, techniques, and strategies

Methodology

Defining the Rules There are many questions that need to be answered before you can begin. Assuming you are roleplaying within the class setting, you must decide such things as what role your classmates will play (how much say they will have before, during, and after roleplaying), what role the teacher will have, how many times the situation will be performed, what roleplaying format will be used, what the maximum length of each situation will be, and how long the discussion will last.

At some point during this discussion you might like to discuss the issue of stage fright. Some of you may feel that you can not be good roleplayers because you don't know how to act. Roleplaying is not a theatrical performance like comedy or drama. The focus in roleplaying is not on your acting ability but on the situation being roleplayed, and on the interaction between you and the other players. If, however, you are nervous about doing roleplaying, try to discuss your feelings with the group. In most cases open discussion will help you deal with your fears.

Selecting the Topic Once you have laid the ground rules you are ready to select your topic. If you are working on problem situations you might want to consult the last part of this chapter. Or, the class might compile a list of problems which tutors have actually been having. If, on the other hand, you want to practice tutoring techniques, you must set up a roleplaying situation in which a particular technique will be necessary.

Choosing Roleplaying Formats Roleplaying can be structured in numerous ways, depending on the experience of the players and the goals of the session. In this chapter we will discuss three effective formats:

FULLY SCRIPTED   Because beginners need structure and information, a full script is recommended for novice roleplayers. A full script consists of a complete outline of both the situation and the desired outcomes. Sometimes each player is given the script, sometimes only one player, sometimes the class group and one player. Clearly, the more that you decide about outcomes beforehand, the greater the number of persons you inform, and the less spontaneous will be the roleplaying. However, if your goal is to practice certain techniques or to discuss specific problems under conditions which eliminate anxiety, a full script is optimum. (See Fig. 7.1. Note that this scenario is based on the case study of Antonia Retamar on p. 58.)

MY LIFE AS A TUTOR

by Marge Baker
Laura Cruz
Antonia Retamar
LaGuardia Community College

Background to Session One
After two weeks of preparation, members of the peer tutoring class were eagerly awaiting the opportunity to meet their tutees. The goal of peer tutoring is to provide the students who come to the Writing

---

Figure 7.1 Full Script Roleplay.

Center with an opportunity to learn and improve their writing skills in an unthreatening, relaxing, and friendly atmosphere, while learning with a friend. The teacher stressed the importance of building a good rapport, so naturally the whole class was very anxious to begin building a foundation for a good and effective learing relationship with their tutees. Following is the scenario of a new tutor's first tutorial relationship.

First Session
TUTOR: Friendly, chatting socially, small talk (i.e., school, job, home).
TUTEE: Business-like. All she will talk about is her paper and errors. Tutee makes it clear that she wants one thing and one thing only from their relationship and that is to improve her writing well enough to pass the course exit-exam.
TUTOR: In reviewing the paper, tutor comes across error. Tutor tells student how to correct error, and tries to explain what the error is.
TUTEE: Does not react favorably in response to tutor's correction; instead tutor is asked a series of questions: "How? . . . Why? . . . Can't be; are you sure? . . . Ask someone . . . Verify it . . . Look it up; I'll look it up too."
TUTOR: Frustrated, disappointed, insecure, intimidated, but hopeful that the next session will be better.

Background to Session Two
Prior to the beginning of the second session, the tutor went to her supervisor for advice on how to handle the situation. The lack of rapport between the tutor and tutee was causing her to feel very insecure and unhappy. Her supervisor volunteered to observe part of the session.

Session Two
TUTOR: Being nice, answering questions, and trying to relax.
TUTEE: Looks to supervisor to verify tutor's answers.
SUPERVISOR: Tells tutee to have more trust and confidence in her tutor. Indicates tutor has made no errors in all the time that he, the supervisor, has been there.
Tells tutor to be confident and secure in her tutoring.
TUTOR: Upset but remains calm. Tutor feels on the spot, because supervisor is watching, even though tutor asked for supervision.
SUPERVISOR: Takes tutor aside and advises her to brush up on her grammar terms, because it may make her feel more confident. He further advises her to feel secure and in control of the session. He tells her that he feels she is doing well, and leaves.
TUTOR: Tries to feel better, but actually feels nervous and discouraged.

Background to Session Three
Tutor and tutee worked on an exercise in *Writing with Confidence*; a tricky question came up, and the tutor was not sure about the answer.

Figure 7.1 (continued)

Session Three
TUTEE: Asks why the word European is circled in her essay.
TUTOR: Tells her it is circled because it should be capitalized.
TUTEE: Asks her if she is sure? Says she will look it up because she has written it this way her whole life. She is sure that it is not capitalized.
TUTOR: Gives her the dictionary and shows her that it is capitalized.
TUTEE: Looks it up in her own dictionary.
TUTOR: Suggests that tutee get another tutor because the tutee has never proven her wrong, but still does not trust her. Tells tutee that she makes her feel both inadequate and insecure and the tutor does not like feeling this way. The tutor admits that she is at fault, for not expressing this before. Her only reason for not doing so is that the tutor did not want to come off as authoritarian.
TUTEE: Facial expression emotionless. Since the session is over the tutee gets up and says good-bye.

Background to Final Session
    Tutor was sure that the tutee would not show up because of what had happened the session before, and because it was the last night of tutoring. Tutee was one-half hour late, so tutor was sure that tutee was not coming.

Session Four
    All of a sudden tutee walks through the door and apologizes for being late. Tutee explains that she was waiting for an advisor so she could register, but when she saw the lateness of the hour, she left because she did not want to miss her last tutoring session. The tutor and tutee go over a paper with twelve errors that the tutee had just gotten back. The tutee corrects her errors with ease. When the session is over the tutee gets out of her chair, walks over to the tutor, puts her hand on the tutor's shoulder, and kisses her on the cheek. The tutee thanks the tutor for being such a good tutor and friend, and then she walks away. The tutor is totally amazed.

Figure 7.1 (continued)

MODERATELY OR PARTIALLY SCRIPTED   As you advance in tutoring expertise (and become more familiar with roleplaying) you may not want as much structure. A moderate script is one in which only partial information is given. (See Fig. 7.2.) You might write a scenario for the tutee role alone and then let the person playing the tutor determine what the problem is and how to deal with it. You might omit some details from the script and let your players improvise. The purpose of a moderate script is to give some structure for the players to follow, while giving them freedom and flexibility to experiment with responses.

UNSCRIPTED   Roleplaying without a script is the most spontaneous, and, therefore, the most advanced form of roleplaying. The group or one of the

"My teacher's misgraded me."
TUTEE: Peer-tutor volunteer
TUTOR: Peer-tutor volunteer

PROBLEM
Tutee brings in a paper which deserves a higher grade. He explains why the grade should be higher, and his argument is good. The tutor is faced with the problem of not wanting to lose the student's confidence by lying and saying the teacher has done no wrong; on the other hand, he doesn't want to destroy the student's confidence in his teacher by implying gross incompetence on the teacher's part.

HINTS TUTOR: Be honest but be generous; remember, you too make mistakes. Also, a grade is a judgment; never comment on it as a professional's judgment is worthy of respect.
TUTEE: Be persistent. Your goal is to convince the tutor to agree with you; then you have ammunition to fight for a higher grade.

PROP Paper with big C on top.

Figure 7.2   Partial Script Roleplay.

players chooses the situation (an example may be—the tutee is habitually late) and gives one or more players background information and character sketches (John is 35, was born in Colombia, and has been in this country for eight years; however, his English is still limited and he has failed the first level English course two times.) and at this point the roleplaying develops extemporaneously. To engender spontaneity, usually some players receive no background information.

Determining the Background and Setting and Establishing Character Roles Any script that you play must be realistic so that players and observers can truly empathize with what is going on; therefore, you must give it a local time and place (a math center, Tuesday night, winter term). Make your characters realistic by giving them a brief but relevant history (sophomore, female, anxious about writing, journalism major).

Warming up The warm-up period is very important because it establishes the context for roleplaying and for the post-roleplaying discussion. You must control the observational process by telling your observers what they need to know (background, setting, characterization) and leaving out what you want them to guess. This is also a time when the group can pose questions for later discussion.

Roleplaying The actual roleplaying may be the shortest part of this whole procedure; many roleplaying situations last no longer than five minutes; few last more than ten. Be certain you have set up a system for ending the roleplaying beforehand so the players know when to stop. For if you wait for the players to "solve" the problem, the roleplaying may go on indefinitely.

Roleplaying Alternative Solutions Sometimes a situation is deliberately scripted "incorrectly" for pedagogic reasons. At other times, your facilitator or members of your audience will not like the way the roleplaying turned out. In cases like these, the group may call upon someone to reenact the situation to find a better solution. This can be tricky, however, since there is no clear right or wrong in roleplaying; every problem solution has *some* motivation behind it that *seemed* valid to the players at the time, probably because tutors (or teachers) once used it successfully. Try to remain aware of the complexity of interpersonal dynamics and avoid labeling something "wrong" unless there is clearly a consensus that the particular approach is a negative one. (Insulting a tutee, for example, would clearly not be "right.") During the post-roleplaying discussion, the group should explore the value of alternative solutions.

Following Up The discussion that takes place after roleplaying is probably the most important part of the whole exercise. During the discussion all the benefits of roleplaying emerge. Tutors get feedback on their tutor-counseling techniques; the players and the group as a whole are able to explore fears and doubts and to open up and, hopefully, explain feelings. Those of you who have been observers should try to be as honest as possible during this discussion so you can learn from it. Even if you don't get to roleplay, you can undoubtedly apply what is happening "on stage" to your own situation.

Concluding As a group you should summarize what the class has learned and make any possible generalizations about tutoring.

Postscript: A Sample Roleplaying Session

Rules

1. Only student will know topic—observers and roleplaying tutor will not.
2. Roleplaying will last no longer than eight minutes.
3. Facilitator will decide when to call time.
4. Someone from group will have opportunity to replay tutor role.
5. Class will hold thirty-minute discussion.

Topic Passive Student

Format Partial script

Background and Character Large math lab at Hatway College. At present there are 15 other students receiving tutoring; you can hear them but you can't see them because everyone is in small cubicles. Each cubicle has a table that seats up to four people.

You are a male sophomore who consistently gets C's because you never ask for help. You don't like to talk in class because it makes you nervous. Anyway, you're not really interested in college, you don't think. You feel you'd much rather be home watching tv than be at the math lab. You are here for your first visit because it is a required part of the course.

Warm-up Discuss setting and role. At this time certain persons should be designated to watch for nonverbal cues from the tutee, and others to watch for the nonverbal gestures of the tutor. Use "What to Look for in Groups," p. 36 to focus your group process activity.

Roleplay The first tutor to roleplay with the "passive" student might try to solve the problem by getting him to talk about personal matters (such as interests, feelings about school, and so forth). Another student might feel it would be better to deal with academic matters by getting the student to do boardwork and to become more actively involved in the learning process.

Follow-Up The discussion that follows the roleplaying might examine the occurrence of nonverbal cues and then go on to analyze the two different approaches to dealing with a passive student, exploring which approach worked better and why. Observers can call upon the players to discuss why they said or acted as they did and how they felt about the responses the other persons had to them. Other group-work concerns can be discussed at this time.

Conclusion Class members might sum up by discussing student passivity and how it generates a number of other tutoring problems; they might also explore how they can apply both roleplaying solutions to solve other tutoring problems. Finally, they may note how the group benefitted from the process activity.

Caution!

Roleplaying has its drawbacks, and you should be aware of them. One particular problem is that roleplaying, by its nature, is spontaneous and dramatic. It will often be very exciting, but it can also make people feel anxious, both because of its public nature and because, if it works, it necessitates an incursion into the psyche which those uncomfortable or unfamiliar with introspection may resent. Also roleplaying is not reality. To roleplay we must focus on selective aspects of the particular situation we are acting out. In life, such "variables" overlap and problems are rarely so clear cut. Do not expect insights you discover while roleplaying to pertain precisely to any given situation.

CLASS PROJECT 1

1. By using a number of formats and situations, these class projects will engage you in roleplaying. In order to get the most out of your practice roleplaying, we suggest you pick a steering committee for each project; the steering committee will be responsible for ordering and summarizing the consequences of each roleplaying analysis. The steering committee might also take responsibility for cueing players when they seem to need help with lines. The roleplayers should be sure to draw on the group process skills developed in chapter 1 and tutor-counseling techniques practiced in chapter 6.

a. Pick one situation from the typical problems described in the following section and then several of you play the role of the tutor in this situation. After all of your versions have been played, discuss similarities and differences between the performances.

   b. Pick two to five situations from Potential Problem Areas (see following) and write partial scripts. (These may be done alone or as a group activity.) Then roleplay one or more of them.

   c. Pick one situation from Potential Problem Areas; write a full script and roleplay it.

   d. Turn a tutoring experience of your own into a full script—omit names, change personal details—and roleplay it with the class.

   2. Pick some of the potential problems and try out the following techniques* in your roleplaying of them:

   Broken Record   When the tutee continually attempts to avoid the subject matter, keep returning to the matter at hand. Use the phrase "But the point is . . . ."

   Disarming Anger   Ignore content and focus attention and conversation on the fact that your tutee is angry. Promise your tutee that you will begin tutoring again when he or she has calmed down. Be sure to maintain eye contact and use a moderate (not loud or soft) tone of voice.

   Negative Inquiry   This is often a way to end a very negative relationship, as when a tutor must respond to a tutee who is highly critical of the tutoring, the lab, the program, or the tutor. In a neutral, inquiring tone the tutor asks if anything else displeases the tutee. The tutor should assure the tutee that he or she would like to know so as to do better in the future. After the list of complaints is complete, the tutor should summarize and then thank the tutee. Finally, the tutor should tell the tutee if he or she thinks of anything else in the future to let the tutor know.

   3. Discuss what effect these techniques have on the roleplaying. Write an analysis of one of the roleplaying situations done in class; include in this analysis as much descriptive detail as possible (dialogue, body language, movements) as well as an evaluation of the outcomes.

LAB APPLICATION

   Where relevant, try out with your tutee one of the roleplayed solutions you have seen in class. Record the experience and how you reacted to it in your journal.

POTENTIAL PROBLEM AREAS

With this chapter, we hope you have gained experience in using roleplaying to understand and resolve both hypothetical and actual problems. As a resource, we have provided a "glossary" of problem situations—to demonstrate that

*These techniques have been borrowed from John V. Flowers, "Simulation and Role-Playing Methods," *Helping People Change*, eds. A. P. Goldstein and F. H. Kanfer (New York: Pergamon Press, 1975), pp. 191–192.

others have experienced similar problems, to give you the benefit of collective insights to these problems, and to make available strategies that have proven helpful to others in the past. We want to emphasize that we do not think of tutoring as a problem—but problems, when they do arise, can be the loneliest and most demanding part of tutoring. Anything that gives you more information and allows you to anticipate conflicts, makes you better able to resolve them. Here are suggestions rather than rules for behavior. Use the glossary as a reference manual, for source material, and as a guide for discussion.

Tutor/Student Conflicts

The first group of problems under discussion is headed tutor/student. This group is the largest because it concerns the primary tutorial relationship. To help you identify the problems when they occur in your own tutoring we have subdivided them into the personal and academic areas; a third subdivision, tutor-generated conflicts, also encompasses these two subdivisions. As with any artificial classification system, some overlap and repetition is inevitable.

Personal Factors

POSSIBLE REASONS

POSSIBLE APPROACHES

The student is passive and contributes little to the session.

The student is insecure and doesn't believe he or she has anything to say.

Ask lots of questions, not "yes" or "no" questions but questions that must be answered after some thought and with a degree of complexity. Ask the tutee to work at the blackboard or on paper to demonstrate what he or she knows.

The student may be overwhelmed by your ease with the subject matter.

Try to elicit an active response from the tutee. Watch yourself to make sure you're not doing all the talking or all the doing. Leave enough time for a response (count to ten).

The tutee lies to you (about grades, understanding, general knowledge).

The student may be too proud to admit failure. If the two of you have a good relationship, the student may not want to let you down by revealing his or her failing at something you have both worked hard at. The student who looks up to you may not want to admit his or her problems in understanding what you are saying. An adult tutee may be especially unwilling to reveal problems in comprehension, especially if you are younger than the tutee.

As with the "passive student," ask for feedback to make certain the student understands what you are tutoring. Don't just ask, "Do you understand?" Work in such a way that the student can *show* understanding. If you know the student has recently taken a big test, ask how he or she did, and then ask if the two of you can go over the test together. If you suspect the student may be misrepresenting his or her grades to you (perhaps "forgetting" to bring in essays or tests), you

POSSIBLE REASONS (*cont.*)   POSSIBLE APPROACHES (*cont.*)

may want to drop the teacher a
note requesting feedback (only do
this if your center permits such
tutor/teacher contact, and be certain
not to betray confidentiality). Never,
of course, call the student a liar;
name-calling usually provokes anger
rather than helping to establish rapport.

The student thinks you can work miracles.

The student would like you to take
responsibility for the work because
of a lack of confidence in his or
her own ability to do it.

The student may prefer to think in
terms of miracles rather than in
terms of the hard, tedious work
that may be necessary.

You must help the student take
responsibility for his or her own
work. Make it clear that, probably,
a miracle is not needed, just solid
work. It may prove helpful to isolate specific manageable tasks, or to
set up a regular, weekly schedule
as a way to help your tutee feel
less overwhelmed and, therefore,
less in need of miracles.

The student blames you for bad grades.

This behavior is just the other side
of the "miracle worker" coin. The
tutee cannot bear to take the responsibility and so blames any
failure on you.

You and the tutee must determine
objective reasons for the bad
grades—and you both must explore
what your tutee can do to amelio-
rate the situation. (See the section
on locus of control in chapter 6.)

The student wants you to write a paper or to do homework for him or her.

The student may be panicked, lazy,
unable to do the work.

Never do the student's class work
or homework; instead, try to help
the student feel capable of doing
the work himself or herself.

The student may not understand
the function of the tutorial session.

Make certain the student is familiar
with tutorial policy regarding tutors
doing papers or homework for students.

*The student continually wants to talk about personal problems rather than do
school work.*

The student may have pressing
problems.

Briefly discuss the problems to determine how bad they are. If the
discussion needs more than about
ten minutes refer the student to a

POSSIBLE REASONS (*cont.*)

POSSIBLE APPROACHES (*cont.*)

counselor. If the problem is severe, do not counsel the student yourself.

The student may be afraid to get down to work.

If the student seems to be inventing personal things to talk about, get down to basics—such as, finding out why the tutee has come for tutoring, and then outlining what tutoring can accomplish. Be certain to do some tangible work that day.

The student doesn't want to be tutored.

The student doesn't feel in need of tutoring.

An examination and diagnosis of the student's work (by you and/or your supervisor) will tell you if tutoring is needed. If you find that the student does, indeed, need tutoring, demonstrate what tutoring can do for the tutee by planning a program outlining tangible goals and a time scheme for accomplishing those goals. Tell the student honestly if you believe he or she doesn't need tutoring at this time. But leave the door open for a time when tutoring might be needed.

The tutee's time is truly limited by other commitments.

Try to work out some arrangements for work at home, telephone conferences, lunch-hour meetings, and so forth.

The student is angry at teachers, or the system, and is taking it out on you.

Focus on what the student wants or needs to accomplish during the tutorial. Make it clear that you are not a teacher; you don't represent the system. While it may be disputable that the system or the teacher in question is all that bad, it is still best to focus on tutoring.

The student doesn't want to spend time outside of class without getting academic credit for it.

If you are tutoring for a course in which lab work is required, show your student how tutoring can help; if that doesn't improve the student's attitude, ask your supervisor to intervene. (It is best not to tutor an unwilling student, but you cannot dismiss a student from lab requirements.)

POSSIBLE REASONS *(cont.)*   POSSIBLE APPROACHES *(cont.)*

The student won't take the session seriously.

The student doesn't need tutoring.	(See p. 205 for approach.)
The student doesn't realize what tutoring can accomplish.	Like the student who is looking for miracles, this tutee needs to see tangible objectives and ways tutoring can meet these objectives.
The student cannot or will not take the tutor seriously because of age, sex or race.	Focusing on a tangible plan and not on attitudes may help (i.e., such as trying not to notice). If the problem persists, ask your supervisor to intervene. Eventually you may have to confront the tutee.
The student is anxious about needing tutoring and tries to hide the anxiety by continually joking about it.	Talking about the student's academic problems, goals, and ways to meet these goals may help. Find out if the student fully understands course requirements.
The student is not serious about school.	Discuss the student's reasons for being in school. If the problem is serious, a counselor may be needed.

The student feels hopeless.

The student may need a skills course and/or may be in a class that is too difficult or one that does not meet his or her academic needs.	Try to explore whether the student's feelings of hopelessness are grounded in reality. (For example, has the student been receiving bad grades?) This student should see an academic counselor and, perhaps, take, or at least sit in on skills courses or lower level courses, where appropriate.
The student may be demoralized by having to repeat a course.	Encourage the student to talk with the instructor.
The student may be having personal problems unrelated to school.	See if you can convince the tutee to see a counselor.

The student flirts with or has a crush on you.

The student wants to equalize the relationship between the two of you. The student is new to dating and misreads your professional interest for social interest.	Try to be professional, that is, to wait until your professional relationship is over before any social contact occurs. Discuss the matter openly with the tutee so that there are no hard feelings and so the tutee understands the reasons for

Courtesy Mark Dandelske

POSSIBLE REASONS (*cont.*)   POSSIBLE APPROACHES (*cont.*)

The student is nervous or embarrassed about being tutored.

The student is attracted to you.

your attitude. If the problem persists, you might consider asking your supervisor to have the tutee switched to another tutor.

The student comes to a session under the influence of alcohol or marijuana.

Nervousness, embarrassment, immaturity, lack of commitment to school, or psychological instability can cause a student to behave this way.

Terminate the session, but first be certain to tell the student why you will not tutor him or her (a student cannot concentrate well, may become hostile under the influence of stimulants or depressants, and is wasting the tutorial hour). Tell the student to come to see you when sober.

The student is consistently late or absent.

The student resents the need for tutoring.

The student doesn't need tutoring.

The student has emotional problems.

The student has personal responsibilities which interfere with his or her academic work.

Lateness or absence is just another manifestation of the lack of seriousness syndrome and the same approaches apply. (See p. 206.) However, be sure to let your tutee know why lateness and poor attendance are problems (it deprives other students of tutoring and wastes your time).

The student doesn't think you are competent.

The student may be older and feel that age brings wisdom.

The student may be sexist or racist.

Do not take the student's attitude personally; "isms," be they sex, age, or race, are based on ignorance and insecurity. Show the tutee that you

POSSIBLE REASONS (*cont.*)   POSSIBLE APPROACHES (*cont.*)

The student may have difficulty taking direction from a fellow student, or anyone who isn't a teacher. The student may realize that you are insecure or do not know a certain topic.

are a professional and that, although you may not know everything, you do know enough to ask questions or to look something up when you don't. Be prepared to discuss your tutoring qualifications without being defensive. If the situation doesn't improve, discuss the possibility of transfer with your supervisor.

The student doesn't seem to like you.

Any of the above "isms" may explain why the tutee doesn't like you.

See the approach directly above.

The student may be shy or insecure.

Try to be warm, undefensive, and, if possible, discuss any specific problems with the student before they become exacerbated. Above all, be friendly.

The student always tries to catch you in a mistake.

The student likes to be in control and is uncomfortable taking advice from others.

The student may not be aware of doing this.

Correcting may be his or her way of showing increased self-confidence.

Find out if the student is aware of his or her behavior and discuss how it interferes with learning, and how it makes you feel. Point out that everyone makes mistakes. Try not to feel personally attacked.

Academic Sources

The student is finding school too difficult.

The student may be taking a course or courses at the wrong level.

The student may need a skills course (reading, writing, ESL, math) before being ready to enter mainstream courses.

The student may not be ready for school at this time.

Talking about some of these reasons may prove helpful. You should also recommend academic counseling.

The student may have personal problems.

Try to get the tutee to see a psychological counselor.

POSSIBLE REASONS *(cont.)*	POSSIBLE APPROACHES *(cont.)*
The student may be overanxious.	If you find that the student's anxieties about school are exaggerated, help the student see this by reviewing together what the student has already accomplished, including essays and tests, and review the feedback from the teacher. (Sharing your own experiences might be particularly helpful here.)
The student may not be studying enough.	If it seems that the student has the ability to do well in the course, find out if the student is putting in the requisite time. Talk about the student's goals for the course and how much time and work is needed to meet these goals.

The student doesn't speak English well enough to be understood.

The student may not be speaking English outside of school and/or may not be getting necessary practice in conversation or grammar.	Check to see whether the student is now taking or plans to take an English conversation class and discuss the value of such a class. Talk to the student about the importance of speaking English whenever possible, reading English newspapers, watching English-language tv, and so forth. (See chapter 5.)

The student doesn't tend to do homework.

The student may not understand the homework assignments (yours or the teacher's). The student may be distracted by social or personal matters. The student may not be interested in the course material. The student may have work or family responsibilities.	Try to go over all homework assignments carefully. Discussing the value of the homework reinforces the material already learned and encourages independent thought on the subject. Help the student to find free time by asking him or her to list responsibilities and to set up priorities.

The student wants to move ahead and do work for which he or she isn't ready.

The student wants you to do his or her homework.	Try to find out the student's homework assignment. (Ask to see a syllabus, if necessary.) Explain why you don't want to work on homework in the lab. (See above.) If you note the student is really anxious

POSSIBLE REASONS *(cont.)*   POSSIBLE APPROACHES *(cont.)*

about the assignment, you may want to go over some of it beforehand, and to promise that you will review it once it is completed.

The student may be anxious to keep up with the rest of the class.

Talk with the student about the importance of understanding basic material before going on to more complex matters. (Find out how important the material in question is to a total understanding of the course; perhaps you can move on without doing the student any damage.)

Tutor Origins

You don't know the answer.

You haven't studied the subject enough.

Try to prepare better for your sessions.

You do not know everything.

Ask another tutor or your supervisor. Look it up yourself.

You feel frustrated or impatient with your tutee.

The student is progressing slowly.

Try to determine why the student is progressing so slowly. See if the student is satisfied with the learning pace. Talk about goals for the term and alternate ways to reach them.

You don't realize how slow the learning process is.

Compare notes with other tutors about what are appropriate rates of learning. Talk to your supervisor. Never let the student know you are disappointed with his or her rate of learning. In some cases, the student may need to revise academic goals and consider alternatives to academic work. (If you suspect such is the case, urge the student to see an academic advisor.)

You don't like your tutee.

You or your tutee might be a sexist, racist, or an ageist.

You may have a truly obnoxious student, or one with whom you simply cannot get along.

Sometimes we are unaware of our own prejudices. Consider carefully your own "isms." If the feelings are mutual, talk to your supervisor; transferring the student to another

POSSIBLE REASONS *(cont.)*

POSSIBLE APPROACHES *(cont.)*

tutor may solve the problem. If *you* are the problem, try to resolve it yourself. Talk to the student; try to find something about him or her you can relate to. Examine your feelings. You will have learned a lot if you can transcend your negative feelings.

You are attracted to your tutee.

A past relationship with a tutee, an attractive tutee, and/or a lack in your social life can all make you susceptible to attraction despite the professional relationship.

Do not act on your feelings unless you are willing to terminate the tutorial; it is unfair to use your position as tutor to further your social life.

You are unsure of the subject area.

The tutee is at a more advanced level than you.

You have not studied the subject in several years and have not brushed up on the subject.

The subject has never been one you were good at.

Unless you can quickly learn the material, have the student switched to someone who does know it.

You discover you gave your tutee incorrect information at a previous session.

You guessed at an answer because you were afraid to say you didn't know.

You thought you knew, but didn't.

Apologize and tell the student why you thought the answer you gave was correct. Discuss how everyone makes mistakes, even tutors.

You just don't feel like tutoring today.

You have other things you would rather be doing.

Personal or social problems are intervening.

If you are so unhappy, distracted, or tired that you can't tutor, don't. However, only cancel if it is utterly necessary. Students often feel personally rejected when tutors don't show up—also, they need you. That's why they come for tutoring.

You feel like a failure.

Your tutee doesn't seem to be making any progress, has failed, or has gotten a low grade in the course being tutored.

You should talk to your supervisor about who is responsible for your tutee's failure. Perhaps you did not do all you could have done to help your tutee; however, using that rea-

POSSIBLE REASONS (*cont.*)

POSSIBLE APPROACHES (*cont.*)

soning, since the tutee was also attending a class, the teacher would be as culpable. Another, and probably the most important, element to be considered is the tutee's own responsibility and/or ability to do the work.

Teacher/Student Conflicts

Problems discussed under the subject heading teacher/student are those concerning dynamics between teacher and student which enter the tutoring arena in some way, either because the student brings them to you or because you learn about them indirectly (from other students or from essays or tests the student shows you). This is the trickiest problem area for you to contend with because you are normally not there when the problem occurs and must rely on third-party evidence, verbal or written, to understand what has occurred; therefore, you must take care to be especially diplomatic and not jump to conclusions. Many of these problems are best resolved by either you or your supervisor talking directly with the teacher. The problems fall into only two major subcategories: personal and academic.

Personal Factors

The teacher doesn't recognize the student's special needs (such as a handicap or a learning disability; shyness, pride, hypersensitivity, or fear of failure).

POSSIBLE REASONS

The teacher may not have confronted your tutee's particular problem before and may not, therefore, know how to deal with it.

The teacher may not want to make special considerations for any student.

POSSIBLE APPROACHES

Encourage your tutee to talk to the teacher about his or her special needs; if the student is reluctant to confront the teacher directly, urge your tutee to speak to his or her counselor. (Also, find out whether teachers are receiving information on how best to approach handicapped students. If they are not, perhaps your lab supervisor can take the matter up with the special counselor for the handicapped.)

The tutee feels that the teacher doesn't like him or her.

The student may be afraid of failing the course and is projecting these negative feelings onto the teacher.

The student may be hypersensitive and/or misreading indifference for dislike.

Try to find out any specific reasons why the student feels "rejected." Explore with the student how he or she feels about the subject and get him or her to verbalize any fears. Encourage the student to meet with

POSSIBLE REASONS (*cont.*)

POSSIBLE APPROACHES (*cont.*)

The teacher may not like the student.

The student may have problems dealing with authority.

his or her teacher to talk over any course problems. (An interview with the teacher may help to demystify him or her.)

The student asks the tutor to intervene with the teacher.

The student is intimidated by the teacher.

The student feels insecure and in need of support.

The student must be encouraged to confront the teacher personally. If the student is too nervous to encounter the professor, try roleplaying the potential encounter to get the student to verbalize reasons for insecurity or fear, or to invent constructive strategies for approaching the faculty member. After the student has seen the teacher you might need to follow up with a visit yourself. (Check with your supervisor first and make sure your tutee approves.) In rare cases you may have to accompany your student to a teacher conference.

The teacher embarrasses the student.

The teacher may not realize how sensitive the student is, or may not care.

The teacher may be sadistic.

Encourage the student to approach the teacher, especially if it is possible that the embarrassing behavior will recur; or if the student prefers not to do that, urge him or her to focus on academic problems.

The teacher's comments on papers are extremely unsupportive.

The student is not doing well and the teacher doesn't wish to mislead him or her.

The teacher does not realize the importance of positive support.

Encourage the student to have a conference with the teacher and thereby get more personal feedback. If possible, get some feedback from the teacher yourself—but only if the student gives permission, and tutorial policy allows such tutor/teacher contact.

The student complains of harassment (sexual or personal).

The incident has actually occurred.

The student may have invented or exaggerated the incident.

The student may have mistaken affection for sex.

Put the student in touch with the lab supervisor and/or counselor. If the student is unwilling to see either, ask his or her permission to speak to your supervisor yourself.

Academic Sources

POSSIBLE REASONS (*cont.*)   POSSIBLE APPROACHES (*cont.*)

The teacher's corrections are incorrect or unfair.

The teacher is overworked and/or careless.

The teacher doesn't know the subject area very well.

The teacher is insensitive.

Discuss the problem with the student only insofar as to correct any misinformation. Do make the student aware that even teachers make mistakes. If the teacher's grading is consistently incorrect or insensitive, discuss the matter with your lab supervisor; never tell your tutee your opinion of the teacher.

The teacher's assignment is too difficult for the student or for the class.

The student is in a class which is too difficult for him or her.

The teacher is not cognizant of the class's learning needs.

Try to find out what the course prerequisites are and see if your tutee has fulfilled those prerequisites. The student may need to be switched out of the class and, if this appears to be the case, urge him or her to see an academic counselor. Also, speak to your lab supervisor about setting up extra tutorials for the student. If the teacher doesn't seem to be dealing with the student's problem, urge the student to set up a conference with the teacher.

The student does not understand the teacher's explanations.

The teacher may be lecturing above the student's head.

The teacher may be lecturing above the heads of all the class members.

The teacher may be a poor speaker or have difficulties with the English language.

Ascertain whether the problem is the student's or the teacher's by determining how other students are doing in the class. Make certain you go over class material slowly, putting everything into very clear language. Suggest that the tutee make an appointment with his or her professor.

The teacher's explanations are different from those of a previous teacher.

The teacher may have a unique approach.

Show the student how different approaches often lead to the same conclusion. (You might try to find examples of different approaches in

POSSIBLE REASONS *(cont.)*

POSSIBLE APPROACHES *(cont.)*

textbooks.) So that the student will not be confused, use the current teacher's approach when tutoring. (A meeting between you and the teacher, if the tutee is comfortable about this, may help you understand the teacher's approach.)

The tutee complains that the teacher is generally not doing his or her job.

The student is being unfair to the teacher and/or doesn't understand what the teacher is trying to do.
The teacher is new and is not fully aware of the course or student requirements.
The teacher is irresponsible.

Try to focus the lab session on your student's academic needs rather than on teacher/student dynamics. If there is overwhelming evidence of teacher culpability, alert your supervisor.

The teacher doesn't give the tutee feedback (on tests, with grades, or in the form of comments on papers).

The teacher does not believe in giving grades until the end of the term.
The teacher is not grading papers quickly enough.

Explain that some teachers believe in deemphasizing grades in favor of content. Encourage the student to make an appointment with the professor as soon as possible to ascertain progress in the course. Give the student ample feedback so that the tutee can get an objective sense of his or her abilities. (Try to find out the course requirements to determine the standards of your tutee's class.) Meet with the teacher to get feedback if your supervisor recommends it and your tutee agrees.

Tutor/Teacher Conflicts

In many colleges, the teacher will be just a name, someone you will hear about from students but may never meet yourself. (It is unfortunate that that should be the case; but the size of some institutions or the demands of academic life often give teachers little time for such meetings.) Sometimes, however, the teacher may seek you out, or you may need to meet with the teacher. In that case, it is well to remain aware that your job is supportive. Try not to get into an adversary relationship with the teacher; you will be of much more service to the student if you have good rapport with the student's teacher.

POSSIBLE REASONS *(cont.)*   POSSIBLE APPROACHES *(cont.)*

The teacher tells the student that your information is incorrect or that you are generally incompetent.

The teacher may have caught you in a mistake.	If you made a mistake, own up to it. Remember, everyone makes mistakes.
The teacher may disagree with you.	If the problem stems from differing interpretations, explain both interpretations to your tutee, but urge the student to adopt the professor's interpretation for class purposes.
The teacher may be threatened by you.	Ask your supervisor if it would be appropriate for either of you to contact the teacher to explore the matter fully.

The teacher is not supportive of you or the tutorial program.

The teacher may have had bad experiences with tutors. The teacher may be unaware of what goes on during tutoring. The teacher may interpret tutoring as interference.	Make certain both teacher and student understand what the tutorial has to offer. Speak to your instructor or lab supervisor about the program's need for public relations.

The teacher demands that you conduct sessions according to his or her methods and ideas.

The teacher uses a methodology (like x-word grammar) which needs to be reinforced in tutoring sessions.	See if you can use the teacher's methodology in your sessions. If not, speak to your instructor or lab supervisor, who may transfer the student to a tutor who is familiar with the teacher's methodology.
The teacher misunderstands the nature of the tutorial. The teacher misunderstands what is going on in tutoring sessions.	If the teacher misunderstands what tutoring does or is supposed to do, speak to your supervisor who may want to contact him or her (or refer the teacher to your supervisor).

The teacher accuses you of doing the student's work for him or her.

You may have been doing too much for the student during the session.	Stop! (See pp. 17 & 52 and chapter 4 for recommendations on how to encourage more student activity during sessions.)
The student's work may have improved drastically, but honestly.	Explain the nature of your tutorial assistance to the teacher or lab su-

POSSIBLE REASONS *(cont.)*

POSSIBLE APPROACHES *(cont.)*

pervisor, whichever is appropriate. Refer to your journal or case study for documentary evidence.

The teacher demands to know the contents of the tutoring session and to be given evaluations of the student's progress.

The teacher is concerned about the student.

The teacher misunderstands the role of the tutorial.

Explain the confidentiality policy to the teacher and refer him or her to your supervisor. Show the teacher any work (like lessons, or text-books) which you feel won't betray confidentiality. (Make sure you obtain the student's permission first. Perhaps you can arrange a meeting to include the three of you.) Discuss this matter with your supervisor if you are unsure of which option to choose.

Student/Student Conflicts

Some tutoring problems can occur as a result of problems among the students in a group-tutoring situation.

One or more students is bored or falls behind.

POSSIBLE REASONS

POSSIBLE APPROACHES

The group is of unequal ability.

See if you can form a more homo-genous group by transferring some students to another group; if you can't do this, use peer-teaching methods to get the students to teach each other in their areas of strength. Use self-paced learning for those students who are "out of sync" with the group.

You have not adequately diagnosed your tutees' needs.

Get feedback from your students frequently enough so that you are sure you are tutoring them at their level.

Not everyone in the group speaks English well.

Your students are not native speak-ers of English.

Speak to your instructor or lab su-pervisor about establishing a special group for second-language learners.

Your students have a handicap that affects their speech.

Encourage all your students to speak slowly and clearly. If your

POSSIBLE REASONS *(cont.)*   POSSIBLE APPROACHES *(cont.)*

tutees are having trouble speaking, see about their getting speech tutoring and/or conversation practice.

Not everyone participates in group discussion.

The students may be bored or may not understand what is going on.

Make certain you're working on a level that can interest and challenge students.

The students may be lazy or academically passive.

Encourage all students to participate by calling on them, getting them to use the board, and to be generally active in session. Assign rotating group leaders. Ask students what they expect from the group. (See approach to "passive" student in this glossary and group techniques in chapter 2.)

Some students form a clique and leave others out.

Some students may know one another personally or have things in common such as race, sex, or language.

Talk to the clique about it, and, if necessary, break it up, transferring these students to other groups. Encourage all students to participate equally and not to socialize during the session.

One student dominates the group.

The student is ahead of others and is impatient.

Transfer the student to a group closer to his or her level.

The student is insecure.

The student is selfish and/or wants attention.

Speak to the dominant student about the problem as soon as possible.

The group is otherwise passive.

Be sure to call on students equally.

Two or more students argue frequently.

The students have strong and opposing feelings about a controversial subject.

The students know each other personally and/or have a personality conflict.

Ask them to stop. If they don't, ask the group to stand up for itself and demand equal time. Do not let this interrupt group work. Ask the dissenting students to work it out, alone or with you present, whatever works. If the problem persists, see if you can get one of them transferred.

CLASS PROJECT 2

The glossary has defined "problems" as functions of individual character or interpersonal relationships; the solutions it proposes are often also individual ones (as in advice to see the instructor or an academic counselor). Do you see any drawbacks to a psychological interpretation of behavior? What differences might social or political analyses make? To explore this, select some specific problems from the glossary that might have social or political causes and discuss different approaches to these problems. (For example: the student who doesn't want to attend lab because there is no credit for it; the adult student who finds class requirements are excessive; problems arising from sexist or racist attitudes.) You may wish to roleplay these situations before discussing the issues.

READING 14

When you consider the amount of discipline—not to speak of the intelligence, imagination, and expressiveness—it takes to be a writer, it always comes as a surprise when we discover that a particular writer was a "problem" student. The distinguished Indian writer, R.K. Narayan, was, by his own admission, the worst of students. Undisciplined, and easily distractable, he preferred to look out the window at cows chewing their cud than to listen to his professors' lectures, as you will see in the selection below from his autobiography.

READING QUESTIONS

1. Narayan clearly had difficulty with formal education. Is our view of this problem student influenced by our knowledge that he has grown up to be a famous writer? How can reading about Narayan's problems make you more sensitive to your tutee's problems with school?

2. What is it that Narayan dislikes about his education? Do his descriptions justify his antagonism?

3. Are you persuaded, as Narayan seems to be, that the best way to lose interest in literature would be to teach (or tutor) it?

14 | MY DAYS: A MEMOIR

R. K. Narayan

Before actually entering the university for my B.A., I had a whole year's reprieve by failing in the university entrance examination held in the high school. I had expected to fare ill in physics and chemistry, both of which had defied my understanding. I never understood what I was expected to do with the "data" provided with the so-called problems, the relevance of "atmospheric pressure" or "atomic weight," or what to do with logarithm tables, or the why or how of a "normal" solution. These points never became clear to me either through my own efforts or through our teacher's explanations. I had been certain of failure in these two subjects, but, as if by a miracle, I had somehow passed in them, though not with flying colours. On the contrary, I had failed where I was most confident—English. I failed so miserably and completely that everyone wondered if I was literate at all. My father, in spite of his strict attitudes in school matters, had one very pleasant quality—he never bothered about the examination results. He always displayed sympathy for a fallen candidate; he had no faith in the examination-system at all. But even he was forced to exclaim in surprise, "Stupid fellow, you have failed in English! Why?" Proficiency in English being a social hallmark, I remained silent without offering any explanation, though I knew why. One of our English texts was a gray-bound book of chilling dullness called *Explorations and Discoveries,* pages full of Mungo Park's expeditions and so forth. In my whole career I have not come across any book to match its unreadability. I had found it impossible, and totally abolished it from my universe, deciding to depend upon other questions in the examination from *Oliver Twist* or *Poetical Selections.* But I found in the examination hall that four out of six questions were based on *Explorations*—that horrible man the question-setter seemed to have been an abnormal explorationist. I gave up, left the examination hall in half an hour, and sat in contemplation on one of the brick monuments beside the lily pond.

My outlook on education has not really improved with the years. A few years ago when my daughter in exasperation threw up her studies, crying, "Why should I bother about arithmetic?" I let her drop out without a word. Thereby she found more time at home for books and music. Now when my grandson shows any disinclination for school, I always support his cause, but of course his parents take a different view. As a grandfather I view his unseen masters as complicated, sinister beings who cannot be trusted. I keep my ears to the ground to find out if there has been any incident at his school. I was opposed to the system of being prescribed a set of books by an anonymous soulless body of textbook-prescribers, and of being stamped good or bad as a result of such studies. My natural aversion to academic education was further strengthened when I came across an essay by Rabindranath Tagore on education. It confirmed my own precocious conclusions on the subject. I liked to be free to read what I pleased and not be examined at all. . . .

In 1926 I passed the university entrance examination and took my seat in the lecture hall of Maharaja's College for my B.A. The college is built in the early French style with octagonal turrets and arched windows on one side and Athenian columns on the other, giving on intoxicating views of the landscape up to the horizon. There was no escape whichever way one turned. A windowed classroom looking out over a landscape is deadly for scholarly concentration. If a student is to listen attentively to lectures he should be cooped up in a windowless classroom in the heart of a city. At Madras the school windows let on a view of nothing more stirring than the wall of the next building, sometimes blank or, worse, plastered with posters. But here in Mysore I found the classroom windows revealing trees and birds, or meadows with cows placidly chewing grass and perhaps the cowherd sitting in the shade. In such a setting, I found the teacher's voice a meaningless drone, which one had to tolerate perforce. From the eastern corridors of the college, one saw Chamundi Hill in all its fullness framed in arches along the parapet; Maharaja's College was on one ridge of the city, with the hill and the Lalitha Mahal Palace on the other; in the valley in between lay the city with the golden dome of the palace standing out. During the political-science hour, one could watch the shadow of clouds skimming the mountainside, alternating with patches of sunlight, or the mirage shimmering across the landscape, and nothing seemed more irrelevant than the Location of Sovereignty in a Modern State or Checks and Balances in Democracy.

For English literature and history, we had to move to the Greek end of the building, on its western side. Now the view was from a gallery seat through a doorway, between tall, fluted columns; one could see the playground and pavilion bounded by a railway line, with a little train whistling and ambling up and down periodically; there was also a glimpse of the Oriental Library, with friezes depicting the life of God Krishna along its walls and inscribed pillars on its lawns, where once again one noticed cows grazing with concentration and contentment. (There are more cows in Mysore than in any other city, though not milk.) During my college years, I became so familiar with the scenic details and their transformations around that I could have drawn up, if need be, a time-table of the natural events. During June and July, for instance, fitful drizzling alternated with sunlight bursting through the clouds, and a rainbow some-times arched over the hill. If a painter had attempted to put all these things on his canvas, he would have been berated for overstatement, but Nature, having no such qualms about criticism, was exuberant and profuse and distracted my attention from my lessons.

I missed a great deal that went on in the classroom, with a couple of exceptions. Shakespeare, taught by Professor Rollo, was enjoyable and edifying. Tall and graceful, Rollo looked like an actor and he read the lines in different tones effectively. He did exquisite monologues. When he trailed and swept his (academic) gown and paced up and down on the platform, you heard the king's voice; when he wrapped his gown close, you heard the fool's remarks, and got at the meaning of Shakespeare's verse. Professor Rollo was an ideal teacher. Even now, from somewhere in Cheshire, he occasionally writes to his old students. The only other professor who sounded interest-ing was Professor Venkateswara, who taught us Indian history. His home was across the play-field and only after he heard the bell for his hour did he leave his study. We crowded beside the Greek column and watched the football field while he emerged on the horizon, clad in dhoti, academic gown, and turban. He had a portly figure and arrived unhurryingly, always late by a quarter of an hour, and entered the lecture hall muttering an apology for being late. When settled, he would produce from somewhere a small strip of paper with a few lines of ancient inscription copied on it. "I came across these lines. . . ."—they could be Asoka's edicts carved on rocks and pillars dated 250 B.C. or a Mughal chronicler's note—but it was always engrossing, bordering on fiction, and would be the starting point of his lecture. He never proceeded chronologically but pursued several channels of historical facts and parallel concepts simultaneously. He would not notice the time passing or the bell going off at the end of his hour, but continued and encroached on the next hour, while Professor Toby hovered outside and made several infructuous attempts to step in and teach Greek drama or eighteenth-century poetry. Professor Toby was shy and timid, looked exactly like Laurel of Laurel and Hardy, and he constantly stroked his chin as if in perplexity. We would not, however, feel sorry that his lectures were delayed, as his teaching made one's mind wander, even if one's body could not actually slip out and relax on the pedestal of Asoka Pillar at the Oriental Library. His accents were peculiar and we never understood a word of his lecture in the class. For his part he never lifted his head or looked at anyone, nor did he take the roll-call, being unable to pronounce a single Indian name. For many years, it was rumoured that he had thought that he was teaching at a women's college, mistaking the men's dhotis for skirts and their tufts for braids. He was a good man, though, and many a venturesome young man visited his house and pleading poverty took loans from him. Since he never looked up or knew a name, he never identified his borrowers and lost money regularly. He spent over a quarter-century in this same isolation, retired, and was not heard of again. His parting message on the last day of his lecture was, "I hope your interest in literature will not vanish with the examinations," or some similar-sounding words. With this farewell, he hopped off the platform and was gone. We lost sight of him after his retirement. A few years ago, however, I was in Leeds and took a trip to visit the home of the Brontë sisters. There I noticed him in a hat shop, trying on a bowler hat. As usual his eyes were fixed like a yogi's on the ground, he was stroking his chin in perplexity. I was on the point of hailing him across the counter, but he left abruptly and I saw him no more.

My inseparable friend at the college was Ramachandra Rao. Slight of build and only five feet tall, wearing thick lenses, he was endowed with an ebullient nature. He sat beside me on the class bench, joined me again for a four-mile walk towards the hill, shared my cigarette expenses, jokes and observations, and was full of humour and laughter. As the final exams approached we "joint-studied." After dinner I walked to his home in Santhepet, a couple of miles away, a vast household teeming with many cousins and aunts where he managed to keep a room for himself. We sat down methodically at nine o'clock, determined to get through Hazen's *European History* or Gilchrist's political theories before the night ended—a fight to a finish with the subject, the heart of the matter to be wrenched out of the book, to recoup all that we had missed in the classroom. One of us read, the other listened by turns—thus we hoped to relieve the tedium of study. But in practice, hardly had one of us read ten pages when the other would interrupt with an observation, "Why waste time on this portion? We won't have any question on Italian unity this year. It was given two years in succession—skip it. Bismarck is more likely." Arguments for and against the view. We would decide to take a quick glance through Italian unity, skipping details, not the heart of the matter but just the outline of the heart. Resuming the study after this interlude, we would start off again and come to a halt when something else came to mind, perhaps the amours of Maria Theresa, or some reminiscences of the classroom, or the farewells on the last day after the "social-gathering," and the group photo. After all this recollection in tranquillity, one of us would notice the Hazen lying open and suddenly declare, "I say, only fifteen days left! Even if we devote twenty hours a day, we will never finish the portion." We would be seized with panic and resolve: "Let us sit up till six A.M. if necessary and finish European history, so that we may go on to other subjects."

"Quite right. What if we don't sleep? Let us have all the sleep after April."

"What about Indian history? Luckily no Greek history this year. Otherwise you would have six hundred pages of Bury!"

"Why go into that now?"

"We must get someone to summarize all the subjects in ten pages each. We must request Seenu to do it; after all, he has no public exam this year."

Seenu, one year our junior in class, always obliging, would willingly undertake such literary tasks (as he still does, as a secretary for whichever maharaja or governor happens to employ him at the moment). This was a sudden, agreeable solution to our problems, bringing such a relief to our minds that we would shut the book and go out in search of a tea shop. A leisurely walk through the streets, marvelling at the tranquil air that the city wore at night, and after one or two cigarettes, we would return to our desk past midnight. Hazen again, but presently Nature would assert itself and make us nod; we would realize that "joint study" was a waste of time and that we should study separately if at all and meet occasionally to discuss and clear doubts, or better still watch for any secret leakage of the question papers through the devious and dark agencies operating in Bangalore, a city full of adventurous possibilities. And so goodnight, one precious day out of the fifteen before the examination gone irrevocably.

Nineteen-thirty, when I attained a belated graduation, became a year of problems.

What should one do with oneself now? Different suggestions came in from different quarters. One could become a lawyer, or a minor civil servant, or what not. At first I toyed with the idea of studying for an M.A. degree in literature and becoming a college lecturer. While I was going up the stairs of the Maharaja's College with my application for a seat in the M.A. class, a friend met me half-way and turned me back, arguing that this would be a sure way to lose interest in literature. I accepted his advice and went downstairs, once for all turning my back on college studies.

READING 15

The following case study was written by a former student in one of the author's peer-tutoring classes. As you will find, Ferguson had a number of problems tutoring Patricia. Some were the tutee's and probably would have been there, no matter who was the tutor; some were a result of their particular tutor-student dynamic.

READING QUESTIONS

1. What were Ferguson's major problems tutoring Patricia? What or who caused these problems? How effective was her approach to her student?

2. Notice that Ferguson decides that a massive effort needs to be made two weeks before the end of the semester. Is this a strategy that you would choose? Why or why not?

3. Why did Ferguson feel it was necessary to work with her student in a large, crowded library some distance from the college?

4. This is the third student case-study in which the tutor had to confront—or thought she had to confront—a hostile tutee. Why are they all so similar in this respect? What might the learning situation, educational system, or social structure have to do with imagined or real tutee hostility?

15 | CASE STUDY: PATRICIA BAUER

Wendy M. Ferguson
LaGuardia Community College

Throughout my brief but fulfilling tutoring experience, I have met all kinds of students: Bold students, shy students and students who just don't care about school. Whatever the category may be there is a tutoring technique for each individual. Some techniques are just a little harder to develop than others, as was the case for me.

I can never forget the day I first met Patricia Bauer. I was sitting in the staff lounge at the Writing Center, when the secretary approached me and asked me if I had a student. My reply was "No." I was then introduced to Patricia, who didn't seem to like the idea that I was going to be her tutor. She had a look of puzzlement on her face and she asked "Is she my tutor?" I took it upon myself to answer her. I said "I am a peer tutor and I can help you with your English if you like."

I led her into one of the small cubicles and decided that I should really use the entire session to break the ice between us. It is a technique that I had relied on plenty of times before and it usually worked. I just knew that Patricia and I were going to be friends, but things did not turn out the way I had anticipated. Instead of gaining ground with Patricia, I felt as though I were losing ground, even in our first session.

I asked her how long she had been attending LaGuardia. She obviously didn't want to discuss it, because she didn't even answer me. I decided to try again, so I asked her where she lived. This time she responded quickly: "Why? What business is it of yours where I live? Do you get paid for asking me stupid questions?" At that moment, I just wanted to walk out of the cubicle and leave her sitting there but I decided against that. Instead I said, "I don't get paid for this but you do get help with English."

Aside from Patricia's negative attitude towards me, she seemed genuinely interested in English. The essays that she'd written in class were beautifully constructed and well-written. Her problem was in the area of verb tense.

After our initial meeting Patricia became very defensive whenever I pointed out an error she had made. At many times during a session she would actually take charge and try to tutor me in English. Whenever Patricia got into one of these moods I would sit back and let her teach. Most of what she was pointing out to me was true, but she never did these things on her papers.

It was hard for Patricia to realize that her work wasn't perfect. It was even harder for her to accept that tutors sometimes make mistakes, too. On one of these occasions, around our sixth session, Patricia pointed out to me that I had made a spelling error. From that point on whenever I told her something or showed her a solution, she would always question my judgment. She asked so often whether I was sure I knew what I was doing, that I felt as though Patricia was beginning to lose what little confidence she had in me. I wanted to be right all of the time for her, but I knew that was next to impossible. So, whenever I was in doubt I asked another tutor. Well, this technique didn't sit too well with Patricia either. She felt as though maybe the other tutor should have been her tutor because they knew "a hell of a lot" more than I did. As our seventh session approached I felt as though I hadn't made any progress with Patricia: I was only prolonging her problem; it was then that I decided to develop my technique.

With the exit exam two weeks away I decided that Patricia and I had to work together for more than 45 minutes a week. I decided that if Patricia did a miniature research paper on verb tense, she would get a chance to practice what she had researched. By learning about the topic Patricia would become more self-conscious and wouldn't make as many verb tense errors as she had in the past.

The next time I met Patricia I laid down some rules and told her that if she was going to pass the exit exam we would have to work together and not against one another. I also suggested to her that we meet at the New York Public Library at 41st Street and 5th Avenue to do the research work. At first Patricia refused, but when she realized that what I was suggesting was really beneficial to her, she agreed.

When I met Patricia at the library I helped her choose some books on English grammar; they were plentiful. After we brainstormed, Patricia worked on the research paper for about five and a half hours. When she finished I went over the paper with her and corrected a few errors. I went over the paper once again to be sure. I was so excited I felt as though a heavy load had been lifted from my heart. Patricia was just as excited as I was. We went out together that night to celebrate. It was to be the beginning of a great friendship between us, I thought.

The next time I saw Patricia was December 2nd. She had already taken her exit exam. I was anxious to hear how she had done on the exit exam. When she told me that she had failed, my heart sank. I began to wonder: "Was it my fault?" "Could I have been more help to her?" All of these crazy thoughts rushed through my mind. Patricia turned and said to me, "Thanks for your help."

Until this day I don't know if Patricia was being sarcastic, or if she really meant what she said. However, whenever I see her in the halls she doesn't even look my way.

READING 16

, Born in Cleveland, Ohio, and educated at Vassar College, Ann Cornelisen went to Italy to study archaeology and instead spent ten years working with a social agency setting up nurseries in impoverished villages there.

In Women of the Shadows (1976), *Cornelisen describes life in one such small town: it is a hard, bitter life, one of fruitless struggle against proverty, ignorance, and isolation. Pinuccia is an elementary school teacher, but the chapter is less about her than about the general problems educating the children of the village.*

READING QUESTIONS

1. What impression do you get of schools in rural Southern Italy? What does education mean to people in this village? How do these attitudes about education compare with those of our own society?

2. What is Pinuccia's attitude towards her students and how do you think it affects her handling of them? Do you agree with Pinuccia's assessment of the children she teaches?

3. Although we do not meet Pinuccia until the chapter is half over, Cornelisen has given the chapter her name. Why has she done this? Further, the writer includes many details about the life of this character that do not seem to bear on her role as a teacher. What purpose do they serve and how do they help us to understand Pinuccia's and Cornelisen's intent?

16 | WOMEN OF THE SHADOWS

Ann Cornelisen

PINUCCIA

What parents or children may think of the *scuola dell' obbligo* (the first eight years of school) is not important, for it is what its name implies—obligatory. If asked, the children shrug. It is something to endure, not to think about, not to like or dislike. The parents will say it is a good thing because there are no jobs now for anyone who does not have "that piece of paper." Some talk about "civilized people," that they must be educated: the skill is less useful than the piece of paper. Others are more openly ambitious. "My children must not work as I have. There are schools now. They can be teachers, or bookkeepers, or surveyors." The same parents would rather feed and clothe their children, letting them drift through drab years, than have them stoop to the physical labor that has been the family curse. They can, at least, be proud that their children are above such work.

Peasants have chosen their models from those around them who appear to succeed, those who condescend to regulate the minutiae of daily existence. The all-enveloping bureaucracy of the government offers safety with the chance to arrange, not be victims of imbroglios. It also offers a certain social position which, though not lofty, requires the automatic civility the parents have never enjoyed. And, at the end of life, there is a pension. They are reaching for the possible, and the school, that piece of paper, is the means.

Because it is so important, they have definite opinions about the school, especially the mothers who watch and hear and resent the half-measure of each school day. Who would listen to them? No one—and besides, there is danger in criticism.

Four hours a morning or afternoon belong to the school. To provide the number of cubic centimeters of "air" deemed vital for each child, the classrooms have the general demensions and acoustics of a squash court. It is a sweet-sour touch of grandiosity when scarcity imposes two shifts. Some ministerial rule of thumb says that, if the building is old, the desks should be new and vice versa, so formica and tubular metal units wobble and clatter on uneven brick floors, while splintery benchdesks with their writing surfaces furrowed by generations of pupils diligently chiseling away with their pens, sit squarely on greenish-white tile floors. The room will have the brief attention of a janitor or janitress, who sweeps up the old football pool tickets, shopping lists and cigarette butts around the teacher's desk and lines up the desks once more, creating the dusty, abandoned order of station waiting rooms.

The children shamble in wearing the leftovers of the family wardrobe, clothes that might keep them warm and were not needed by the others. Some who suffer from chronic ooze of yellow matter from their noses have their heads swathed in wool scarves. Others shuffle along in rubber boots so worn that their naked toes stick out the tips. When finally they sit down, the raggle-taggle gypsy look is camouflaged by rusty black smocks with white plastic lace collars. Reforms come, reforms go, but the black *grembiule* remains inviolate. A few regularly forget to wear theirs and a few wait month after month for the School Aid Committee to give them one. It becomes a point of honor on all sides. Each morning the teacher shouts out the rule requiring the smock, and so the day begins. Attendance is taken, a few remarks about homework, more often than not untouched by children who live in houses with one bulb hanging in the center of a single room, and then problems are put up on the blackboard.

Conditions remain remarkably static in the elementary schools of Southern towns. Once the pupils are more or less occupied, the women teachers settle down to plan dinner, writing out the shopping list. The men collect in the hall for a cigarette and send the janitor to the nearest café to bring back coffee—after making sure the director has left. If he has, they can count on him to stay away for at least two hours: he has a number of small farms worked by tenants and is convinced that peasants will not work unless supervised. The teachers have plenty of time to read the newspapers. Everything takes time. All compositions and problems are done twice—the *brutta copia*, a marked-up first draft, and the *bella copia*, a final, clean version. It is a doubling-up that conditions the mind for life, but in school it helps the hours to pass. From one class a little girl is sent off with the list of the teacher's chores; from another, a boy, one who, as the teacher would say, will not profit from class, but who knows how to ingratiate himself, will spend the rest of the morning running for cigarettes, taking messages, even marketing for his teacher's wife. That is the best. He may have a chance to steal some fruit off a vendor's counter.

Days, five years of them, trip one after the other, varied only by the local religious ceremonies or the chance arrival of a Minister, which requires the mobilization of the school children, two by two, in long snake lines to swell whatever collected multitude.

Late in the winter of 1972 I asked eight children I have known since they were born to come to see me, bringing their school books with them. They were all in the first class. Their parents have had little schooling and most have forgotten how to read or write anything other than their names, which in practice is all they are ever asked to do. The fathers of those eight children have spent a total of thirty-six years in Germany. The mothers have stayed at home, taking care of these children who continue to be born with alarming regularity.

The children came, some suddenly timid, others echoing what their mothers had probably said: "Do we get a candy?" They did and then showed me their composition books filled with neat pages of A's and B's and C's. No one admitted to enjoying those endless rows of letters; one said words were better. Further on they had reached syllables, neat rows of them, which never became words. They were exercises to show the adjustments which are necessary to maintain the original sound of consonants as they are followed by the various vowels. Each child read me the next day's lesson. There were three different texts being used in as many sections of the first grade. (Teachers are free to choose texts from an "approved" list and usually do so on the basis of which salesman offers the largest "premium.") They shared certain sim-ilarities—brightly colored pictures of things outside the experience of mountain children—a little girl chasing a butterfly, which boys and girls alike said was stupid, a sailboat which one boy refused to believe could be a boat at all, and an airplane one girl said could not be one because it was a plain old bus with wings. The texts used very long words which invariably hit the end of the line and so had to be hyphenated. The children's concentration as they read out loud was an actual physical strain: their little bodies quivered with tension. The index fingers pressed so hard under each printed syllable that the nails turned white and the lit-tle voi-ces that fin-al-ly pronounced the words just did escape from vocal cords as taut as bailing wire. And the words they managed to read, pronouncing them properly, were astounding. Because Italian is written as it is pronounced, I imagined compositions of precocious brilliance. Little Carmela was looking at me with her large, sad brown eyes. She had finished, and I seemed not to approve. I told her how well she had read, how clever she was and asked how she had learned so fast. She stuck her head down in my lap, then looked up and giggled happily.

"Tell me, Carmela, what is the story about? You must know the rest of it too."

Her look of complete mystification told me the answer, that was reinforced as, one by one, the other children read. They could pronounce the words. Nothing had been said about any meaning the words might have. And so another step toward learning by rote had been masterfully accomplished.

I should not have been surprised. I had spent the evening before with a peasant family I have known for fifteen years. One of their sons, Salvatore, had just finished his military service and was looking for a job. When I first remembered him, he was perhaps nine, a small sturdy boy with delicate features, gray eyes and dry blond hair, like a new broom, that stuck up and out from an amazing number of cowlicks. He was shy, and I think, people puzzled him, for he never looked directly at them except to decide whether they were serious or teasing. Then, as though their faces held the answers to all mysteries, he would stare at them. He did not talk a lot either. Once he took me for a walk along the boundaries of his father's fields, which he knew followed a line sighted from the top of the hill, down between two oak trees, along a bean field as far as the copse where a fox lived, and from below the well to that stretch off to the right where the third branch of one particular fig tree points. He also showed me the trap he had built to catch the fox, who was eating their chickens. So far it had not worked. He had made himself a slingshot in case the fox showed himself in daylight. He never did. Before I left he fed the chickens and explained the economic advantages of raising pigeons. His mother teased him for being so willing at home and such a mule at school.

He shrugged. "I want to be outside," was all he said.

Perhaps two years later he volunteered to show me a brigands' cave, which turned out to be a black slit under a large rock ledge. He instructed me in just how to crawl through the narrow passage so that he could prove to me there was a big room behind where the brigands hid, that is what the shepherds had said. I did as I was told and found enough sheep droppings to prove, at least, that the shepherds and their flocks had escaped from the winter winds. He told me the band kept its guns there, and I nodded solemnly.

As he grew older he still liked to be outside, to work with his father, and school was still a punishment for him. He was not stupid; no one had ever managed to connect school subjects with the world that interested him. He repeated the fifth grade and went reluctantly into the middle school, where he stumbled again in the seventh grade, but did take and pass the final examination. He had his piece of paper.

He was sixteen then. The delicate features had coarsened and his voice had become a rasping basso profondo. Only his hair reminded me of the nine-year-old boy with the slingshot and the brigands' cave. He worked all summer for his father. In the fall he repaired shovels and picks, cut wood and then there were no more chores. His father said he could not sit out the winter, so he did what his friends had done: he went to Germany. The night before he left, he came to call on me, wearing a new white shirt with a collar so starched it seemed the points would perforate the cloth, and a pair of tight beige wool trousers, also new, already too tight for him and too cheap to last the month. This was his finery for the trip. On his feet he still wore the dung-caked farm boots of other years. He muttered over and over again,

"I'll get along. Don't know what I'm going to do exactly, but I'll get along. Don't worry."

He did for four years, carrying stones on a construction job. When he was called up for military service, he left Germany and put in his fifteen months without complaint. The night I met him again he was one of six hundred young men twenty-one years old to be examined for nine jobs in a factory some fifty kilometers away in the valley. Someone in the family had wheedled a recommendation from a local man, supposed to be influential, who had also obligingly provided a list of probable questions. When I arrived Salvatore was sitting in front of the fire puzzling over the questions. Syllable by syllable he muttered the words to himself, then shook his head and started again. He was reading as little Carmela did the next evening. The sounds were right, but they meant nothing to him. He was twenty-one, she, six. Trying to make a joke of it, I offered to be the Grand Inquisitor and read the questions to him.

"What form of government does Italy have? Italy is a . . ."(Republic)

"It's in Rome. Those people in Rome . . ." He went no further.

"Who is the President of Italy?" (This was sixty days after the last presidential election: Leone.)

"How should I know? DeGasperi. Wasn't he the famous one?"

"How is the President elected?" (By Parliament with a two-thirds majority of the voting members.)

"I guess in the elections. Next May we have elections."

"Who is the President of the United States?"

"Nixon."

"Who is the Pope and what is he?" (Pope Paul.)

"It's Pope John. He's the Bishop's boss."

"Where does he live?" (The Vatican.)

"Rome."

"No, they don't mean just Rome. More specific than that. Where?" He did not know.

We ran aground forever on "What are your social responsibilities?" They had become fashionable since he left school: the concept meant nothing to him. His younger sister found a textbook of hers with a single paragraph defining social responsibilities and told him to memorize it. He went off into the bedroom for twenty minutes. When he joined us again, he was sweating and red-faced.

"I can't memorize that. I don't understand the words."

Nor could he write the answers to the other questions in anything resembling Italian. He is not stupid, but after ten years in school, four years in Germany and fifteen months of military service, he is a functional illiterate. When I asked him if he had changed his mind about farming, he said.

"No, but you know how it is. Mamma's right. Everyone makes fun of peasants. I thought if I could get this job, maybe it would be better. I wouldn't just be a peasant."

I do not think Carmela and her little friends will be any more at ease with the mechanics of reading and writing than Salvatore, but I cannot feel that it is entirely their fault. Nor can their mothers do a great deal to help them. They know the teachers pay perfunctory attention to their classes. They see their children running errands and they hear the teacher screaming in dialect, but when they ask how they can help their children, they are told they are illiterate and can do nothing. They must wait until the end of the year to see if their children pass or fail. And at the end of five years those same illiterate mothers know their children do not write properly, still speak dialect, and read only comic books with ease. They have that first piece of paper. If they are sent on to finish the *scuola dell' obbligo,* the three years of the lower middle school with French and English and worst of all more Italian, they may have another piece of paper, but the question cannot be avoided—will they know how to do anything? Will they speak enough Italian to get around Rome or Milan where they must go to find work? Will they be able to answer questions on Salvatore's quiz? Will they get jobs? Apparently not. Each spring I find more young girls hoeing beans with their mothers, and when I ask if they have finished school, whether the girl nods yes or no, the mother always adds:

"But what's the difference? The choice is still the same. She can sit up there and learn to embroider, while she waits to find a husband, or she can come down here and learn to work—and make some money besides."

And the boys go to Germany.

Several days after my misadventures with reading and writing I ran into a young teacher I know. Years ago we saw each other every day or so in the way normal to village life, and since then we have met four or five times a year, sometimes casually at shops or in the market, sometimes at formal meetings and at other times, when, for no particular reason, we have talked alone at length. I know odd things about her that I would not know, would not expect to know, in a different sort of community.

Pinuccia was next to the youngest child in a family of three sons and four daughters. Her father was a tailor. He died ten years ago, shortly after ready-made clothes became available in the weekly market, but his trade had never produced a living in a town where old suits are more often turned than new ones ordered. Every morning of his life he peddled slowly down the Corso on his bicycle and just as slowly out to a few acres of land he owned. He plowed, hoed, planted or picked as the season dictated and then in the late afternoon pushed the bicycle, now piled high with bundles of firewood, slowly back to town and up the Corso. It was the land that fed the family, but his wife and children always maintained that he was a professional man whose hobby was farming and arranged the façade of their lives accordingly.

Signora Di Santis, Pinuccia's mother, is considered very devout. Each morning with her black lace veil firmly twisted under her chin, she settles into a particular seat on a particular aisle to await the beginning of Mass. She is always early, but something about her stiff, disapproving back suggests everyone else, even the priest, is late. She repeats the performance in the evening for Rosary. She is so regular that children ask their mothers very seriously if the church is Signora Di Santis' house. Between functions she is at home, invisible, cooking one assumes, mending probably, and though she thinks it is a secret, she used to spend that time making the trousers of the occasional suit commissioned from her husband. It is not strange that her nickname should be *La Pantalonaia*—the pants-maker—nor that her husband's nickname was Bartoli, after Gino Bartoli, one of the great Italian bicycle racers.

Their ambition was to raise seven "*Professori*," but financial pressure and nature, most especially nature, worked against them. Of the sons one is a bookkeeper, one a driver for the government insurance agency and one is unemployed, but has stood for every civil service examination posted in the last eight years and so is said to be "waiting." Of the girls, one is a nursery teacher, unemployed, two went to Normal School, Pinuccia being the one who managed to *win* a place as a permanent elementary teacher, and the fourth and youngest did not make it through the upper middle school and remains in her early thirties *una signorina da maritare,* a young lady to be married, which is more tactful than saying bluntly that she is a spinster. She is very much under her mother's command. The other six have married, not as well as they should, according to their mother, who now enjoys the luxury of a small pension paid in Money and the services of two full-time attendants—her youngest daughter and her daughter-in-law, the one married to the "waiting" son. He has been allowed to take up farming as a hobby.

Twelve years ago, when she first started teaching, Pinuccia was a small-boned, solid young woman with a broad face, not really round, high checkbones and large brown eyes, so dark they conceal her most fleeting interest. She turns them full on anyone who talks to her, but they never betray what she sees, much less what she thinks. Bright red cheeks were her one natural asset, which, probably believing high color to be a sign of low birth, she disguised with sallow, opaque makeup. In her enthusiasm she sometimes applied it so heavily that, when it dried, brownish lines checked it like china exposed too long to heat. She was always neatly and simply dressed except for *feste* when she could be astonishing in tight violet satin aswirl with rainbow peonies. Her one external defeet, not that she has ever considered it such, is a hoarse, rough voice, which time and the strains of marriage have made raucous.

The local euphemisms of refined speech bellowed out by Pinuccia sound like jokes, but she is serious when she calls feet "extremities" or excuses the term "pork" when discussing meat. She would never get in the front seat of a car without saying to the passengers in back, "*Scusate le spalle*"—Excuse the shoulders," i.e., my turning my back— and she is always coyly *in stato interessante,* never pregnant. From the young woman who used to say, "In the city they do such and such," knowingly and then add, "Don't they?" in a quiet plea for information, she has become an imitation of what she thought she wanted to be. At times she does not convince herself, but her inferiors will never be allowed to guess it.

She married a clerk in the tax office ten years older than she and balding. He is almost a parody so much does he look what he is in his sturdy, formless suit and his shoes with the heavy rubber soles. An inspection of his hands will show deepset splodges of ink and a long, not very clean nail on the little finger. He used to drift around town aimlessly in the afternoon and evening, neither gentry or peasant. Now he has a battered Fiat 600 and a little tweed hat and he *drives* aimlessly around town. It is not out of character that he is a vicious gossip. They have had three children in five years, but no matter how many more may come, Pinuccia will never resign her job any more than she will ever approve of birth control or divorce.

Pinuccia is an authority on her "rights" and always arranges for her full quota of maternity leave and the daily time off allowed for nursing her new baby. She also talks a great deal about the more or less intimate arrangements of her household. So it is that I know her husband wears undershirts she knits for him, which he changes once every two weeks when he bathes (if it is not too cold). She still uses washable sanitary towels and does not touch water on "those days." Her husband loves *baccalà* (dried cod), insists on unrefined olive oil and drinks a liter of wine with lunch. One of her children suffers from liver trouble. She swaddles her babies for at least the first six months and feels that as long as she is nursing, she is safe from pregnancy.

Much of her physical neatness has disappeared. Blouses are apt to be spotted; buttons are often missing. Her hair is only washed for holidays and her figure bulges with strange lumps and protuberances. Everything about her has sagged into lethargy except her tongue. Recently she told me that her mother-in-law had moved into their two bedroom flat with them. When I asked how it was working out, she did not understand why her answer amused me.

"Well, she's a help in the house, of course, but she's always telling my husband what to do and that makes me mad. My mother is right—one family, one house. You can't put two feet in one shoe."

She is neither better nor worse than the others. She does her work well, as she understands it, but, if she were to tell the truth, it is a source of income and social standing, not a vocation. This is the conversation I had with her about Salvatore and the children who had read to me. Clearly if there is to be a change, she will not initiate it.

"Of course I teach because I love my work, but if you only knew how impossible it is with *these* children. They come to school dirty, half asleep with their homework not done, and they're pigheaded as well. If I ask them why they didn't do their work, they just shrug. They don't care. They don't see any point in going to school. You can't expect any help from their families either. They're all illiterate, or almost all. I have three or four children out of thirty who are bright—*oh Dio*, not brilliant, but what you might call teachable—who try to speak well and they write well too, but, of course, their families are different. One's the daughter of another teacher, one's the son of a doctor, another the son of a colleague of my husband's. The rest of them—well—I do my best, but you end up screaming at them, and I admit it—in dialect. They're too thick to understand Italian, or they pretend to be. By the end of the morning I'm exhausted. It's hard to teach and look after a house and a family too. That's why I ask for the morning turn. Then by the time my husband comes home at two, everything's ready for lunch and the day can go on normally. But it's hard work.

"Sometimes they insist we go to courses. Then my husband doesn't like it. They're usually a waste of time too. *Scuola Attiva, Scuola Democratica*, all those social workers running around, finding out if children are healthy and wanting us to find out. I say that's up to doctors and for the rest, school-this or school-that may be fashionable for a time, but they pass, and we're still left teaching them to read and write.

"They've just put nursery schools under public instruction and everything's still disorganized, but in a few years, as I see it, children will learn their letters at nursery and the elementary schoolteacher's work will be easier—that is if the Ministry in Rome doesn't change the program. They change things, sometimes just to change them. I mean from a way that worked to one that just shouldn't be—like—for instance—having mixed classes—boys and girls together, using the same texts too. Now that may be all right in Anglo-Saxon countries. We always copy them as though their ideas and ways of doing things were better than ours. I don't like all this foreign influence—present company excluded, of course. *He* wasn't wrong when *he* said Italy for the Italians! As I say, mixed classes may be all right in Anglo-Saxon countries, but not in Italy. There's nothing you can do about it—we're hot-blooded. You put children together and they're just like animals, leaving out how these live at home. They start playing nasty games and then where does it stop? That's what they don't realize in Rome. Hot blood, I tell you. Hot blood! Boys and girls should not be mixed in classes together.

"And the textbooks. It's the same thing. I'm teaching them what is right, no? That's the job of a teacher, no? What a boy needs to know is different from what a girl needs. They have to know what's expected of them. I always used such a good book with the girls—I can't now, but before, yes—about the Madonna being a mother, just like our own and someday we too will be mothers, so we must respect ours, help them take care of the house and the babies. It wasn't a sermon, but it was right for these girls. After all, why do they need to read and write? They don't really, except—yes, agreed, everyone should know *how*—but what they need to know is how they are supposed to act. If we don't tell them, who will?

"No, I don't feel I should be preparing the girls for work in a factory or any other career—not even the boys. These are peasant children. Their minds aren't refined like city children's. Peasants are not civilized people, and making them restless for something they can't have, couldn't do if they had the chance—why—it would be silly. All right, the world is changing, but not that much and not down here. Listen to me, I know these people. The children need to know what is Right and Wrong without blowing up their heads with ideas they can never understand, and if you don't agree, I'm sorry, but *we* know what they need."

"We never did find one of the copper boilers. My little boy left the old house carrying it, but he doesn't remember where he stopped along the way. All I know is he went down into the valley and up, and we had to take the long way around with the furniture. It was bad enough hauling the heavy things without making the climb. A truck? After we bought light fixtures and a stove—with a fireplace and a gas burner, we'd never needed a stove before—there wasn't any money left. Besides, the truck couldn't get to our old house, so everything had to be carried as far as the Piazza anyway. My sisters and my mother helped. It took all day, but we finished before dark. We don't have enough furniture, and what we have is old and beaten up, but I don't care—just to have two bedrooms and a toilet with water, sometimes. That's enough for now.

"If I buy two piglets maybe by Christmas I can begin to think about a real bed for the children, that is, if my husband doesn't take the money. The only reason he agreed to move was the rent. It's a thousand lire ($1.50) a month cheaper. In his mind he's already spent it more times than there are months left in his life. He didn't want to come over here to the new houses. He says we're too far from the Piazza, there aren't any stores. We're second class citizens, he says, with no postman, no garbage collection, no protection. But men always talk about unimportant things. We never get any mail and there'll be garbage collection—someday. As for the Piazza, he can walk there, just like me. Men are like that, always holding out for the unimportant things. They don't spend much time in a house, and all they really want is their pasta ready when they come in. Beyond that, separate bedrooms, toilets, water in the house, they don't care. If they don't have them, they talk about them, mind you, but we care. We have to. We're the ones who have to make do—however it is."

BIBLIOGRAPHY

Bales, Robert F. et al., eds. *Small Groups: Studies in Social Interaction*. Rev. ed. New York: Alfred A. Knopf, 1965.

Moreno, Jacob L. *Psychodrama*. 3 vols. Boston: Beacon House, 1959–1977.

Patton, Bobby R. and Kim Griffin. *Problem–Solving Group Interaction*. New York: Harper & Row, 1973.

Schein, Edgar and Warren G. Bennis, eds. *Personal and Organizational Change Through Group Methods*. New York: John Wiley & Sons, 1965.

Sharan, Shloma and Yael Sharan. *Small Group Teaching*. Englewood Cliffs, N.J.: Educational Technology Pubs., 1976.

Shaw, M. E. *Group Dynamics: The Psychology of Small Group Behavior*. 2d ed. New York: McGraw-Hill, 1976.

Thelen, Herbert A. *Dynamics of Groups at Work*. Chicago: Univ. of Chicago Press, 1963.

Thompson, J. E. *Using Role-Playing in the Classroom*. Bloomington, Ind.: Phi Delta Kappa, 1978.

8 | *LEARNING*

A TUTORIAL PROTOCOL

The following dialogue—called a "protocol" by social scientists—is a typical one between tutor and tutee. They review homework and material from a previous lesson, discuss new material and, finally, the tutee does a writing assignment and so gets a chance to expound on all that was learned.

TUTOR: I'm glad you read the chapter on women's roles. (*S-R reinforcement*)

TUTOR: It certainly made me feel that our society has a lot of different models for women. (*cognitive hypothesis*)

TUTOR: What do you mean? (*S-R stimulus*)

TUTEE: Well, that women can have ideals; women can do a lot of good things in society. (*concept formation; definition*)

TUTOR: Give me some examples of what you mean. (*recall*)

TUTEE: Like being a mother, but also being a nurse, or a teacher, or a social worker. (*acquisition; encoding, storage, recall*)

TUTOR: Are those the only roles women can play? (*concept or category; create expectancies*)

TUTEE: What do you mean?

TUTOR: Well, what do you know about sexism? (*link to previous learning*)

TUTEE: Sexism is when the society represses women. It means that they can't work. (*definition—essential feature of concept*)

TUTOR: I dunno. I think sexism might be a little broader. You think it *only* means that they can't work.
How much do you think women make on an average? (*present novel item*)

TUTEE: As much as anybody—but maybe you wouldn't be asking me if that was so.

TUTOR: Right. On the average, they earn about two-thirds as much as men do. (*novel item*)

TUTEE: Wow. I guess a woman might still be able to work in a sexist society. But how can these women be models? (*concept*)
Teacher, nurse, social worker ... I guess that's not like being in business. They're all pretty low-paying. And you know, the chapter said something about women ... wait, let me find it. Here it is ". . . tend to develop in occupations that are related to traditional

233

female roles." I didn't really understand that. But part of what that's saying is that women still are in sexist roles. (*redefinition to fit a new concept; gain in meaning*)

TUTOR: What did you think the chapter meant by models?

TUTEE: Ideals, you know, like when you're a role model for your little sister, but now I see they just meant what we see is available in society. (*new concept*)

TUTOR: Good, I'm glad to see that. (*reinforcement*) Remember the chapter that talked about the role of tradition in "so-called primitive societies." Why don't you take the last twenty minutes to write about the role of tradition regarding women in modern society? (*link to previous learning; encoding*)

TUTEE: Now I can see how what we've been talking about fits in. (*self-reinforcement*)

Since you have probably been tutoring for some time now, the structure of the session should have been familiar to you. You may have wondered, however, about the words in parentheses. These terms, which we will discuss in the present chapter, are from the field devoted to the study of how we learn. Knowing words like "reinforcement" and "encoding" will not make you a better tutor; however, recognizing the processes of learning, and exploring educational applications of research into these processes, should help you to understand better *your* role in your tutee's learning.

STIMULUS-RESPONSE THEORY

Classical Conditioning

The classical psychological model of learning is based on a theory of conditioning called stimulus-response. This approach evolved from famous experiments in animal behavior which were conducted by the Russian scientist Ivan Pavlov (1849–1936) in the late nineteenth century. While dogs normally salivate at the sight and smell of food, Pavlov trained them to salivate at the sound of a bell by getting them to associate the sound with the smell of food. Salivation, then, is the conditioned response, and the response the animal now makes automatically to the sound of the bell, the conditioned stimulus, rather than to food, the unconditioned stimulus. In approaches derived from this model, learning is not a result of understanding. It is, instead, a response to a stimulus.

Although stimulus-response is primarily used to explain the acquisition of motor skills (like learning to swim) or habits (like learning to brush your teeth), it is also the theory underlying teaching and tutoring strategies that stress practice and repetition to ensure an "automatic" response, or to strengthen and improve a skill. In this way, it can be very useful. Drill work, for example, helps students remember facts and figures. However, stimulus-response models of education have, unfortunately, often been used in a way that was detrimental to learning. The material to be learned was presented in

Courtesy Mark Dandelske

isolation and context was disregarded (for instance, students learned vocabulary words without seeing them in sentences). The following excerpt from George Orwell's essay "Such, Such Were the Joys. . . ." presents us with a classic example of a stimulus-response model of education. In it Orwell recalls the mindless memorization of material which otherwise had no meaning for him:

> History was a series of unrelated, unintelligible but—in some way that was never explained to us—important facts with resounding phrases tied to them. . . . I recall positive orgies of dates, with the keener boys leaping up and down in their places in their eagerness to shout out the right answer, and at the same time not feeling the faintest interest in the meaning of the mysterious events they were naming.
>
> "1587?"
>
> "Massacre of St. Bartholomew!"
>
> "1707?"
>
> "Death of Aurangzeeb!"
>
> "1713?"
>
> "Treaty of Utrecht!"
>
> "1773?"
>
> "The Boston Tea Party!"

"1520?". . . .

"Field of the Cloth of Gold!"

And so on.

Orwell's education as depicted here certainly represents the triumph of Gradgrind (p. 19). We do not recommend you use such a system with your tutee. However, rote learning and drills are sometimes necessary when the bulk of material is great or certain elements of the subject matter are basic to any further understanding of it. (For example, memorizing the multiplication table is crucial to progressing further in arithmetic.) Vocabulary in a foreign language, chemical elements of the periodic table, historical names, dates, and places are some examples of things your tutees can learn using stimulus-response, for these are building blocks a person needs to think or work within a certain discipline. Repeated association may help students build up a reserve of material to draw from when working on more complex material. For instance, if students automatically learn to identify a simile whenever they hear *like* or *as* used in a comparison, they may understand more easily the literary work in which it is found. This automatic response may also help them retain material longer.

CLASS PROJECT 1

1. Form into groups with those in your discipline or related disciplines to:
   a. discuss what aspects or topics of your discipline might benefit from drill;
   b. as a group, write a drill;
   c. use the drill with someone who is not familiar with the drill material;
   d. discuss the results with your group.

2. Some theorists have suggested that classical conditioning may explain the formation of *attitudes* towards learning. Think about a subject you particularly dislike or like. If it is a subject you do not like, try to remember if there was a "punishment" connected to your learning of the subject? How did this punishment make you feel? If it is a subject you do like, did you receive a reward to perform well in this subject? Or did you reward yourself? Which punishments and which rewards do you associate with learning in general? Discuss your conclusions with your group.

LAB APPLICATION

Have your tutee prepare flashcards with items to be drilled on one side and their meaning or related information on the other, for example, a foreign word on one side and its English translation on the other. These flashcards can be used in a variety of ways: you can drill your student at the beginning of a session; your tutees can drill themselves at home or while travelling to and from school—especially to review for tests.

Operant Conditioning

Conditioning theory took a significant step forward when American psychologist B. F. Skinner developed the theory of "operant behavior." His experiments focused on *reinforcing* the initial stimulus, with the reinforcement *contingent* upon the subject's response. (For example, if a child, when learning to swim, is reinforced by praise and hugs for going into the water, the child is likely to *decide* to *continue* going into the water because doing so reproduces the reinforcement.) While in classical conditioning the subject automatically responds to a positive or negative stimulus, in Skinner's model, the subjects play a more active role. They gain a measure of control because their own actions trigger certain consequences. Since the subjects "operate" on their environment, the repeated reinforcement of certain kinds of responses is called operant conditioning.

Psychologists who think operant conditioning is at the core of human learning insist that learners have to feel they control or stimulate all reinforcement of learned behavior for learning to take place. In other words, learners must see that if they learn they will be *reinforced* positively—that is, rewarded.

The Role of Reinforcement Operant conditioning lends great weight to the importance of reinforcement in learning—especially positive reinforcement. In general, reinforcement tends to increase the rate of the operant's response. *Positive reinforcement* means rewarding or satisfying the person in some way, so that the desired response or behavior will be repeated. *Negative reinforcement* involves ending or removing something hurtful or painful. Practically, in human learning, negative reinforcement implies *deemphasizing* or *ignoring* a response—most usually the incorrect answer—in effect, withdrawing the positive reinforcement; thus, negative reinforcement is different from punishment. If you were to punish a student, you might actually embarrass or penalize your tutee for a "wrong" answer; however, Skinner believed that punishment was an unreliable basis for conditioning behavior and created negative side effects, as well. In human learning, for example, students who are "punished" for incorrect behavior may learn to avoid incorrect responses but they also may develop antagonism toward school or hostility to the teacher or tutor. Besides, in the effort to avoid punishment, people may not risk an answer, even if it's the right one. Positive reinforcement remains the most consistent and reliable means for developing "right-answer" responses.

Not only is the nature of reinforcement important in Skinner's scheme; timing is an essential consideration as well. For reinforcement to be unambiguous, it needs to be given within five seconds so that it is clearly linked to the event, or, if there is a delay, the reinforcement must be distinct enough so as to be connected to remembrance of the event. Moreover, Skinner documents that 100 percent reinforcement is necessary to establish behavior; once behavior has been established, partial reinforcement maintains the desired behavior. In sum, 100 percent reinforcement means saying "That's right. Good work!" *immediately* after a right answer *every* time a student produces one until you are sure that the tutee knows the concept or can produce the right answer every time, then responding in this way intermittently to be sure your learner retains the learning. For Skinnerians, immediate *feedback* in the form of positive reinforcement is not only a desireable but a necessary condition for learning. (Obviously tutors can do this well because they usually have a one-to-one relationship with their tutees.)

Reinforcement in the Skinnerian scheme also influences how much we learn and how learning is structured. That is, Skinnerians break learning into small pieces and arrange the pieces in order of increasing complexity. The simpler and more distinct the information is, the more likely it is that it will be learned or acquired without error, and therefore with continuous reinforcement. For example, learning simple pieces of knowledge permits the student *to discriminate* one learned response from another (as when a subject learns to press the lever only when a red—not a green—light goes on or when a person can distinguish the *that* used to initiate an indirect quotation [He said that he was leaving] from other relative clauses beginning with *that* [Stop at the house that has the blue door]).

Skinnerian educators also make use of *generalization,* the reverse phenomenon of discrimination. Generalization happens when a fact or idea is seen in a wide variety of contexts before one statement encompasses all the contexts. For example, a student will learn that oxidation is a process that affects aluminum, copper, iron, and so on, after which he or she will learn that oxidation occurs in the presence of oxygen to form oxides. Finally, the student will be able to generalize that oxidation occurs when metals are exposed to oxygen to form metal oxides. In that way, the student is able to incorporate the smaller, simpler pieces into a more complex whole.

Because the rate of learning depends on the individual's desire for reinforcement, Skinnerians argue that learning must be, by definition, individually directed and self-paced. It is not surprising that their theories stimulated the growth of labs and centers and of the development of modularized forms of instruction, teaching machines, and programmed learning (See chapter 4). Teaching and tutoring methods have been influenced by Skinnerian techniques as well. As an extreme example, in some labs or programs, tutors are trained to question only, and *never* to give information (or the "answer") until the tutee has replied, and sometimes not even then. Central to all Skinnerian theory, then, is the active role of the learner: and as you will see in later sections, psychologists, who would otherwise have little in common with Skinner and other behavioral theorists, also acknowledge and confirm its importance.

LAB APPLICATION

Periodically review material your tutee has previously learned with you. Discuss the effects of this partial reinforcement in your journal.

COGNITIVE THEORY

Although stimulus-response theory is concerned with learning, it has traditionally said little or nothing about cognitive processes, such as understanding, attitudes, and emotions. For this reason, it has often been called the "black box" theory: "We know what went into it; we know what came out of it; we don't know—or care—what went on inside." That is, the theory is concerned only with "input" (stimulus) and "output" (response), and not with changes that go on inside the box, or the mind. Some psychologists have argued that ignoring these cognitive processes is both simplistic and destructive, and believe that studying them could yield new and more effective learning strategies. Thus, many learning theorists, linguists, and computer scientists have focused on how people think, how thinking changes, and what patterns of thought are necessary for certain kinds of learning to take place. The model we are about to discuss, derived from cognitive theory, is more concerned with *process* and *understanding* than with content and performance; it not only deals with the interaction between the learner's *response* and the environment, but also the *mind* as it shapes and is shaped by the environment.

CLASS PROJECT 2

Form into groups and choose a leader. The leaders should:

a. read one of the lists of items indicated in Figures 8.1, 8.2, or 8.3;

b. ask group members to count backwards from a given number by threes for a given number of seconds (the numbers are arbitrary: from 236 for 7 seconds, for example);

c. ask group members to recall the items on the list by writing them down.

Discuss the results of your trials: how many of the words did each of you recall; in what order? from what part of the list? If you repeated the experiment with different lists and/or different times for counting backwards, did there seem to be any improvement as a result of repeated efforts? A recorder should assume responsibility for indicating what patterns, if any, existed, and whether or not they seemed related to any strategies that members of the group were aware of using to remember the words on the list. Be prepared to share the collective insights of the group with the class.

The Mind as an Information-Processing System

Because it stresses the integrative and dynamic interaction of the mind with its environment, information processing is one of the most widely used models of cognitive psychology.

The Structure of Memory In the information-processing model, the mind has three components: the sensory information system, which is involved in perception (such as the visual or auditory recognition of a sign or object); the short-term memory, which is involved in recall and comprehension; and the long-term memory, which gathers, synthesizes, and stores information and is the system to which information, or knowledge, is transferred and from which it must be retrieved. You as a tutor are primarily concerned with the last two components, which are the conscious mechanisms of verbal learning. The project experiment you have just completed should offer some insight into the features of these mechanisms and how they operate.

Mechanisms of Memory You may have noticed, first, that the length of the interference task (counting backwards) significantly affected your ability to recall by limiting your *attention*. That is, the task was intentionally supposed to distract you from learning the very material you were asked to master. If you were able to recall a number of items, especially the last words on the list, then the interference probably was only a few seconds long, and these items remained in your short-term memory, perhaps maintained there by your *rehearsal* (mentally repeating the items over and over again). Yet disruption of more than five seconds or so affected your ability to form a more permanent record of the incoming information or to transfer the information to storage in the long-term memory. Consequently you forgot some, many, or most of the words on the list.

The short-term memory is limited in its capacity; besides holding items in the mind for only a brief time (up to twenty to thirty seconds *without* interference), it cannot hold more than five to ten items, whether these are taken from the external environment or retrieved from storage in the long-term memory. Your ability to retain even five to ten items or *acquire* new learning is probably related to how well you can transfer information from short- to long-term memory. In the previous exercise you may have used *mneumonics* (a variety of memory devices) such as alliteration, to recall *h*ammer and *h*older or *p*aper clip, *p*lunger, and *p*aper in List 1 (Fig. 8.1). These devices represent a way to *cluster*, or group, related ideas, thus allowing you to reduce the number of items in the short-term memory: instead of remembering *paper clip, paper, plunger*, you need only to remember words beginning with P.

Clustering involves relating an item to some general idea or category which encompasses the essential features of that item. It is the most effective way we have to store and retrieve information; its effectiveness depends on how *meaningful* the items are to the person. Thus in List 1, the concept *gem*, as mineral, or as *semiprecious jewel*, may have allowed you to remember *rubies, emeralds, opal*, and *diamond*; you might have used the category of plumbing tools to group *hammer, wrench*, and *plunger*. Another group in this list was the most difficult to conceptualize, perhaps because desk or writing materials is an amorphous category, perhaps because the first word of this group on the list, "holder," is too vague to suggest clearly a specific category. Another obstacle to clustering may be that some terms are less tied to an object or to visual memories than others, such as the many abstract terms related to media formats in List 3 (Fig. 8.3) (binding, serial, cliffhanger, repertory); or they may be capable of being confused with other more common

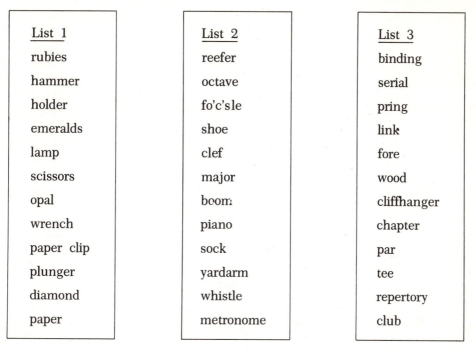

List 1	List 2	List 3
rubies	reefer	binding
hammer	octave	serial
holder	fo'c'sle	pring
emeralds	shoe	link
lamp	clef	fore
scissors	major	wood
opal	boom	cliffhanger
wrench	piano	chapter
paper clip	sock	par
plunger	yardarm	tee
diamond	whistle	repertory
paper	metronome	club

Figure 8.1   Figure 8.2   Figure 8.3

terms. For example, most of us, hearing "serial," probably think the word meant is "cereal" because concrete terms of daily experience are easier to remember. In fact, we probably store memories of these in a way different from the way we store information derived from books and verbal learning. *Novelty* is also an aid to memory, and some of you stored items like fo'c'sle or metronome in List 2 (Fig. 8.2) or the made-up word "pring" in List 3 precisely because they were unknown or bizarre to you and, thus, stuck out. One other important element to note is the degree to which past knowledge created a context or *expectancies*. That is, your previous learning—or the lack of it—helped or hindered your ability to anticipate, group, store and then retrieve the musical or sailing terms in List 2.

We have spent a long time analyzing the exercise in order to touch on important learning processes—attention, acquisition, interference and forgetting, storage and recall. The importance of clustering in transferring information from short-term memory to long-term memory for storage and retrieval, in particular, suggests that the mind does not merely act as a memory bank but is an active mechanism seeking to understand and make sense of what it remembers.

The Importance of Understanding When you related the words on the list, you isolated critical aspects of meaningfulness and linked them to a network of concepts, definitions, and categories you had already formed. At the same time you were forced to reorganize your memory to accommodate the new information, and in doing this, you created new concepts. To take a very simple case, when we discussed the list-recall experiment, you first saw discrete items, then learned that some words really could be grouped under a category heading such as "technical knowledge of sailing," which in turn could be considered a subcategory of some broader concept; you may also have connected these items to actual sailing experiences, and you may have mentally reviewed the image of a boat, and attempted to fit the words to the parts of that boat. This process of embedding new knowledge in long-term memory is called *encoding*, and it underlies all human thought. It seems to ensure that a person will be able to incorporate into his or her long-term memory all the bits or discrete pieces of information he or she is bombarded with daily (See Fig. 8.4).

While such mental processes underlie all human thinking, your mental structures are built up from your own experiences, information, and knowledge—memories that are uniquely your own. Consequently, your way of thinking about things is unique. Even our lengthy discussion about the exercise didn't exhaust all possible patterns and strategies of recall. Had the items on the lists been even more complex, it might have been more difficult—but more interesting—to trace the complex associations which resulted in the way each individual arranged the items. The point is, learning is a dynamic process which functions within an incredibly flexible and complex system—a system that works differently for each individual. The mind is capable of making distinctions meaningful to others, yet capable of creativity and originality as it simultaneously expands its capacity for storage. At the same time, these processes result in a somewhat unreliable system, one in which we may be unable to remember a fact or idea because it isn't meaningful, or doesn't fit any of our preconceived notions. As a result we may encode concepts only partially, or distort them from what they originally were.

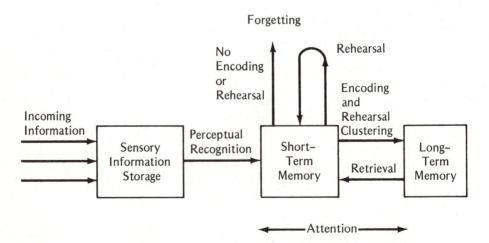

Figure 8.4 The Structure and Mechanisms of Memory. This model shows the components of memory along with the processes that contribute to different levels of "understanding" and learning. Like Freud's model of the mind, the diagram does not refer to actual areas in the brain; it merely offers a visual presentation of a concept.

CLASS PROJECT 3

1. Each of you make a list of all items that you can recall from the lists in Class Project 2. In your groups, discuss the differences between this recall and the kind of recall required in Class Project 2. Be prepared to discuss in class how both of these recalls differed.

2. As a writing project, some of you might do an autobiographical study of a particular learning experience, how it involved both a change in your mental processes, and an awareness of a conceptual reorganization of your thought in a given area. One jumping-off point might be an experience you had which you originally thought about in one way and subsequently came to think about or to interpret in another. You may also wish to consider how this relates to the model of memory presented here, and to the model developed by Piaget, presented later in this chapter.

Cognitive Tutorial Strategies It has been said that we remember

10 percent of what we read (passive)
20 percent of what we hear (passive)
30 percent of what we hear and see (passive)
70 percent of what we say or write (active)
90 percent of what we say as we do (active)

The information processing model hypothesizes that the mind constantly interacts with its environment and establishes concepts which expand and are modified by knowledge, which then, in turn, modify the knowledge; it makes sense that the more active the mind, the greater the chance that new knowledge will be permanently integrated or encoded into the memory. If you give your tutees a diagram to accompany a reading (or your explanation of a reading) they will be likely to retain only 30 percent of your tutoring aid; on the other hand, if you create learning structures which require your tutees to be active, it is far more likely that they will connect one item to another, items to a concept, concepts to other concepts—and thus will permanently encode the new information in their long-term memory.

Letting your students solve their own learning problems, having your students write an essay, urging them to always explain what they are doing and why they are doing it, are all ways to encourage your tutees' active participation in their learning. Getting your tutee to be active is an important part of the Skinnerian model, but the information-processing model takes it still further because it suggests that you as a tutor promote the tutee's mental processes.

What techniques and strategies can ensure this? The tutorial excerpt in Figure 8.5 below shows how you can *help your students to fit their knowledge to what they already know*. You can also help them to make meaningful conceptual links, to relate one example or item to others, or link these to some more general process or structure.

TUTOR: Do you remember the picture we talked about today?
TUTEE: Yeah, it was Modigliani's "Reclining Nude."
TUTOR: Did it remind you of anything else?
TUTEE: That one we saw by Renoir, and oh, yeah, another one by Rubens.
TUTOR: What do we call that in art: when we have pictures that fall into a certain group?
TUTEE: Genre painting.
TUTOR: Yeah, that's right. Can you tell me some of the characteristics of the genre paintings of the nude? And you might want to think about different forms of the genre, too.

Figure 8.5. Tutoring That Makes Significant Conceptual Links.

Use the idea of the meaningful concept to get at problem errors. If you have a student who chronically makes a particular mistake, instead of correcting the particular error, as in the following examples ("You forgot to add an *s* to the third-person singular verb" or "Your equation should be reversed"), point out that there is a *pattern* to the errors that are made. The fact that there is a pattern suggests that the student has mislearned or misunderstood an underlying concept. If you correct the error yourself the students will probably fail to *understand* the general concept, and will be unable to correct the error or to apply the concept intelligently.

Constantly urge your students to conceptualize, that is, to articulate principles and processes, not only to indicate the solution but to explain how they arrived at it. Create situations which give the student the opportunity to develop a theory, tell a story, or establish an hypothesis. This will allow you to see where your tutee has omitted or ignored relevant material—which is critical to good understanding or to concept formation.

Problem-solving Methods What we have been suggesting are actually applications of problem-solving methods. Practice alone may not be sufficient to improve your student's performance, whether it be in writing, math, or history. It may be necessary for you as an "expert" problem solver in your discipline to discuss and to *explicitly* demonstrate the strategies you use to find "solutions": the response to an interpretive question; the answers to word problems; the formulation of an hypothesis, and so forth.

Delineating how one solves problems is by no means easy, especially in areas of verbal reasoning. Often our knowledge of certain processes and procedures is not verbalized, and our application of these processes and procedures is apparently automatic. Sometimes introspection can help us to acquire a more conscious, articulate knowledge; more often we must train ourselves by talking to others explaining how we go about thinking about something, why we choose one approach over another, and what exactly is involved in these "decisions" we make. Such training can take a long while. In mathematics and the sciences, thinking about problem solving has been going on for some time and so a great deal of information has already been made available about how to go about it.

Heuristics, as this accumulated information is called, are descriptions of what you need to do or the steps you go through in order to solve a problem. Thus, the heuristics for the *analysis* of a scientific problem might include drawing a diagram, examining special cases, simplifying the problem. A different set of heuristics would be used to *explore* a problem or to *verify* an answer.

Heuristics are not rules or formulas, although they may involve routines which yield further information. Problem-solving strategies or heuristics have been extended to a variety of disciplines to designate procedures or techniques for problem solving. In your own tutoring, *explicitly* telling your students the way you cluster or formulate a particular set of relationships or how you relate particular new information to what you already know may teach them ways to understand or remember material. This may also give them the additional structure they need to make practice effective. Again, if you discuss the writing strategies of brainstorming, invention, and editing, encouraging your tutees to be aware of and use these processes, they may internalize these heuristics so that they become part of their own mental structures, effecting the way in which they will go about developing their ideas and shaping their writing style.

The processes of understanding and solving problems were clarified by the work of the Swiss-born cognitive psychologist, Jean Piaget. By looking at his work you may be able to deepen and extend your knowledge of these cognitive strategies so you can understand better how to relate them to your tutorial work.

The Contribution of Piaget

The cognitive model developed by computer and information-processing theorists has relied significantly on the research of Jean Piaget (1896–1981). Like, these theorists, Piaget assumes the mind is actively engaged with its environment and is constantly building and revising an internal structure of the outside world. The child, and later, the adult, is constantly forced to confront and to accommodate new aspects of reality to his or her model. This dynamic interaction goes both ways: *assimilation* is the process by which aspects of the environment (or knowledge) are adapted to or assimilated into the mental structure; simultaneously, the mind is forced by new knowledge to revise its structure through the process of an *accommodation* to reality.

As a result of these processes, Piaget argued, the mind moves through a more or less orderly progression of stages: chronological, hierarchical, and cumulative. Yet these stages do not occur at the same time in all persons. Nor do they emerge full-blown: instead, assuming that appropriate physical maturation takes place, these stages are stimulated by the environment or certain aspects of it, and evolve only gradually. From the point of view of a Piagetian, tutors can use their close relationship with their tutees to appropriately structure the way in which tutees learn, thus stimulating the students' mental development, and extending their reasoning abilities.

The Four Stages of Thought For purposes of analysis, Piaget schematized mental processes into distinct stages. These stages are marked by the person's ability to carry out certain mental operations.

The first stage is the level of *sensory-motor intelligence*, which develops from birth to about age two. At this stage, children develop the notion of "object permanence," which we recognize in children's delight in playing "peek-a-boo" because they know that the face which has disappeared will, in fact, reappear. *Preoperational thought* is the next stage, the one of language acquisition; language enables the development of reasoning processes characterized by egocentrism. For example, at the beginning of this stage a child may know John is her brother but will deny she is his sister (or that there are two children in the family); likewise John can point to the right and left parts of his own body without being able to point to anybody else's. Later, he will recognize that, of two objects on the table, one is on the left, the other on the right *from his point of view*; but he will be unable to say how three objects relate to one another *independent* of his own perspective. If children at this stage are asked to explain how a bicycle works, their explanations, instead of indicating proper cause and effect, sound like narratives ("And then . . . , and then . . . , and then. . . .") When asked if natural phenomena like stones, water, or the sun are alive, the children give inconsistent answers or cannot explain their answers. Their ideas are formed by a "logic of action," which depends on their immediate perception and empirical reality. This way of thinking produces a series of discontinuous judgments characterized by what Piaget, in *Judgment and Reasoning in the Child* (1924), calls *juxtaposition*:

> The child is given . . . a test of the form: "If this animal has long ears it is a mule or donkey; if it has a thick tail it is a mule or a horse. Well, this animal has long ears and a thick tail, what is it[?]" . . . The child [or adult operating at this level] begins by considering the existence of long ears, and concludes that the animal must be a donkey or a mule. He then considers the existence of the thick tail. If this new condition were made to interfere with the preceding one, the child [or adult] would eliminate the donkey since it has not got a thick tail. But the child [or adult] considers this new condition separately, he *juxtaposes* it instead of contrasting it with the former condition, and he concludes that the animal may be a horse or a mule. Each judgment is therefore *juxtaposed* and not *assimilated* [italics ours] to the judgment that precedes it. Finally the child [or adult] merges these two judgments into a single whole, but this whole . . . [is] not a hierarchy. For the child [or adult] comes to the conclusion that all three cases are possible. (p. 101)

Probably Piaget's most famous experiments are those he conducted to illustrate the third level, that of *concrete operations*. In one experiment, in which liquid is poured from a short, squat beaker into a tall, thin one, the subject is able first to say—and later to predict—that the amount of liquid will remain the same, thus demonstrating a mastery of the principle of conservation. In another, illustrating the principle of invariance, the same number of discs spaced widely apart are understood by the child to be the same quantity as those placed close to one another. A final experiment illustrating one-to-one correspondence, involves the subjects' ability to recognize that both blue and red discs can be grouped under the category of circles.

How does achieving this level affect learning capacities? The ability to group classes and relations and to understand numbers prepares the student to learn algebra and geometry. In writing, a student at the level of concrete operations has the intellectual framework for mastering narrative sequence and topic-and-supporting-detail patterns of organization, since these are based on deductive reasoning skills developed at this stage.

The final stage is that of *formal operations* and the reasoning processes accompanying them. These reasoning abilities will make possible wide varieties of understanding necessary to all academic subject matter. Thinking up to this stage has become increasingly systematic; this level of thought permits reflecting or theorizing. At this level persons can use the logical processes of induction and deduction together; formulate and test hypotheses; and orchestrate a number of operations in solving problems. They can use combinatorial logic, for example, which means considering one of several factors at a time while excluding others ("All other things being equal, I'd rather eat out than eat at home.") and systematically varying it to determine its influence. In verbal reasoning or writing, the ability to explain things in a complex way reflects such logical power. Because these operations *may* involve a high degree of abstraction, or the separation of form and content (as in mathematical logic), Piaget defined this stage as formal: no longer focusing on (concrete) reality, this level instead stresses *possibility*. It is at this stage that people become capable of thinking about ideals, such as humanity or intellectual freedom or human justice, their implications, and the changes that the applications of such principles might effect within institutions and social structures.

Piagetian Tutoring Strategies What does an understanding of Piaget's stages contribute to tutoring theory? First, we can gain a more subtle understanding of the developing mind. Although the stages occur in a certain order, they do not appear predictably at a certain time or in a set form; therefore, the very inconsistency of mental operations within the structure of the mind generates discrepancies (what Piaget calls *disequilibrium*) that lead to further intellectual growth. In other words, seeing discrepancies between different ideas allows people to learn things better than if they didn't see them. (You can find an example of this in the student protocol at the beginning of the chapter where the tutee realizes that women still suffer from sex role stereotyping.) However, in order for your tutees to gain access to or awareness of these discrepancies, you must be willing to emphasize *process,* stimulating your tutees to think aloud and to hear themselves, to see ideas from other perspectives and come to recognize the possible disparities inherent in their own. Secondly, then, the theory shows the mechanism in the mind that helps people learn.

The third significance of Piaget for tutoring has specifically to do with the development of learning stages. Since Piaget argues that the mind goes through sequential stages to learn or develop certain mental processes, it seems to follow that people will go through these stages each time they learn something. Therefore, we should *structure* learning to reflect goals at each stage of thought. (See Fig. 8.6.) The Piagetian model of instruction is often called a learning cycle.

The Learning Cycle The first stage of the learning cycle might be called *exploration* and parallels the sensory-motor and preoperational levels of thought. If you are working with your student to master the formula for measuring the area of a four-sided figure, you might use a rubber band or string and a geoboard on which the student forms various shapes that match

Piaget's Stages of Thought	The Learning Cycle
Sensory-motor and Preoperations	Exploration
Concrete Operations	Invention
Formal Thinking	Discovery

Figure 8.6 The diagram shows the parallels between mental processes, structures, or stages and the instructional model derived from Piaget's psychology.

diagrams. In helping your student write a literary analysis, you might emphasize the *process* of organizational development, *beginning* with a haphazard brainstorming on the topic and not distinguishing between or ordering in any way persons, events, "facts," and ideas, themes or motifs that come to mind.

Invention, the second part of this cycle, corresponds to the level of concrete operations. Using the geoboard, you might have your students form different four-sided figures—rectangles, parallelograms, trapezoids; systematically, they might vary the length of one side, then another, drawing up a column that shows what changes occur when the size is increased by one, two, three pegs, and so on. You might then ask students if they can make mathematical or algebraic statements that describe the "events." Similarly, in the writing tutorial, you can ask students a series of related questions intended to help develop or extend a concept about a single character in a book. In this case, as in the mathematical one, the student is led to abstract hypothesizing: "X is a symbol of compassion."

In the last stage, *discovery,* the learning corresponds to the mental operations of formal thinking. The student might engage in active experimentation and confirmation; for example, the student might apply a math formula to specific cases to ensure that the formula always pertains; in the literary analysis, you might explore with your tutee how *each* of the characters in the book is symbolic of certain Christian vices and virtues. Active experimentation might help the tutee understand these difficult concepts well enough to "translate" them into an essay to support and confirm a thesis. (Another more extended example of the learning cycle, this time applied to a topic in Earth Science, may be found in the reading selection on p. 265).

CLASS PROJECT 4

1. In your groups, summarize the following:
   a. the common points of all the cognitive models discussed in this chapter.
   b. the relationship between stimulus-response and cognitive models.
2. Discuss with your group members your own thought process.

LAB APPLICATIONS

1. As a group or term project, you may develop some learning cycles to use with your tutee.

2. Provide a heuristics fact sheet for your tutees based on problem-solving procedures developed in the group-work class project above.

READING 17

The life of the Soviet psychologist A. R. Luria (1902–1977) spans the same period as that of Jean Piaget and to a degree his research and interests were also quite parallel. Both psychologists show a concern for higher psychological functioning and the more complex processes of knowledge and motivation (rather than elementary sensations and their associations); both develop new sorts of experimental methods which illuminate these processes and at the same time vindicate psychology as a science. Like Piaget, Luria was influenced by Freud who used clinical methods of "free association" to *discover the unconscious structures that determined or made sense of people's patterns of behavior. (Later in life, Luria found the information processing model congenial to his view of the mind as a dynamically organized system.) But he was also influenced by the demands of the Communist state in which he lived and was concerned with the social determinants of the mind's functioning. He was therefore led to explore the impact of learning on the processes of thought. Given these considerations, it is not surprising that Luria adapted, for at least some of his experimentation, the field model of cultural anthropology, in which the experimenter is a participant-observor, collecting data to substantiate his theories.*

The following excerpt is taken from an autobiographical account of Luria's research: he applies some experimental (laboratory) standards, selecting from both village and urban populations: some in each group having no education, others, some education. As Luria tells us, such scientific field research was possible because it was a period of transition, a time of social ferment. After the 1917 Revolution, Russian society underwent profound socioeconomic and cultural changes, which included the establishment of village schools, the beginnings of the collectivization of agriculture, as well as the emancipation of women.

READING QUESTIONS

1. How do Luria's ideas relate to those of Piaget?

2. What cultural factors discussed in the Kleinfeld article (p. 144) (resistance to outsiders, discomfort with "tests," and so forth), might be playing a

role in the exchanges between the experimenter and his "subjects"? Do you think Luria has anticipated cultural interference? How effectively?

3. How does this selection relate to the issues raised in Rodriguez's essay (p. 136)?

---

17 | THE MAKING OF MIND

A. R. Luria

A somewhat different way of characterizing these results is to say that the primary function of language changes as one's educational experience increases. When people employ a concrete situation as a means of grouping objects, they seem to be using language only to help them recall and put together the components of the practical situation rather than to allow them to formulate abstractions or generalizations about categorical relations. This raised the question of whether abstract terms in their language, such as "tool," "vessel," or "animal," actually had more concrete meaning for them than for better educated subjects. The answer turned out to be yes.

For example, we presented three subjects (1-3) with drawings of an ax, a saw, and a hammer and asked, "Would you say these things are tools?"

All three subjects answered yes.

"What about a log?"

1: "It also belongs with these. We make all sorts of things out of logs—handles, doors, and the handles of tools."

2: "We say a log is a tool because it works with tools to make things. The pieces of logs go into making tools."

"But" we remarked, "one man said a log isn't a tool since it can't saw or chop."

3: "Some crazy fellow must have told you that! After all, you need a log for tools, together with iron it can cut."

"But I can't call wood a tool?"

3: "Yes, you can—you can make handles out of it."

"But can you really say wood is a tool?"

2: "It is! Poles are made out of it, handles. We call all the things we have need of 'tools.' "

"Name all the tools you can."

3: "An ax, a mosque [light carriage on springs], and also the tree we tether a horse to if there's no pole around. Look, if we didn't have this board here, we wouldn't be able to keep the water in this irrigation ditch. So that's also a tool, and so is the wood that goes to make a blackboard."

"Name all the tools used to produce things."

1: "We have a saying: take a look in the fields and you'll see tools."

3: "Hatchet, ax, saw, yoke, harness, and the thong used in the saddle."

"Can you really call wood a tool?"

2: "Yes of course! If we have no wood to use with an ax, we can't plow and we can't build a carriage."

The answers of these subjects were typical of the group of illiterates with whom we worked, and they indicate that in attempting to define the abstract, categorical meaning of a word, subjects began by including things that in fact belonged to the designated category. But they soon exceeded the limits of the category and added objects that were simply encountered together with items that were members of the designated class, or objects that could be considered useful in an imagined situation in which such items were used. Words for these people had an entirely different function from the function they have for educated people. They were used not to codify objects into conceptual schemes but to establish the practical interrelations among things.

When our subjects had acquired some education and had participated in collective discussions of vital social issues, they readily made the transition to abstract thinking. New experiences and new ideas change the way people use language so that words become the principal agent of abstraction and generalization. Once people are educated, they make increasingly greater use of categorization to express ideas about reality.

This work on word definition, when added to work on classification, led us to the conclusion that the modes of generalization which are typical of the thinking of people who live in a society where rudimentary practical functions dominate their activities differ from the generalization modes of formally educated individuals. The processes of abstraction and generalization are not invariant at all stages of socioeconomic and cultural development. Rather, such processes are themselves products of the cultural environment.

On the basis of the results showing a shift in how people categorized the objects encountered in their daily lives, we speculated that when people acquired the verbal and logical codes that allowed them to abstract the essential features of objects and assign them to categories, they would also be able to do more complex logical thinking. If people group objects and define words on the basis of practical experiences, one might expect that the conclusions they draw from a given premise in a logical problem would also depend on their immediate practical experience. This would make it difficult, if not impossible, for them to acquire new knowledge in a discursive and verbal-logical fashion. Such a shift would represent the transition from sensory to rational consciousness, a phenomenon that the classics of Marxism regard as one of the most important in human history.

The presence of general theoretical concepts to which more practical ones are subordinated creates a logical system of codes. As theoretical thought develops, the system becomes more and more complicated. In addition to words, which take on a complex conceptual structure, and sentences, whose logical and grammatical structure permits them to function as the basis of judgment, this sytem also includes more complex verbal and logical "devices" that make it possible to perform the operations of deduction and inference without reliance on direct experience.

One specific device that arises in the course of cultural development is syllogistic reasoning, in which a set of individual judgments give rise to objectively necessary conclusions. Two sentences, the first of which makes the general proposition and the second of which gives a specific proposition, comprise the major and minor premises of the syllogism. When educated adults hear the two premises of a syllogism together, they do not perceive them as two isolated phrases in juxtaposition. Rather, they "hear" the premises as a logical relation implying a conclusion. For example, I may say:

"Precious metals do not rust.

Gold is a precious metal."

The conclusion "Gold does not rust" seems so obvious that many psychologists were inclined to regard the drawing of such a logical conclusion as a basic property of human consciousness. The phenomenologists or adherents of the Wurzburg school, for instance, spoke about "logical feelings" and implied that such feelings existed throughout the history of mankind. Piaget raised doubts about the ubiquitousness of such "logical feelings" in his studies of the development of intellectual operations. But at the time we did our studies no one had bothered to determine whether or not such logical schemas are invariant at different stages of social history and social development. We

therefore set out to study the responses of our subjects to syllogistic reasoning problems.

To determine whether people's judgments were being made on the basis of the
logic of the major and minor premises or whether they were drawing conclusions from
their own practical experience, we created two types of syllogism. First, we included
syllogisms whose content was taken from the immediate practical experience of the
people. Second, we created syllogisms whose content was divorced from such experience so that conclusions could be drawn only on the basis of logical deduction.

We were afraid that if the subjects did not perceive the major and minor premises
as parts of a single problem, they might forget or distort either element of the problem,
in which case their conclusion would be based on evidence other than that which we
had presented. To guard against this possibility, we developed a procedure in which we
first presented the major and minor premises and then asked subjects to repeat the
entire syllogism. We paid particular attention to distortions in the premises and to any
questions of the subjects. These distortions would be important evidence of the extent
to which syllogisms were perceived as a unified system. After a subject was able to
repeat a syllogism correctly, we went on to see whether he could draw the proper
deduction.

One of the first things we found was that the nonliterate subjects often failed to
perceive the logical relation among the parts of the syllogism. For them, each of the
three separate phrases constituted an isolated judgment. This was manifested when
subjects attempted to repeat the separate sentences of the problem, because they
recalled them as if they were unrelated and separate, frequently simplifying them and
modifying their form. In many cases the sentences virtually lost all syllogistic character.

This can be demonstrated with examples from subjects who were presented the
syllogism:

"Precious metals do not rust.
Gold is a precious metal.
Does it rust or not?"

The recall of three subjects (1-3) was as follows:

1. "Do precious metals rust or not?
Does gold rust or not?"
2. "Precious metals rust.
Precious gold rusts.
Does precious gold rust or not?
Do precious metals rust or not?
Does precious gold rust or not?"
3. "These are all precious.
Gold is also precious.
Does it rust or not?"

These examples show that the syllogisms were not perceived by the subjects as a
unified logical system. The different parts of the syllogism were remembered as isolated, logically unrelated phrases. Some subjects grasped the interrogative form of the
last sentence, which they then transferred to the formulation of both premises. In other
instances, the question formulated in the syllogism was repeated regardless of the
preceding premise. Thus, the question was perceived as unrelated to the two intercon-
nected premises.

These results made us realize that further study of logical operations required us
to do preliminary work on syllogisms with our subjects in order to stress the universal
nature of the premises and their logical interrelations so that subjects would focus their
attention on these relations and better recall the basic problem when it came time to
make a deduction. In this later work, we contrasted reasoning from syllogisms with
familiar and unfamiliar content. When the syllogisms were drawn from the subject's

practical experience, our only transformation was to change the particular conditions to which they applied. For example, a syllogism of this type would be:

"Cotton grows well where it is hot and dry.

England is cold and damp.

Can cotton grow there or not?"

The second type of syllogism included material unfamiliar to the subjects so that their inferences had to be purely theoretical. For example:

"In the far north, where there is snow, all bears are white.

Novaya Zemlya is in the far north.

What color are the bears there?"

Subjects living under the most backward conditions often refused to make any inferences even from the first kind of syllogism. In such cases, they were likely to declare that they had never been in such an unfamiliar place and did not know whether cotton grew there or not. Only after extended discussion, when they were requested to answer on the basis of what the words suggest, would they reluctantly agree to draw a conclusion: "From your words, it should be that cotton can't grow there, if it's cold and damp. When it's cold and damp, cotton doesn't grow well."

Such subjects refused almost entirely to draw inferences from the second type of syllogism. As a rule, many refused to accept the major premise, declaring, "I've never been in the north and never seen bears." One of our subjects told us, "If you want an answer to that question, you should ask people who have been there and have seen them." Frequently they would ignore the premise that we gave and replaced it with their own knowledge, saying such things as, "There are different kinds of bears. If one is born red, he'll stay that way." In short, in each case they would avoid solving the task.

These reactions were demonstrated in our discussion with a 37-year-old villager. We posed the syllogism: "Cotton can grow only where it is hot and dry. In England it is cold and damp. Can cotton grow there?"

"I don't know."

"Think about it."

"I've only been in the Kashgar country. I don't know beyond that."

"But on the basis of what I said to you, can cotton grow there?"

"If the land is good, cotton will grow there, but if it is damp and poor, it won't grow. If it's like the Kashgar country, it will grow there too. If the soil is loose, it can grow there too, of course."

The syllogism was then repeated. "What can you conclude from my words?"

"If it's cold there, it won't grow. If the soil is loose and good, it will."

"But what do my words suggest?"

"Well, we Moslems, we Kashgars, we're ignorant people; we've never been any-where, so we don't know if it's hot or cold there."

READING 18

The article synthesizes much of the cross-disciplinary research that has been conducted on learning in the past sixty years and shows some of the connections among the American psychologist Jerome Bruner, the Swiss Jean Piaget and the Russian A. R. Luria. At the same time its concern is to show what future directions research should take and what some of the practical implications of the research might be.

READING QUESTIONS

1. How would you fit tutoring as a concept into the discussion in this article?

2. Do you agree or disagree with the distinction drawn between how words operate in the context of daily life and of formal schooling, that is between their scientific and mundane use? Can you provide examples from your own experience which substantiate or refute this distinction?

3. From your own experience give examples of three categories of learning situations in which you have participated. On what basis did you categorize them (as compared to the groupings in the article)?

18 | COGNITIVE CONSEQUENCES OF FORMAL AND INFORMAL EDUCATION

Sylvia Scribner and Michael Cole

The study of formal education is one of the perennially popular topics that have consistently created more heat than light among social scientists. A little reflection suggests why this should be so: Every theory of education clearly requires a theory of society as a whole and of how social processes shape education. A theory of formal education also requires a theory of how learning and thinking skills develop in an individual member of society, and how educational processes contribute to the shaping of these skills.

Our special interest as psychologists is the cognitive consequences of education. More particularly, we are interested in investigating whether differences in the social organization of education promote differences in the organization of learning and thinking skills in the individual. It is our hypothesis that this is indeed the case. We will review some of the evidence favoring this hypothesis and examine current theories of informal and formal learning. It is our belief that these theories overestimate the continuity between formal and informal education. We will also argue for the necessity of distinguishing school-based education from the broader category of formal education. Our thesis is that school represents a specialized set of educational experiences which are discontinuous from those encountered in everyday life and that it requires and promotes ways of learning and thinking which often run counter to those nurtured in practical daily activities. In making this argument, we will accentuate the contrasting features of school learning and everyday learning although, in fact, the two are constantly intermingled. We will also be positing an idealized version of school learning, not describing learning as it actually occurs in a New York City school or in a Mexican village school. We hope in this way to illuminate some of the contradictions inherent in the different ways society organizes education and so to help deepen our understanding of current educational problems in our own and other countries.

SCHOOLING AND COGNITIVE CHANGE

We will begin with a very condensed review of some of the evidence pointing to the differential intellectual consequences of formal learning embodied in the school and the informal learning of practical life. In presenting this evidence, we want to make clear what we mean when we talk about cognitive skills. Skills are to be distinguished from capacities. We think that this distinction, which has not always been clearly made, is of great importance to interpreting the intellectual consequences of formal education. In our view, cross-cultural psychological research confirms anthropological findings of the universality of basic cognitive capacities. All culture groups thus far studied have demonstrated the capacity to remember, generalize, form concepts, operate with abstractions, and reason logically. [This material is reviewed in Cole *et al.* and Cole and Scribner (1); for a contrasting interpretation see Greenfield and Bruner (2).] On this level, it is clear that a great diversity of informal social learning contexts all nurture the same fundamental psychological capacities. What we have found, however, is that there are differences in the way these capacities are brought to bear in various problem-solving situations. We will use the terms "functional learning system" and "skills" to designate the different ways in which basic capacities are integrated and brought into play for the purposes at hand.

The evidence that different educational experiences give rise to different functional learning systems comes primarily from the work of contemporary psychologists in cross-cultural settings. Best known is the work of Jerome Bruner and Patricia Greenfield (3, 4). In studies among the Wolof of Senegal, Greenfield repeatedly found differences between village children with a few years of education and uneducated children on a variety of classification and Piagetian reasoning tasks. On a concept-formation problem, school children who were older and had attended school longer were more likely to form classes of items on the basis of form and function than were the younger school children, whereas the unschooled children showed no such difference with age, simply becoming more consistent in their use of color as a basis of classification. When presented with a standard Piagetian conservation task, children who attended school showed a developmental curve similar to that found in European and U.S. children, whereas the unschooled ones did not necessarily manifest conservation as they grew older. Greenfield summarized her results in the generalization that Wolof school children thought and performed more like Boston school children on these tasks than like their unschooled brothers and sisters.

A leading Soviet psychologist, Alexander R. Luria, found similar changes in concept formation associated with a change from informal to formal education among Central Asian peasants (5). His two contrasting groups were traditional, uncollectivized peasants living in small villages and peasant farmers who had moved onto collective farms. The latter generally had had a few years of schooling of some kind and were participating in the planning and management of large farm enterprises. In one study the subjects were shown four pictures, three being of members of a well-defined category and the fourth clearly not a member, and were asked to pick out the three that belonged together. One set of pictures, for example, depicted three tools—saw, ax, and shovel—and a piece of wood. Collectivized farmers commonly selected the three tools as the items belonging together, forming what Luria called an "abstract category." Not one of the traditional farmers did so. Their choices were made on the basis of concrete, practical situations in which the various objects could be used together; thus the piece of wood, the saw, and the ax might be grouped because "it is necessary to fell the tree, then to cut it up, and the shovel does not relate to that, it is just needed in the garden" (5, p. 268). Luria also investigated the way in which the two groups went about solving verbal reasoning problems. When presented with logical syllogisms, the traditional people refused to accept the system of assumptions embodied in the problems and to draw conclusions from them, while slightly educated people readily drew such conclusions.

Our own cross-cultural investigations (1) have also pointed to the special significance of school-based learning experiences. At the outset, we have to say that schooling did not make a difference on all the tasks we experimented with and that different levels of education influenced certain tasks differentially. The complexity of education-task interaction prohibits any sweeping generalizations about the "effects of schooling." Nevertheless, we did find certain characteristics that distinguished the performance of schooled and unschooled populations over a wide variety of seemingly unrelated tasks. The pervasiveness of these characteristics requires some attention.

First, unschooled populations tended to solve individual problems singly, each as a new problem, whereas schooled populations tended to treat them as instances of a class of problems that could be solved by a general rule. For example: Kpelle children from central Liberia were given a series of discrimination problems involving geometrical figures that differed in color, form, and number. For some groups of children, the problems could be solved only by attending to color and ignoring variations in form and number. When these children solved the first problem correctly (for example, learned to select all the cards with red figures), they were given additional problems in which color remained the basis for solution but the right answer was now blue or black. Overall results of these studies were that young, unschooled children tended to show little improvement, whereas school children of the same age solved later problems considerably faster than the earlier ones, demonstrating that they had grasped a rule of solution that yielded the correct answer in one problem after another.

Two other striking instances of failure to generalize a solution rule were found in studies with adults who had never attended school. In the first, villagers were given a set of 14 leaves—seven from the natural-language category of vines and seven from that of trees—and were asked to classify them one at a time. Their classification was called correct if they accurately sorted the leaves into the vine and tree categories. When they were told that the leaves came from vines and trees, they accomplished this task with virtually no errors. When they were told that some of the leaves "belong to Togba" and some "belong to Sumo" (names of persons), they failed to use the knowledge of the tree-vine distinction to help them solve the problem. In a somewhat different kind of study, adults were given a classification problem based upon the familiar Kpelle distinction of forest animals and town animals. After they solved the first problem, they were given a new one, to classify different instances of the same two classes. Solving of the second problem was no faster than solving of the first, and no faster than the performance of a control group that had completely different classes for each of two problems. This failure to transfer a rule of solution from the first to the second problem was all the more remarkable in that (i) internal evidence indicated that these people were using conceptual rules to solve the initial problem, and (ii) a group of adults who were asked to free-associate to the names of the animals given in the first problem spontaneously named animals used in the second. We can infer from this that the experimental subjects knew and recognized the common class membership of the items in the two problems but this knowledge did not figure in their solution strategy.

Other examples of nongeneralization of solution principles could be cited, but we will turn instead to the second feature that distinguishes the performance of schooled and unschooled groups in a wide variety of tasks—their use of language to describe the tasks and what they are doing with them. In a recent sorting experiment (6), various populations of Kpelle adults were asked to put 25 familiar objects into groups so that "those that belong together are in the same group." After the subjects completed sorting, they were asked why the items belonged together. There were more consistent and more striking group differences in the verbal explanations given for the groupings than in the nature of the groups per se. Most of the high schoolers referred to some physical or semantic property of the objects as the criterion for classification. Most of the villagers gave idiosyncratic or arbitrary reasons ("my sense told me") which were unrelated to an analysis of the task materials or the operational requirements of the task.

The same pattern emerged when these same subjects were asked to spend two minutes doing anything they wanted to help them remember a set of common objects and later were asked how they had tried to remember. High schoolers in most cases reported activities they were actually observed carrying out (such as rehearsing the names of objects), whereas the majority of unschooled villagers had great difficulty with the question and frequently fell back on a nonspecific explanation such as "God helped me." We have consistently obtained these kinds of responses whenever uneducated, traditional people have been asked to explain the nature of their learning activities or "the principle of solution" (7).

If we are going to have an explanation for these different performance patterns, we need to know how they are generated. What is the connection among forms of societal organization, their dominant values, the characteristics of the learning contexts they furnish, and the functional learning systems that develop in them? Anthropological studies offer much helpful information about these relationships and important clues about the characteristics distinguishing different forms of social organization of education. These forms are generally classified as informal education, formal education in noninstitutional settings, and the formal education of the school. Is there anything different going on in these different contexts?

INFORMAL EDUCATION

Informal education is the subject matter of most major works on children in primitive societies (8-10). Such learning is called informal because it occurs in the course of mundane adult activities in which the young take part according to their abilities. There is no activity set aside solely to "educate the child." Social processes and institutions are structured to permit the child's acquisition of the basic skills, values, attitudes, and customs which define appropriate adult behavior in the culture. It is informal learning that Margaret Mead celebrates in her descriptions of little Manus children piloting around their elders in outsized canoes, Arapesh children engaging in a hunt with minature bows and arrows, and Balinese children learning to dance.

A number of anthropological descriptions of informal learning tend to converge around the following three characteristics, which Cohen (11) argues are its distinctiive traits:

1) Because informal education (Cohen uses the word "socialization") occurs in the family, it is particularistic. That is, "expectations for performance ... are phrased in terms of who a person is instead of *what* he has accomplished" (11, p. 25). Furthermore, this particularism is connected to how evidence is evaluated—the value of information is closely related to who imparted it.

2) Informal education fosters traditionalism. This conclusion follows rather directly from the preceding one, since the elders are accorded the highest status in the group.

3) Informal education fuses emotional and intellectual domains. As Cohen puts it (11, p. 34),

> One of the most outstanding characteristics of socialization ... is the high affective charge that is associated with almost everything that is learned within that context. The reason for this is that the content of learning, especially in children, is often inseparable from the identity of their teachers.

Almost all anthropological descriptions of informal learning also make some kind of statement about the learning mechanisms involved. Fortes, for example, talks about the "three fundamental learning mechanisms, mimesis, identification, and cooperation" (8). Mead lists empathy, imitation, and identification as the cornerstones of informal education (12). Cazden and John emphasize the importance of "learning through looking" among young American Indian children (13). These labels and terms are often used with little precision, but what is important for the present discussion is that they all refer to a general domain which we may call "observational learning." Observational learning, in general, is contrasted with learning that is acquired primarily through the means of language. Mead points out, for example, that in informal learning the adult model rarely formulates a particular practice in words or rules, but instead provides a demonstration of it. Fortes adds the complementary observation from his study of education in Taleland that children there were rarely heard to ask "why" questions. He concludes that such questions are absent because much of the child's learning occurs in real situations where the meaning is intrinsic to the context. We are not certain about the generality of Fortes's observations or his conclusions, but they are important for one of the generalizations to which they have given rise—the idea that informal learning does not promote verbal formulation on the part of the learner any more than it does on the part of the model.

NONINSTITUTIONAL FORMAL EDUCATION

When we turn to formal education in traditional societies, we find less evidence concerning its nature or the dynamic processes involved. Drawing on recent anthropological discussions (14), we can provisionally define formal education as any process of cultural transmission that is (i) organized deliberately to fulfill the specific purpose of transmission, (ii) extracted from the manifold of daily life, placed in a special setting and carried out according to specific routines, and (iii) made the responsibility of the larger social group.

Anthropological discussion of formal education tends to emphasize the presence of at least some formal education even in the most primitive societies. Cohen, for example, tells us that informal and formal education are aspects of growing up in all social systems although their roles vary quantitatively from one society to another (11, p. 21). The formal learning situations most often analyzed by anthropologists are those intended to educate the young in values and attitudes rather than knowledge and skills. Cohen's example is aborigine initiation rites in which the adults conduct a complex, prerehearsed sequence of behaviors that is more or less invariant from year to year and is viewed as an essential part of the child's education.

Not much scholarly attention has been given to detailed studies of formal education in nonliterate societies that focus on the transmission of knowledge and skills. There are intriguing, but brief, references to the formal nature (in certain societies) of such diverse instructional activities as military training, teaching of music, dissemination of geographic information (15), transmission of totemic names (16), and language teaching (12), among others.

One of the most complete descriptions of a formal learning situation in a nonliterate society is Thomas Gladwin's analysis of the procedures and the materials used by Puluwatan navigators to teach novices the complex skills of navigation (17). He makes abundantly clear that formal instruction of this kind represents more than apprentice training; it involves didactic teaching and the deliberate, disciplined mastery of large bodies of information which are embedded in well-developed theoretical frameworks. Unfortunately, Gladwin's study, like others, fails to illuminate the dynamics of the teaching and learning processes. He tells us only that (i) no "general heuristic principles" are involved, (ii) that the "logic" of the teaching process is different from ours, and (iii) that rote memory may be involved, but that the nature of the learning goes beyond this. Similarly, we have no idea whether new principles are involved in the learning that takes place in an aboriginal initiation ceremony, or when an Iatmul boy commits to memory the extensive esoteric lore that will be demanded of him as an adult. In the absence of such information, we cannot judge whether formal learning situations in traditional societies are merely an extension of ways of learning that operate in the course of everyday life or whether they represent "something new." If they are in fact discontinuous in respect to techniques of teaching and learning, studies thus far indicate that they are continuous with informal learning in respect to other characteristics: they transmit traditional knowledge and skills with a highly positive social value; the learning is not depersonalized but continues to be bound up with the social status of the persons acting as teachers; and it is bounded learning in the sense that it deals with a demarcated set of activities or skills with the result that the learning processes are inseparably related to the given body of material.

SCHOOL LEARNING

When we turn to the schools, the evidence seems much clearer that its demands are *not* continuous with those of everyday informal learning. Sifting through the mountains of achievement and evaluation studies which constitute the bulk of research on the schools, we find very few penetrating analyses of the learning and teaching processes actually going on in the school environment (18). Our procedure here will be to select and discuss some of the characteristics of schooling that we speculate are of special significance to the development of functional intellectual skills. We make no claim that these are characteristics that are uniquely to be found in schools. It is more likely that there are some informal, everyday learning situations showing one or another feature of school learning. But we think that it is the combination of these features and the frequency of their occurrence that bring about a learning environment that is qualitatively new.

Anthropologists have long emphasized contrasts between the values, attitudes, and content transmitted by informal education and by the school. To this, we shall add a discussion of the way in which values and content interact to influence the organization of functional learning systems.

Whereas informal education rests upon a system of person-oriented values, "the essence of [formal] education . . . is that one of its principal emphases is on universalistic values, criteria, and standards of performance" (11). What is being taught, instead of who is doing the teaching, becomes paramount. Children are expected to learn by relating themselves solely to subject matter and by disregarding their relationship with the teacher; they are likely to see a new teacher each semester, if not each hour. When schools introduce these universalistic values into traditional societies where particularistic, person-oriented values dominate, the resulting value discrepancy may create obstacles to learning. Considerable attention has been devoted to this situation. But in addition to the value conflicts that are inherent in formal schooling, other, more pernicious conflicts arise from the fact that schools have often represented a culture that oppresses and denigrates the indigenous culture. Success in school may become identified with despising one's parents and heritage, school failure with resistance to injustice. Under such circumstances, as Wax and Wax (19) describe, value conflicts may transform the school into a place where very little formal education can take place.

When comparing school learning to informal learning, anthropologists and psychologists most commonly emphasize differences in content. "Dick and Jane" readers, textbooks and materials that do not reflect the child's actual living circumstances, have been justifiably criticized. But the conflict between the knowledge the school seeks to impart and the knowledge most children bring to school runs much deeper than this

(20). In some subject matter the information dispensed by the school contradicts commonly accepted knowledge and beliefs. The history curriculum obliterates the oral tradition and replaces it with a "world history" whose people and events were previously undreamed of in the child's culture. The subject called geography transforms the child's known physical universe into an unfamiliar one whose properties are not derived from the senses. These changes in overlapping content areas have been epitomized in the saying that in school "science lays common sense to rest."

In addition, school introduces new subjects, such as grammar, mathematics, and the sciences, which may have no cultural counterparts at all. Not only the content but the basic organizing concepts of these fields of knowledge may conflict with the traditional culture's way of understanding and interpreting the world. Robin Horton brings this out in a touching anecdote from his teaching career in Nigeria (21). He describes the absolute disbelief that greeted him when he told his students that he loved chemistry as a youth because the rules for combining elements and compounds were so regular and knowable. Horton preferred the laboratory to socializing with his schoolmates, whom he found confusing and difficult to understand. His Nigerian students, on the other hand, came to school believing, and got all the way to college confirmed in the belief, that the natural world is disorderly and uncontrollable, whereas the human world can be understood and controlled.

All these changes in content are of obvious importance to a theory of formal education. But the discussion cannot rest here. We need to go on to consider the possibility that changes in the content of education are closely connected with changes in the basic organization of learning.

FUNCTIONAL LEARNING SYSTEMS

A useful starting point for comparing the functional learning systems developed in school and nonschool settings is Bruner's description of the school (3, p. 62.):

> ... the important thing about school as now constituted is that it is removed from the immediate context of socially relevant action. This very disengagement makes learning an act in itself and makes it possible to embed it in a context of language and symbolic activity ... words are the major invitations to form concepts rather than the action.

The two principal attributes of the school mentioned in this passage are that language is the predominant mode of transmitting and acquiring information and that teaching and learning occur "out of context." We shall discuss each in turn.

Some discussions about the crucial role of language in school learning seem oversimplified because they ignore the many different functional uses of language in everyday life. Children and adults are always learning through the medium of language, outside the school as well as in it. What is special about the school situation is that there language becomes almost the exclusive means of exchanging information. It is self-evident that when linguistic forms carry the full burden of communication, the amount of information available to the learner is restricted. Compare the many rich sources of information available to the child who learns to weave by watching and doing: he sees particular bits of material varying in width and flexibility, feels their tension and resistance, compares his physical movements to those of the modeler, and integrates all these inputs from different sense modalities into his cognitive scheme of what weaving is all about. Learning to weave by hearing a discourse on it is quite a different situation. As visual and other modalities of information disappear in the classroom, the skills for processing them become irrelevant to the learning situation and possibly become impediments. "Observation" is a limited technique in the overwhelming linguistic environment of the school.

A far more interesting aspect of language use in the school is that its relationship to practical activities and concrete referents seems to be the exact converse of the relationship obtaining in everyday life. We have cited anthropologists' observations that informal learning proceeds in the main by demonstration without accompanying verbal statements of "rules" or "principles." The child sees or participates in a number of demonstrations of the "same event" and from these accumulated instances he acquires some generalized ways of performing the activity in question. This knowledge may regulate his subsequent behavior in this domain without being formulated verbally or generalized to related but different events. In school the contrary often happens. Teaching frequently begins with a verbal formulation of a general rule or a generalized verbal description. Ideally, the verbal schema is eventually connected with the empirical referents from which it has been abstracted. Unfortunately, we all know too many examples of school learners who "know the words" but not the referents, who are limited by their empty verbal constructs just as informal learners may be limited by their inarticulated practical constructs.

Vygotsky drew attention to these different courses of learning in his well-known comparison of "everyday" and "scientific" concepts (22). He maintained that the concepts we acquire in everyday life (he used "brother" as an example) are built from the bottom up through our experience with many concrete exemplars. They are rich in content but often difficult to define and to incorporate in a coherent conceptual system. Scientific concepts transmitted in the school ("exploitation" was his example) proceed in the opposite direction, from the top down. The student begins by knowing the verbal definition, and the course of his learning consists in overcoming his ignorance about the specific aspects of reality to which this definition refers. This analysis suggests the origin of one of the prime characteristics that distinguish educated and uneducated subjects in psychological experiments. Given extensive participation in concept formation on a purely linguistic level, it is not surprising that school populations tested in a variety of psychological tasks give fuller and more accurate verbal descriptions of their classifying operations and rules of solution than do their unschooled counterparts.

Bruner's idea that learning in school is best characterized as "learning out of context" is an important idea, but it needs further clarification. Everyday life also presents occasions in which the child learns material through the use of language when the referents of the words are not physically present—when someone tells a story, for example, or recalls his family genealogy. But the referents to the words used are familiar natural and social entities, and in that sense the new information can be assimilated "in context." What is special about learning out of context in the school is that the child is asked to learn material that has no natural, that is, nonsymbolic, context. A prototype for this kind of learning is mathematics. In informal learning, numbers are used to count things and are learned in connection with the particular things counted. Among the Kpelle the translation of the numbers 1, 2, 3, is "one of a thing, two of a thing," and so on (23). Similarly, the metrics for length depend upon the thing being measured. By contrast, when the school child is asked to learn numbers the operation has changed. He is no longer using numbers for the purpose of manipulating particular things; he is manipulating numbers qua numbers; they are themselves the things.

A substantial part of school learning may be seen as the process of becoming competent in the use of various symbol systems of this kind. A great deal of attention is devoted to teaching the child new techniques for processing information (how to read, to write, to "figure," for example) which mediate later learning. This independent learning of techniques or instrumental skills, apart from the ends to which they will later be functionally related, does not seem to have many parallels in everyday life. At a simple level of technology, the use of a specific tool is ordinarily mastered in the course of exercising it for some particular purpose. This is another sense in which school learning can be considered to occur "out of context."

The intellectual tools of the school seem to differ from the tools used in practical activity in at least one other respect. We know that in daily life learning in different practical domains is mediated by different instruments—a knife for carving, a sickle for cutting grass, an ax for chopping. Within a single conceptual domain—measuring, for example—instruments may vary according to the object being measured—a pinch of salt and a teaspoon of vanilla. By contrast, the intellectual tools used in school range over a wide variety of tasks and contents; how one operates with a book or ruler is not much affected by the subject-matter or goal. An inch of cloth is equivalent to an inch of wood in a special sense. We believe that the existence of common operations that are applied to a multitude of tasks underlies the tendency we reported of school populations to generalize rules and operations across a number of problems. This tendency to treat a wide class of problems as examples of some general class or rule is an excellent example of what we have been referring to as a functional learning system. Further, we would like to suggest that such learning systems are acquired by the principle of "deutero-learning" or learning-to-learn which Bateson long ago suggested to explain cultural differences in memory (24); learning-to-learn occurs when people are repeatedly presented with "problems of the same type." No better summary of our description of school learning could be wished for.

SOME PROBLEMS FOR RESEARCH

Before discussing the implications of our analysis, we need to emphasize that it rests upon a shallow empirical base. At each step of the way we have had to deal with insufficient data and conceptual confusion.

In the area of informal learning, there are many gaps in ethnographic data and a great deal of uncertainty about the mechanisms associated with observational learning. These should not remain unattended by anthropologists or ignored by psychologists. Greenfield and Childs (25) provide a research example which we think might serve as a model for future efforts. Beginning with the observation that Zinacantecan girls are expected to learn to weave three traditional patterns, they were led to inquire whether this traditional task brought about any generalized ability to represent patterns. They found, consistent with our analysis of skills acquired in informal learning contexts, that their young weavers had not developed generalized pattern-representation skills. They also found some, but by no means a great deal of, influence of schooling on pattern representation. This work raises many important questions which simply cannot be answered on the basis of current evidence: Is the failure to generalize patterns a consequence of the way in which weaving is taught, or a result of the fact that there are only three acceptable patterns in Zinacantecan? Would generalized pattern-representation skills be found in people who had learned to weave many patterns? Our discussion of learning-to-learn suggests that only where many examples of a principle are present does generalized learning occur. Is this proposition testable within a traditional, informal educational framework?

A quite different set of questions arises in connection with learning by observation. If a person has grown up in a society where a wide variety of tasks are learned by observation, does he develop special skills in "observational learning"? If such skills could be demonstrated, could they be turned to good use in formal educational settings?

When we turn to the question of formal learning outside the school, our known data base is even more restricted. Gladwin has pointed the way, but more scrupulous accounts of the teaching-learning process and, of course, a variety of examples must be provided. Completely neglected have been studies of the consequences of attending such institutions as the Koranic School in West Africa, where children spend long hours learning to read the Koran with little or no knowledge of Arabic (26).

We have been treating formal and informal learning as disjoint for didactic purposes. But we know that they are constantly interacting in the classroom and we need detailed studies of this interaction with an eye to its impact on the organization of learning systems. For example, we have characterized teaching in the schools as a process that emphasizes scientific concepts and generalization from superordinate categories to instances. But in the real world, a great deal of teaching in the school derives its style directly from the informal learning background of the teacher. How else can we intepret the heavy reliance on authority and rote teaching methods applied to problems that we have characterized as central to formal education? This mixture of formal and informal elements must also underlie the great resistance Peace Corps volunteers meet when they try to introduce discovery techniques into the classroom; their students' basic conception of what it means to learn makes it "unfair" to ask for the solution to $x + 4 = 7$ if they were given $x - 5 = 10$ as an example.

A study of the interaction of formal and informal learning systems is also a prerequisite to resolving the current arguments among psychologists about the cognitive consequences of education. As we mentioned earlier, we have not found school-nonschool differences in all the tasks we have studied, and other investigators have not always replicated seemingly well-established effects of education on particular cognitive tasks (27). We need to seek the resolution of these contradictions in careful studies of the kinds of informal and formal learning situations that exist in the society outside of school and the mixture of informal and formal learning that goes on in the school. We would expect measurable influences of education only where the school presents a clear contrast in its dominant educational methods.

IMPLICATIONS

We have maintained that the problems and techniques of the school are not the problems and techniques of practical life or the traditional home. The school's knowledge base, value system, and dominant learning situations and the functional learning systems to which they give rise are all in conflict with those of the student's traditional culture. If we take this opposition seriously, certain implications follow for educational policy.

For one thing, it is not necessary to look further for explanation of the difficulties formal education may present to people who rely heavily on informal education as their basic method. The problem does not lie "in them." Searches for specific "incapacities" and "deficiencies" are socially mischievous detours.

Second, if many of the demands of formal schooling are by their very nature discontinuous with those of everyday life, it seems unreasonable to expect masses of children to cope successfully with them so long as they perceive the school to be a hostile institution. Yet this is exactly the situation in many poor and minority neighborhoods in the United States and in many third-world countries. The antagonism the schools generate by their disrespect for the indigenous culture and by ignorance of its customs almost guarantees the production of nonlearners. While indigenous control of the schools cannot by itself undo the basic opposition between informal and school-based education, it is surely a necessary precondition for their reconciliation.

Finally, we think our analysis points to the need for serious and basic changes in the social organization of education. Changes in textbooks, curricula, and teaching techniques are all needed and important, but they cannot be counted on to bridge the gulf between school and practical life by themselves. A two-way movement is necessary here. The first, which is already under way in some experimental schools (28), is to move everyday life into the school so that its subject matter and activities deal with some of the same aspects of social and physical reality that the pupils confront outside of school.

The second has been little attempted. The techniques of the modern school need to be introduced into the context of recognized practical problems. Education must be stripped from the schoolroom and made instrumental in traditional settings. We take this to be the message behind Paolo Freire's writings on literacy (29) and the import of the changes reported by Luria when modern planning and management techniques were introduced into traditional Russian agriculture. We have seen such approaches work when applied to helping Liberian farmers get a better price for their rice.

These suggestions bring us back to the problem with which we opened this paper. A complete theory of formal education requires analysis of phenomena at several levels of social organization, as well as their interactions. We have only sketched our own theory of how certain social phenomena are related to educational performance. It is painfully clear to us that the facts at hand can do no more than lend credibility to the assertions we have been making. On one matter, however, we can be relatively confident: to expect massive changes in educational outcomes without a readiness to change the social organization of education is to invite cynicism and disillusionment.

References and Notes

1. M. Cole, J. Gay, J. Glick, D. Sharp, *The Cultural Context of Learning and Thinking* (Basic Books, New York, 1971); M. Cole and S. Scribner, *Culture and Cognition: An Introduction to Ethnographic Psychology* (Wiley, New York, in press).
2. P. M. Greenfield and J. S. Bruner, *Int. J. Psychol.* 1, 89 (1966).
3. J. S. Bruner, in J. S. Bruner, R. R. Olver, P. M. Greenfield, *Studies in Cognitive Growth* (Wiley, New York, 1966).
4. J. S. Bruner, *Am. Psychol*, 19, 1 (1964); P. M. Greenfield and J. S. Bruner, in *Handbook of Socialization Theory and Research,* D. A. Goslin, Ed. (Rand McNally, New York, 1969).
5. A. R. Luria, *Int. J. Psychol.* 6, 259 (1971).
6. S. Scribner, "Organization and memory among traditional west Africans" (unpublished report, Rockefeller Univ., 1973).
7. T. Ciborowski and M. Cole, *J. Exp. Child Psychol.* 15, 193 (1973).
8. M. Fortes, *Africa* 11, suppl. (1938).
9. M. Mead, *Growing Up in New Guinea* (Morrow, New York, 1930); *Coming of Age in Samoa* (Morrow, New York, 1928); *Am. J. Sociol.* 48, 633 (1943); O. F. Raum, *Chaga Childhood* (Oxford Univ. Press, London, 1940); J. W. M. Whiting, *Becoming a Kwoma* (Yale Univ. Press, New Haven, 1941).
10. In trying to make comparisons between learning skills involved in formal and informal learning we are limited by a curious discrepancy: most of our knowledge about informal education is based on field work in traditional, nonliterate societies, whereas most of our knowledge of formal education is based on studies of educational institutions in industrialized, literate societies. When we draw on illustrations, it may appear as though we are making comparisons between cultures or societies, whereas we mean to draw attention to the possible differential consequences of the several kinds of education within one culture or society.
11. Y. A. Cohen, in *Anthropological Perspectives on Education*, M. L. Wax, S. Diamond, F. O. Gearing, Eds. (Basic Books, New York, 1971).
12. M. Mead, *Continuities in Cultural Evolution* (Yale Univ. Press, New Haven, 1964).
13. C. B. Caden and V. P. John, in *Anthropological Perspectives on Education*, M. L. Wax, S. Diamond, F. O. Gearing, Eds. (Basic Books, New York, 1971).
14. G. D. Spindler, *Education and Anthropology* (Stanford Univ. Press, Stanford, 1955); M. L. Wax, S. Diamond, F. O. Gearing, Eds. *Anthropological Perspectives on Education* (Basic Books, New York, 1971).
15. N. Miller, *The Child in Primitive Society* (Kegan Paul, London, 1928).

16. G. Bateson, *Naven*. (Stanford Univ. Press, Stanford, 1965).

17. T. Gladwin, *East Is a Big Bird* (Harvard Univ. Press, Cambridge, 1970).

18. Studies we have found stimulating are those of E. B. Leacock, *Teaching and Learning in City Schools* (Basic Books, New York, 1969); A. V. Murray, *The School in the Bush* (Cass, London, 1967); R. Thabault, *Education and Change in a Village Community* (Shocken, New York, 1971); M. L. Wax, R. H. Wax, R. V. Dumont, Jr., *Soc. Probl.* 2, suppl. (1964).

19. M. L. Wax and R. H. Wax, in *Anthropological Perspectives on Education*, M. L. Wax, S. Diamond, F. O. Gearing, Eds. (Basic Books, New York, 1971).

20. We are excepting here children whose position in society is such that their families and social milieus hand down a basically academic tradition.

21. R. Horton, *Africa* 37, 157 (1967).

22. L. S. Vygotsky, *Thought and Language* (Wiley, New York, 1962).

23. J. Gay and M. Cole, *The New Mathematics and an Old Culture* (Holt, Rinehart & Winston, New York, 1967).

24. G. Bateson, in *Steps to an Ecology of Mind*, G. Bateson, Ed. (Ballantine, New York, 1972).

25. P. M. Greenfield and C. P. Childs, "Weaving, color terms, and pattern representation," unpublished manuscript.

26. J. R. Goody, Ed., *Literacy in Traditional Societies* (Cambridge Univ. Press, Cambridge, England, 1968).

27. P. Dasen, *J. Cross-Cultural Psychol.* 3, 23 (1972).

28. J. Kozol, *Free Schools* (Bantam, New York, 1972).

29. P. Freire, *The Pedagogy of the Oppressed* (Herder & Herder, New York, 1971).

30. Preparation of this article was supported in part by grant OEG-0-71-1965 from the Office of Education and grant 5-29179 from the Carnegie Corporation of New York, both to M.C.

READING 19

The following learning cycle grew out of a project designed to develop reasoning skills in science and is part of a course book in formal thinking. Yet it might also be easily adapted to a tutorial setting for an earth science session.

READING QUESTIONS

1. This learning cycle calls for the use of proportional reasoning. Does this skill have any application to the subject you tutor? (One example, in chemistry, might be the reasoning skill needed to determine the density of liquids.)

2. For those of you who have mastered the area covered in this learning cycle, can you recall how you learned it? How does this cycle differ from your own learning experience?

19 | DEVELOPMENT OF REASONING IN SCIENCE

Gaylen Carlson

REASONING SKILL: Proportional Reasoning
CONTENT TITLE: Sizes and Distances of Astronomical Objects
OBJECTIVES: When completed with this lesson, the student will be able to:

   A. *REASONING SKILL*: Calculate the diameters of three balls (when the diameter of one is given) using the law of proportions for similar triangles.

   B. *CONTENT*: (1) Position 4 balls and 4 coins of different diameters along a line so they have the same apparent diameters when viewed from one point. (2) Recognize that the diameters of these balls form the short side of similar isosceles triangles. (3) Extend the knowledge of proportions of similar triangles to the sun, earth, and moon system and to calculate unknown parts of triangles formed from this system.

PREREQUISITES: A. *REASONING SKILL*.

   B. *CONTENT*: Knowledge of subtended angles

EQUIPMENT OR SUPPLIES REQUIRED:

   For each pair of students:

   1 penny, nickel, quarter and poker chip

   4 different sized balls (diameters ranging from approximately 2 to 4 centimeters)

   1 meter stick

EXPLORATION ACTIVITY

Part I

Place two meter sticks together to form a wedge ————— . Place a penny, nickel, quarter and poker chip inside the wedge until they touch both sides of the wedge. Position an eye so it is at the imaginary point where the wedge would meet:

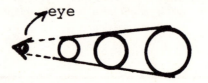

How many different ways can you position the two sticks and the four cylinders? Draw diagrams of two ways. Show how the position of your eye changes.

Part II

Place 4 different sized balls on the table in a line so they all appear to have the same size when viewed from one point on the edge of the table. (Use only one eye and have your partner check your locations.) How many different ways can you position the balls so they all appear to have the same size? List two ways.

INVENTION ACTIVITY

The diameter of each of the coins (or the balls) forms the short side of a series of similar isosceles triangles:

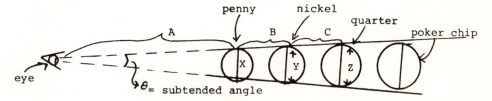

A is the length of the long side of the shortest isosceles triangle which has a short side equal to X. A + B is the long side of a *similar* triangle which has a short side equal to Y, etc.

When A/X gives the same mathematical results as A + B / Y, we say the sides of these two triangles are directly proportional. This is written mathematically as

$$\frac{A}{X} = \frac{A + B}{Y}$$

The observer sees the four coins as having the same apparent size in the observer's field of view. Because the subtended angle of each of the coins is equal, the balls have the same apparent diameter. The apparent diameter is stated in degrees of arc and is equivalent to specifying the subtended angle.

How does the apparent diameter for the coins differ from the apparent diameter for the balls?

List all of the factors which can affect the apparent diameter of the balls or the coins.

DISCOVERY ACTIVITY

I. Calculate the diameters of balls if the diameter of the second smallest ball (B) is 10 cm. Draw a diagram showing the position of the balls and the measurements you made. Show how you calculated the diameters of balls A, C, and D. Show all of your work and answers.

Apparent Diameters of:

Ball A (smallest ball) =

Ball C =

Ball D (largest ball) =

Calculations:

II. During a total solar eclipse the moon is directly between the sun and the earth. The moon exactly "covers-up" the sun. The sun and moon have the same apparent diameter. Calculate the diameter of the sun. Make a diagram and show your calculations.

> Data: Diameter of moon = 3456 km
> Diameter of earth = 12.7×10^3 km
> Avg. distance from earth to moon = 38.2×10^4 km
> Avg. distance from earth to sun = 15×10^7 km

Solution:

III. During a lunar eclipse the earth is between the moon and the sun (the full moon position). The sun is larger than the earth and thus a cone of total darkness (the umbra) extends into space on the dark side of the earth. The moon passes through the umbra during a lunar eclipse. Part of the shadow cone of the earth is cast on the moon and the moon appears as shown below:

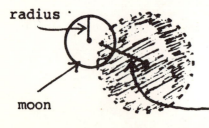

radius ·

moon

radius of umbra cone at the moon's distance from the earth

Calculate the ratio of the diameters of the two circles shown in the diagram above. Make another diagram showing the side view of the sun, moon, and the earth and its shadow. Show how you calculated your answer.

BIBLIOGRAPHY

Atkinson, R. C. and J. A. Paulson. "An Approach to the Psychology of Instruction." *Psychological Bulletin*, 78 (1972), 49–61.

Berlyne, D. E. *Structure and Direction in Thinking*. New York: John Wiley & Sons, Inc., 1965.

Bloom, Benjamin S. and Lois J. Broder. *Problem-Solving Processes of College Students: An Exploratory Investigation*. Supplementary Educational Monographs Published in Conjunction with *The School Review* and *The Elementary School Journal*, 73 (July 1950). Chicago: Univ. of Chicago Press, 1950.

Bruner, J. S. "The Nature and Uses of Immaturity." *American Psychologist*, 27 (1972), 687–705.

Bruner, Jerome. *The Process of Education*. Cambridge, Mass.: Harvard Univ. Press, 1960; 1977.

Bruner, Jerome S., P.M. Greenfield, and R.R. Olver. *Studies in Cognitive Growth*. New York: John Wiley & Sons, Inc., 1966.

Estes, W. K. *Introduction to Concepts and Issues*. Vol. I of *Handbook of Learning and Cognitive Processes*. Hillsdale, N.J.: Lawrence Erlbaum Associates, Publishers, 1975.

Gruber, Howard H. and J. Jacques Volècke. *The Essential Piaget: An Interpretive Reference and Guide*. New York: Basic Books, Inc., 1977.

Hill, Winfred F. *Learning: A Survey of Psychological Interpretations*. 3rd ed. New York: Harper & Row, 1977.

Hulse, Stewart H., James Deese, and Howard Egeth. *The Psychology of Learning*. 4th ed. New York: McGraw-Hill, 1975.

Kleinmuntz, Benjamin. *Problem Solving: Research, Method and Theory*. Papers from Symposium in the Area of Cognition Under the Sponsorship of Carnegie Institute of Technology. 15–16 April, 1965. New York: John Wiley & Sons, Inc., 1966.

Lindsay, Peter H. and Donald A. Norman. *Human Information Processing: An Introduction to Psychology*. New York: Academic Press, 1972.

Lockhead, Jack and John Clement, eds. *Cognitive Process Instruction: Research on Teaching Thinking Skills*. Philadelphia: The Franklin Institute Press, 1979.

Luria, Alexander R. *The Role of Speech in the Regulation of Normal and Abnormal Behavior*. Ed. J. Tizard. New York: Liveright Publishing Corp., 1961.

McKeachie, Wilbert J., ed. *Learning, Cognition, and College Teaching*. New Directions for Teaching and Learning, No. 2. San Francisco: Jossey-Bass, Inc., 1980.

Pankowski, Mary L., Wayne L. Schroeder, and Irwin Jahns. "The Relationship Between Group Process Training and Group Problem Solving." *Adult Education* 14, 1 (Fall 1973), 20–42.

Slamecka, Norman J., ed. *Human Learning and Memory: Selected Readings*. New York: Oxford Univ. Press, 1967.

Whimbey, Arthur and Jack Lockhead. *Problem Solving and Comprehension: A Short Course in Analytic Reasoning*. Philadelphia: The Franklin Institute Press, 1979.

Wood, David, J. S. Bruner, and Gail Ross. "The Role of Tutoring in Problem Solving." *Journal of Child Psychology and Psychiatry*, 17 (1976), 89–100.

9 | *TUTORING ADULTS*

Adult learners, those who are continuing their education, usually on a part-time basis after several years of working or raising a family, are the single largest and fastest growing segment of the college population. By 1975 more than 17 million adults had been involved in some organized learning activity (some estimates go as high as 30 million), and 37 percent of these learning projects were undertaken at two- and four-year institutions. Some of these adults were continuing their higher education on a part-time basis; others were returning to school after some years of being employed or raising a family. Since adults represent such a large proportion of the college population, and since you stand a good chance of having an adult tutee (or being an adult tutor) you should benefit from a look at some of the social, intellectual, and physiological factors of adult learning.

CLASS PROJECT 1

As a term research paper or topic for group discussion, you may wish to explore the reasons for this burgeoning population. Use the following questions to focus your reading: What social and economic factors have contributed to the growth of adult education? What changes in attitude and social policy does the growth of adult education reflect? What impact does adult education have on the educational system—its structure, programs, and policies? What are the effects—actual or potential—on the larger social and economic structure?

SOCIAL ASPECTS: WORK, FAMILY, AND TRADITION

Previous commitments and responsibilities will probably be much more important to adults than to "college-age" students because adults have had more time to form a large and varied network outside of school. If your adult tutee is female she may be caught by the many demands which she makes on herself, and by those others make on her. Balancing the multiple roles of parent, wife, child, and wage earner may create stress and guilt about the time taken by school (as well as the practical difficulties she may have to face). As her tutor, you will need to help her plan her time most effectively, suggesting efficient techniques for studying and producing work. Next, you want to put her in touch with a support group which will give her a network within school: persons with whom she can share common concerns and fears, and from whom she can learn solutions.

While women have now established a tradition of group problem-sharing and consciousness-raising, most men still do not feel comfortable expressing their concerns or forming and using support networks. However, men returning to school suffer from the same or related pressures: fear of not performing well, fears of failure, and embarrassment at not having adequate credentials. One of your roles, then, may be to encourage and support male adults by discussing such feelings with them and to suggest that they may benefit from networks similar to those established by women.

For some adults, education may represent discontinuity because it threatens to cut them off from their past culture, class, and roots, even as it links them to the larger society and to the future. Education, although important in a highly technological, rapidly changing society, weakens the authority of the older generation. Experience, past experience, may no longer be sufficient; therefore, communication between generations becomes increasingly difficult. (This problem is further compounded when language as well as experience separates generations.) Adults may resist new learning as a response to a *seeming* condemnation of their tradition. ("Why aren't my ways—the old ways—good enough?" they may ask.) Yet this response is too often justified by a curriculum's *real* denial or negation of their reality and past experience (for example, a history or economics course which talks about the post-war prosperity of America and overlooks the poverty of many Americans, or a 20th century American literature course which excludes immigrant writers).

The point is, the social aspect will play a large part in your adult tutees' lives and this social world will probably make strong demands on them. The journal and case studies you've read all reflect the impact of life experiences. If you recognize this and give it due credit, your tutees will probably feel more open to discussing social conflicts that might be inhibiting their learning.

CLASS PROJECT 2

1. Write a paper in which you explore your reasons for seeking an education. Include the values of your family and peer group that were influential in your making your educational decisions.

2. Write an essay about your mother's or father's education from their point of view. (Use their voice, for example, "I was born in 1913, in Germany and moved to this country when I was three.") Read it aloud to your group. After everyone has read his or her essay, discuss the similarities and differences of the experiences described.

3. Interview an adult relative, friend, or neighbor who has returned to school about his or her learning experiences and difficulties or problems in pursuing a formal education.

PHYSIOLOGICAL FACTORS

Given reasonably good health, appropriate diet, and exercise, physical limitations which result from age should be minimal and have little or no effect on one's intellectual functioning. Reaction time may decrease with age and older adults may generally slow down; however, this adult's increased interest and attention span and greater concentration and accuracy will probably compensate for these changes. In tutoring older adults, then, you should be aware that the effort of concentration and time pressure may tire them. To minimize fatigue, therefore, you may want to vary the rate and presentation of material. Also, vision and hearing are often affected by age, and you should take care to

126 COMPUTERIZING AND MANAGING YOUR MAILING LIST

24th St. & Sixth Ave.
Today most businesses and organizations use mailing lists to sell products, publicize events, circulate information, collect marketing data or to communicate with customers and other businesses. This course is designed to teach you the latest methods for computerized mailing list creation and management to increase your sales, income and public awareness. Learn how to computerize, how to build and clean your list, ways to earn additional income from list rentals, how to collect marketing data from your list and how to select and purchase lists from other companies. The economics of computerization will be explored and evaluated for your business or organization. This course will take place at Comarco Data Services, one of the city's most sophisticated mailing list managers. Students will be able to see computers, printouts and input terminals at work.
Louis J. Loglisci *is the Data Processing Manager at Comarco Data Services, Inc.*
Course fee $40   **Materials $2**
Sec.A:Tu.   Sept.9,16,23,30   6:00-8:00pm

111/FUNDRAISING AND GRANTSMANSHIP

77th St. & Third Ave.
Millions of dollars are available each year to a variety of worthwhile community groups and non-profit organizations. This class will explore how that money is obtained. It will take you through all stages of grantsmanship from the initial research to the submission of your final proposal. How do you prepare a budget? How much money can you ask for? What sources are available to you — foundations, corporations, government. Also, importantly, it will help your organization expand its possibilities for raising money through a detailed look at a variety of other fundraising techniques. By the end of the course each student will have prepared a draft proposal for their organization's project and a fundraising plan.
Gilda Dangot *is a Director of Information & Resource Development for the New York City Human Rights Commission, she is the author of the forthcoming book "So Your Organization Needs Money".*

Course Fee $40
Sec.A:Tu.   Sept.9,16,23,30   7:30-9:30pm

Figure 9.1 Many institutions have been developed to cater to the adult's learning needs. One such is The Network for Learning, an informal structure established to offer courses of interest, at times and places convenient to adults, and in formats congenial to their capacities and interests: the sample course descriptions and information here show this.

avoid strain on these key senses by making sure that your environment is well lit and quiet. Keeping the chalkboard within close range, writing in large print, and facing your tutee when you speak are details you should keep in mind as you work. Finally, other conditions, such as physical disabilities, chronic diseases, or short-term illnesses, are much more likely to be factors in an older person's life than in that of an adolescent: if your older adult tutee is on medication, his or her physiological state may be affected.

CLASS PROJECT 3

1. Discuss the following questions in class or in your log; or use them as the basis of an essay. (Do this before reading ahead, if possible.)

a. Give your own definition of an adult. Describe how your definition has changed in the past years. Using your own definition, decide how close you come to being an adult.

b. Is adult intelligence different from childhood intelligence, and in what ways might it be different?

c. Should such differences affect educational experiences. If so, how?

ADULT INTELLIGENCE

Most early work on intelligence was done with children because psychologists felt the adult's ability to learn was limited physiologically. Research into adult intelligence only came later, and when it did, it tended to rely on findings and theoretical models based on children's capacities and childhood school experi-

---

977/TENANTS' RIGHTS

74th St. & Amsterdam Ave.   Course Fee $15
Are you paying more rent than you should be? How do you find out and if necessary, have it adjusted? This course will also cover signing, renewing and breaking leases, sublets, rent strikes and eviction.
Michael Beltrami *(see biography for Course #223)*
Sec. A: Wed.   Sept. 17   7:00-10:00pm

Figure 9.2 Education can become a force for social change or political activity, as evidenced in this description of a course offered as a part of an adult education program.

ence. Moreover, research on adults which did occur was often guided by practical concerns rather than by theoretical ones: the goal of many studies was not to investigate critical components of adult intelligence but to develop tests that could predict performance on certain specialized tasks. Thus the first large-scale study of adult intelligence used the so-called Army Alpha Tests, developed in World War I to weed illiterates out of the Army. The study emphasized speed and discounted completely the test components of information and vocabulary, which remain stable over a person's life span. As a result the study concluded that adult intelligence declined with age. Needless to say, these findings discouraged many adults from taking advantage of educational opportunities.

In this context, the importance of Edward L. Thorndike cannot be overestimated. In 1927, already an eminent psychologist at Columbia Teachers' College, he published *Adult Learning*, a book that summarized the research conducted primarily since World War I. The title and focus of the book took for granted that learning in adulthood did occur, and that it had distinctive characteristics worthy of attention and study. Moreover, Thorndike provided empirical evidence to show that adult performance did not peak until age 40, some 20 years later than most others had indicated was the case.

By dint of his considerable prestige, Thorndike's belief in adult capacities gave scientific credibility to the beginnings of the adult education movement. (In a parallel way, the formation of the Adult Education Association the year before, recognized and certified this new force in education.) Thorndike's study and teaching stimulated research which proved that he was right. For instance, later studies found that adults' reaction time is slower, and therefore, negatively influences test scores. (Intelligence tests are timed.) These experiments evaluated *efficiency* and found that the number of *correct* responses on intelligence tests increased with age. New tests designed to account for a wider range of abilities showed that adults' test scores remain the same over time in all factors that predict intellectual attainment: vocabulary, information, comprehension. (Adults decline in tasks related to motor performance: object assembly, digit symbol, and block design.) The results of this research suggest that adults can perform well in educational settings. Academic work confirms this; records prove that adults do as well as or better than adolescents. One of the most important of these new studies sorted intelligence scores by generations; the tables showed that those of one age, but born at a later date, tended to have higher scores than those of the same age born earlier. (Thirty-year-olds born in 1940 had, on the average, higher scores than adults tested at age 30 but born in 1930.) That is, intelligence correlated with date of birth rather than with age. Since education levels rise with each succeeding generation, it is clearly education (and other environmental factors) that is "breeding" intelligence. Ironically, Thorndike and those before him may have been right in setting peak performance earlier than we do. However, given relatively longer life spans, higher levels of education, and greater intellectual involvement, Thorndike's theory that the adult's intelligence ability peaks at 40 years of age is now far too conservative.

While modern theories of adult intelligence testify to the full intellectual capacity of the adult, the earlier assumptions did succeed in short-circuiting the intellectual efforts of many adults, and still constitute obstacles to be overcome. As a tutor, you can help your adult tutee by talking about his or her negative self-evaluation when you find it is interfering with his or her learning. When your adult says, "I'll never get it," that's the time to dispel any notion the adult has about innate capacities—or stupidity. The next time an adult learner reminds you that her 12-year-old could rattle off those dates without thinking or that those complicated formulas are easy for *you* because you're 20 years her junior, remind *her* that it's easy for you because you've been studying it since high school, and high school is only two years ago—and besides, you aren't raising a 12-year-old at the same time. In other words, affirm the adult's intelligence and his or her capacity to learn.

There are differences, however, between adult intelligence and that of children. Studies have shown that as people mature their intellectual processes change in several ways:

Adult thought is less bound to language. If children do not have the words or language, they do not have the concept. Adults, however, have ideas, and yet may not be able to express them if their vocabulary is limited or they lack knowledge of, and practice in, forms of oral and written expression. Thus, it is especially important that you encourage adult learners to express ideas, emphasizing that new skills will enable them to communicate their ideas more effectively.

As people mature they tend to organize their thinking. That is, they tend to process information systematically in terms of what they already know; therefore, your adult's thinking will be more organized than a child's. (This of course fits with what you read in the chapter on learning.) In general, you can take advantage of the adult's conceptual understanding to set learning in a context. Instead of treating what is to be learned in isolation, connect new knowledge to what has already been learned or to how it relates to the entire construct. Telling your learner that this *x* is just another form of *y* which the student learned last week, or that learning *x* and *y* will enable the student to do the end-of-term project by giving him or her the formulas to analyze the accumulated data, will allow the learner to see that the exercise is connected to what he or she has learned in previous sessions and will need to know in the future.

As the above paragraphs suggest, *adults not only organize their thinking, they organize it in terms of their own experiences and commitments:* a fact may be less a fact for them than the expression of an idea. For example, an adult learning about the American writer Henry Thoreau may become angry because he or she interprets Thoreau's life as typical of today's "hippies who just live off other people like parasites." In this instance, a conceptualizing tendency interfered with learning, preventing the student from "hearing" or fully understanding what Thoreau had to say. Adults are not the only people guilty of jumping to conclusions, of course, but they are more likely to have considered judgments and values; and these are more likely to be tied up with their sense of identity. Consequently, your tutees may be somewhat rigid, often insisting on seeing things their own way. In exploring why adults think what they do, you should be able to help them unlearn a wrong or old concept by appealing to their understanding, for example, to distinguish between Thoreau as an historical character and Thoreau's ideas as they have evolved over the years. (Group work may prove helpful, in this case, by providing a non-threatening opportunity for the learner to consider other possible perspectives, and to become disengaged from habitual responses.) Sometimes, however, it may be easier to supply your student with other, more neutral examples that will make the same point.

CLASS PROJECT 4

1. In a term research paper or group discussion those interested may pursue questions related to adult intelligence and learning: How is it measured? How and under what circumstances were measurements developed? What are their consequent limitations (or controversies surrounding them)? How do they affect our understanding of and attitudes toward the adult's intelligence and capacity to learn? What impact do you think such understanding and changing attitudes have had on the growth of the adult learning population? What influence do you think they have had on your adult tutee?

2. Many institutions have sought to take into account the role of the adults' life experience and sometimes they offer academic credit for past learning or projects related to past experience. In your group, consider how your own education has handled the students' life experience. Discuss with your group what life experiences you have had which are relevant to your education, and how they are relevant.

3. Review your school catalogue and assess how your institution has adapted to the adult learner. Specifically, what provisions are there for independent study or credit for life experience? Check the student handbook, as well as the bulletin, to determine what, if any, support services are available to older students. Discuss how your school responds or might respond to the needs of learners who have family and work responsibilities.

4. One of the conclusions Scribner and Cole came to in their article (p. 253) was that there is a great lack of continuity between formal schooling and everyday life. Discuss alternative academic programs and support services in this context. Do they, can they, bridge the gap?

LAB APPLICATIONS

1. Explore some of the above ideas regarding adult learning with your adult tutees. Record samples of this dialogue in your journal for possible use in your case study.

2. Share what you have learned regarding adult intelligence and learning with your adult tutees. Ask them what it is like to be back in school. Encourage them to explore their feelings about school.

3. Find out what your adult tutees know about special options or services available to them. Fill them in on those that may interest them.

READING 20 ·

In "Me and Miss Mandible" American writer Donald Barthelme creates an uncanny replica of the American classroom; at the same time he shows the reader how little difference there is between children and adults. "Me and Miss Mandible" was originally published in Come Back, Dr. Caligari, *one of several collections of short stories by this writer.*

READING QUESTIONS

1. Why is the narrator in Miss Mandible's class? And why doesn't he do something about it?

2. What do Sue Ann and Miss Mandible represent to the narrator?

3. How do the narrator's experiences relate to those of the adult learners that you know?

4. What role is the narrator expected to play in the classroom and how does it differ from the roles he played in his former life?

5. What do you think of the narrator's idea that school is a place you go to when you have failed at life?

20 | ME AND MISS MANDIBLE

Donald Barthelme

13 September

Miss Mandible wants to make love to me but she hesitates because I am officially a child; I am, according to the records, according to the gradebook on her desk, according to the card index in the principal's office, eleven years old. There is a misconception here, one that I haven't quite managed to get cleared up yet. I am in fact thirty-five, I've been in the Army, I am six feet one, I have hair in the appropriate places, my voice is a baritone, I know very well what to do with Miss Mandible if she ever makes up her mind.

In the meantime we are studying common fractions. I could, of course, answer all the questions, or at least most of them (there are things I can't remember). But I prefer to sit in this too-small seat with the desktop cramping my thighs and examine the life around me. There are thirty-two in the class, which is launched every morning with the pledge of allegiance to the flag. My own allegiance, at the moment, is divided between Miss Mandible and Sue Ann Brownly, who sits across the aisle from me all day long and is, like Miss Mandible, a fool for love. Of the two I prefer, today, Sue Ann; although between eleven and eleven and a half (she refuses to reveal her exact age), she is clearly a woman with a woman's disguised aggression and a woman's peculiar contradictions. Strangely neither she nor any of the other children seems to see any incongruity in my presence here.

15 September

Happily our geography text, which contains maps of all the principal landmasses of the world, is large enough to conceal my clandestine journal-keeping, accomplished in an ordinary black composition book. Every day I must wait until Geography to put down such thoughts as I may have had during the morning about my situation and my fellows. I have tried writing at other times and it does not work. Either the teacher is walking up and down the aisles (during this period, luckily, she sticks close to the map rack in the front of the room) or Bobby Vanderbilt, who sits behind me, is punching me in the kidneys and wanting to know what I am doing. Vanderbilt, I have found out from certain desultory conversation on the playground, is hung up on sports cars, a veteran consumer of *Road & Track*. This explains the continual roaring sounds which seem to emanate from his desk; he is reproducing a record album called *Sounds of Sebring*.

19 September

Only I, at times (only at times), understand that somehow a mistake has been made, that I am in a place where I don't belong. It may be that Miss Mandible also knows this, at some level, but for reasons not fully understood by me she is going along with the game. When I was first assigned to this room I wanted to protest, the error seemed obvious, the stupidest principal could have seen it; but I have come to believe it was deliberate, that I have been betrayed again.

Now it seems to make little difference. This life role is as interesting as my former life role, which was that of a claims adjuster for the Great Northern Insurance Company, a position which compelled me to spend my time amid the debris of our civilization: rumpled fenders, roofless sheds, gutted warehouses, smashed arms and legs. After ten years of this one had a tendency to see the world as a vast junkyard, looking at a man and seeing only his (potentially) mangled parts, entering a house only to trace the path of the inevitable fire. Therefore when I was installed here, although I knew an error had been made, I countenanced it, I was shrewd; I was aware that there might well be some kind of advantage to be gained from what seemed a disaster. The role of The Adjuster teaches one much.

22 September

I am being solicited for the volleyball team. I decline, refusing to take unfair profit from my height.

23 September

Every morning the roll is called: Bestvina, Bokenfohr, Broan, Brownly, Cone, Coyle, Crecelius, Darin, Durbin, Geiger, Guiswite, Heckler, Jacobs, Kleinschmidt, Lay, Logan, Masei, Mitgang, Pfeilsticker. It is like the litany chanted in the dim miserable dawns of Texas by the cadre sergeant of our basic training company.

In the Army, too, I was ever so slightly awry. It took me a fantastically long time to realize what the others grasped almost at once: that much of what we were doing was absolutely pointless, to no purpose. I kept wondering why. Then something happened that proposed a new question. One day we were commanded to whitewash, from the ground to the topmost leaves, all of the trees in our training area. The corporal who relayed the order was nervous and apologetic. Later an off-duty captain sauntered by and watched us, white-splashed and totally weary, strung out among the freakish shapes we had created. He walked away swearing. I understood the principle (orders are orders), but I wondered: Who decides?

29 September

Sue Ann is a wonder. Yesterday she viciously kicked my ankle for not paying attention when she was attempting to pass me a note during History. It is swollen still. But Miss Mandible was watching me, there was nothing I could do. Oddly enough Sue Ann reminds me of the wife I had in my former role, while Miss Mandible seems to be a child. She watches me constantly, trying to keep sexual significance out of her look; I am afraid the other children have noticed. I have already heard, on the ghostly frequency that is the medium of classroom communication, the words *"Teacher's Pet!"*

2 October

Sometimes I speculate on the exact nature of the conspiracy which brought me here. At times I believe it was instigated by my wife of former days, whose name was . . . I am only pretending to forget. I know her name very well, as well as I know the name of my former motor oil (Quaker State) or my old Army serial number (US 54109268). Her name was Brenda, and the conversation I recall best, the one which makes me suspicious now, took place on the day we parted. "You have the soul of a whore," I said on that occasion, stating nothing less than literal, unvarnished fact. "You," she replied, "are a pimp, a poop, and a child. I am leaving you forever and I trust that without me you will perish of your own inadequacies. Which are considerable."

I squirm in my seat at the memory of this conversation, and Sue Ann watches me with malign compassion. She has noticed the discrepancy between the size of my desk and my own size, but apparently sees it only as a token of my glamor, my dark man-of-the-world-ness.

7 October

Once I tiptoed up to Miss Mandible's desk (when there was no one else in the room) and examined its surface. Miss Mandible is a clean-desk teacher, I discovered. There was nothing except her gradebook (the one in which I exist as a sixth-grader) and a text, which was open at a page headed *Making the Processes Meaningful*. I read: "Many pupils enjoy working fractions when they understand what they are doing. They have confidence in their ability to take the right steps and to obtain correct answers. However, to give the subject full social significance, it is necessary that many realistic situations requiring the processes be found. Many interesting and lifelike problems involving the use of fractions should be solved . . ."

8 October

I am not irritated by the feeling of having been through all this before. Things are done differently now. The children, moreover, are in some ways different from those who accompanied me on my first voyage through the elementary schools. *"They have confidence in their ability to take the right steps and to obtain correct answers."* This is surely true. When Bobby Vanderbilt, who sits behind me and has the great tactical advantage of being able to maneuver in my disproportionate shadow, wishes to bust a classmate in the mouth he first asks Miss Mandible to lower the blind, saying that the sun hurts his eyes. When she does so, *bip!* My generation would never have been able to con authority so easily.

13 October

It may be that on my first trip through the schools I was too much under the impression that what the authorities (who decides?) had ordained for me was right and proper, that I confused authority with life itself. My path was not particularly of my own choosing. My career stretched out in front of me like a paper chase, and my role was to pick up the clues. When I got out of school, the first time, I felt that this estimate was substantially correct, and eagerly entered the hunt. I found clues abundant: diplomas, membership cards, campaign buttons, a marriage license, insurance forms, discharge papers, tax returns, Certificates of Merit. They seemed to prove, at the very least, that I was *in the running*. But that was before my tragic mistake on the Mrs. Anton Bichek claim.

I misread a clue. Do not misunderstand me: it was a tragedy only from the point of view of the authorities. I conceived that it was my duty to obtain satisfaction for the injured, for this elderly lady (not even one of our policyholders, but a claimant against Big Ben Transfer & Storage, Inc.), from the company. The settlement was $165,000; the claim, I still believe, was just. But without my encouragement Mrs. Bichek would never have had the self-love to prize her injury so highly. The company paid, but its faith in me, in my efficacy in the role, was broken. Henry Goodykind, the district manager, expressed this thought in a few not altogether unsympathetic words, and told me at the same time that I was to have a new role. The next thing I knew I was here, at Horace Greeley Elementary, under the lubricious eye of Miss Mandible.

17 October

Today we are to have a fire drill. I know this because I am a Fire Marshal, not only for our room but for the entire right wing of the second floor. This distinction, which was awarded shortly after my arrival, is interpreted by some as another mark of my somewhat dubious relations with our teacher. My armband, which is red and decorated with white felt letters reading FIRE, sits on the little shelf under my desk, next to the brown paper bag containing the lunch I carefully make for myself each morning. One of the advantages of packing my own lunch (I have no one to pack it for me) is that I am able to fill it with things I enjoy. The peanut butter sandwiches that my mother made in my former existence, many years ago, have been banished in favor of ham and cheese. I have found that my diet has mysteriously adjusted to my new situation; I no longer drink, for instance, and when I smoke, it is in the boy's john, like everybody else. When school is out I hardly smoke at all. It is only in the matter of sex that I feel my own true age; this is apparently something that, once learned, can never be forgotten. I live in fear that Miss Mandible will one day keep me after school, and when we are alone, create a compromising situation. To avoid this I have become a model pupil: another reason for the pronounced dislike I have encountered in certain quarters. But I cannot deny that I am singed by those long glances from the vicinity of the chalkboard; Miss Mandible is in many ways, notably about the bust, a very tasty piece.

24 October

There are isolated challenges to my largeness, to my dimly realized position in the class as Gulliver. Most of my classmates are polite about this matter, as they would be if I had only one eye, or wasted, metal-wrapped legs. I am viewed as a mutation of some sort but essentially a peer. However Harry Broan, whose father has made himself rich manufacturing the Broan Bathroom Vent (with which Harry is frequently reproached; he is always being asked how things are in Ventsville), today inquired if I wanted to fight. An interested group of his followers had gathered to observe this suicidal undertaking. I replied that I didn't feel quite up to it, for which he was obviously grateful. We are now friends forever. He has given me to understand privately that he can get me all the bathroom vents I will ever need, at a ridiculously modest figure.

25 October

"*Many interesting and lifelike problems involving the use of fractions should be solved ...*" The theorists fail to realize that everything that is either interesting or lifelike in the classroom proceeds from what they would probably call interpersonal relations: Sue Ann Brownly kicking me in the ankle. How lifelike, how womanlike, is her tender solicitude after the deed! Her pride in my newly acquired limp is transparent; everyone knows that she has set her mark upon me, that it is a victory in her unequal struggle with Miss Mandible for my great, overgrown heart. Even Miss Mandible knows, and counters in perhaps the only way she can, with sarcasm. "Are you wounded, Joseph?" Conflagrations smolder behind her eyelids, yearning for the Fire Marshal clouds her eyes. I mumble that I have bumped my leg.

30 October

I return again and again to the problem of my future.

4 November

The underground circulating library has brought me a copy of *Movie-TV Secrets*, the multicolor cover blazoned with the headline "Debbie's Date Insults Liz!" It is a gift from Frankie Randolph, a rather plain girl who until today has had not one word for me, passed on via Bobby Vanderbilt. I nod and smile over my shoulder in acknowledgement; Frankie hides her head under her desk. I have seen these magazines being passed around among the girls (sometimes one of the boys will condescend to inspect a particularly lurid cover). Miss Mandible confiscates them whenever she finds one. I leaf through *Movie-TV Secrets* and get an eyeful. "The exclusive picture on these pages isn't what it seems. We know how it looks and we know what the gossipers will do. So in the interest of a nice guy, we're publishing the facts first. Here's what really happened!" The picture shows a rising young movie idol in bed, pajama-ed and bleary-eyed, while an equally blowzy young woman looks startled beside him. I am happy to know that the picture is not really what it seems; it seems to be nothing less than divorce evidence.

What do these hipless eleven-year-olds think when they come across, in the same magazine, the full-page ad for Maurice de Paree, which features "Hip Helpers" or what appear to be padded rumps? ("A real undercover agent that adds appeal to those hips and derriere, both!") If they cannot decipher the language the illustrations leave nothing to the imagination. "Drive him frantic . . ." the copy continues. Perhaps this explains Bobby Vanderbilt's preoccupation with Lancias and Maseratis; it is a defense against being driven frantic.

Sue Ann has observed Frankie Randolph's overture, and catching my eye, she pulls from her satchel no less than seventeen of these magazines, thrusting them at me as if to prove that anything any of her rivals has to offer, she can top. I shuffle through them quickly, noting the broad editorial perspective:

"Debbie's Kids Are Crying"
"Eddie Asks Debbie: Will You . . .?"
"The Nightmares Liz Has About Eddie!"
"The Things Debbie Can Tell about Eddie."
"The Private Life of Eddie and Liz"
"Debbie Gets her Man Back?"
"A New Life For Liz"
"Love Is a Tricky Affair"
"Eddie's Taylor-Made Love Nest"
"How Liz Made a Man of Eddie"
"Are They Planning to Live Together?"
"Isn't It Time to Stop Kicking Debbie Around?"
"Debbie's Dilemma"
"Eddie Becomes a Father Again"
"Is Debbie Planning to Re-wed?"
"Can Liz Fulfill Herself?"
"Why Debbie Is Sick of Hollywood"

Who are these people, Debbie, Eddie, Liz, and how did they get themselves in such a terrible predicament? Sue Ann knows, I am sure; it is obvious that she has been studying their history as a guide to what she may expect when she is suddenly freed from this drab, flat classroom.

I am angry and I shove the magazines back at her with not even a whisper of thanks.

5 November

The sixth grade at Horace Greeley Elementary is a furnace of love, love, love. Today it is raining, but inside the air is heavy and tense with passion. Sue Ann is absent; I suspect that yesterday's exchange has driven her to her bed. Guilt hangs about me. She is not responsible, I know, for what she reads, for the models proposed to her by a venal publishing industry; I should not have been so harsh. Perhaps it is only the flu.

Nowhere have I encountered an atmosphere as charged with aborted sexuality as this. Miss Mandible is helpless; nothing goes right today. Amos Darin has been found drawing a dirty picture in the cloakroom. Sad and inaccurate, it was offered not as a sign of something else but as an act of love in itself. It has excited even those who have not seen it, even those who saw but understood only that it was dirty. The room buzzes with imperfectly comprehended titillation. Amos stands by the door, waiting to be taken to the principal's office. He wavers between fear and enjoyment of his temporary celebrity. From time to time Miss Mandible looks at me reproachfully, as if blaming me for the uproar. But I did not create this atmosphere, I am caught in it like all the others.

8 November

Everything is promised my classmates and I, most of all the future. We accept the outrageous assurances without blinking.

9 November

I have finally found the nerve to petition for a larger desk. At recess I can hardly walk; my legs do not wish to uncoil themselves. Miss Mandible says she will take it up with the custodian. She is worried about the excellence of my themes. Have I, she asks, been receiving help? For an instant I am on the brink of telling her my story. Something, however, warns me not to attempt it. Here I am safe, I have a place; I do not wish to entrust myself once more to the whimsy of authority. I resolve to make my themes less excellent in the future.

11 November

A ruined marriage, a ruined adjusting career, a grim interlude in the Army when I was almost not a person. This is the sum of my existence to date, a dismal total. Small wonder that reeducation seemed my only hope. It is clear even to me that I need reworking in some fundamental way. How efficient is the society that provides thus for the salvage of its clinkers!

Plucked from my unexamined life among other pleasant, desperate, money-making young Americans, thrown backward in space and time, I am beginning to understand how I went wrong, how we all go wrong. (Although this was far from the intention of those who sent me here; they require only that I *get right*.)

14 November

The distinction between children and adults, while probably useful for some purposes, is at bottom a specious one, I feel. There are only individual egos, crazy for love.

15 November

The custodian has informed Miss Mandible that our desks are all the correct size for sixth-graders, as specified by the Board of Estimate and furnished the schools by the Nu-Art Educational Supply Corporation of Englewood, California. He has pointed out that if the desk size is correct, then the pupil size must be incorrect. Miss

Mandible, who has already arrived at this conclusion, refuses to press the matter further. I think I know why. An appeal to the administration might result in my removal from the class, in a transfer to some sort of setup for "exceptional children." This would be a disaster of the first magnitude. To sit in a room with child geniuses (or, more likely, children who are "retarded") would shrivel me in a week. Let my experience here be that of the common run, I say; let me be, please God, typical.

20 November

We read signs as promises. Miss Mandible understands by my great height, by my resonant vowels, that I will one day carry her off to bed. Sue Ann interprets the same signs to mean that I am unique among her male acquaintances, therefore most desirable, therefore her special property as is everything that is Most Desirable. If neither of these propositions work out then life has broken faith with them.

I myself, in my former existence, read the company motto ("Here to Help in Time of Need") as a description of the duty of the adjuster, drastically mislocating the company's deepest concerns. I believed that because I had obtained a wife who was made up of wife-signs (beauty, charm, softness, perfume, cookery) I had found love. Brenda, reading the same signs that have now misled Miss Mandible and Sue Ann Brownly, felt she had been promised that she would never be bored again. All of us, Miss Mandible, Sue Ann, myself, Brenda, Mr. Goodykind, still believe that the American flag betokens a kind of general righteousness.

But I say, looking about me in this incubator of future citizens, that signs are signs, and that some of them are lies. This is the great discovery of my time here.

23 November

It may be that my experience as a child will save me after all. If only I can remain quietly in this classroom, making my notes while Napoleon plods through Russia in the droning voice of Harry Broan, reading aloud from our History text. All of the mysteries that perplexed me as an adult have their origins here, and one by one I am numbering them, exposing their roots.

2 December

Miss Mandible will refuse to permit me to remain ungrown. Her hands rest on my shoulders too warmly, and for too long.

7 December

It is the pledges that this place makes to me, pledges that cannot be redeemed, that confuse me later and make me feel I am not *getting anywhere*. Everything is presented as the result of some knowable process; if I wish to arrive at four I get there by way of two and two. If I wish to burn Moscow the route I must travel has already been marked out by another visitor. If, like Bobby Vanderbilt, I yearn for the wheel of the Lancia 2.4-liter coupé, I have only to go through the appropriate process, that is, get the money. And if it is money itself that I desire, I have only to make it. All of these goals are equally beautiful in the sight of the Board of Estimate; the proof is all around us, in the no-nonsense ugliness of this steel and glass building, in the straightline matter-of-factness with which Miss Mandible handles some of our less reputable wars. Who points out that arrangements sometimes slip, that errors are made, that signs are misread? *"They have confidence in their ability to take the right steps and to obtain correct answers."* I take the right steps, obtain correct answers, and my wife leaves me for another man.

8 December

My enlightenment is proceeding wonderfully.

9 December

Disaster once again. Tomorrow I am to be sent to a doctor, for observation. Sue Ann Brownly caught Miss Mandible and me in the cloakroom, during recess, and immediately threw a fit. For a moment I thought she was actually going to choke. She ran out of the room weeping, straight for the principal's office, certain now which of us was Debbie, which Eddie, which Liz. I am sorry to be the cause of her disillusionment, but I know that she will recover. Miss Mandible is ruined but fulfilled. Although she will be charged with contributing to the delinquency of a minor, she seems at peace; *her* promise has been kept. She knows now that everything she has been told about life, about America, is true.

I have tried to convince the school authorities that I am a minor only in a very special sense, that I am in fact mostly to blame—but it does no good. They are as dense as ever. My contemporaries are astounded that I present myself as anything other than an innocent victim. Like the Old Guard marching through the Russian drifts, the class marches to the conclusion that truth is punishment.

Bobby Vanderbilt has given me his copy of *Sounds of Sebring*, in farewell.

BIBLIOGRAPHY

Adkins, Winthrop, R. "Life Skills Education for Adult Learners." *Adult Leadership*, June 1973.

Brandenburg, Judith Berman. "The Needs of Women Returning to School." *Personnel and Guidance Journal,* 53, 1 (Sept. 1974), 11–18.

Dubin, Samuel S. and Morris Okun. "Implications of Learning Theories for Adult Instruction." *Adult Education*, 14, 1 (Fall 1973), 3–19.

Gessner, Robert, ed. *The Democratic Man: Selected Writings of Eduard C. Lindeman.* Foreword by Max Otto. Boston: Beacon Press, 1956.

Kidd, J. R. *How Adults Learn*. Revised and Updated. New York: Association Press, 1977.

Klevins, Chester, ed. *Materials and Methods in Continuing Education.* Los Angeles: Klevins Publications, Inc., 1978.

Knowles, Malcolm. *The Adult Learner: A Neglected Species.* 2nd ed. Houston: Gulf Publishing Co., 1978.

Knox, Alan B. *Adult Development and Learning: A Handbook on Individual Growth and Competence in the Adult Years for Education and the Helping Professions.* The Jossey-Bass Higher Education and Social and Behavioral Science Series. San Francisco: Jossey-Bass Pub., Inc., 1977.

Neugarten, Bernice. "Adult Personality: A Developmental View." *Human Development*, 9 (1966), 61–73.

Peterson, Richard E. et al. *Lifelong Learning in America*. San Francisco: Jossey-Bass Pub. Inc., 1979.

Pollard, W. Grosvenor III, "Implications of the Rank Concession Syndrome for Adult Education Programs: An Exploration in Social Roles and Program Effectiveness." *Adult Education*, 14 (Summer 1974), 255–269.

Smith, Robert M., George F. Aker, and J. R. Kidd. *Handbook of Adult Education*. New York: Macmillan Publishing Co., Inc., 1970.

Srinivason, Lyra. *Perspectives on Nonformal Adult Learning: Functional Education for Individual, Community, and National Development.* New York: World Education, 1977.

Tough, Allen. *The Adult's Learning Projects. A Fresh Approach to Theory and Practice in Adult Learning.* 2nd ed. Research in Education Series No. 1. Toronto: The Ontario Institute for Studies in Education, 1979. Orig. published 1971.

10 | *EVALUATION*

THEORETICAL CONSIDERATIONS

Who Evaluates?

Three agents are likely to evaluate a tutor's work: the tutee, the tutoring service, and you, the tutor. Although the motives for doing so may vary, each of you wants to know what, if any, progress the tutee has made, how much you, as the tutor, are responsible for that progress, and, ultimately, what the value is of the program under which you both have worked. All of you, at many different levels, are working at trying to determine whether "it was worth it." What needs to be decided first, however, is what the "it" actually was.

The "it" will depend on whom you ask. You, for one, may decide that the "it" was the readings in psychology, or the relationship you established with a tutee of another ethnic background. The "it" for the program may have been the number of students who came for tutoring and the percentage of students who passed the relevant courses. For one tutee, "it" may have been passing Introduction to Sociology, while for another "it" may have been developing research skills which were useful for a variety of courses. None of these are necessarily mutually exclusive. Yet the standards of success, and from whose perspective we define such standards, is of considerable importance.

A student's dropping out, for instance, may reflect his or her inability to complete a course of study but may also be an expression of growth in self-assessment—the ability to determine real needs, to establish goals more appropriate to those needs and capacities, and to make decisions about his or her own life. You and the tutee may concur that success should be measured by personal growth while the tutorial program's administrators may insist that the tutorial was a failure because the student did not attend tutoring regularly and never completed the academic program. There are other standards, however, over which you and your tutee may differ. One tutee may have found the actual tutoring you offered inadequate but felt good about remaining in tutoring because he or she developed important habits of self-discipline. Another tutee may consider passing the course the only measure of success and will disregard his or her improvement.

Evaluation is conditioned by your tutee's values and your own; it is also conditioned by the philosophy of your tutoring program and the nature, context, and priorities established by your institution. It should be a cooperative venture. Beginning on the first day of tutoring and continuing all term, you, your tutee, and the administrative staff of your program all work interdependently to evaluate yourselves and each other.

Goals and objectives must be established together, allowing for accommodations to be made as you work toward those goals and objectives, and final evaluations regarding them shared. Such a team effort can determine not only whether the goals were achieved but whether they were appropriate, necessary, and valuable in the first place.

What to Evaluate

Tutoring can be evaluated by measuring the success that tutor, tutee, and the program has had in meeting goals in three areas: the academic, counseling, and professional domains. *Academic goals* are concerned with whether the tutor knew what he or she needed to know in order to tutor the tutee, and whether the tutee learned the required material. *Counseling goals* address changes in attitude and motivation, and the emotional impact and meaningfulness of the tutorial experience. *Professional goals*, like scheduling, attendance, and record keeping, seem trivial in comparison to those established in other areas; but they are quite essential in providing the framework within which the other goals can be accomplished. Fulfilling these tasks is an obligation students take on when they assume the role of tutee and which you take on when you assume the professional role of tutor.

PRACTICAL APPLICATIONS: THE END-TERM EVALUATION

Winding Down

As you near the end of the term you must begin thinking about your tutoring sessions differently. Your tutees' thoughts will probably be on evaluation anyway: they will want to know how well they have performed this term, and will be concerned that what they know is measurable in terms of final exams, essays, and finally, in end-term grades. Your responsibility, as tutor, is to help the tutees evaluate themselves and to make the process of evaluation a positive one, one which reinforces knowledge, helps the students discover what they need to know, and alleviates anxiety about what is often an excruciatingly painful process: finals! Be sure to do this early enough so that your tutees can benefit most from such an evaluation, late enough so that the pressure to perform well will motivate your tutees to work extra hard.

Tutor-Tutee Evaluation Conference About three or four weeks before the end of tutoring you should designate a session as an evaluation conference. Prepare your tutees for this conference by asking them to gather together all the work which they have done in and out of class that will be able to help you and your tutees figure out how they are doing in the class, and what they still need to accomplish in tutoring. During this conference, you should also try to gather the following information relevant to your counseling role:

1. How your tutees feel about the course (this will allow them to express any emotional problems they are having with the course or the teacher).

2. How your tutees feel about their progress in the class (this will allow you to determine how realistic they are being).
3. What your tutees feel are their weaknesses—in terms of the course—and what they have planned to do regarding them (this will allow you to ascertain whether or not they are preparing for the end of the term).
4. How the tutees feel tutoring has helped them this term (which is for your benefit) and how they feel tutoring can help them in the next few weeks (which is for their benefit).

Then, during the same session, if possible, carefully analyze the following four areas in the academic domain. As you can see, they will be accessible only if both of you have been keeping good records.

Class Grades Although students' grades on tests and papers during the term should not be the only indicators of progress, they will, inevitably, be the most important determinants of the final grade; they are also the easiest way to see what students learned and how relevant tutoring has been.

During the term you undoubtedly discussed grades with your tutees, determining what the grade meant in terms of class standards and what needed to be done, if anything, to improve the grade. You might have used the test or essay as a basis for tutoring sessions (and these were probably particularly good sessions because tutees were very motivated to find out why they got the grade they got). Since you are nearing the end of the term you should discuss graded work with tutees again to see if there is any material they still don't understand. Pay particular attention to error patterns—areas in which students are recurrently weak. A complete understanding of performance on previous tests or papers is essential in preparation for a final test or essay.

Now you have several options. You might want to give tutees a mock-final exam (or assignment, if it is a writing course), based on material from all the tests. Or you might try to get hold of previous tests, either by the tutees' teachers or other course instructors, and administer that. (Your program may keep a file of such material.) The results of such a test will help to indicate how well your tutees have mastered their classwork and what still needs to be done. Also, it will give students a realistic sense of their standing. A good performance will help them to build needed confidence for the upcoming final test period.

Course Review At this point, you should check students' course descriptions and syllabi again to determine whether you and your tutees have covered all important material. Make certain students have a clear understanding of what will be on the final (or in the final paper). Sometimes students do not realize that they may be responsible for everything on their syllabi, *whether or not it has been covered in class.* Go over any areas the students still don't know.

Assignments In rechecking the syllabi, ask to see any required assignments, such as small projects that are neither tests or essays. Since these assignments rarely have equal weight with tests or essays, students at times neglect them; but if not done, their absence may affect the final grade. Make certain your tutees have handed in all required work (including any rewritten assignments), have made up any missed quizzes, and so on.

Tutee Folder Aside from work tutees have done in or for their classes, it should be helpful to review work tutees have done for you. Again, look through tests and exercises for any persistent weaknesses. Note where students have improved and reinforce their strengths by testing them in those areas. If you concentrate on strengths first, the work you do on persistent weaknesses will not be so demoralizing. Look at your own journal. Did you cover all the areas you thought were important?

Next, set up a schedule of what needs to be accomplished during the final weeks of tutoring. You can call it a battle plan or a contract; call it anything that will help students feel excited about the project. A team effort such as this, with clear objectives, can provide the motivation your tutees need to put in that extra effort. For evaluation can be extremely painful, especially if a student hasn't been doing very well. Your role is to help students believe that an extra effort is actually going to make a difference despite past problems, or even failures.

If you have your end–term conference sufficiently early, if you have a complete review, and if you make sure the last few sessions profit from that review, you will have a much better chance of bringing to fruition everything that you have been working for all term.

The Final Session: Evaluation as Closure

In most relationships and experiences it is important to provide for some ceremony and ritual that will seal them, lending them importance and dignity. Anthropologists have designated such occasions rites of passage because they signal important transitions that individuals make in moving into new activities, and toward taking on new roles. Inherent in the rite of passage is the notion that there comes a time when a person leaves something or some part of his or her old self behind. So there comes a time when the semester ends and the tutee must leave tutoring behind. You, too, must provide a kind of ritual to give your tutees a sense of what they have accomplished. Bringing closure, if done well, will support your tutees' efforts to act independently of tutoring or, at least, of you.

Closure is actually a kind of evaluation, for it occurs at the end of the term, when final grades are known and you and each of your tutees are reviewing what you have accomplished, both for yourselves and each other. Now is the time to make specific recommendations for the future: what do the tutees still need to know in order to pass the course or to do well in the second half of the course; what should the tutees read; how much time might they devote to what kinds of practice; what courses would build on and help to develop their strengths? How might you have helped them more? Be sure to share feelings as well, and what you've learned beyond the subject matter in working together. Finally, even though the course has been (perhaps) completed successfully, you should encourage tutees to continue to think of tutoring as a service that they may always use, and assure them that asking for tutoring again is a sign of strength rather than weakness. If the tutee wants to continue with tutoring next term and you won't be available, give your student the name of another available tutor; in this way, the tutee won't feel abandoned. (The task-centered model case is a good reference point for what we've been talking about, and you might wish to review it for its concrete handling of the process of both winding-down and closure. See p. 184).

Self-Evaluation

A self-evaluation involves closure as well; it allows a tutor to take pride in past accomplishments and also to move to a new level of training. It is, in some ways, a graduation. If you are like the typical tutor, you have probably been evaluating yourself constantly, in some ways probably too much. In the beginning of the term, you were probably very hard on yourself. Now, however, you are at the end of the term, and, one hopes, less self-critical. Each session is not a crisis because you are beginning to recognize your own expertise. You are now ready to develop a systematic assessment of yourself as a tutor, to bring closure to your term as a tutor, and to prepare the way for future tutoring experiences.

Here's how to do it. Take all your records concerning your case-study tutee and prepare to examine yourself in the three areas that we've surveyed—academic, counseling, professional—as outlined in the following pages. Once you have finished your self-evaluation you will have a lot of the material for your case study.

TUTOR–COUNSELING SELF–EVALUATION

I.   Academic Function

   a. Diagnosis

   List below all the methods you used to analyze your tutee's problems.

   _____

   _____

   _____

   _____

   _____

Now check the discussion in Chapter 2 which explains diagnosis and evaluate

your diagnostic skill. Did you get a writing sample as early in the term as

possible? Did you check to see whether the teacher had left a referral?

_____

_____

Was your diagnosis accurate? (Compare your initial and end–of–term analyses.)

What did you miss and why? (What in your diagnostic mechanism was faulty?)

_____

_____

b.   Plan

Write down your term tutoring plan (goals and objectives).

_____

_____

_____

_____

_____

Again, look at the student's final work. Did your plan cover all it needed to?
What should you have included that you didn't? What did you include that wasn't
necessary?

_____

c.   Strategies and Techniques

Write up any methodologies that you used. (Check your journal for
this information.) Explore whether they helped you tutor the subject.
If the strategy or technique worked, determine why and how it worked. If
it wasn't successful, try to determine why it went wrong and whether the
problem lay with the strategy or technique itself, with the student, or
with you. Wherever possible, recommend alternates, always explaining
why what you are recommending would be more appropriate. (What you may
find is that the reason something works or not is usually quite complex,
and cannot be attributed to a single cause.)

II. Counseling Function

Analyze the counseling strategies you used. Your journal should give you the information you need to evaluate this part of your function (see Chapter 6).

a. Sensitivity to student's emotional needs

Make a list of what personal characteristics you feel helped or impeded your tutee from functioning well during tutoring (such as intelligence, passivity, assertiveness, anxiety).

_____

_____

_____

_____

_____

Analyze how you responded to meet the student's needs in these areas.

_____

_____

b. Skill at handling problem situations

Describe any problem situations that occurred during your tutoring (see Chapter 7). Analyze how you handled them. What could you have done to resolve them more successfully?

III.   Professional Function

Being a professional means filling the role you agreed to fill with utmost skill, integrity, and precision. As a tutor you are both a learner and a professional, a tricky position because you fill two complex roles. How well were you able to maintain the balance between your two roles?

a.   Rules

Every organization has rules. A lab is no exception. Did you arrive on time, leave on time, call when late or sick? Did you follow your lab's code of ethics (see Chapter 1)? Write a paragraph below in which you analyze how well you obeyed your lab's rules (and reasons for any lapses).

---

b. <u>Paperwork</u>

The larger and more bureaucratic the tutoring program, the more
paperwork it probably has developed (such as attendance forms, registration
forms, session reports).   How prompt and efficient were you in doing the
paperwork?   List here the administrative tasks you hated the most (if any)
and why?

_____

_____

_____

_____

_____

c.   <u>Training</u>

Examine the training you received. How well were you able to apply what you learned to your tutoring? List training that seemed especially useful to tutoring and explain how it was useful.

_____

_____

Look at your command of your subject matter at the beginning of your training. What did you do this term to improve on your weak areas? How successful were you? What areas still need work? What are you going to do about it? Outline a program of self study for next term.

_____

_____

Now consider the affective changes that have resulted from this experience. Focus on your attitudes, commitment, and other aspects of your own growth. In what ways would you like to develop further? What do you need to do to accomplish those goals?

_____

_____

READING 21

Here is an evaluation completed by a college junior after her second year as a tutor. Note that the evaluation is general and does not refer to a specific tutee but to her tutoring experience with several students. Read it and see if it can help you formulate your own evaluation.

TUTOR-COUNSELING SELF-EVALUATION

I.   Academic Function

    a. Diagnosis

Kathy Blasius
School of Arts and Sciences
College of New Rochelle

List below all the methods you used to analyze your tutee's problems.

1. Writing sample. (especially for inconsistent mistakes)
2. Student's attitude and behavior (just lack of interest?)
3. Student's definition of the problem.
4. The tutee's instructor.
5. Distractions while writing and time alloted for writing.

Now check the discussion in Chapter 2 which explains diagnosis and evaluate your diagnostic skill. Did you get a writing sample as early in the term as possible? Did you check to see whether the teacher had left a referral?

1. I usually have the student write a sample for me at the beginning of the first session.
2. Before I get a chance to ask the student, either the form is waiting for me in my box or "self" has been written beside "Referred by" in the log book.

Was your diagnosis accurate? (Compare your initial and end-of-term analyses.)

What did you miss and why? (What in your diagnostic mechanism was faulty?)

I found that the majority of the time I was able to get to the base of the problem. I did have some difficulty where emotions were concerned.

b.   Plan

Write down your term tutoring plan (goals and objectives).

Mainly, I try to help the student understand her mistakes, and through application see if she really does understand. I also try to give students a healthy outlook on writing and the importance of being a good writer.

Again, look at the student's final work. Did your plan cover all it needed to? What should you have included that you didn't? What did you include that wasn't necessary?

I feel that the majority of the time the students did come a long way with their writing problems. Usually, after the problem areas had been worked out, we would work on more creative writing and writing techniques.

I think I should have included more specific things, but that could only have been done if I had looked at one individual at a time. The goals also change several times in the semester as new things come up.

c.   Strategies and Techniques

Write up any methodologies that you used. (Check your journal for this information.) Explore whether they helped you tutor the subject. If the strategy or technique worked, determine why and how it worked. If it wasn't successful, try to determine why it went wrong and whether the problem lay with the strategy or technique itself, with the student, or with you. Wherever possible, recommend alternates, always explaining why what you are recommending would be more appropriate. (What you may find is that the reason something works or not is usually quite complex, and cannot be attributed to a single cause.)

One technique I used that proved to be very effective was turning any lesson into a game. The only competition the student had was herself. It was fun for both of us and the material was often learned quickly and easily.

Using the material in every day situations was also helpful. It was easy for the students to relate the information to a subject they were interested in.

(I think both were successful as they didn't make the lesson dry and lifeless.)

(I also write practically everything on scrap paper as we go along, as the visual work helps the student to understand more quickly.)

II. Counseling Function

Analyze the counseling strategies you used. Your journal should give you the information you need to evaluate this part of your function (see Chapter 6).

a. Sensitivity to student's emotional needs

Make a list of what personal characteristics you feel helped or impeded your tutee from functioning well during tutoring (such as intelligence, passivity, assertiveness, anxiety).

Helped - a seemingly apparent willingness to learn
Impeded - lack of self-confidence
          emotional preoccupation, which led
          to a short attention span.

Analyze how you responded to meet the student's needs in these areas.

. I tried to boost her ego wherever it could justifiably be done. To keep her attention, I prepared many different types of material to use, so we were constantly starting something different. For the material she seemed most interested in, I would spend more time on. I didn't press her to tell me any problems, because I thought she would feel uneasy and hesitant to come back.

b. Skill at handling problem situations

Describe any problem situations that occurred during your

tutoring (see Chapter 7). Analyze how you handled them. What

could you have done to resolve them more successfully?

1. One student arrived very angry because her instructor gave her a referral slip. She wanted me to say what I had to say, teach her everything about grammar in half an hour and send back my slip to her writing teacher saying she did okay. I was taken aback, as she really seemed to think she was doing me the favor. After I had asked if she would like to talk about the purpose of the slip and her writing, she became more indignant. She said plainly that she didn't want to be here. I told the student it wasn't my fault she had to be there, so to begin with, not to push her anger on me. I then went on to say that she would not benefit from tutoring with such an attitude and basically it was change it or fail. I guess I handled it okay. Her mouth fell open for a second, and she then apologized. We worked very well together after that.

2. A student came in feeling dejected and very much like "... the big dummy who didn't know a thing about writing." She tended to regard me as the all-knowing tutor who knew everything about anything. It was an uncomfortable situation for me, and it often affected our tutoring sessions. I tried to remedy the situation by nonchalantly admitting my faults. Saying that I was a poor speller, and that I really had to work to improve it, was a surprise yet almost a relief to her. When she finally realized that I was not perfect and indeed not all-knowing, our sessions went much better and the progress was on a much faster level.

III. <u>Professional Function</u>

Being a professional means filling the role you agreed to fill with utmost skill, integrity, and precision. As a tutor you are both a learner and a professional, a tricky position because you fill two complex roles. How well were you able to maintain the balance between your two roles?

a. Rules

Every organization has rules. A lab is no exception. Did you arrive on time, leave on time, call when late or sick? Did you follow your lab's code of ethics (see Chapter 1)? Write a paragraph below in which you analyze how well you obeyed your lab's rules (and reasons for any lapses).

I usually arrive on time, but Charlotte had to call me twice to wake me up to come down. I called, or had someone call for me, or called the tutee when I couldn't make it. In the beginning of the semester, I mixed up my schedule and missed a few sessions. I am sure I obeyed all the other rules. (Most of the time I forgot to write down my hours, but Charlotte fixed me of that dirty habit very soon.)

b. <u>Paperwork</u>

The larger and more bureaucratic the tutoring program, the more paperwork it probably has developed (such as attendance forms, registration forms, session reports).   How prompt and efficient were you in doing the paperwork?   List here the administrative tasks you hated the most (if any) and why?

I always filed my schedule and remembered to write in the log book. The task I <u>hate</u> most is filing, but there wasn't that much to do, thankfully.

c.   <u>Training</u>

Examine the training you received. How well were you able to apply
what you learned to your tutoring? List training that seemed especially
useful to tutoring and explain how it was useful.

Training in defining the problem was very useful.
I saw that I was wasting time without the proper
two-way dialogue.

Look at your command of your subject matter at the beginning of your
training. What did you do this term to improve on your weak areas? How
successful were you? What areas still need work? What are you going to do
about it? Outline a program of self study for next term.

I worked on the time allotment for tutoring,
realizing that an hour is usually not enough for going
over long term papers, and too long for simple essays
that don't require much tutoring. I also have a better
understanding of how emotions affect someone's writing.

Now consider the affective changes that have resulted from this
experience. Focus on your attitudes, commitment, and other aspects of
your own growth. In what ways would you like to develop further?
What do you need to do to accomplish those goals?

I would like to try working with more than one
tutee at a time, but as of yet I have not had
two people at the same time who would benefit
from it.

SUMMARY

If you have evaluated yourself carefully, you will probably find that you know a lot more now than you did before you started this text—but you still don't know enough. Good! Use this evaluation as a starting point for future development. Perhaps your last journal entry for this term should include some resolutions on what you can do to improve your tutoring. And don't be dejected if your list is long. The real failure is to have a short list, one which doesn't recognize that the best tutors are those who continue to learn and grow.

BIBLIOGRAPHY

Bloom, Benjamin S. *Taxonomy of Educational Objectives: Book I, Cognitive Domain.* New York: Longman, 1980.

Ebel, R. L. *Measuring Educational Achievement.* Englewood Cliffs, N. J.: Prentice-Hall, 1965.

Krathwohl, David R. et al. *Taxonomy of Educational Objectives Handbook II: Affective Domain.* New York: David McKay Co., Inc., 1974.

Mager, R. F. *Preparing Objectives for Programmed Instruction.* San Francisco: Haron, 1962.

Thorndike, R. L. and E. P. Hagen. *Measurement and Evaluation in Psychology and Education.* New York: John Wiley & Sons, 1969.

INDEX

"About New York," 14–15
Acceptance, 165–66
  class project, 167
Acculturation, 127–28
Adult education, 270–84
  adult intelligence and, 273–76
  class projects, 270, 271–72, 273, 276
  lab applications, 276
  physiological factors, 272–73
  reading questions, 277
  social aspects, 270–72
Adult Education Association, 274
Adult Learning, 274
Alternation method, 94
American English Sign Language
    (AMESLAN), 66, 67
American Manual Alphabet, 67
American Sign Language (ASL), 66
Anxiety, 130, 168
Aphasia, 72
Application of tutoring to course of
    study, 94
Appointments, 17
Arkin, Marian, 17*n*
Army Alpha Tests, 274
Articulation, 65–66
Assertiveness, 171–72
  class project, 172
  lab application, 173
Attitudes, tutees', 5–6
  potential problem areas in, 203–18
Audio-tutorial learning, 94–95
Audiovisual aids, 105–8
  class project, 108
  lab application, 108
Autobiography and the Classroom
    (excerpt), 23–28

Barthelme, Donald, 277

Benefits of tutoring, 4–6
  class projects, 3, 6
"Benjamin: Reading and Beyond,"
    29–35
Berne, Eric, 165
Black English, 129
Boardwork, 98–99
Bounded Figure, 73
Braille, 69–70
Braille, Louis, 70
Braille Alphabet, 70
Bresnick, Renee, 61
Bruffee, Kenneth A., 57
Bruner, Jerome, 253

Calculator Game Book (excerpt),
    117–20
Calculator Saturnalia (excerpts),
    115–17, 120–26
Career development, 5
Carlson, Gaylen, 266
Case study, autobiographical, of deaf
    student, 75–83
"Case Study: Patricia Bauer," 233–25
Case study, task-centered social work,
    185–93
Case study, tutorial relationship,
    54–62
  class project, 56
  critique, 57
  guide, 55–56
  reading questions, 57–58
  in self-evaluation, 174
Case Study Critique, 57
Cerebral palsy victims, 72
Classical conditioning, 234–36
  class project, 236
  lab applications, 236–37
Closure, evaluation as, 288

Clustering, 240–41

Coding, 100

"Coffee Break," 134–36

"Cognitive Consequences of Formal
  and Informal Education," 254–64

Cognitive theory, 239–48
  class project, 248
  consequences, 254–64
  tutorial strategies, 243–44

Cole, Michael, 254

Collaborative learning, 6–9
  class project, 8–9

Community, classroom as, 23

Computer-assisted education, 106–7

Concept formation, 244

Concrete operations, as level of
  thought, 246–47

Conditioning. *See* Classical conditioning; Operant conditioning

Confidentiality, 17

Conflicts, potential, for roleplaying:
  student/student, 217–18
  teacher/student, 212–15
  tutor/student, 203–12
  tutor/teacher, 215–17

Confrontation, in tutor-counseling,
  169–70

"Conjugal Reluctance," 124–26

Content, preparing tutorial session,
  42–43

Cornelisen, Ann, 225

Counseling, 154–93
  approaches, 160–70
  caution in, 171
  class projects, 161–62, 164, 165–66,
    167, 169, 170, 172, 175
  lab applications, 164, 166, 169, 173
  motivation and, 154–59
  reading questions, 175, 185
  self-evaluation outlines, 290–306
  self-understanding and, 171–75

Course review, 287

Cross-age tutoring, 4

Culture, understanding others', 127–28
  class project, 128–29

Deaf students, 65–69
  articulation with, 65–66
  autobiographical case study, 75–83
  class project, 69
  lipreading, 65–66, 67
  sign languages, 66–68
  tutorial services, 66
  word problems, 67–68

Demonstration, as tutoring technique,
  98

"Development of Reasoning in Science," 266–69

Dewey, John, 78n

Diagramming, 98–99, 100
  sample, 99

Dialect problems, 129–33

Dickens, Charles, 18, 19

Didion, Joan, 11

Discovery method, 93

Discriminating between learned responses, 238

Disequilibrium, 247

Don't Look Now, 98

Drill, 94

Drop-in students, 43

Dyslexia, 72

"Edward," 61–62

Ego states, 165

Eisenstadt, Bert, 13n

Empathy, 160–61

Encoding, 242

Environment, physical, 41–42

Ethics of tutoring, 16–17
  class project, 18

Evaluation
  as closure, 288
  early, 53–54
  end-term, 286–88
  guidelines, 16
  theoretical considerations, 285–86
  use of case study in, 54–62, 174
  see also Self–evaluation

Expectations, tutoring, 18, 52–53

Experimenter bias, 52

"Experiment in Preschool Education,
  An," 75–83

Farrell, William E., 14

Feedback, 87, 160, 168, 174

Feelings, "owning," 171–72

Ferguson, Wendy M., 223

"Fibonacci Follies," 118

Filmstrip-Tape Projector, 106

Fishbowl technique, 10
  class project, 43–44

Flowers, John, 172n, 202n

Formal operations, as level of thought,
  247

"Freedom to Learn," 176–85

Friedman, Paul G., 156n

Full Script Roleplay, 196–98

Games, 90, 114–26
  class project, 91
  reading questions, 114–15
"Gauss' 'Gimmick,'" 118
Generalization, in operant conditioning, 238
Glanville, Ranulph, 115, 120
Goals, 47, 285–86
"Going Home Again: The New American Scholarship Boy," 136–43
"Golden Ratio, The," 119
Grades, 16, 287
Group work, 9–11
  adult, 275–76
  class projects, 10–11, 43–44
  reading questions, 35–36
  techniques, 10
Guidelines, tutoring, 16–17

Handicapped persons, 64–83
  class projects, 64, 69, 74
  deaf students, 65–69
  lab application, 74
  learning disabled, 72–73
  other physical impairments, 72
  reading questions, 75
  visually, 69–72
Hansen, Philip G., 36
Hard Times (excerpt), 19–23
Hartman, Arlene, 117
Hawkins, Thom, 28, 29
Heuristics, 245
  lab application, 249
Hierarchy of Needs, 155
Hofsteater, Howard T., 74, 75
Homework, 87
Hughes, Langston, 133, 134

Information-processing system, mind as, 239–45
Information retrieval, 99
Instruction, tutorial session, 88–89
"Intellectual Strengths in Culturally Different Groups: An Eskimo Illustration," 144–51
Intelligence, adult, 273–76
  class project, 276
Interaction, tutor–tutee, 52–53, 89
Internal-External Conrol Scale, 157
Interviews, initial, 44–52
  defining student problem, 45–46
  ending, 51
  lab application, 50, 53
  learning contract, 47–50

planning from, 46–47
  problems with, 51–52
"Is It 11 or 9?," 117

Journal keeping, 11–15
  class project, 14–15
  comparing case study with, 54–55
  guidelines, 12–13
  lab applications, 13–14, 44
  reading questions, 28–29
  in self-analysis, 173–74
Judgment and Reasoning in the Child, 246
Juxtaposition, 246

Kleinfeld, J. S., 144

Language, learning a second, 129–33
Large-type formats, 69–70
Lazarus, A. A., 172*n*
Learning, 233–69
  cognitive theory, 239–48
  collaborative, 6–9
  formal and informal, 254–64
  improved through tutoring, 5
  reading questions, 249–50, 254, 265
  stimulus-response theory, 234–38
Learning contract, 47–50
  class project, 48
Learning cycle, 247–48
  diagrammed, 248
  lab application, 249
  reading questions, 265
Learning disabilities, 46, 72–73
Learning module, 94–95
Lecturing, 98
Lipreading, 65–66
Locus of control concept, 158–59
Luria, A. R., 249, 250, 253

McDermott, Dermod, 161*n*
Making of Mind, The (excerpt), 250–53
Manual alphabet, 66–67
Maslow, Abraham, 154–56, 184
Math Tutor, The, 17
Maturity, tutoring and, 4–5
"Me and Miss Mandible," 277–84
Media, instructional, 89–90
Memory, 240–41, 242
Meno (excerpt), 109–14
Methodology, roleplaying, 195–200
Microteaching, 10
Mind, as information-processing system, 239–45

Modeling, 53
"More Odds in Your Favor," 119
Motivation, 87, 88, 154–59
  class projects, 91, 156, 158
  devices to improve, 89–91
  hierarchy of needs and, 154–56
  lab applications, 91, 157
  locus of control and, 158–59
  tutoring strategies, 159
Multicultural settings, 127–53
  class projects, 128–29, 133
  lab applications, 133
  reading questions, 134, 136, 144
  second-language learners, 129–33
  understanding, 127–28
"My Days: A Memoir," 220–23

Narayan, R. K., 219–220
Needs hierarchy, 154–56
Network for Learning, The, 272
Nondirective listening, 160
  class project, 161–62
Nonverbal communication, 66–68, 167
"Numerical Intuition," 115–17

Observer-critic method, 10
"Odds Are in Your Favor, The," 119
"101 Revisited," 117
Operant conditioning, 237–38
Oral communication
  with deaf students, 66–68
  with second-language learners,
    129–30
  with visually handicapped, 70–71
Orwell, George, 235–26
Overhead Projector, 107

Paraphrase, 10
  class project, 164
  in Rogerian psychology, 160–63
  as tutoring technique, 97–98
Paraplegic students, 72
Partial Script Roleplay, 199
"Partridge in a Pear Tree," 119
Pask, Gordon, 115, 120
Pavlov, Ivan, 234
Peer teacher technique, 10
Peer tutors, defined, 2
Perception of Handicapped Persons, 64
Personality, theories of, 160–70
"Physically challenged," as term, 65*n*
Piaget, Jean, 245–48, 249, 253
Piagetian theory, 245–48
  learning cycle, 247–48

reading questions, 249–50
stages of thought, 245–47
tutoring strategies, 247
Planning
  after tutoring, 87
  before tutoring, 86
  chart, 101–4
  class projects, 85, 102
  from initial interviews, 46–47
  lab applications, 86, 87, 102
  role of, in tutorial session, 84–87
  while tutoring, 86–87
Plato, 108, 109
PLATO Computer-Based Education, 95
Porter, Roger, 23
Preoperational thought, 246
Preparation, tutorial session, 41–44
  content, 42–43
  environment, physical 41–42
  planning chart, 101–4
  program mechanics, 42
Problem(s)
  areas for roleplaying, 202–18
  defining student's, 45–46
  first-session, 51
  of handicapped students, 65–73
  language, 129–33
  reading questions, 219, 223, 225
  -solving methods, 244
Processes of learning, 234–69
  cognitive theory, 239–48
  formal and informal, 254–64
  stimulus-response theory, 234–38
Professional tutors, defined, 1–2
Program, mechanics of tutoring, 42
Programmed instruction, 94
Projectors, use of, 105–6, 107
Protocol, tutorial, 233–34
Psychological insight, 5

Quadraplegic students, 72
Questioning techniques, 45–46, 92

Reading problems, second-language
  learner, 131
Reassurance, 167–68
  class project, 169
  lab application, 169
Recall, 239–42
  class projects, 239, 243
Record player, 105
Referral, 17
  forms, 43
  as tutoring technique, 99

Reflecting skills, 160–63
    class project, 161–62
Reid, William J., 185
Reinforcement, 89, 93, 101, 237–38
Relationship, tutorial, 52–53, 89
    case study, 54–62
Relevance in instruction, 88–89
"Reluctance," 120–23
Retamar, Antonia, 58
Robinson, Mike, 115, 120
Rodriguez, Richard, 136
Rogerian psychology, 160–63
    class projects, 161–62, 164
    nondirective listening, 160
    reflecting skills, 160–63
Rogers, Carl, 160, 175, 176, 184
Roleplaying, 90, 194–232
    caution in, 201
    class projects, 201–2, 219
    lab application, 202
    methodology, 195–200
    problem areas for, 202–18
    reading questions, 219, 223, 225
    sample session, 200–201
    scripted, 196–98
    in self-evaluation, 174
    unscripted, 198–99
Rosenthal, Robert, 52
Rosnick, Peter, 17*n*

Scribner, Sylvia, 254
Scripted roleplaying, 196–98
Second-language learners, 129–33
    class project, 133
    emotional problems, 129, 131, 133
    lab applications, 133
    oral communication, 129–30
    reading problems, 131
Self-actualization, 155
Self-esteem, 155, 166
Self-evaluation, 173–75, 289
    outlines, 290–306
Self-instructed learning, 94–95
Self-understanding, 171–75
    assertiveness in, 171–72
    class project, 175
    sources for, 173–75
Sensory-motor intelligence, 245–46
Session, tutorial
    audiovisual aids, 105–8
    class projects, 85, 91, 96, 101, 102, 108
    components of good, 88–89
    final, 288

initial, 44–52
    lab applications, 86, 87, 88, 91, 96, 102, 108
    motivational devices, 89–91
    planning chart, 101–4
    reading questions, 109, 114–15
    strategies, 91–95
    structuring, 53
    techniques, 96–101
    tutor-tutee relationship in, 54–62
Session Planning Chart, 103–4
Shollar, Barbara, 17*n*
Sign languages, 66–68
Silence, 167
    as tutoring technique, 96–97
Simulations, 90
Skills acquisition, tutoring and, 4
Skinner, B. F., 94, 237–38
Socratic method, 92–93
Steering committee, use of, in group work, 10
Stereotyping, 128
Stimulus-response theory, 234–38
    classical conditioning, 234–36
    operant conditioning, 237–38
Strategies
    cognitive theory, 243–44
    model tutoring, 91–95
    Piagetian theory, 247
Structure and Mechanisms of Memory, The, 242
Structuring, role expectancy, 53
    lab application, 53
Student
    -student conflicts, 217–18
    -teacher conflicts, 212–15
    -tutor conflicts, 203–12
    see also Tutee(s)
Subjective Units of Disturbance (SUDS)
    Scale, 172
Summarizing, 100
Supervision, 173

Talking machines, 71
Tape recorder, 71, 105
    lab application, 74
Task(s), 47
    -centered social work, 184, 185–93
"Task–Centered Casework," 185–93
Teacher(s)
    defined, 2
    -student conflicts, 212–15
    -tutor conflicts, 215–17

Techniques
  group work, 10
  questioning, 45–46, 92
  tutorial session, 96–101
  with visually handicapped, 69–70
Tests, 91, 101, 287
Thorndike, Edward L., 274
Transactional analysis, 165–70
  acceptance, 165–66
  class project, 165–66
  confrontation, 169–70
  reassurance, 167–68
Tutee(s)
  benefits of tutoring to, 5–6
  defined, 3
  demonstration, 98
  folder, 288
  initial interview with, 44–52
  relationship to tutor, 54–62, 203–12
  -tutor evaluation conference, 286–87
  see also Tutoring
Tutor(s)
  -counseling, 154–93, 290–306
  kinds of, 1–3
  meetings, 174–75
  -student conflicts, 203–12
  -teacher conflicts, 215–17
  -tutee evaluation conference, 286–87
  -tutee protocol, 233–34
  see also Counseling; Tutoring
Tutor-Counseling Self-Evaluation
  outlines, 290–306
Tutoring, *passim*
  adults, 270–84
  audiovisual aids, 105–8
  benefits of, 4–6
  components of good, 88–89
  -counseling, 154–93
  cross–age, 4
  deaf students, 65–69
  evaluation, 285–88
  expectations, 18, 52–53

guidelines, 16–17
initial interviews, 44–52
kinds of, 1–3
learning disabled, 72–73
in multicultural settings, 127–53
planning, 41–44, 84–87
process of learning and, 234–69
protocol, 233–34
relationship, 54–62
roleplaying in, 194–232
second-language learners, 129–33
self-evaluation, 289–306
session, 44–52, 84–126
strategies, 91–95, 243–44, 247
techniques, 96–101
visually handicapped, 69–72
Tutoring ESL Students, 17
"Tutoring Maria: A Case Study," 58–60
Tutoring Reading and Academic Survival Skills, 17n
Tutoring That Makes Significant Conceptual Links, 244
Typical Features of Learning Disabilities, 73

Understanding, importance of, 241–42
Unscripted roleplaying, 198–200

Values, cultural, 127–28
Videotape player, 105, 173, 174
Visually handicapped, 69–72
  Braille and, 69–70
  class project, 74
  equipment for, 71–72
  oral communication with, 70–71

"What to Look For in Groups," 36–39
Wolf, Howard, 23
Wolpe, J., 172n
"Women of the Shadows," 225–32
Writing Tutor, The, 17n